Fifth Edition

PRINCIPLES OF CRIMINAL LAW

Harvey Wallace

Cliff Roberson

LLM, Ph.D.
Academic Chair, Graduate School of Criminal Justice, Kaplan University
Emeritus Professor of Criminal Justice, Washburn University

Prentice Hall
Boston   Columbus   Indianapolis   New York   San Francisco   Upper Saddle River
Amsterdam   Cape Town   Dubai   London   Madrid   Milan   Munich   Paris   Montreal   Toronto
Delhi   Mexico City   Sao Paulo   Sydney   Hong Kong   Seoul   Singapore   Taipei   Tokyo

Editorial Director: Vernon Anthony
Senior Acquisitions Editor: Eric Krassow
Editorial Assistant: Lynda Cramer
Media Project Manager: Karen Bretz
Director of Marketing: David Gesell
Senior Marketing Manager: Adam Kloza
Senior Marketing Coordinator: Alicia Wozniak
Project Manager: Holly Shufeldt
Creative Director: Jayne Conte
Cover Designer: Bruce Kenselaar
Cover Photo: Fotolia
Image Permission Coordinator: Karen Sanatar
Full-Service Project Management/Composition: Mohinder Singh/Aptara®, Inc.
Printer/Binder: RR Donnelley & Sons, Inc.

Pearson Education LTD.
Pearson Education Australia PTY, Limited
Pearson Education Singapore, Pte. Ltd
Pearson Education North Asia Ltd
Pearson Education, Canada, Ltd
Pearson Educación de Mexico, S.A. de C.V.
Pearson Education–Japan
Pearson Education Malaysia, Pte. Ltd

Library of Congress Cataloging-in-Publication Data

Wallace, Harvey.
 Principles of criminal law / Harvey Wallace, Cliff Roberson. — 5th ed.
   p. cm.
 Includes bibliographical references and index.
 ISBN-13: 978-0-13-512158-0
 ISBN-10: 0-13-512158-2
 1. Criminal law—United States. I. Roberson, Cliff, II. Title.
KF9219.W35 2012
345.73—dc22

                                          2010041476

10 9 8 7 6 5 4 3 2

Prentice Hall
is an imprint of

www.pearsonhighered.com

ISBN-13: 978-0-13-512158-0
ISBN-10:   0-13-512158-2

CONTENTS

PREFACE

Principles of Criminal Law was first published in 1992. More than eighteen years later, the fifth edition is published. Harvey Wallace was the coauthor of the first four editions. Harvey died in 2007. Harvey and I were close friends and fellow Marines. We wrote ten books together over a sixteen-year period.

In a continuing effort to improve each edition, we have consulted with our colleagues, professionals in the field, and students who have used it as a learning vehicle. Most reviewers suggested leaving the majority of the text the same—if it isn't broken, don't fix it. However, we have received other feedback that included recommendations for improvement, most of which have been incorporated into the fifth edition. New topics added to this edition are discussed later.

The study of substantive criminal law is actually a study of human behavior. It is more than a study of specific crimes; it is also an examination of the rules of human behavior and criminal responsibility. Criminal law is based on moral values, and many of our crimes are also violations of our moral standards. The study of criminal law is controversial and exciting. For example, what subject is more controversial than the issue of whether abortion is the exercise of a woman's right to privacy or simply murder? As with many other criminal law issues, the answer to that question depends on one's values and beliefs. As for being exciting, notice how many of our movies and television programs are based on criminal behavior (e.g., *Law and Order* and *CSI*).

An important but seldom mentioned function of criminal law for social scientists is to define the subject matter of criminology. Criminology is the sociological and psychological study of the causes of crime, the control of crime, and the reasons for crime. Accordingly, defining certain acts as criminal and others as noncriminal directly affects the subject matter of criminology. As a comedian once stated, the only way to eliminate crime is to abolish our criminal laws—then there could be no crime.

Too often, books on general criminal law devote a considerable portion of the text to comparing majority and minority positions on specific issues. The result is that most readers are confused and lack a general understanding of settled concepts. For the most part, we have presented the prevailing positions with only an occasional reference to the majority–minority conflicts.

This book is designed as an introductory text on criminal law and not as a research book. Accordingly, to reduce its size and enhance its readability, endnotes are used sparingly in chapters involving noncontroversial subjects. The text presents basic concepts or principles of criminal law in definitions, focus boxes, and practicums. All of these features are designed to assist the student in understanding this often confusing area of the law.

We have chosen to present this material in a narrative form rather than approach it from a traditional law school casebook perspective. While we believe both techniques may be used to teach criminal law, our goal is to present a clear, concise text that discusses background information necessary to understand the principles involved in criminal law and sets forth the elements of the major crimes.

The fifth edition contains several significant changes. Those changes include

- Each chapter starts with a list of what you should know after you reading the chapter.
- A new section on terrorism has been added.
- The discussion on the Racketeer Influenced and Corrupt Organizations Act (RICO) has been expanded.

- A section on home invasion robbery has been added.
- The key words section of each chapter has been expanded.
- The section on counterfeiting has been rewritten in an effort to increase student understanding of the issues involved.
- A discussion on assisted suicide has been added.
- New discussions on the crimes of incest, bigamy, and polygamy were added.
- In most chapters, a student exercise "How would you rule?" has been added.
- Cases and legislation have been updated where appropriate.

Comments, corrections, or suggestions for improvement of the text should be forwarded to Cliff Roberson at cliff.roberson@washburn.edu. Enjoy the fascinating world of criminal law.

ACKNOWLEDGMENTS

We would like to express our appreciation to the following persons at Pearson for their support and understanding during this project: Eric Krassow, Senior Acquisitions Editor Criminal Justice; Lynda Cramer, Editorial Assistant for Criminal Justice; Jessica Sykes, Production Project Manager; Holly Shufeldt, Project Manager and Mohinder Singh, Project Manager at Aptara. Without their assistance, encouragement, and advice, this text would not have been possible. In addition, we extend our appreciation to the manuscript reviewers from the fourth edition: Bonnie Black, Mesa Community College; David Briscoe, University of Arkansas at Little Rock; and Lisa Nored, University of Southern Mississippi. Finally, thanks to our colleagues and families for their understanding and support.

Final note: Harvey Wallace, my friend, fellow Marine, and coauthor, died during the revision process for the fourth edition. Harvey, I miss you.

—Cliff Roberson

CHAPTER 1

Sources of Criminal Law

Chapter Outline

What you should know about the sources of criminal law. After reading this chapter, you should know

- The origins of criminal law.
- The definition of the term *crime*.
- The various classifications of criminal law.
- The development of common law.
- The importance of case law.
- The difference between moral lapses and crimes.

- The sources of criminal law.
- The basic theoretical concepts of punishment.
- The concept of administrative crimes.
- The differences between crimes and torts.
- The principles involved in the reform of criminal statutes.

Key Terms

After reading this chapter, you should understand the following key terms:

common law: Early English law, developed by the judges, into which were incorporated Anglo-Saxon tribal customs, feudal rules, and everyday rules of the villages. Common law became the standardized law of the land in England and later in the United States.

crime: A violation of an existing societal rule of behavior as expressed in a criminal statute, for which a criminal punishment may be imposed.

criminal code: The codification of the criminal law of the jurisdiction into one code that allows the criminal law to be more accessible and more democratically made and amended.

customs: Social rules of conduct or norms that do not arouse the intensity of feelings that mores do; generally, their violation will result in less severe reactions.

felony: A serious crime for which the accused, if convicted, may be sentenced to a prison term or the death penalty.

folkways: Social rules of conduct or norms that, when violated, carry the least intense feelings when compared to customs and mores.

infraction: The least serious violation of a criminal statute, normally punishable only by a fine. In many states, minor traffic offenses are considered infractions.

jail: A local place of confinement for those awaiting trial and those who have been convicted of misdemeanors.

misdemeanor: A crime that is punishable by fine and/or jail confinement. Less serious than a felony.

mores: Social rules of conduct or norms that arouse intense feelings and are subject to extreme consequences when violated.

police power: The authority of a state to enact and enforce a criminal statute.

procedural criminal law: That part of the criminal law that specifies the methods to be used in enforcing substantive criminal law.

stare decisis: The legal principle that binds courts to stand by prior decisions and use them as the standards by which to judge subsequent cases.

statutory law: Law created by legislative bodies to meet changing social conditions, customs, and public opinion.

substantive criminal law: The part of criminal law that establishes what conduct constitutes a crime and prescribes the punishment for violations of the crime.

In this chapter, we will examine the sources of criminal law. The study of criminal law is a study of crimes, moral principles, and common law. Our system of criminal law should be viewed not as a set of rules for memorization, but as a cluster of ideas, principles, and values about which reasonable persons can and do disagree. The system is not fixed in stone; it is changing and flexible. Understanding our concept of justice requires a thoughtful comprehension of the historical background, social values, moral standards, and political realities that give direction to our system.

Criminal law is used to fully define and to establish the limits of prohibited criminal behavior. Roscoe Pound describes two needs that can be considered the controlling force behind most philosophical thinking in the area of criminal law.[1] First is society's need to maintain security in the community by regulating and controlling governmental and individual activity. Second is the need to provide for and allow changes in the law in response to changes in the society.

What is a crime? As noted by a federal court in 1847, it is not enough to constitute an act a crime, that it is opposed to some law or the Constitution, unless Congress declares it to be criminal or punishable. It often is but a civil injury or wrong. [*United States v. New Bedford Bridge,* 27 F. Cas. 91 (C.C.D. Mass. 1847)]

A simple definition is that a crime is any act that has been so designated by the lawmakers. For our purposes, we will define crime as conduct that has been prohibited by law and that subjects the offender to criminal punishment. To understand our criminal law, it is necessary to focus on the one characteristic that differentiates it from civil law. That characteristic is punishment.[2]

PUNISHMENT

> *If you did not punish crimes you would help wickedness.*
>
> PUBLILIUS SYRUS, LATIN WRITER, C. 43 BC

One of the core functions of criminal law is to punish wrongdoers. This section presents a brief introduction to the concepts of punishment. Chapter 15 discusses punishment in greater depth. While almost everyone advocates that criminals should be punished for their criminal behavior, any definition of punishment can be criticized as being arbitrary. Joshua Dressler defines punishment as the suffering imposed on a defendant by an agent of the government pursuant to the authority given to that agent by reason of the defendant's criminal conviction.[3]

All societies punish those who have committed crimes. There is a lack of agreement, however, on the purposes of punishment, which may include rehabilitation, incapacitation, retribution, and deterrence.

The belief that punishment will cause a wrongdoer to reform is a noble one, but is it realistic? Most criminologists contend that punishment generally does not reform. This conclusion is supported by the high degree of recidivism among those persons presently serving time in jails and prisons.

Incapacitation as the rationale for punishment is based on denying the criminal the opportunity to commit other crimes by virtue of his or her restraint (confinement).

The theory of punishment for retribution purposes is different from the other theories in that its goal is to take revenge on the individual rather than to reform an offender or restrain the would-be criminal. Under the concept of retribution, the criminal has committed a wrong to society and, therefore, must pay his or her debt to society. As one nineteenth-century scholar wrote in support of retribution, "criminal law thus proceeds upon the principle that it is morally right to hate criminals . . . and that it is highly desirable that criminals should be hated . . ."[4]

There are two types of deterrence: general and specific. General deterrence is based on the idea that punishment of a criminal will cause other people to forgo criminal behavior in the future. Special deterrence is the punishment of a wrongdoer to deter that individual from misconduct in the future.

In many cases, one of these purposes would suggest severe punishment, whereas another purpose would suggest limited or no punishment. The concepts involving punishment are explored in depth in Chapter 15.

Factors to be considered in imposing a sentence:

18 U.S. Code § 3553. Imposition of a sentence

(a) The court shall impose a sentence sufficient, but not greater than necessary, to comply with the purposes set forth in paragraph (2) of this subsection. The court, in determining the particular sentence to be imposed, shall consider—

   (1) the nature and circumstances of the offense and the history and characteristics of the defendant;

   (2) the need for the sentence imposed—

      (A) to reflect the seriousness of the offense, to promote respect for the law, and to provide just punishment for the offense;

      (B) to afford adequate deterrence to criminal conduct;

      (C) to protect the public from further crimes of the defendant; and

      (D) to provide the defendant with needed educational or vocational training, medical care, or other correctional treatment in the most effective manner;

   (3) the kinds of sentences available;

   (4) the kinds of sentence and the sentencing range established for [the crime].

PRINCIPLES OF CRIMINAL RESPONSIBILITY

Laws undertake to punish only over acts.

de Montesquieu, The Spirit of Laws, 1748

The criminal law of a state includes not only a list of crimes but also a body of principles that help us to decide under what circumstances individuals should be considered criminally responsible for their conduct. These principles are also used to determine when it is fair to impose criminal sanctions on individuals. In general, a person is criminally responsible only for voluntary acts of misconduct. There are, however, some rules that hold persons guilty for nonvoluntary acts. In addition, the rules regarding self-defense and justification are used to excuse certain behavior that would otherwise be criminal. The principles of criminal responsibility determine which acts will be considered criminal and under what circumstances the law will excuse an otherwise criminal act. The principles of criminal responsibility include the following:

• Those defenses that excuse conduct that would otherwise be criminal—for example, insanity, self-defense, and necessity

• The requirements for *actus reus* and *mens rea*

• The requirement for joinder of intent and act

MORALS VERSUS LAW

A creep is not a criminal.

ANONYMOUS

While the criminal statutes are in general a reflection of our moral codes and values, there is often a difference between what is morally wrong and what is legally prohibited. Many acts that are considered criminal may not be morally wrong. For example, insider trading on the stock market is a statutory crime that does not violate everyone's moral code. In addition, some acts that most of us would consider morally wrong are not illegal. If you are standing on a boat dock and see a young man (a stranger) drowning, you are normally under no duty to rescue him even if you could without endangering yourself. There may, however, be a moral duty to do so. Crimes that are also violations of our moral and ethical codes receive the strongest condemnation from the public—for example, rape, murder, and child sexual abuse. As a general rule, the standards that we set for moral and ethical reasons are higher than the standards required by our criminal laws. This is based on the fact that our moral and ethical codes attempt to establish perfect personal character, whereas the criminal codes tend to establish minimal levels of conduct. In addition, criminal conduct is ordinarily considered unjustifiable and inexcusable.

Practicum 1.1

Is the Filming of Bustlines and Bottoms in Public a Crime?

A bridge tender in South Florida used a camcorder for months to film close-ups of the breasts and buttocks of women as they crossed the bridge where he worked. Apparently, he videotaped the women from his station on the bridge. Evidence indicated that he would step outside the bridge tender's house to follow unsuspecting women with his camera lens focused on their bustlines and bottoms. He explained that at various times he would gather his coworkers to watch his videos of the women.

ISSUE: *Most of us would agree that his conduct is not morally acceptable, but has he committed a crime?*

After watching his videotapes, the police of Delray Beach, Florida, concluded that the bridge tender had committed no crime, because the video had taken place in public places and was thus protected under the First Amendment. Note: He was subject to disciplinary action by his employer.

Miami Herald, March 2, 2007, p. 3B, Col. 1.

Use of Sanctions to Regulate Morality and Societal Rules

Before the American Revolution, the American colonies were subject to the law handed down by the English judges. Accordingly, the common law of England with its Anglo-Saxton concepts became the basic criminal law of the colonies. After the revolution, the common law was modified and changed by the state legislatures. During the modifications, the colonies' religious beliefs became a part of our criminal code, and criminal law was used to regulate morality. According to Norval Morris and Gordon Hawkins, our present criminal codes in the United States are some of the most moralistic criminal laws in history.[5]

Societal rules—norms—are used by society to regulate behavior in a given situation and at a given time. Norms are also considered as rules of conduct and approved blueprints for behavior. Norms have great power to motivate behavior. They carry with them positive and negative sanctions: When we behave according to norms, we are rewarded; when we behave in ways that do not meet normative expectations, we may be punished. Most people do not obey norms just because of the sanctions. There would never be enough police officers to enforce all laws if everyone was determined to break them.

Formal norms are imposed on us from above or outside and are often codified or written down. Criminal law is an example of a formal norm. Categories of norms include mores, customs, and folkways. **Mores** are behaviors that arouse intense feelings and are subject to extreme consequences. They involve the basic moral judgments and ethical rules of a society. They are the strongest norms and have great power over us. An example of a more is the belief that we should not kill other people.

Customs do not arouse the intensity of feelings that mores do, and generally their violation will result in less severe reactions. Usually people will react with disgust, repulsion, and shock to the violation of a custom. An example of a violation of a custom would be using vulgar language in a chapel.

Folkways are norms that, when violated, carry with them the least intense feelings. Folkways are trivial conventions and are generally concerned with taste and good manners, dress, politeness, and speech. They do not involve feelings of disgust or repulsion.

CLASSIFICATION OF CRIMES

A crime is anything that a group in power chooses to prohibit.
FREDA ADLER, SISTERS IN CRIME, 1974

Crimes may be classified in many ways. First, they are classified as either *mala in se or mala prohibita. Mala in se* crimes are those acts that are not only crimes but are also considered morally wrong—for example, rape, murder, and theft. Generally, all common law crimes are considered *mala in se* crimes. *Mala prohibita* crimes are those that are not considered morally wrong even though they are crimes—for example, insider trading or failure to have a business license. *Mala prohibita* crimes are wrong simply because they are prohibited by statutes.

Crimes are also classified as crimes against the person, crimes against property, sex crimes, victimless crimes, professional or white-collar crimes, and crimes against public order.

White-collar crime is a term originated by Edwin Sutherland in the 1930s to describe nonviolent crimes of personal or corporate gain committed by people in their work, occupation, or business or in defrauding other people or the government.[6] White-collar crimes are also called business crimes, commercial crimes, or occupational crimes.

Victimless crimes are those in which there are no direct victims, such as gambling, prostitution, and using drugs. Unlike murder, rape, or robbery, a victimless crime is usually committed by two or more people, all of whom readily participate in the crime. In some cases, it is also called a "public order" crime. While many of these offenses are called "victimless crimes," some authorities believe that society is the victim. Additionally, some crimes, such as drug use, lead certain people to commit other crimes, such as prostitution, to pay for their addiction.

Substantive or Procedural Law

Criminal law is divided into substantive criminal law and procedural criminal law. **Substantive criminal law** refers to that part of the criminal law that creates and defines crimes and specifies punishment. It can be found generally in the penal codes of each state and the federal government. **Procedural criminal law** is that part of the criminal law that establishes the rules by which the accused is brought to trial. Procedural criminal law includes the rules related to searches, seizures, arrests, interrogations, and the manner in which the case is tried and appealed. Procedural criminal law does not establish crimes or prescribe punishments.

Felony or Misdemeanor

The most popular classification of crimes uses four categories: treason, felonies, misdemeanors, and infractions. Treason, since it threatens the very existence of the nation, is considered the most serious. Because of its rarity, treason will not be further discussed in this text. The majority of our crimes are classified as either felonies or misdemeanors. The key to distinguishing between a felony and a misdemeanor is not the punishment actually given in court but the punishment that could have been imposed. For example, X commits the crime of burglary and could receive ten years in prison. The judge sentences him to only six months in the local **jail**, the sentence typically given for a misdemeanor. X has been convicted of a felony even though he received only a jail sentence.

In common law, a **felony** was considered any crime for which the offender would be compelled to forfeit property to the king. Most common law felonies were punishable by the death penalty. The common law felonies include murder, rape, assault and battery, larceny, robbery, arson, and burglary. Presently, only aggravated murder may subject the offender to the death penalty.

Most states distinguish between **misdemeanors** and felonies on the basis of place of incarceration. If the offense carries a punishment of incarceration only in a local jail, then the offense is a misdemeanor. Felony offenders can be imprisoned in prisons or correctional institutions. Other states use a combination of place of incarceration and character of offense to make the distinction between felonies and misdemeanors. The Model Penal Code (MPC) provides that a crime is a felony if it is so designated, without regard to the possible penalty. In addition, any crime for which the permissible punishment includes imprisonment in excess of one year is also considered a felony under the code. All other crimes are misdemeanors.

Several states, such as California, have crimes that are referred to as "wobblers" based on the fact that the court can treat them as either a felony or a misdemeanor.

Felonies and misdemeanors are frequently subdivided into classes. For example, in Texas misdemeanors are subdivided into classes A, B, and C, and felonies are subdivided into classes of first, second, and third degree. Under this classification, promotion of prostitution is a felony of the third degree, and forcing someone to commit prostitution is a felony of the second degree. The burglary of an inhabited building is a felony of the first degree, whereas the burglary of an uninhabited building is a burglary of the second degree. The MPC also creates degrees of felonies. A first- or second-degree felony under the MPC carries a $10,000 fine plus imprisonment and a third-degree felony carries a $5,000 fine plus imprisonment.

In many states, **infractions** are the lowest level of criminal activity. An infraction is an act that is usually not punishable by confinement, such as a traffic ticket. In several states, the term *petty misdemeanor* is used in lieu of infraction.

Similar to infractions are violations of municipal ordinances. In some states, ordinance violations are not considered crimes based on the theory that a crime is a public wrong created by the state and thus prosecuted in the name of the state. An ordinance is a rule created by a public corporation (the municipality) and prosecuted in the name of the municipality.

The classification of a crime as a felony or misdemeanor is important for several reasons. First, a felony conviction on a person's record can prevent the individual from entering many professions and obtaining certain jobs. A felony conviction has been used to deny a person the right to enter the armed forces or obtain employment with a law enforcement agency, and it may even affect one's ability to obtain credit or adopt a child. In one state, a felon (a person who has been convicted of a felony) may not obtain a license to sell chickens wholesale. In addition, conviction of a felony can be grounds to impeach a public official. At one time, many states did not allow a convicted felon to vote, hold office, or serve on a jury. Today, in all but eight states, many of the disabilities commonly associated with a felony conviction have been abolished.

Administrative Crimes

The Supreme Court, in *United States v. Grimaud*, held that Congress could delegate to an administrative agency the power to make regulations that may be enforced by criminal penalties.[7]

Today, state legislatures and the U.S. Congress have delegated to certain administrative agencies the power to make rules and enforce them by criminal penalties. For example, a private airplane pilot may be subject to criminal penalties for violation of the Federal Aviation Administration's regulations regarding flying rules. In delegating the authority to an agency, the legislature must provide specific guidelines to be observed by the agency. The delegation of such authority is generally constitutional if the following steps or guidelines are followed:

- The legislative delegation of authority must be limited and contain sufficient standards to guide the actions of the agency.
- The agency must operate within the specific guidelines established by the legislature.
- The agency rules must be explicit and unambiguous and within the standards established by the legislature.

Crimes and Torts Distinguished

Not all legal wrongs are crimes. Private wrongs are usually considered either a tort or a breach of contract. A crime is a public wrong, since it involves the violation of the peace and dignity of the state. In theory, it is committed against the interest of all of the people of the state. Accordingly, crimes are prosecuted in the name of the "State," the "People," or the "Commonwealth."

A tort is a wrong that violates a private interest and thus gives rise to civil liability. The same conduct, however, may be both a crime and a tort. For example, if a woman is forcibly raped by a neighbor, the criminal aspect of the conduct is a violation of the peace and dignity of the state. It is, therefore, a crime against all the people in the state. It is also a violation of the private interest of the victim, and she may file a civil suit and obtain civil damages against the offender.

An offender may be acquitted at a criminal trial, where proof of his or her guilt is required to be established beyond a reasonable doubt, yet may be held accountable at a civil trial, where the degree of proof required is much smaller.

Public and Private Laws and Wrongs

Our laws are also classified as either public or private laws. Generally, private laws deal with relationships between people, in which the government has only an indirect interest. Family law (marriage, divorce, etc.), real property law, and probate law (wills and trusts) primarily regulate the relationships between individuals and companies. The government has only an indirect interest. Public laws are those in which the government has a more direct interest. Public laws include constitutional law, criminal codes, vehicle codes, and public health laws.

At one time in early England, rules prohibiting crimes against the individual, such as rape, robbery, and theft, were considered private laws, on the theory that these crimes did not affect the state. Eventually, English law recognized that crime was not a personal affair but a wrong against society, a violation of the peace and dignity of the people.

A few public wrongs are, however, prosecuted in civil court. Usually, the statutes that establish certain crimes provide the state or federal government the option to proceed civilly rather than criminally. The matters in which the government has this option include civil rights, antitrust, obscenity, and consumer fraud. In civil court, the offender may be found civilly liable and ordered to pay compensatory and punitive damages.

ORIGINS OF CRIMINAL LAW

The first requirement of a sound body of law is, that it should correspond with the actual feelings and demands of the community, whether right or wrong.
JUSTICE OLIVER WENDELL HOLMES, THE COMMON LAW, 1881

American criminal law has been described as "English in heritage and judicial in its origin." Our present criminal codes grew out of custom, tradition, and actual written codes. One of the first known criminal codes was the Code of Hammurabi. This code was a comprehensive series of laws covering not only crime but property rights, family law, and other civil matters. The Code of Hammurabi also contained rules protecting victims of crimes. The concept of "an eye for an eye and a tooth for a tooth" was first introduced by King Hammurabi with his *lex talionis* (punishment by retaliation) based on the premise that the punishment should fit the crime. As we will discuss later, our criminal law was in large measure adopted from the English common law, which was first recorded by judges. Today, however, criminal law is formulated by the legislatures rather than judges. Accordingly, in both state and federal jurisdictions, to be a crime the conduct must be prohibited by a criminal statute, and there must be some form of prescribed punishment that may be imposed on a person who is convicted of a violation of the prohibited act.

The two major legal systems are the common law and the civil law systems. The common law system is used primarily in England and North America. The civil law system, known as Roman law, is the predominant system used in the rest of the world today. Under civil law, the laws are written and codified by the rules of the state.

Common Law

> *The common law is nothing else but statutes worn out by time . . .*
> English Chief Justice John Wilmot, 1686, Rex v. Clement, 4 Barn. & Aid.
> 218, 233, 106 Eng. Rep. 918, 923 (K. B. 1686)

Common law developed from the customs of the people. Certain customs became so entrenched that they were considered accepted norms of behavior. As the courts developed in England, judges made their decisions based on customs and recorded them. Other judges looking for assistance started following those decisions.

Since the original source of common law was the customs of the people, it is often stated that common law was developed by the common people and imposed on the kings. On the contrary, civil law, since it was based on rules published by the state, was handed down to the common people by the rulers.

Most people consider the legal systems of all states except Louisiana to be common law systems. They are, however, a mixture of the common law and civil law systems. Acts that are considered crimes are written and codified as in civil law, but courts rely on the common law concept of *stare decisis* to interpret the meanings of the written statutes. Even in those states that have expressly abolished common law, prior case law is still examined for definition purposes.

Development of Common Law

> *Common law is that body of law and juristic rules which was originated, developed,*
> *formulated, and administered in England . . . common law comprises the body*
> *of principles and rules of action . . . which are derived from usages and*
> *customs of immemorial antiquity.*[8]

As we noted earlier, most of our criminal law principles are traceable to the common law of England. This is especially true of the underlying philosophy of criminal law. There are, however, no "common law crimes" in most states. Accordingly, there must usually be in existence some statute, ordinance, or regulation prohibiting the conduct in question prior to the commission of the act. The common law principles regarding the interpretation of criminal statutes are still used. For example, in defining a crime, the legislature may use words that are well known and defined by criminal law.

The first known English code was written in the seventh century by King Aethelbert. The proclamations of the code were called dooms, which were related to social class. For example, theft was punishable by fines that varied widely in magnitude according to the status of the victim. Stealing from the king was punishable by a fine equal to nine times the value of the property stolen. Theft from a person of the holy order was punishable by a fine three times the value of the property taken. Crimes committed in the presence of the king were considered a violation of the "king's peace," which increased the punishment. The code was rewritten in the ninth and eleventh centuries, but little new was added.

Most historians trace the common law of England to William the Conqueror, who invaded England in 1066. At the time of the invasion, each county was controlled by a sheriff (shire-reeve), who also controlled the courts in that county. Accordingly, there was no uniform English system. William took over the courts and made them royal courts, that is, under the control of the king. He sent representatives to the many courts in England to record their decisions and distributed selected decisions to all the judges to use in making their own decisions. As the routine of these courts became firmly established, it was possible to forecast their decisions by reference to similar cases they had decided in the past. From this the doctrine of stare decisis developed in the eighteenth century.

William also compiled the law of crimes that most areas of the kingdom observed in common. These crimes became the common law crimes of England. Later, new statutory crimes were added by the king and Parliament. The concept of common law crimes was so ingrained in England that the traditional crimes of burglary, larceny, murder, and so forth were not defined by statute in England until the 1960s.

During William's time, very few people could read or write. The king, the judges, and the church authorities determined the elements and the scope of criminal offenses. In some cases, they even created new crimes. As William made England a unified nation rather than a collection of isolated villages, the judges developed familiarity with the general customs, usages, and moral concepts of the people. Judicial decisions began to be based on these general customs, usages, and moral concepts.

The Trial of William Penn

WILLIAM PENN TO JUDGE: I desire you would let me know by what law it is you prosecute me, and upon what law you ground my indictment.

JUDGE: Upon the common law.

PENN: Where is that common law?

JUDGE: You must not think that I am able to run up so many years, and over so many adjudged cases, which we call common law, to answer your curiosity.

PENN: This answer I am sure is very short of my question, for if it be common, it should not be so hard to produce.

JUDGE: The question is, whether you are guilty of this indictment?

PENN: The question is not, whether I am guilty of this indictment, but whether this indictment is legal. It is too general and imperfect an answer to state that it is the common law, unless we knew both where and what it is. For where there is no law, there is no transgression and that law which is not in being, is so far from being common, that it is no law at all.

JUDGE: You are impertinent, will you teach the court what the law is? It is "Lex non scripta," that which many have studied 30 or 40 years to know, and would you have me tell you in a moment?

PENN: Certainly, if the common law be so hard to understand it is far from being common.

Trial of William Penn as reported in 6 How. St. Trials 951 (1670).

By the 1600s, the primary criminal law of England was based on the mandatory rules of conduct laid down by the judges. These rules became the common law of England. Prior decisions were accepted as authoritative precepts and were applied to future cases. When the English settlers came to America in the 1600s, they brought with them the English common law. With a few modifications, English common law became the common law of the colonies. During the American Revolution, there was a great deal of hostility toward the English in America. This hostility extended to the common law system. Thus, most of the new states enacted statutes defining criminal acts and establishing criminal procedures. The statutes, however, basically enacted what was formerly English common law.

As we noted earlier, many aspects of our present criminal law system are based upon English common law. All states except Louisiana can trace their legal systems to the English common law system. In 1805, Louisiana, whose system was originally based on French and Spanish legal concepts, officially embraced the common law of England as a further basis for its system.

CASE LAW

Case law is the term used to indicate appellate court interpretations of the law.[9] A substantial majority of "law" is case law, that is, court opinions that interpret the meaning of constitutions and statutes. Case law also helps clarify and apply statutory law. For example, the U.S. Constitution (Fourteenth Amendment) provides that no state shall deprive any person of life, liberty, or property without due process of law. What constitutes "due process of law" is decided almost daily in the courts. Hundreds of opinions on this subject are issued by federal and state appellate and supreme courts each year.

A court decision on a code provision may interpret its scope and effect, the meaning of the words, the legislative intent, its relationship to other laws, and whether it violates any constitutional restrictions.

Precedent

A court decision on a legal principle may be a precedent (guide) for similar situations. There are two basic types of precedent—mandatory and persuasive. Mandatory precedent means that when a higher appellate court renders a decision on an issue, the lower courts under its supervision must follow the ruling or face reversal on appeal.[10] For example, if the Arizona Supreme Court decides an issue, state courts in Arizona must follow that precedent. Persuasive precedent means that, although a court decision is not legally binding on a second court, its analysis may be persuasive. For example, a court in New Mexico is faced with an issue that has never been decided by a New Mexico court. There is, however, a court in Nevada that has considered the same issue. The Nevada court decision is not binding on the New Mexico court, but it may have some persuasive authority. Precedent is based on the principle of stare decisis, which is discussed next.

Stare Decisis

The common law practice of following precedents (other court decisions) is termed **stare decisis**, which means to abide by or adhere to decided cases.[11] The original version of stare decisis was *stare decisis et non quieta movere*, which means to adhere to precedents and not to unsettle things that are established. Blackstone, in his famous commentaries, described the process as one in which the older cases are examined to find whether the same points are once again being questioned. He contended that this practice keeps the scales of justice even and steady and does not allow them to waver with each new judge.[12]

The doctrine provides that, when a court has once laid down a principle of law as applicable to a certain state of facts, it will adhere to that principle and apply it to all future cases where the facts are substantially the same.[13] Stare decisis is founded on the theory that security and certainty require following established legal principles, under which rights may accrue.[14]

Statutory Law

Statutory law is law that is enacted by legislative bodies of government. The primary statutory laws dealing with crimes and criminal procedure are the state penal codes. Other statutes that set forth crimes include the vehicle, government, and business codes. Under our democratic system, the legislative branch enacts the criminal laws, the executive branch administers and enforces them, and the judicial branch determines the guilt or innocence of defendants and their punishment, if any.

Legislatures frequently give the following reasons for designating certain acts as crimes:

- To protect the public from violent conduct by others
- To safeguard property rights
- To maintain public order
- To protect public health
- To protect our concepts of public morality
- To protect the right of privacy

Reasons that are commonly given for not making certain acts criminal include the following:

- Inability of the state to control the acts
- Constitutional protection for the acts
- Political considerations
- Lack of demand by influential people or groups
- Economic infeasibility
- Voter opposition

Model Penal Code

The American Law Institute, a nonprofit organization sponsored by the American Bar Association, drafted the Model Penal Code (MPC). This code was developed by a group of judges, lawyers, and scholars and is designed to reflect in general the criminal law of the United States. The project was started in 1952, its rationale being that states enacted criminal laws in a piecemeal fashion, often based on public perceptions of need without a thorough examination of the situation. The project was basically completed in 1962 after thirteen tentative drafts. Since 1962, approximately two-thirds of the states have adopted new criminal codes greatly influenced by the MPC. While some states have adopted this code with slight changes, other states refer to it when redrafting criminal laws.

REFORM OF CRIMINAL LAW

As we noted in the preface, criminal law is constantly changing as our moral values change. Reform of criminal law is guided by several principles. Andrew Ashworth divides those principles into two groups: the virtues of codification (including the values of certainty, consistency, comprehensibility, and accessibility of the criminal law) and the social and moral issues that are being raised by the changing values of our society.[15]

Certainty is important because it provides a foundation on which to base our conduct. If the definition of criminal behavior changed daily, we would be unable to conform our conduct to the expected norm, because the norm would always be shifting. Therefore, we expect that our rules of conduct will be consistent and that each of us will be required to conform to the same rules of conduct. In order to be law-abiding citizens, we need to have access to our criminal laws and be able to comprehend them. Regarding the social and moral issues that are being raised, we should not forget that our criminal laws are to a great extent a codification of our social and moral beliefs.

According to Ashworth, in any reform of criminal law, there are certain questions about the shape and form of the criminal legislation that we should be concerned with. First is the choice between defining the offense as a result of crime or defining it in an inchoate mode.[16] The former would prohibit an act causing X, whereas the latter would prohibit the doing of an act with the intent to cause X. Second is the choice of whether to use one or a few broad-based crimes to cover a sphere of criminal activity or to establish a number of narrowly defined subdivided offenses. Third is whether to impose strict criminal liability and allow conviction without proof of fault (an exception to the usual principle of *mens rea*). Fourth is the allocation of the burden of proof. Despite the presumption of innocence, many statutes place the burden of proving certain facts on the defendant. For example, in most states, the defendant has the burden of establishing self-defense.

William J. Chambliss and Thomas F. Courtless state that the process of creating criminal laws (or reforming present ones) can be understood as a function of one or more of the following processes:[17]

- The act of describing prevailing values and norms of a society
- The act of looking at the historical context in which the laws are created
- An arbitrary decision of those in power
- A reflection of the changing needs of society
- A reflection of the desires of those with the power to get inside the heads of the lawmakers

Practicum 1.2

Ramsey County deputy sheriffs responded to a report of a car in the ditch near Gem Lake in Minnesota. The car was stuck in a snow-filled ditch. The headlights were on, but the motor was not running. As the deputy approached the driver's side of the car, he found the defendant Sandra Starfield sitting in the driver's seat. The deputy opened the car door and asked Sandra for her driver's license. She could not find her purse. From the odor of alcohol and bloodshot eyes, the deputy concluded that Sandra was intoxicated. He noticed that the keys were not in the ignition. He asked Sandra for the keys. She stated she could not find them. The Minnesota statute made it a crime to "drive, operate, or to be in 'physical control' of a motor vehicle while under the influence of alcohol" (Minn. stat. 169.121).

At her trial, Sandra stated that her son had driven the car into the ditch and had gone for help when the police arrived. While deliberating, the jury returned with the following question: "Does the car have to be able to be moved for a person to have physical control of the vehicle?" The trial judge responded by repeating the below instruction:

A person is in physical control of a motor vehicle when he or she is present in a vehicle and is in a position to either direct the movement of the vehicle or keep the vehicle moving. It is not necessary for the engine to be running in order for a person to be in physical control of a motor vehicle.

Should Sandra be convicted of being in physical control of a motor vehicle while intoxicated in violation of the Minnesota statute?

The Supreme Court of Minnesota upheld Sandra's conviction and held that the statute includes a motor vehicle so stuck in a snow-filled ditch that it cannot move and that the state is not required to prove operability of the motor vehicle. The court also remarked that "Drunk-driving cases, especially those where the officer comes upon a stationary car with an inebriated person inside, seem to provoke a remarkable variety of explanations to test the factfinder's credibility-determining powers."

State v. Starfield, 481 N.W. 2d 834 (Minn. 1992).

POLICE POWERS OF GOVERNMENT

The **police power** of a government is the authority of that government to enact legislation to protect the public health, safety, order, welfare, and morality. Under the U.S. system of federalism, the police power of government is primarily vested in the state legislatures. States have comprehensive power to adopt laws regulating the activities of individuals and business entities as long as those laws do not violate limitations contained in the state and federal constitutions. State legislatures, in turn, may delegate some of this power to local governments, which enact ordinances defining crimes within their jurisdiction.

Case on Point

Raich v. Gonzales

Throughout our history, the several States have exercised their police powers to protect the health and safety of their citizens. Because these are primarily, and historically, . . . matter[s] of local concern, the States traditionally have had great latitude under their police powers to legislate as to the protection of the lives, limbs, health, comfort, and quiet of all persons.

2007 U.S. App. LEXIS 5834 (9th Cir. Cal. Mar. 14, 2007).

Under our system of federalism, the U.S. Congress does not possess plenary legislative authority except in the District of Columbia and federal territories. The U.S. Constitution enumerates certain powers that it grants to the U.S. Congress. These enumerated powers include the power to establish rules governing immigration and naturalization, to "define and punish piracies and felonies committed on the high seas," and "to provide for the punishment of counterfeiting the securities and current coin of the United States."

The U.S. Congress is also granted certain implied powers by the "Necessary and Proper Clause" of Article I, Section 8, of the U.S. Constitution. While the implied powers expand the legislative authority of the Congress, they do not confer on Congress the general police powers that are possessed by the states. To qualify as a valid implied power, the federal legislation must be "plainly adapted" to the goal of furthering one or more of Congress's enumerated powers.

In the area of criminal law, Congress's most significant power is enumerated power to regulate the "commerce between the states." While Congress cannot make prostitution a crime, it can make it a crime to transport a person across state lines for "immoral purposes." Congress has expanded the concept of interstate commerce to justify broader authority to enact criminal statutes, but the authority is not unlimited. Criminal laws enacted by the U.S. Congress under the commerce clause include the following:

- Interstate transportation of stolen automobiles, 18 U.S. Code 2312
- Interstate transportation of kidnapped persons, 18 U.S. Code 1201
- Computer crimes, 18 U.S. Code 1030
- Environmental crimes
- Loan sharking, 18 U.S. Code 891
- Carjacking, 18 U.S. Code 2119
- Manufacture, sale, distribution, and possession of controlled substances, 21 U.S. Code 801 et seq.
- Racketeering and organized crime, 18 U.S. Code 1961–1963

HOW WOULD YOU DECIDE?

Defendant Burch appealed the decision of the United States District Court for the Southern District of Texas, which imposed the maximum prison term allowable under 21 U.S.C.S. § 846, following his plea of guilty to one count of conspiracy to possess marijuana with the intent to distribute.

The court justified the sentence on two stated reasons—Burch's social history and his criminal past. The court noted Burch's education, apparent intelligence, maturity, and social background. The court contrasted Burch with "people who are 17 years old and don't know better," and stated, "the system has not been harsh with you . . ." The court described Burch as "one of the top persons, scholastically speaking, all your education pursuits, an extremely gifted, talented individual. You are not the ordinary person who walks through here." The district court also noted Burch's previous involvement in drug activities. It was on the basis of these factors that the court imposed the maximum statutory punishment.

Question: Was it proper to consider the high educational level of the defendant as one of the reasons to impose the maximum statutory punishment?

SEE: UNITED STATES V. BURCH, 873 F.2D 765 (5TH CIR. TEX. 1989)

Summary

The study of criminal law is a study of crimes, moral principles, and common law. Our system of criminal law involves ideas, principles, and values about which reasonable persons can and do disagree. The system is a flexible one. Criminal law defines and establishes the limits of prohibited criminal behavior.

A crime may be defined as any act that has been designated a crime by lawmakers. We will define crime as conduct that has been prohibited by a statutory code and that subjects the offender to punishment. One of the core functions of criminal law is to punish wrongdoers. Almost everyone advocates that criminals should be punished for their criminal behavior. Any definition of punishment can be criticized as being arbitrary.

The criminal law of a state includes principles that indicate under what circumstances individuals should be considered criminally responsible for their conduct. The principles are also used to determine when it is fair to impose criminal sanctions on individuals. While the criminal statutes in general reflect our moral codes and values, there is often a difference between what is morally wrong and what is legally prohibited. Many acts that are considered criminal may not be morally wrong.

Crimes may be classified in many ways. First, they are classified as either *mala in se* or *mala prohibita*. *Mala in se* crimes are those acts that are not only crimes but that most people consider to be morally wrong—for example, rape, murder, and theft. Generally, all common law crimes are *mala in se* crimes. *Mala prohibita* crimes are those that are not usually considered morally wrong even though they are criminal— for example, insider trading or speeding. The most popular classification of crimes is by the categories of treason, felonies, misdemeanors, and infractions.

Additional Assignments

1. Read the selected cases and associated material for Chapter 1 posted at www.mycrimekit.com
2. Complete the online study guide material for Chapter 1 posted at www.mycrimekit.com
3. Discussion and thought questions:
   a. Explain the functions of criminal law in our society.
   b. Why is the classification of crimes important?
   c. What factors may be considered by our lawmakers when they take up the reform of substantive criminal laws?
   d. Contrast "moral values" and "criminal law."
   e. Explain the development of common law.
   f. Why is the concept of stare decisis important?

Practicum

1. Log on to the Internet and go to www.findlaw.com
2. Click on the tab for "Search cases and codes."
3. Search for the U.S. Supreme Court decision *Hoke v. United States*, decided in 1913.
4. Briefly explain why this case is important to the study of criminal law.

Notes

1. Roscoe Pound, "Justice According to the Law," 14 Colum. L. Rev. 1–26 (1914).
2. Arnold H. Loewy, *Criminal Law* (St. Paul, MN: West, 1987).
3. Joshua Dressler, *Understanding Criminal Law* (New York: Matthew Bender, 1989), 5.
4. James Stephens, *A History of the Criminal Law in England*, vol. 2 (London: Macmillan, 1883), 82.
5. Norval Morris and Gordon Hawkins, *The Honest Politician's Guide to Crime Control* (Chicago: University of Chicago Press, 1969).
6. Edwin H. Sutherland, "White-Collar Criminality," 5 Am. Sociological Rev. 40–46 (1940).
7. *United States v. Grimaud*, 220 U.S. 506 (1911).
8. *Black's Law Dictionary*, 4th ed. (St. Paul, MN: 1951).
9. Id.
10. Lower courts are "under supervision" of a higher court when the lower court's decisions may be appealed to the higher court.
11. There are instances in which courts do not follow the doctrine of stare decisis—for example, when a court overrules one of its prior decisions.
12. William Blackstone, *Commentaries on the Laws of England* 168 (7th ed., 1775).
13. *Moore v. City of Albany*, 98 N.Y. 396 (1967).
14. *Otter Tail Power Co. v. Von Bank*, 72 N.D. 497 (1974).
15. Andrew Ashworth, "Towards a Theory of Criminal Legislation," 1 Crim. L. J. 41 (1989).
16. Inchoate crimes are crimes that involve incomplete or unfinished acts, for example, attempts. See Chapter 4 for a more detailed explanation.
17. William J. Chambliss and Thomas F. Courtless, *Criminal Law, Criminology, and Criminal Justice* (Pacific Grove, CA: Brooks-Cole, 1991), 7.

World Wide Web Sites for Legal Resources

AllLaw: For researching federal and state law questions. http://www.alllaw.com

ALSO: American Law Sources Online: A comprehensive, uniform, and useful compilation of links to online law resources. http://www.lawsource.com

FedLaw: Resource for online legal research. http://www.legal.gsa.gov

FindLaw: Links to both state and federal laws and cases. http://www.findlaw.com

Law.com: Resource for both lawyers and researchers. http://www.law.com

MegaLaw: A useful starting place for online legal research. http://www.megalaw.com

Nolo's Legal Encyclopedia: Excellent general-purpose resource for nonlawyers. http://www.nolo.com/legal-encyclopedia/

LEGAL RESEARCH

Indiana University School of Law: http://www.law.indiana.edu/v-lib

Washburn Law Library: http://www.washlaw.edu

LAW DICTIONARIES

http://www.dictionary.law.com

http://www.dictionary.findlaw.com

http://www.nolo.com/dictionary.htm

http://www.courttv.com/legalterms/glossary.html

COURTS RESOURCES

Conference of State Court Administrators: http://cosca.ncsc.dni.us/

Courts Net: http://www.courts.net

Federal Judiciary: http://www.uscourts.gov

National Center for State Courts: http://www.ncsc.org

U.S. Supreme Court: http://www.supremecourtus.gov

CHAPTER 2

Limitations on Criminal Liability

Chapter Outline

What you should know about the limitations on criminal liability. After reading this chapter, you should know

- The constitutional limitations on criminal liability.
- The relationship between social harm and criminal liability.
- Which crimes are federal crimes and which crimes are considered as state crimes.
- The meaning of the due process limitations in the Constitution.
- When a statute is void for vagueness.
- The issues involved with the right to privacy.
- The protections against "cruel and unusual" punishments and "double jeopardy."

Key Terms

After reading this chapter, you should understand the following key terms:

Bill of Rights: The first ten amendments to the U.S. Constitution that set forth certain rights guaranteed to individuals.

conviction: A judgment of guilt; verdict by a jury or by a judge in a nonjury or bench trial.

cruel and unusual punishment: Physical or mental punishment in excess of that given to the people under similar circumstances; banned by the Eighth Amendment to the U.S. Constitution.

double jeopardy: A protection in the Fifth Amendment to the U.S. Constitution, enforceable against states through the Fourteenth Amendment, which protects an individual against second prosecution for the same offense after acquittal or conviction and against multiple punishments for the same offense.

due process: A basic constitutional principle based on the concepts of privacy of the individual, limitations on governmental power, and a safeguard against arbitrary and unfair governmental actions. Due process includes the basic rights of a defendant in a criminal proceeding.

equal protection: A clause in the Fourteenth Amendment to the U.S. Constitution that requires that persons under like circumstances be given equal protection in the enjoyment of personal rights and the prevention and redress of wrongs. The constitutional guarantee of "equal protection of the laws" means that no person or class of persons shall be denied the same protection of the laws that is enjoyed by other persons or other classes in like circumstances.

ex post facto law: A law that makes an act criminal after the act was committed, retroactively lessens the evidence required for a conviction, or increases the punishment for a previously committed criminal act.

jurisdiction: The power and authority of a court to hear and determine judicial proceedings; and the power to render a particular decision in question.

legality: A guide for judges based on the common law principle that sets limitations on the formation, creation, and interpretation of criminal laws.

right to privacy: The right to be left alone, the right to be free from unwarranted publicity, and the right to live without unwarranted interferences by the public in matters with which the public is not necessarily concerned. The right is a generic term encompassing various rights recognized to be inherent in the concept of ordered liberty, preventing governmental interference in intimate personal relationships or activities, and the freedom of an individual to make fundamental choices regarding himself or herself and family.

social harm: The proposition that, before an act may be declared a crime, there must be some harm to society resulting from the commission of the act.

venue: The geographic location where a trial should be held. The Sixth Amendment to the U.S. Constitution provides that a defendant has a right to be tried in the judicial district in which the alleged criminal act occurred.

void-for-vagueness principle: A constitutional principle that refers to the requirement that any statute which in defining a crime is so unclear that a reasonable person of at least average intelligence could not determine what the law purports to prohibit is unconstitutional.

To understand criminal law concepts, it is necessary to have a basic understanding of the limitations on criminal liability. Accordingly, the goal of this chapter is to provide you a brief overview of those limitations that are critical to an understanding of criminal law concepts. (Although the statute of limitations is a limitation of criminal liability, it is also an affirmative defense, as discussed in Chapter 5.)

BILL OF RIGHTS

Bad men, like good men, are entitled to be tried and sentenced in accordance with the law . . .

JUSTICE HUGO BLACK, GREEN V. UNITED STATES, 1961

The first ten amendments to the U.S. Constitution compose our federal "**Bill of Rights**." The Bill of Rights and the Fourteenth Amendment to the Constitution limit the actions of the government. In general, the amendments place restrictions on the procedures that the government may use against a person accused of a crime. Most of the restrictions apply to criminal procedural matters. Few directly affect substantive criminal law. The two major restrictions against substantive criminal law are the due process clause, which is also important in the criminal procedural context, and the Eighth Amendment prohibition against cruel and unusual punishment. Both of these restrictions are discussed later in this chapter.

The Bill of Rights was drafted as a protection against the powers of a federal government. The Supreme Court has used the due process clause of the Fourteenth Amendment to apply to the states most of the Bill of Rights limitations on governmental actions.

EIGHTH AMENDMENT

There is a point beyond which even justice becomes unjust.

TERENCE, THE SELF-TORMENTOR, C. 185–189 BC

In *Robinson v. California*, the Supreme Court held that the prohibition in the Eighth Amendment against **cruel and unusual punishment** not only limits the amount and types of punishment that may be inflicted, it also limits the legislative authority to make some conduct criminal.[1] For example, while the state may make it a crime to possess or use drugs, the state may not make it a crime to be addicted to drugs or to be afflicted with a disease.

While Robinson could not be punished for being a drug addict, it is clear that he could be punished for possessing or using illegal drugs. This is based on the concept that in possessing or using drugs he was engaged in behavior that society has an interest in preventing. In contrast, punishment for being an addict is based merely on status. The Court, in comparing drug addiction with leprosy, failed to consider that a leper may have that condition without displaying any criminal behavior, whereas Robinson and the majority of other drug addicts become addicted because of their illegal activities in using prohibited drugs.[2]

DUE PROCESS

Whatever disagreement there may be as to the scope of the phrase "due process of law," there can be no doubt that it embraces the fundamental conception of a fair trial, with opportunity to be heard.

OLIVER WENDELL HOLMES, FRANK V. MANGUM, 1915

The federal and state constitutions protect against the deprivation of life, liberty, or property without due process of law under the U.S. Constitution, Amendment XIV. Due process means that a defendant is entitled to fundamental fairness that includes the right to notice and an opportunity to be heard. However, due process is also a flexible concept, and the procedural protections available are based on the particular situation at issue. When determining the procedural protections required to protect due process rights, one must examine the private interest at stake, the risk of deprivation of interests through the procedure used, the value of other procedures, and the state or government interest, including the administrative burden imposed by substitute procedures. [*People v. Noboa*, 2008 Mich. App. LEXIS 783, 7-8 (Mich. Ct. App. Apr. 17, 2008)]

There are two **due process** clauses in the U.S. Constitution. The one in the Fifth Amendment protects an individual from actions by the federal government, and the one in the Fourteenth Amendment protects an individual from actions by state governments.

One aspect of due process requires that crimes be described such that an individual is reasonably aware of what conduct is prohibited by the statute. Accordingly, if the statute establishing certain conduct as criminal is vague or overbroad, the statute violates due process. What makes a statute indefinite and thus vague is hard to define. As Justice Felix Frankfurter once stated: "Indefiniteness is not a quantitative concept. It is itself an indefinite concept."[3] In general, the statute must be sufficient to provide reasonable persons with "fair" notice as to what conduct is illegal. The U.S. Supreme Court stated that "the root of the vagueness doctrine is a rough idea of fairness."[4]

One of the problems in this area is the fact that most penal statutes must necessarily be vague. Accordingly, the void for vagueness limitation is triggered only when laws become so vague that reasonable people must necessarily guess as to their meaning and application. Criminal laws are designed to protect reasonable, law-abiding persons, not put them at risk of prosecution.

Case on Point

Robinson v. California

Facts: California enacted a statute making it a crime for a person to be addicted to the use of narcotics. The offense was punishable by ninety days to one year in jail.

Question: Was the statute constitutional, since no act was required by the defendant and the defendant's condition of drug addiction was sufficient for conviction?

Holding: The statute in question was cruel and unusual punishment in violation of the Eighth and Fourteenth Amendments to the U.S. Constitution. Robinson's "crime" consisted only of his status as a person suffering from the "disease" of drug addiction. It was unlikely that a state would attempt to punish a person for being afflicted with mental illness, leprosy, or venereal disease. If a state attempted to punish a person for one of those problems, it would "doubtless be universally thought to be an infliction of cruel and unusual punishment." The same regard should be shown to those persons suffering from drug addiction. Limited punishments were provided for in this statute, but even one day in custody because of a person's "status" would be cruel and unusual punishment.

In explaining the Robinson case, Justice Thurgood Marshall later stated:

The entire thrust of Robinson's interpretation of the cruel and unusual punishment clause is that criminal penalties may be inflicted only if the accused has committed some act, has engaged in some behavior, which society has an interest in preventing, or perhaps in historical common law terms, has committed some actus reus.

---

370 U.S. 660 (1962).

JURISDICTION

Jurisdiction is the power of a court to exercise its authority over the subject matter or person. If the court has no jurisdiction over either the defendant or the subject matter of the proceeding, the court is without power to act in the matter. Jurisdiction over the subject matter refers to the power of the court to decide matters pertaining to that subject matter. For example, a family law court with no jurisdiction over criminal matters cannot issue a ruling or make a decision in a criminal case. Likewise, a justice court in most states cannot try an accused for a felony offense. In addition, a Florida court cannot try a defendant for violation of a North Carolina statute, since the Florida court lacks jurisdiction over North Carolina statutes.

Practicum 2.1

ISSUE: *Is a state "stop and identify" statute, which requires a person to "stop and identify" himself or herself with "credible and reliable" identification, a violation of the U.S. Constitution?*

A police officer responded to a call reporting that a man had assaulted a woman. The officer found the defendant standing outside a parked truck with a woman inside the truck. The officer asked for defendant's identification eleven times and was refused each time. The officer arrested the defendant. The defendant was convicted for obstructing the officer in carrying out his duties under Nev. Rev. Stat. 171.12, a "stop and identify" statute that required the

defendant only to disclose his name. The U.S. Supreme Court determined that the Terry stop, the request for identification and the state's requirement of a response did not contravene the guarantees of the Fourth Amendment because the request for identity had an immediate relation to the purpose, rationale, and practical demands of the Terry stop. Also, the request for identification was reasonably related in scope to the circumstances that justified the Terry stop. The Court also determined that defendant's conviction did not violate the Fifth Amendment's prohibition on compelled self-incrimination because disclosure of his name presented no reasonable danger of incrimination.[5]

Question: After Mr. Hiibel was arrested, was he advised of his Miranda rights, which included "the right to remain silent"?

An essential element of any criminal charge is that the court has subject matter jurisdiction over the offense. For example, in *Gardner v. State*, the defendant was charged in an Arkansas court with rape under an Arkansas statute.[6] It appears that the defendant raped a young girl on the backseat of a moving car that was being driven from Arkansas to Texas and then to Oklahoma. The defendant's counsel argued that the Arkansas court did not have jurisdiction because the rape actually occurred in either Texas or Oklahoma. The Arkansas Supreme Court upheld the rape conviction, saying it was not essential that all elements of a state crime take place within the state as long as at least one of them did. Thus, under this concept the defendant also may have violated the rape statutes of Texas and Oklahoma.

Limits on Jurisdiction

There are limits, however, on the ability of a state court to control the actions of citizens in other states. For example, suppose a judge in Arizona does not like Nevada's gambling laws. Accordingly, the judge convinces the city council to pass an ordinance to punish persons who travel from the local area to Nevada for the purpose of gambling. While part of the statutory violation occurs within the jurisdiction of the local city, an appellate court would probably hold that the city does not have jurisdiction to control the conduct of its citizens while they are in another state and performing actions legal in that state. In addition, there is a constitutional right for citizens to travel between the states. It would appear under the same rationale that a state could not make it illegal for its citizens to travel to a second state to obtain an otherwise legal abortion.

Case on Point

Papachristou v. City of Jacksonville

Question: When is a statute void for vagueness?

Justice William O. Douglas:

This case involves eight defendants who were convicted in a Florida municipal court for violating a . . . vagrancy ordinance. . . . At the time of the arrest, four of the defendants were riding in a car on the main thoroughfare. The four were charged with "prowling by auto". . . . The other defendants were arrested for "loitering." . . .

The ordinance is void for vagueness, both in the sense that it "fails to give a person of ordinary intelligence fair notice that his contemplated conduct is forbidden by statute" . . . and because it encourages arbitrary and erratic arrests and convictions. . . .

Living under a rule of law entails various suppositions, one of which is that all persons are entitled to be informed as to what the State commands or forbids. . . . While not mentioned in the Constitution or Bill of Rights, the unwritten amenities have been in part responsible for giving our people the feeling of independence and self-confidence, the feeling of creativity. These amenities have dignified the right of dissent and have honored the right of nonconformists and the right to defy submissiveness. . . . The due process implications are equally applicable to the States and to this vagrancy ordinance. . . . Where the list of crimes is so all-inclusive and generalized as that one in this ordinance, those convicted may be punished for no more than vindicating affronts to police authority.

---

405 U.S. 156 (1972).

Jurisdiction over the Person

As a general rule, to have jurisdiction over the person the court must have the defendant before the court. There are exceptions. For example, if the defendant is present at the start of a trial, his voluntary absence later in the trial does not cause the court to lose its jurisdiction over him. In criminal cases involving minor offenses, often the accused will waive her presence and will have an attorney appear on her behalf. In these situations, the fact that an attorney appears on the defendant's behalf constitutes a waiver and gives the court personal jurisdiction over the defendant.

State versus Federal Jurisdiction

The majority of criminal laws in the United States are state-made laws, that is, penal laws that were enacted by state legislatures. Federal laws must be based on powers granted or implied by the U.S. Constitution. Most federal statutes are based on the "interstate commerce clause." State criminal law statutes are generally based on the right of a state to secure and promote the welfare of its residents. Most criminal trials take place in state courts. There are at least five counties in the United States—for example, Los Angeles, Harris (Houston), Cook (Chicago), Dallas, and New York—that try more criminal cases in each county than are tried in the entire federal court system. As discussed later in this chapter and in Chapter 5 on defenses, the same act may be both a federal and a state crime because the act violates both federal and state statutes.

Case on Point

Koon v. United States

Facts: On the evening of March 2, 1991, Rodney King and two of his friends sat in King's wife's car in Altadena, California, and drank malt liquor for a number of hours. Then, with King driving, they left Altadena. King was intoxicated. California Highway Patrol officers observed King's car traveling at a speed they estimated to be in excess of 100 mph. The officers followed King with red lights and sirens activated and ordered him by loudspeaker to pull over, but he continued to drive. The highway patrol officers called for help on the radio. Units of the Los Angeles Police Department joined in the pursuit, one unit manned by officers Laurence Powell and trainee Timothy Wind. King left the freeway, and after a chase of about eight miles, stopped at an entrance to a recreation area. Powell ordered King and his two passengers to exit the car and assume a felony prone position—that is, to lie on their stomachs with legs spread and arms behind their back. King's two friends complied. King got out of the car but did not lie down. Los Angeles Police Officer Stacey Koon arrived while King was resisting. Koon fired Taser (stun) darts into King. The officers were later videotaped assaulting King. Koon, Powell, Wind, and Briseno were tried in state court for assault with a deadly weapon and excessive use of force by a police officer. The officers were acquitted of all charges, with the exception of one assault charge against Powell that resulted in a hung jury.

Question: Can the officers be tried in federal court based on the same acts for which they were acquitted in state court?

Holding: Yes. The officers were tried in the state courts for violations of state laws. They may be tried in federal court for violations of federal laws, that is, violation of King's civil rights under 18 U.S.C. 242. In fact, that is exactly what happened.

---

518 U.S. 81 (1996).

Venue

Venue, often associated with jurisdiction, refers to the geographic location where the trial should be held. Venue is derived from the Sixth Amendment of the U.S. Constitution, which provides that "the accused shall enjoy the right to a . . . public trial . . . by an impartial jury of the State and district wherein the crime shall have been committed. . . ." Since jurisdiction refers to the power of a court to take certain actions, jurisdiction cannot be waived by a defendant. Venue can, however, be waived. In highly publicized cases, the court, on motion by the defendant, may change venue and transfer the case to a different district for trial.

SOCIAL HARM

> *The aim of the law is not to punish sins, but is to prevent certain external results . . .*
> OLIVER WENDELL HOLMES, COMMONWEALTH V. KENNEDY, (170 MASS. 1897)

Does the Constitution require that, before conduct may be declared illegal, there must be **social harm**?

Many have contended that, for behavior or conduct to be a crime, there must be some "social harm" attached to it. Social harm involves the proposition that, before an act may be declared a crime, there must be some harm to society resulting from the commission of the act. No state requires social harm as a necessary element of a criminal act. The U.S. Supreme Court has been silent on this question in cases in which the conduct involves voluntary action. This failure to rule may be because the concept of social harm is vague, and the Court hesitates to take over the state's customary role of determining what conduct constitutes social harm.

As the Court held in *Robinson v. California*, an individual cannot be punished for being addicted to drugs.[7] Accordingly, if no voluntary act is involved, the Constitution prohibits punishing a person because of the person's status (in this case, as a drug addict). In Robinson, however, the court seemed to imply that deciding what conduct constitutes social harm is for the states to decide.

RIGHT TO PRIVACY

A man has the right to pass through this world, if he wills, without having his pictures published, his business enterprises published, his successful experiments written up for the benefits of others, or his eccentricities commented upon, whether in handbills, circulars, catalogues, newspapers or periodicals.

JUSTICE ALTON B. PARKER, N.Y. COURT OF APPEALS,
ROBERSON V. ROCHATER FOLDING BOX CO., 1901

The "right to privacy" is not explicitly guaranteed by the U.S. Constitution. The Supreme Court, however, has held that the **right to privacy** is a substantive right protected by the Constitution under the due process and freedom of association clauses. The Court has held that the framers of the Constitution intended that an independent right of privacy exist and that it protect citizens from undue government encroachment.[8]

In the *City of Chicago v. Wilson*, 75 Ill. 2d 522, defendant Wilson was arrested for violating a section of the city's municipal code which prohibited a person from wearing clothing of the opposite sex with the intent to conceal his or her gender. Wilson was a transsexual preparing for a sex-reassignment operation. The state supreme court reversed his conviction and held that the code was unconstitutional as it applied to him. The court stated that there exist unspecified constitutionally protected freedoms, which include the right to choose one's appearance.

In *Sterling v. Cupp*, [290 Ore. 611 (Or. 1981)], the Supreme Court of Oregon held that it was an invasion of privacy for male officers to conduct a body search of a female absent exigent circumstances.

Case on Point

Stanley v. Georgia

Question: Do adults have the right to possess obscene pictures in their home under the "right to privacy"?

Holding: The mere possession of obscene pictures cannot constitutionally be made a crime. When this obscene matter is located in the privacy of one's own home, the "right of privacy" takes on an added dimension. Even though the states are free to regulate or even ban obscene matter, "that power simply does not extend to mere possession by an individual in the privacy of his own home."

The Court observed:

The makers of our Constitution undertook to secure conditions favorable to the pursuit of happiness. They recognized the significance of man's spiritual nature, of his feelings and of his intellect. . . . They sought to protect Americans in their beliefs, their thoughts, their emotions. . . . They conferred . . . the right to be let alone.

394 U.S. 557, 564.

The precise contours of the right to privacy have not been fully outlined by the courts. At one time, the right was perceived as a limitation on the authority of a legislature to prohibit socially harmful conduct. Recent court decisions, however, have indicated that this right has limited viability.[9] In *Stanley v. Georgia*, the Court discussed the right of Americans "to be free, except in very limited circumstances, from unwanted governmental intrusions into one's privacy."[10] The Stanley case indicated that we have a right to possess obscene material in our homes without fear of governmental intrusion. If it is not illegal to possess obscene material, is it permissible to possess illegal drugs in the privacy of our homes? As of this date, no court has held that we have such a right. The Stanley case may be limited only to obscene material.

The right to privacy, discussed in the Roberson case, protects a person from having his or her private matters made public. This particular aspect of the right to privacy, however, does not generally apply to a "public figure" such as a congressperson or a senator.

In *Board of Education v. Earls* (536 U.S. 822 [2001]), students sued the board of education, alleging that the board's policy requiring all students participating in extracurricular activities to submit to drug testing violated the students' constitutional right to be free from unreasonable searches. The U.S. Supreme Court, in holding the requirement constitutional, discussed the issue of privacy. The court stated that: "Considering the nature and immediacy of the government's concerns and the efficacy of the Policy in meeting them, the Court concludes that the Policy effectively serves the School District's interest in protecting its students' safety and health." The Court noted that preventing drug use by schoolchildren is an important governmental concern.

LEGALITY

We can afford no liberties with liberty itself.
JUSTICE ROBERT JACKSON, UNITED STATES V. SPECTOR, 1952

The principle of **legality** is a common law principle that sets limitations on the formation, creation, and interpretation of criminal law. It is not so much a rule of law as it is a guide for judges, who in earlier times were the creators and overseers of the criminal law. The principle reached its zenith in the seventeenth and eighteenth centuries in both America and Europe. The principle was developed to move the operation of law farther away from historical barbarism toward the rule of law. It promotes the concept of *nullum crimin sine lege* (no crime without law).

The fact that certain conduct is considered immoral or harmful does not necessarily mean that the conduct constitutes criminal behavior. According to the principle of legality, there is no crime unless the legislature makes the conduct a crime. One purpose of the principle is to prevent the government from punishing a person for conduct that was lawful when performed. The second aspect of this principle is that government must give prior notice of what conduct it considers a crime. The Constitution prohibits *ex post facto laws,* meaning those that would retroactively criminalize actions that were innocent when they were done. The ex post facto limitation also prohibits any law that aggravates a crime (that is, makes it more serious than it was when committed) or inflicts a greater punishment than the law allowed when the crime was committed.[11]

The third aspect of the legality principle is the prohibition against bills of attainder. A bill of attainder is a special law that declares a specific person to be guilty of a crime and thus subject to punishment without a trial or conviction.[12]

The ex post facto and bill of attainder restrictions apply only to legislative action, that is, statutes and laws. The courts, using common law concepts, may expand the definition of a crime, possibly resulting in conviction and punishment that is retroactive in its effect. The judicial expansion is, however, rare, and most states have abolished common law crimes.

EQUAL PROTECTION

The law, in its majestic equality, forbids all men to sleep under bridges, to beg in the streets, and to steal bread—the rich as well as the poor.

ANATOLE FRANCE, CRAINQUEBILLE, 1902

The Fourteenth Amendment to the U.S. Constitution prohibits states from denying individuals the **equal protection** of their laws. This constitutional right implies that all persons will be treated with substantial equality. This does not mean that a state must treat all persons exactly the same. A state may distinguish in its treatment of persons according to acceptable criteria or classifications. For example, the state may require large businesses to provide certain benefits to their employees while exempting smaller businesses from this requirement.

Common classifications in criminal law are based on the state of mind of the offender, type of person involved, and occupation. For example, the state may prohibit sex between an adult and a person under the age of eighteen years while not prohibiting sex between two consenting adults. A state may not, however, use an unacceptable criterion to justify the difference in treatment of individuals. For example, a state may not make it a crime for a person from a certain racial group to be in specified parts of a city.

Suspect classifications (those that appear to be illegal) are usually based on race or religion. A gender differential, while not a suspect classification, must also be based on a rational difference. For example, a statute that treats males and females differently violates the equal protection clause unless the classification is substantially related to achieving an important government objective.[13] If the classification is based on one of the suspect

---

Practicum 2.2

Shaw v. Director of Public Prosecutions

The defendant decided to water his garden while wearing only his underwear. He is charged and convicted of the crime defined only as "committing a public mischief."

ISSUE: Does his conviction violate the principle of legality?

Holding: Yes. There appears to be no fair warning or notice that watering your garden in your underwear constitutes a public mischief. The court in this case appeared to have acted retroactively, deciding what constitutes a public mischief.[14]

classifications or on gender, the state has the burden to show both the existence of an important objective and the substantial relationship between the discrimination in the statute and that objective. If the classification is not based on sex, national origin, or race, generally there is a presumption that the statute is valid, and the person attacking the statute has the burden of proving that the criteria are impermissible.

One aspect of the equal protection requirement is the concept of "equality of punishment." This is discussed in Chapter 15.[15]

DOUBLE JEOPARDY

> . . . [N]or shall any person be subject for the same offense to be
> twice put in jeopardy of life or limb . . .
>
> U.S. CONSTITUTION, AMENDMENT V

The above-quoted constitutional guarantee against **double jeopardy** involves three separate restrictions on governmental conduct. First, the accused is protected from prosecution for the same offense after an acquittal. Second, the accused is protected from prosecution for the same offense after a **conviction**. Third, the accused is protected from multiple punishments for the same criminal conduct. The purpose of the doctrine is to protect a person from the harassment of multiple trials.

For double jeopardy to apply, the prosecution must be for the same offense as that involved in the earlier proceeding. Accordingly, if an individual is tried in state court for robbing a bank and is acquitted (a state crime), the individual may later be tried in a federal court for robbing a federally insured bank (a federal crime). In this example, although only one bank was involved, the crimes are different, and therefore the doctrine does not apply. Note the Koon case discussed earlier in this chapter on this point. Double jeopardy also does not apply when a case is reversed on appeal or a mistrial is declared for valid reasons. Double jeopardy is an affirmative defense, so the burden of raising the issue rests with the defendant.

Case on Point

In Re Michael M.

Facts: The defendant, a seventeen-year-old male, was charged with having unlawful sexual intercourse with a female under the age of eighteen, in violation of California's statutory rape law. The statute described statutory rape as "an act of sexual intercourse with a female not the wife of the perpetrator, where the female is under the age of 18 years. . . ." The defendant, prior to trial, petitioned for relief in the California Court of Appeal and the California Supreme Court, asserting that the statute unlawfully discriminated on the basis of gender. The appellate courts denied his petition.

Question: May a state make it a crime for a seventeen-year-old male to have sex with a seventeen-year-old female while not making it a crime for the female involved?

Justice William H. Rehnquist:

A Legislature may not make overbroad generalizations based on sex which are unrelated to any differences between men and women or which demean the ability of the social status of either gender. . . . The Equal Protection Clause does not demand that a statute necessarily apply equally to all persons or require things which are different in fact to be treated in law as though they were the same. . . . This court has consistently upheld statutes where the gender classification is not invidious, but rather realistically reflects the fact that the sexes are not similarly situated in similar circumstances. . . .

Applying these principles to this case, the fact that the California Legislature criminalized the act of illicit sexual intercourse with a minor female is an indication of its intent or purpose to discourage the conduct. . . .

We are satisfied not only that the prevention of illegitimate pregnancy is at least one of the purposes of the statute, but also that the State has a strong interest in preventing such pregnancies. . . .

Accordingly, the judgment of the California Supreme Court is affirmed. [Justice John Paul Stevens dissented.]

450 U.S. 464 (1981).

HOW WOULD YOU RULE?

First Case:

In 1917, while the United States was involved in World War I and sugar was a scarce commodity, the defendant was indicted pursuant to § 4 of the Lever Act, codified at 41 Stat. 297, which imposed a fine or imprisonment upon any person who willfully exacted excessive prices for any necessaries. The defendant allegedly violated this statute by charging an unreasonable price for sugar.

The defendant appealed, contending that the statute was vague and did not provide fair notice of what conduct was prohibited. As a justice of the U.S. Supreme Court, how would you rule?

SEE: *UNITED STATES V. L. COHEN GROCERY CO., 255 U.S. 81 (U.S. 1921)*

Second Case:

On March 11, 2004, terrorists' bombs exploded on commuter trains in Madrid, Spain, killing 191 people and injuring another 1,600, including three U.S. citizens. Shortly after the bombings, the Spanish National Police (SNP) recovered fingerprints from a plastic bag containing explosive detonators. The bag was found in a Renault van located near the bombing site. On March 13, 2004, the SNP submitted digital photographs of the fingerprints to Interpol Madrid, which then transmitted them to the Federal Bureau of Investigation (FBI) in Quantico, Virginia.

The FBI searched fingerprints in its own computer system, attempting to match the prints received from Spain. On March 15, 2004, an FBI computer produced twenty candidates whose known prints had features in common with what was identified as Latent Finger Print # 17 (LFP # 17). The FBI performed background checks on each of the candidates, one of whom was Brandon Mayfield.

On March 17, 2004, FBI Agent Green, a fingerprint specialist, concluded that Mayfield's left index fingerprint matched LFP # 17. Green then submitted the fingerprints for verification to Massey, a former FBI employee who continued to contract with the FBI to perform forensic analysis of fingerprints. Massey verified that Mayfield's left index fingerprint matched LFP # 17. The prints were then submitted to a senior FBI manager, Wieners, for additional verification. Wieners also verified the match.

On March 20, 2004, the FBI issued a formal report matching Mayfield's print to LFP # 17. The next day, FBI surveillance agents began to watch Mayfield and follow him and members of his family when they traveled to and from the mosque, Mayfield's law office, the children's schools, and other family activities. The FBI also applied to the Foreign Intelligence Security Court (FISC) for authorization to place electronic listening devices in the "shared and intimate" rooms of the Mayfield family home; searched the home while nobody was there; obtained private and protected information about the Mayfields from third parties; searched Mayfield's law offices; and placed wiretaps on his office and home phones. The application for the FISC order was personally approved by John Ashcroft, then the attorney general of the United States.

In April 2004, the FBI sent Mayfield's fingerprints to the Spanish government. The SNP examined the prints and the FBI's report, and concluded that there were too many unexplained dissimilarities between Mayfield's prints and LFP # 17 to verify the match. FBI agents then met with their Spanish counterparts in Madrid, who refuted the FBI's conclusion that there was a match.

On October 4, 2004, Mayfield, his wife, and his children filed suit against the government in the United States District Court for the District of Oregon. The complaint alleged claims for unlawful arrest and imprisonment and unlawful searches, seizures, and surveillance in violation of the Fourth Amendment; a claim under the Privacy Act, 5 U.S.C. § 552a, for leaking information from the FBI to media sources regarding Brandon Mayfield's arrest.

Mayfield claims that his constitutional right to privacy was violated by the FBI's erroneous conclusions regarding the fingerprint match. As federal judge in the case, how would you rule?

SEE: MAYFIELD V. UNITED STATES, 2009 U.S. APP. LEXIS 26889 (9TH CIR. OR. DEC. 10, 2009)

Summary

The first ten amendments to the U.S. Constitution constitute our federal Bill of Rights. The Bill of Rights and the Fourteenth Amendment to the U.S. Constitution restrict the procedures that the government may use against a person accused of a crime. While most of the restrictions apply to criminal procedural matters, the two major restrictions against substantive criminal law are the due process clause and the Eighth Amendment prohibition against cruel and unusual punishment.

The Supreme Court has held that the Eighth Amendment limits not only the amount and types of punishment that may be inflicted but also legislative authority to make some conduct criminal.

The due process clause in the Fifth Amendment protects an individual from actions by the federal government, and the one in the Fourteenth protects an individual from actions by state governments. Among other things, due process requires that crimes be described so that an individual is reasonably aware of what conduct is prohibited by the statute.

Jurisdiction is the court's power over the subject matter or person before it. If the court has no jurisdiction over either the defendant or the subject matter of the proceeding, it is without power to act in the matter. An essential element of any criminal charge is that the court has jurisdiction over the offense. To have jurisdiction over the person, the court usually must have the defendant before the court.

While many have contended that a crime must have some "social harm" attached to it, the U.S. Supreme Court has not ruled on this question in cases in which the conduct involves voluntary action.

The right to privacy is not included as such in the U.S. Constitution. The Supreme Court, however, has found authority for privacy as a substantive right under the due process and freedom of association clauses.

Conduct is not necessarily criminal just because it is considered immoral or harmful. The principle of legality states that there is no crime unless the legislature makes the conduct a crime. The government may not enact ex post facto laws, which make an action criminal after it is performed or raise the penalty for a crime after it is committed.

The Fourteenth Amendment to the U.S. Constitution prohibits states from denying individuals equal protection of the law. A state need not treat everyone exactly the same, but it may distinguish between persons only on the basis of permissible criteria.

The constitutional guarantee against double jeopardy involves three separate restrictions on governmental conduct. The state may not prosecute an accused for the same offense after an acquittal or for the same offense after a conviction or apply multiple punishments for the same criminal conduct. The purpose of the doctrine is to protect a person from the harassment of multiple trials.

Additional Assignments

1. Read the selected cases and associated material for Chapter 2 posted at www.mycrimekit.com.
2. Complete the online study guide material for Chapter 2 posted at www.mycrimekit.com.
3. Discussion and thought questions:
   a. Explain the relationship between "social harm" and "criminal conduct."
   b. Define the various types of jurisdiction.
   c. Why is the concept of jurisdiction important in criminal cases?
   d. What basic restrictions does the Bill of Rights place on state governments?
   e. Why should it be unconstitutional to punish someone for having a disease?

Practicum

1. Log on to the Internet and go to www.findlaw.com.
2. Click on the tab for "Search cases and codes."
3. Search for the U.S. Supreme Court decision *Stanley v. Georgia*, decided in 1969.
4. Why is this case important?

Notes

1. *Robinson v. California*, 370 U.S. 660 (1962).
2. *Powell v. Texas*, 392 U.S. 533 (1966).
3. *Winters v. New York*, 333 U.S. 507 (1948).
4. *Colten v. Kentucky*, 407 U.S. 104 (1972).
5. *Hiibel v. Sixth Judicial Dist. Court*, 124 S. Ct. 2451 (decided June 2004).
6. *Gardner v. State*, 569 S.W. 2d 74 (1978).
7. *Robinson v. California*, 370 U.S. 660 (1962).
8. *Griswold v. Connecticut*, 381 U.S. 479 (1965).
9. Joshua Dressler, *Understanding Criminal Law*, 2nd ed. (New York: Matthew Bender, 1995), 91.
10. *Stanley v. Georgia*, 394 U.S. 557 (1969).
11. *Calder v. Bull*, 3 U.S. 386 (1798) at 390.
12. U.S. Constitution, Article I, section 9, clause 3, provides, in part, "No state shall . . . pass any Bill of Attainder." See also *Cummings v. Missouri*, 71 U.S. 277 (1867).
13. *People v. Liberta*, 474 N.E. 2d 567 (N.Y. 1984).
14. *Shaw v. Director of Public Prosecutions*, 2 All E.R. 46 (1961) [Decided by the British High Court of Justice].
15. Cal. Penal Code 161.5.

CHAPTER 3

Basic Requirements of a Criminal Act

Chapter Outline

What you should know about the basic requirements of a criminal act. After reading this chapter, you should know

- The two requisites of each crime.

- The meaning of *actus reus* and *mens rea*.

- What constitutes an act for purposes of criminal behavior.

- The concept of a legal duty to act.

- The requirements of a voluntary act.

- The distinction between intention and intent.

- How motive differs from intent.

- The different types of intent involved in criminal behavior.

- The differences between "willful" and "knowingly."

- What constitutes recklessness and criminal negligence.

- The rationale for strict liability crimes.

Key Terms

After reading this chapter, you should understand the following key terms:

actus reus: An illegal act; the act or failure to act that constitutes the crime.

constructive intent: A principle of law that refers to those situations where the actor does not intend any harm but should have known that his or her behavior created a high risk of harm to others.

criminal negligence: Behavior in which a person fails to reasonably perceive substantial and unjustifiable risks of dangerous consequences; negligence of such a nature and to such a degree that it is punishable as a crime; or flagrant and reckless disregard for the safety of others or willful indifference to the safety and welfare of others.

criminal sanction: The punishment that is associated with being convicted of a crime.

culpability: Blameworthiness for criminal conduct based on mens rea.

elements of a crime: The parts of a crime that the prosecution must establish to obtain a conviction. If any one element of a crime cannot be established by the prosecution, then a finding of not guilty must be entered as to that crime.

general intent: A concept employed by the courts to explain the required criminal intent for a defendant to be convicted of a certain crime, by which the government is not required to prove that the defendant intended to bring about a particular intent.

legal causation: A cause recognized by law as necessary to impose criminal liability.

mala in se: Crimes that are inherently bad: for example, murder, rape, and theft.

mala prohibita: Acts that are crimes only because the government has declared them criminal. Acts that are not inherently bad: for example, hunting without a license.

mens rea: The required mental state necessary to constitute a crime.

Model Penal Code (MPC): A model code of criminal laws developed by the American Law Institute for the purpose of standardizing general provisions of criminal liability, sentencing, defenses, and the definitions of specific crimes between and among the states.

negligence: The unconscious creation of risk, or the mental state in which the actor unknowingly creates a substantial and unjustifiable risk of harm to others.

recklessness: The conscious creation of substantial and unjustifiable risk.

specific intent: The intent to accomplish a specific purpose as an element of a crime.

strict liability crimes: Those crimes that require no proof of culpability or state of mind and are justified on the basis of the need to encourage extremely high standards of care for the protection of the public.

transferred intent: A principle of law that transfers the intent to harm to the person actually harmed. Involves a situation where a person intends to injure one person and mistakenly injures a third person.

There are two requisites of each crime: the required act or failure to act (actus reus) and the required mental state (mens rea). To state this another way, a defendant is not guilty of an offense unless he or she committed the wrongful act with the required mental state or culpability. Accordingly, before a defendant may be found guilty in a criminal trial, the prosecution must establish beyond a reasonable doubt the required actus reus and the required mens rea. In this chapter, we will examine those two requisites along with the associated rules of criminal responsibility.

A man may have as bad a heart as he chooses, if his conduct is within rules.
OLIVER WENDELL HOLMES, "NATURAL LAWS," IN COLLECTED LEGAL PAPERS, 1921

ACT—ACTUS REUS

If the law was so restricted (to punish bad thoughts), it would be utterly intolerable:
all mankind would be criminals, and most of their lives would be
passed in trying and punishing each other . . .
JAMES FITZJAMES STEPHEN, HISTORY OF CRIMINAL LAW IN ENGLAND, 1883

The Latin term **actus reus** was not actively used by scholars prior to the twentieth century.[1] It is currently used in most works on criminal law in the United States. Unfortunately, it has no single accepted meaning. Since it has no universally accepted meaning, many courts and commentators use the term more narrowly to simply describe the defendant's conduct or the results of that conduct rather than the combination of both. The term actus reus literally means "guilty act." It is more than voluntary muscular contractions (voluntary movement). The actus reus includes three ingredients of a crime:

1. a voluntary act or a failure to perform a voluntary act that one has a legal duty to perform
2. that causes
3. social harm

Actus reus can be conceptualized as including both muscular contractions and the circumstances and consequences associated with the contractions.

The justification for requiring actus reus is to prevent punishing a person merely for his or her thoughts. An old legal maxim says that you cannot be punished for your evil thoughts, but you may be punished for any actions associated with your evil thoughts. An additional justification is based on the concept that criminal law should not be so broad as to reach those people who entertain criminal schemes in the mind only but never allow the thoughts to govern their conduct. The practical reason for the actus reus requirement is that, until a person does something, we have no objective proof of the seriousness of his or her thoughts. Haven't we all at one time or another thought about "choking someone"?

Voluntary Acts

The act necessary to constitute a crime varies with each crime and is generally specified in the statute that establishes it. For example, as this text will discuss, burglary is the entering of a building with the intent to commit certain offenses. In this crime, the actus reus is the entering of the building with the required criminal intent.

Involuntary movement normally is not sufficient to cause criminal liability. For example, C shoves A into B. A has not committed the act necessary to establish an assault on B, since A's act was involuntary. A classic example of an involuntary movement is a muscle spasm that causes a pistol to discharge, thereby killing someone; this is not an act sufficient to establish murder. Most authorities acknowledge that mere reflex is not a voluntary act.[2]

In some crimes, the act of speaking can be the act underlying the crime. In others, possession of something that is illegal may be an act sufficient to constitute a crime.

Acts of Omission

Criminal liability can be based on a failure to act (act of omission) when the individual has a legal duty to do so. Note that there must first be a legal duty to act. A moral duty is insufficient to establish criminal liability. For example, if a medical doctor is a bystander who witnesses an automobile accident, he has no legal duty to render medical assistance to the injured persons. If, however, the doctor causes the accident by his negligence, then he has a duty to render aid. In the first situation, the duty to render aid is a moral duty only. In the second situation, since the doctor caused the accident, he is under a statutory duty in most states to render aid.

Legal duty to act arises in most cases from statutory sources. For example, most state vehicle codes require persons involved in an automobile accident to render aid or assistance to persons injured in the accident. Under the Internal Revenue Code, most of us are required to file tax returns. The failure to file when required is a crime.

Practicum 3.1

Defendant was drunk in his home. He was arrested by the police and taken out onto a public highway.

The court held that his appearance in public was involuntary, and therefore he had not committed the crime of public drunkenness.[3]

ISSUE: On these facts, can he be convicted of public drunkenness?

In some cases, the duty may result from the relationship of the parties. For example, parents have a duty to protect and safeguard their children. Thus, a parent generally has a duty to rescue his or her endangered child. The legal duty may also result from a contractual relationship between the parties. If a childcare worker accepts the care of a child, the worker has a reasonable duty to rescue if the child is in danger.

If one has no duty to act, but does act, then there is a legal duty to act in a reasonable manner.

Model Penal Code (MPC 2.01)

REQUIREMENTS OF VOLUNTARY ACT

1. A person is not guilty of an offense unless his liability is based on conduct which includes a voluntary act or the omission to perform an act of which he is physically capable.

Practicum 3.2

A husband was convicted of first-degree rape upon his daughter based on a sexual relationship that had been going on for some time.

ISSUE: Can a wife who knows of the illegal sexual relationship be convicted as an accomplice for her failure to take any action to stop the relationship?

The court held that the wife had a duty to protect her daughter and that her failure to intervene on behalf of the child made her an accomplice.[4]

Case on Point

The Murder of Kitty Genovese

Kitty Genovese was murdered in New York City. She was killed on the sidewalk in front of her apartment in Queens. The attack started at 3:20 a.m. and continued until she died some thirty-five minutes later. During this period, at least thirty-seven law-abiding citizens watched the killer stalk and stab her three times. Twice during the series of assaults on Genovese, lights turned on in nearby bedrooms interrupted the killer and frightened him off. Each time he returned to continue the assaults. Despite her cries for help, not one of the thirty-seven citizens attempted to help—not one even called the police during the attacks, although one called after her death. When asked why he did not call the police, one man stated, "I was tired."[5] Since none of the thirty-seven citizens had a legal duty to help, their inaction, while morally wrong, was not criminal behavior.

2. The following are not voluntary acts within the meaning of this section:
   a. a reflex or convulsion;
   b. a bodily movement during unconsciousness or sleep;
   c. conduct during hypnosis or resulting from hypnotic suggestion;
   d. a bodily movement that otherwise is not a product of the effort or determination of the actor, either conscious or habitual.
3. Liability for the commission of an offense may not be based on an omission unaccompanied by action unless:
   a. the omission is expressly made sufficient by the law defining the offense; or
   b. a duty to perform the omitted act is otherwise imposed by law.

Case on Point

Jones v. United States

Circuit Judge Wright:

. . . . There are at least four situations in which the failure to act may constitute breach of a legal duty. One can be held criminally liable: first, where a statute imposes a duty to care for another; second, where one stands in certain status relationship to another; third, where one has assumed a contractual duty to care for another; and fourth, where one has voluntarily assumed the care of another and so secluded the helpless person as to prevent others from rendering aid.

---

308 F.2d 307 (D.C. Cir. 1962).

---

4. Possession is an act, within the meaning of this section, if the possessor knowingly procured or received the thing possessed or was aware of his control thereof for a sufficient period to have been able to terminate his possession.

INTENT—MENS REA

> *Actus non facit reum nisi mens sit rea.*
> "AN ACT DOES NOT MAKE (AN INDIVIDUAL) GUILTY, UNLESS THE MIND BE GUILTY."[6]

The general concept of *mens rea* is that **criminal sanctions** should not be imposed on those who innocently cause harm. As Justice Oliver Wendell Holmes, Jr., stated in *The Common Law*: "even a dog distinguishes between being stumbled over and being kicked."[7] Accordingly, for an act to be criminal, it must be accompanied by the required mens rea, also referred to as **culpability**. Although this concept appears clear and is generally accepted, there are many problems in applying it to particular cases. One legal scholar says that the term mens rea is fraught with greater ambiguity than any other legal term.[8]

As we will show, different crimes require different degrees of intent. In addition, substantial problems are caused by the traditional use of imprecise terminology.

If a person has sufficient mens rea to commit a crime, but commits a lesser one, he or she will be held accountable only for the actual crime committed. A classic example in this area is the following:

If one from a housetop recklessly throws down a billet of wood upon the sidewalk where persons are constantly passing, and it falls on a person passing by and kills him, this would be murder. If instead of killing him, it inflicts only a slight injury, the party would not be convicted of murder since murder was not committed.[9]

The term mens rea has been difficult for the courts and the legislatures to define: The U.S. Code takes seventy-nine words to define it. A restatement of the U.S. Code's definition serves only to confuse readers. Many scholars consider intent and mens rea to be the same.

Others argue that intent is only a part of mens rea, since it does not cover those situations where recklessness or negligence is sufficient to establish the mental requirement.

The easiest way to understand mens rea is to understand the four mental states that qualify as mens rea: general intent, specific intent, transferred intent, and constructive intent. As we will note later in this chapter, constructive intent includes those situations in which recklessness or negligence is sufficient to establish mens rea.

In criminal law, there is a significant distinction between the words *intention* and *intent*. Intention is often equated with the mental state of specific intent, which is discussed below. Intent is also different from motive.

Motive is the desire that compels or drives a person to intend to do something. Unlike intent, motive is not an element of the crime and therefore does not need to be proven in order to find a defendant guilty. Evidence of a motive, however, is often used to establish the existence or absence of intent.

General Intent

Arnold Loewy, in attempting to describe **general intent**, states: "General intent is an extraordinarily esoteric concept. It is usually employed by courts to explain criminal liability when a defendant did not intend to bring about a particular result."[10]

General intent, for the most part, refers to the intent to commit the act (actus reus) required for the crime. General intent is sufficient mens rea for most criminal offenses. To establish general intent, it must be shown that the defendant acted with a malevolent purpose; that is, the accused committed the required act while knowing that it was wrong. Once it is proven that the accused committed the required act, it is presumed that he or she had the necessary general intent.

It is often stated that a person is presumed to intend the natural and probable consequences of his or her knowing and deliberate acts. There is no presumption, however, that a person intended results that are not natural, reasonable, or probable consequences of voluntary acts.

Specific Intent

Specific intent refers to doing the actus reus with the intent to cause a particular result. The term specific intent is often used by the courts for crimes that require proof of a particular mental state of intent or knowledge. Unlike general intent, specific intent is not presumed but must be proven. Associated with specific intent is the requirement of *scienter*. Scienter is a legal term meaning the degree of knowledge that makes a person criminally liable for his or her physical acts.[11] When a certain state of knowledge (scienter) is required, the prosecution must allege the existence of the scienter in the indictment (charges) against the accused. For example, in most states, the offense of battery or assault upon a police officer requires showing that the defendant knew that the victim was a police officer. This is the scienter, and it must be alleged in the pleadings. Other examples of scienter include

- Aiding a felon (must allege and prove that the defendant knew that the person he or she was aiding was a felon).
- Refusing to assist a law enforcement officer (must allege and prove that the defendant knew that the person requesting assistance was a law enforcement officer).

Also associated with specific intent is the term willful. This is another one of those terms that is very perplexing. At times, it means nothing more than "intentional." At other times, it means more, namely that the defendant intentionally caused the social harm with a bad motive. This latter meaning was applied by the U.S. Supreme Court in *United States v. Murdock*.[12] In this case, the defendant refused to answer questions by a governmental agency, based on his belief that he had a constitutional privilege not to answer the questions. The Court held that, while he did not have a constitutional privilege to avoid the questions, his refusal to answer was based on an honest but erroneous belief, and therefore his refusal was not willful.

Practicum 3.3

Defendants were prosecuted in the County of Maui, Hawaii, for indecent exposure. They admitted that they were sunbathing in the nude on a beach but contended that there was no intent to expose themselves indecently. In addition, defendants contended that there was no evidence to show an intent to expose themselves indecently. The statute in question required a general intent for the essential **elements** of the offense. Evidence was presented in court to establish that the beach was isolated and away from the view of the adjoining road and beaches. It was accessible by a well-worn path and known to be a favorite fishing location.

ISSUE: Are the facts sufficient to justify an inference of intent on the part of the defendants to be seen by others?

The court held that the defendants' actions in exposing themselves on a public beach under circumstances where they might be seen by others was sufficient to infer a general intent to offend the community's common sense of decency.[13]

Constructive Intent

Constructive intent refers to those situations in which the actor does not intend any harm but should have known that his or her behavior created a high risk of harm. The Model Penal Code (MPC) substitutes "recklessness" for constructive intent. Under the MPC, a reckless state of mind implies that one acts without intending harm but with complete disregard for the rights and safety of others, causing harm to result.

Criminal Negligence

Usually, a person is not criminally liable for negligent acts. To establish criminal liability, the **negligence** must amount to criminal negligence. Criminal negligence, however, has no single meaning at common law. In most cases, it constitutes a gross deviation from the standard of care required of an individual. Frequently, courts describe criminal negligence as gross negligence or culpable negligence.

One court described a criminally negligent person as one who creates a substantial unjustified risk of harm to others.[14]

Is it criminal negligence to drive with extremely worn tires on your automobile? In *Ison v. Commonwealth*, 271 S.W.3d 533 (Ky. Ct. App. 2008), a jury convicted defendant of three counts of reckless homicide (Ky. Rev. Stat. Ann. § 507.050) among other charges. The facts of the case were that on the rainy afternoon of October 21, 2005, Ison was driving his Ford Mustang on Highway 15 in Letcher County. An eyewitness in the vehicle behind Ison testified that Ison drove within the speed limit and safely negotiated a curve before losing traction and crossing lanes into oncoming traffic, where his vehicle collided with a vehicle driven by Tracy Craft. Ison's three passengers died as a result of the collision. On appeal, Ison argued that because there was insufficient proof of the necessary mental states for the offenses of reckless homicide charges. The appellate court agreed and noted that wanton behavior generally requires a person to be aware of, but consciously disregard, "a substantial and unjustifiable risk" which is "of such nature and degree that disregard thereof constitutes a gross deviation from the standard of conduct that a reasonable person would observe in the situation." The court noted that while Ison's vehicle was described as having rear tires that were extremely worn, the eyewitness to the collision testified that Ison was not speeding or driving erratically before the tires lost traction immediately prior to the collision. And the toxicology report showed no alcohol or drugs in Ison's blood.

To be liable in civil cases for negligence, one should be but is not necessarily aware that his or her conduct constitutes an unjustified foreseeable risk. Generally, the criminal defendant is aware of the unjustified risk but proceeds anyway.

In many states, "recklessly" is a synonym for "criminally negligent." In other states, *recklessly* differs from *criminally negligent* in that it involves greater risk taking. In those states where there is a difference between criminal negligence and recklessness, recklessness additionally requires that the defendant's fault be subjective, in that he or she is aware that there is unjustifiable risk of danger in his or her conduct.

In *West v. Commonwealth*, 935 S.W. 2d 315 (Ky. Ct. App. 1996), a Kentucky court of appeals stated that one acts "recklessly" with respect to a result or to a circumstance when he fails to perceive a substantial and unjustifiable risk that the result will occur or that the circumstance exists. The risk must be of such nature and degree that failure to perceive it constitutes a gross deviation from the standard of care that a reasonable person would observe in the situation.

Transferred Intent

Transferred intent refers to the situation in which one intends to harm one person and instead harms another. In these cases, the law transfers the intent to harm to the person actually harmed. Transferred intent cases are often called "bad aim" cases because a large number involve an offender firing at one person and accidentally hitting someone else.

The doctrine of transferred intent has long been recognized in common law. For example, Sir William Blackstone stated in his commentaries on the law of England:

> Thus if one shoots at A; and misses him, but kills B; this is murder; because of the previous felonious intent, which the law transfers from one to the other. The same is the case where one lays poison for A; and B, against whom the prisoner had no malicious intent, takes it, and it kills him; this is likewise murder.[15]

In *Henry v. State*, 184 Md. App. 146 (Md. Ct. Spec. App. 2009), defendant argued that the trial court committed error by instructing the jury on the doctrine of transferred intent where both the intended victim and the unintended victim were killed. The defendant shot his intended victim with a shotgun, killing him and also killing another person. The appellate court disagreed, holding that transferred intent doctrine applied even when defendant killed the intended target. In *State v. Anderson*, 2009 Minn. App. Unpub. LEXIS 305 (Minn. Ct. App. Mar. 31, 2009), defendant's conviction for murder and assault with a dangerous weapon was affirmed where the defendant shot the intended victim killing him and at the same time injuring two bystanders. The conviction for assault with a dangerous weapon on the bystanders was affirmed based on the doctrine of transferred intent.

Strict Liability Crimes

As Chapter 1 discussed, common law crimes are considered moral wrongs in themselves (*mala in se*). Traditionally, these crimes require proof of either general or specific intent. Some of the *mala prohibita* crimes, however, require no proof of culpability. These offenses are called "strict liability" offenses because mere proof that the act was committed is sufficient to convict an individual. No culpability or state of mind need be proven. Some criminal law writers contend that these crimes are not really crimes but only regulatory offenses.

Strict liability crimes often involve one of the following types of conduct: selling impure or adulterated food, selling prohibited beverages to minors, selling articles that are misbranded, and driving without a license.

Similar to the strict liability offenses are the vicarious liability crimes. In these crimes, the defendant is held accountable for the conduct of another, usually an employee. For example, if a waiter serves adulterated food in a restaurant, the owner of the restaurant may be vicariously liable for the actions of the waiter even though the owner did not know of the conduct. In some cases, vicarious liability is extended to the employer even in situations in which the employee deliberately disobeys the orders or instructions of the employer—for example, when a bartender disobeys the owner and sells beer to minors.

In *Pelayo-Garcia v. Holder*, 2009 U.S. App. LEXIS 27096 (9th Cir. Dec. 14, 2009), an appellate court noted that Cal. Penal Code § 261.5(d) contains the following elements: (1) sexual intercourse with another person; (2) the defendant was at least twenty-one years of age at the time of intercourse; and (3) the other person was under the age of sixteen years at the time of intercourse. The statute does not expressly include a scienter requirement, and courts have concluded that Cal. Penal Code § 261.5(d) is a strict liability crime that does not require any showing of scienter.

Case on Point

Establishing defendant's mental state: State v. Williams

Excerpt from the trial judge's instructions to the jury:

> Often a defendant's mental state is not conducive to demonstration through direct evidence. In criminal prosecutions, proof of a defendant's mental state often must be inferred from the circumstances, and the jury must make its determination by both

the act and by the surrounding circumstances. The key to circumstantial evidence generally, and as applied to state-of-mind questions specifically, is whether it bears a logical connection to the disputed fact. When an individual's state of mind is at issue, a greater breadth of evidence is allowed. A court will admit circumstantial evidence that has a tendency to shed light on a defendant's mental state or which tends fairly to explain the defendant's actions, notwithstanding that the evidence relates to conduct that occurred before the offense. Similarly, conduct that occurs after the charged offense circumstantially may support inferences about a defendant's state of mind.

The relevance of post-crime conduct to a defendant's mental state is recognized when the conduct demonstrates consciousness of guilt. Flight is recognized as being a type of post-crime conduct that can demonstrate consciousness of guilt. Evidence of flight occurring after the commission of an offense has been held probative of guilt and admissible. A defendant's post-crime conduct evidencing a guilty conscience provided a sound basis from which a jury logically could infer that a defendant was acting consistent with an admission of guilt or that the conduct was illuminating on a defendant's earlier state of mind.

When the State alleges criminal recklessness, it must demonstrate through legally competent proofs that defendant had knowledge or awareness of, and then consciously disregarded, a substantial and unjustifiable risk.

The element of criminal recklessness differs from knowing culpability in that the latter requires a greater degree of certainty that a particular result will occur. Recklessness can generally be distinguished from purposely and knowingly based on the degree of certainty involved. Purposely and knowingly states of mind involve near certainty, while recklessness involves an awareness of a risk that is of a probability rather than certainty. Even when recklessness is the mens rea element of the crime charged, a defendant's knowledge or awareness is material to the determination of culpability. Recklessness resembles knowledge in that both involve a state of awareness.

N.J. LEXIS 346 (N.J. Apr. 11, 2007).

Practicum 3.4

In a dispute over the quality of heroin, the defendant fired at the drug dealer. He missed the dealer but hit and killed a twelve-year-old bystander.

ISSUE: Is the defendant guilty of murder with intent to kill?

Despite the argument by his counsel that the defendant had no malice toward the victim and did not intend to kill him, the defendant was convicted of murder with intent to kill. The Maryland appellate court stated that the doctrine of transferred intent has been a part of American common law since before the Revolution and continues today as part of our law.[16]

The justifications for strict and vicarious liability crimes are the need to encourage extremely high standards of care required for the protection of society and the difficulty of proving culpability in those cases.

Model Penal Code (MPC 2.02)

General Requirements of Culpability

1. ***Minimum Requirements of Culpability.*** Except as provided in Section 2.05, a person is not guilty of an offense unless he acted purposely, knowingly, recklessly, or negligently, as the law may require, with respect to each material element of the offense.

2. ***Kinds of Culpability Defined.***
    a. ***Purposely.*** A person acts purposely with respect to a material element of an offense when:
        i. if the element involves the nature of his conduct or a result thereof, it is his conscious object to engage in conduct of that nature or to cause such a result; and
        ii. if the element involves the attendant circumstances, he is aware of the existence of such circumstances or he believes or hopes that they exist.
    b. ***Knowingly.*** A person acts knowingly with respect to a material element of an offense when:
        i. if the element involves the nature of his conduct or the attendant circumstances, he is aware that his conduct is of that nature or that such circumstances exist; and
        ii. if the element involves a result of his conduct, he is aware that it is practically certain that his conduct will cause such a result.
    c. ***Recklessly.*** A person acts recklessly with respect to a material element of an offense when he consciously disregards a substantial and unjustifiable risk that the material element exists or will result from his conduct. The risk must be of such a nature and degree that, considering the nature and purpose of the actor's conduct and the circumstances known to him, its disregard involves a gross deviation from the standard of conduct that a law-abiding person would observe in the actor's situation.
    d. ***Negligently.*** A person acts negligently with respect to a material element of an offense when he should be aware of a substantial and unjustifiable risk that the material element exists or will result from his conduct. The risk must be of such a nature and degree that the actor's failure to perceive it, considering the nature and purpose of his conduct and the circumstances known to him, involves a gross deviation from the standard of care that a reasonable person would observe in the actor's situation.

3. ***Culpability Required Unless Otherwise Provided.*** When the culpability sufficient to establish a material element of an offense is not prescribed by law, such element is established if a person acts purposely, knowingly, or recklessly with respect thereto.

4. ***Prescribed Culpability Requirement Applies to All Material Elements.*** When the law defining an offense prescribes the kind of culpability that is sufficient for the commission of an offense, without distinguishing among the material elements thereof, such provision shall apply to all material elements of the offense, unless a contrary purpose plainly appears.

5. ***Substitutes for Negligence, Recklessness, and Knowledge.*** When the law provides that negligence suffices to establish an element of an offense, such element also is established if a person acts purposely, knowingly, or recklessly. When recklessness suffices to establish an element, such element also is established if a person acts purposely or knowingly. When acting knowingly suffices to establish an element, such element also is established if a person acts purposely.

6. ***Requirement of Purpose Satisfied If Purpose Is Conditional.*** When a particular purpose is an element of an offense, the element is established although such purpose is conditional, unless the condition negatives the harm or evil sought to be prevented by the law defining the offense.

7. ***Requirement of Knowledge Satisfied by Knowledge of High Probability.*** When knowledge of the existence of a particular fact is an element of an offense, such knowledge is established if a person is aware of a high probability of its existence, unless he actually believes that it does not exist.

8. ***Requirement of Willfulness Satisfied by Acting Knowingly.*** A requirement that an offense be committed willfully is satisfied if a person acts knowingly with respect to the material elements of the offense, unless a purpose to impose further requirements appears.

9. ***Culpability as to Illegality of Conduct.*** Neither knowledge nor recklessness or negligence as to whether conduct constitutes an offense or as to the existence, meaning, or application of the law determining the elements of an offense is an element of such offense, unless the definition of the offense or the Code so provides.

10. ***Culpability as Determinant of Grade of Offense.*** When the grade or degree of an offense depends on whether the offense is committed purposely, knowingly, recklessly, or negligently, its grade or degree shall be the lowest for which the determinative kind of culpability is established with respect to any material element of the offense.

Comments on Model Penal Code Sections

Section 2.02 has been called the most important section of the MPC since it contains a number of rules for resolving conceptual difficulties with regard to culpability. Under the section, strict liability is provided only for violations, which are punished only by financial penalties. The code stresses that the required degree of culpability must exist with respect to each essential element of the offense.

The traditional terms "willfully" and "maliciously" have been replaced by four types of culpability: purposely, knowingly, recklessly, and negligently. Knowingly means voluntarily and intentionally, not by accident or mistake. Phillip E. Johnson illustrates the differences between the types by the use of an old English case:

An anarchist throws a bomb into the royal carriage, killing the king, the king's valet, the royal coachman, and a bystander on the street. The assassin's purpose was to kill the king (purposely). He knew that the bomb would also kill the king's valet who was riding in the coach (knowingly). He told a friend that his actions might kill the coachman, but he hoped the coachman would survive (recklessly—aware of the risk). He was unaware, however, that the bomb would also kill a bystander (negligently).[17]

The code also makes a significant distinction between reckless and negligent. Under this section, **recklessness** involves the conscious creation of a risk, whereas negligence involves the failure to recognize a risk that one should be aware of. Recklessness under the MPC is equivalent to the traditional culpability state of general intent. Negligence is the only one of the four types of culpability that involves no conscious wrongdoing.

With respect to ignorance of the existence of a statute prohibiting the conduct in question, the section provides that the knowledge of the existence of a criminal prohibition is not an element of the offense.

JOINDER OF INTENT AND ACT

The *actus reus* and the *mens rea* must be joined in time. For example, if X decided to murder someone one week, then changed her mind but accidentally killed the person the next week, this would not be murder, since the intent to kill and the act did not exist together at any one time. There is no specific length of time, however, that the *mens rea* must exist before the act as long as they exist concurrently at some time. In fact, the necessary mental element may be formed at the exact time that the requisite act is committed.

CAUSATION

Causation is an implicit element of a crime's *actus reus*. This is based on the fact that the *actus reus* is considered a voluntary act resulting in the harm to society prohibited by the offense. For example, before X can be convicted of murder, his act must have been the cause of the victim's death. Most causation issues arise in criminal homicide cases. The presence of causation is usually an issue only when the harm caused was an unwanted result—for example, the unintended death of a victim.

Actual cause exists if the result would not have occurred when it did in the absence of that factor. This can be stated another way: But for the defendant's act, would the social harm have occurred when it did?

The determination that the defendant's conduct was an actual cause of the result, however, does not necessarily mean that the defendant is criminally liable for the harm. For the defendant to be guilty, not only must she have acted with the required *mens rea,* but she must also be the proximate cause of the harm. Proximate cause is also defined as the **legal causation** of the harm. That cause is legally considered the act that was directly responsible for the harm.

In most crimes, it is easy to assign the direct cause of the social harm. There may, however, be intervening causes that are also linked to the event. Intervening causes are classified as either dependent or independent. A dependent intervening cause is a force that occurs in response to an earlier causal force. Dependent causes do not relieve the defendant of causal responsibility for the resulting harm. An independent intervening cause is a force that does not occur in response to the wrongdoer's initial conduct. An independent cause may relieve the defendant of the causal responsibility for the resulting harm.

Consider the following examples:

1. X shoots V. V is being transported to the hospital when the ambulance is involved in a wreck that kills V. Is X guilty of murder?
2. X shoots V. V is taken to the hospital, where he receives negligent treatment. V dies. Had V received adequate treatment, he would have survived the shooting. Is X guilty of murder?

In the first situation, X probably would not be guilty of murder, since the wreck was an independent intervening cause. The wreck was not in response to the defendant's conduct. In the second situation, X probably would be guilty of murder, since poor medical treatment is considered a dependent intervening cause. In the latter example, medical treatment is in response to the defendant's conduct.

Case on Point

People v. Rideout

Excerpts from the trial judge's instructions to the jury on causation:

In criminal jurisprudence, the causation element of an offense is generally comprised of two components: factual cause and proximate cause. The concept of factual causation is relatively straightforward. In determining whether a defendant's conduct is a factual cause of the result, one must ask, "but for" the defendant's conduct, would the result have occurred? If the result would not have occurred absent the defendant's conduct, then factual causation exists. The existence of factual causation alone, however, will not support the imposition of criminal liability. Proximate causation must also be established. Proximate causation is a "legal colloquialism." It is a legal construct designed to prevent criminal liability from attaching when the result of the defendant's conduct is viewed as too remote or unnatural. Thus, a proximate cause is simply a factual cause of which the law will take cognizance.

For a criminal defendant's conduct to be regarded as a proximate cause, the victim's injury must be a "direct and natural result" of the defendant's actions. In making this determination, it is necessary to examine whether there was an intervening cause that superseded the defendant's conduct such that the causal link between the defendant's conduct and the victim's injury was broken. If an intervening cause did indeed supersede the defendant's act as a legally significant causal factor, then the defendant's conduct will not be deemed a proximate cause of the victim's injury. The standard by which to gauge whether an intervening cause supersedes, and thus severs the causal link, is generally one of reasonable foreseeability. The linchpin in the superseding cause analysis is whether the intervening cause was foreseeable based on an objective standard of reasonableness. If it was reasonably foreseeable, then the defendant's conduct will be considered a proximate cause. If, however, the intervening act by the victim or a third party was not reasonably foreseeable—e.g., gross negligence or intentional misconduct—then generally the causal link is severed and the defendant's conduct is not regarded as a proximate cause of the victim's injury or death.

In criminal law, a superseding intervening cause does not need to be the only cause. Indeed, while a defendant's conduct might have been a factual cause of an accident, the victim's conduct might also have been a cause and, more to the point, potentially a superseding cause.

272 Mich. App. 602 (2006).

PRESUMPTIONS

Often, it is difficult to prove the requisite intent required to convict the defendant of a certain crime. For example, in one state, first-degree murder may be defined as the unlawful and intentional killing of a human being with malice. How do you establish that the defendant actually intended to kill the victim, especially when the defendant claims that the killing was accidental? To overcome this difficulty, legislatures and courts establish rules of presumption. A presumption operates in the following manner: Upon proof of fact A, the court may or must presume fact B. One of the most commonly accepted presumptions is that a person is presumed to have intended the natural and probable consequences of his or her act. Many states have enacted "bad check" statutes that create the presumption that, if an individual has not made "good" the bad check within a certain number of days after notification, that the individual is presumed to have intentionally defrauded the individual who accepted the bad check. In this situation, to prove the intent to defraud (fact B), you would need to establish notification of the check's dishonor (fact A). There are two types of presumptions: permissible or rebuttable ones and mandatory or conclusive presumptions. With a permissible or rebuttable presumption, the fact-finder (judge or jury) may find fact B after fact A is established. With mandatory or conclusive presumptions, if fact A is established, the fact-finder must accept the existence of fact B.

Case on Point

United States v. Bailey

In the early morning hours of August 26, 1976, respondents Clifford Bailey, James T. Cogdell, Ronald C. Cooley, and Ralph Walker, federal prisoners at the District of Columbia jail, crawled through a window from which a bar had been removed, slid down a knotted bed sheet, and escaped from custody. Federal authorities recaptured them after they had remained at large for a period of time ranging from one month to three and one-half months. Upon their apprehension, they were charged with violating 18 U.S.C. § 751 (a), which governs escape from federal custody. At their trials, each of the respondents adduced or offered to adduce evidence as to various conditions and events at the District of Columbia jail, but each was convicted by the jury. The Court of Appeals for the District of Columbia Circuit reversed the convictions by a divided vote, holding that the District Court had improperly precluded consideration by the respective juries of respondents' tendered evidence.

Respondents' defense of duress or necessity centered on the conditions in the jail during the months of June, July, and August 1976, and on various threats and beatings directed at them during that period.

Criminal liability is normally based upon the concurrence of two factors, "an evil-meaning mind and an evil-doing hand . . ." *Morissette v. United States*, 342 U.S., at 251. In the present case, we must examine both the mental element, or mens rea, required for conviction under § 751 (a) and the circumstances under which the "evil-doing hand" can avoid liability under that section because coercive conditions or necessity negates a conclusion of guilt even though the necessary mens rea was present.

Few areas of criminal law pose more difficulty than the proper definition of the mens rea required for any particular crime.

At common law, crimes generally were classified as requiring either "general intent" or "specific intent." This venerable distinction, however, has been the source of a good deal of confusion. "Sometimes 'general intent' is used in the same way as 'criminal intent' to mean the general notion of mens rea, while 'specific intent' is taken to mean the mental state required for a particular crime. Or, 'general intent' may be used to encompass all forms of the mental state requirement, while 'specific intent' is limited to the one mental state of intent. Another possibility is that 'general intent' will be used to characterize an intent to do something on an undetermined occasion, and 'specific intent' to denote an intent to do that thing at a particular time and place." (Chief Justice Rehnquist quoting from the *Morissette* opinion; case also discussed on p. 47)

A person who causes a particular result is said to act purposefully if he consciously desires that result, whatever the likelihood of that result happening from his conduct, while he is said to act knowingly if he is aware that that result is practically certain to follow from his conduct, whatever his desire may be as to that result. . . . In the case of most crimes, the limited distinction between knowledge and purpose has not been considered important since there is good reason for imposing liability whether the defendant desired or merely knew of the practical certainty of the results. . . . In certain narrow classes of crimes, however, heightened culpability has been thought to merit special attention. Thus, the statutory and common law of homicide often distinguishes, either in setting the "degree" of the crime or in imposing punishment, between a person who knows that another person will be killed as the result of his conduct and a person who acts with the specific purpose of taking another's life.

444 U.S. 394 (1980).

VERTICAL GROWTH OF CRIMINAL CODES

Robert Johnson, County Attorney for Anoka County, Minnesota, and a member of Minnesota's Crime Volunteer Advisory Committee, points out that the vertical growth of criminal codes occurs in three ways. The most direct way is simply declaring a crime, such as interference with privacy, to be a felony rather than a gross misdemeanor. Another way is to declare that a misdemeanor crime, such as domestic assault or driving while impaired, becomes a felony upon a second or third violation. The third method by which vertical growth has been achieved is increasing the penalty when the victim is a member of a particular interest group, such as police, probation officers, or jailers.

According to Johnson, the broad criminalization of conduct since the 1970s means many more lives are impacted by the criminal justice system and the collateral consequences of conviction. Some individuals are swept unexpectedly into the criminal justice system unaware that their conduct is now considered worthy of a criminal charge. Johnson notes that, when we use the criminal justice system to regulate offensive behavior, we employ a system that is enormously expensive and slow. Police, prosecutors, jailers, defenders, judges, and corrections officials all must deal with an offense. Cases often take months or years to work through the system. By the time a criminal charge is resolved, the penalty is often no longer as meaningful to the people involved.

Johnson opines that overcriminalization may also undermine deterrence—a primary purpose of the criminal justice system. When a code cannot possibly be evenly enforced as written, it is likely to be enforced differently from jurisdiction to jurisdiction, and even within a locality. He contends that deterrence becomes much less effective when the public receives a mixed message as to the seriousness of a crime, or the gravity of its consequences.[18]

HOW WOULD YOU DECIDE?

Defendant argued that his prior conviction for possession of a sawed-off shotgun under Ark. Code Ann. § 5-73-104 (1987) was unconstitutional because he was not aware that the shotgun had been modified. And therefore this earlier conviction should not have been considered as a prior conviction under the Armed Career Criminal Act, 18 U.S.C.S. § 924(e). If you were the judge in the present case and required to sentence him for conviction of being a felon in possession of a firearm in violation of 18 U.S.C.S. § 922(g), would you consider the prior conviction?

SEE: UNITED STATES V. VINCENT, 575 F.3D 820 (8TH CIR. ARK. 2009)

Summary

Every crime has two requisites: the required act or failure to act (*actus reus*) and the required mental state (*mens rea*). *Actus reus* literally means "guilty act." It is more than voluntary movement. It includes both muscular contractions and the circumstances and consequences associated with the contractions. The requirement of *actus reus* prevents punishing one merely for his or her thoughts.

The act necessary to constitute the crime is generally specified by statute. Involuntary movement normally does not constitute sufficient *actus reus* to cause criminal liability. The act of speaking or the possession of something illegal may be a sufficient act to constitute a crime.

Criminal liability can be based on a failure to act, but only when the individual has a legal duty to act. A moral duty is insufficient to establish criminal liability.

Mens rea involves the concept that criminal sanctions should not be imposed on those who innocently cause harm. For an act to be criminal, it must be accompanied by the required *mens rea*, also referred to as culpability. This principle can be hard to apply in some cases.

Four mental states qualify as *mens rea*: general intent, specific intent, transferred intent, and constructive intent. Criminal law distinguishes between intention and intent. Intention is often equated with specific intent. Intent also differs from motive. Motive is the desire that drives a person to intend to do something. Unlike intent, motive is not an element of a crime and therefore need not be proven in order to find a defendant guilty.

General intent is the intent to commit the act (*actus reus*) required for the crime. General intent is sufficient *mens rea* for most criminal offenses. To establish general intent, the prosecution must show that the accused committed the required act and knew that it was wrong. If the accused committed the required act, the law presumes that he or she had the necessary general intent.

Specific intent refers to the intent to cause a particular result. It often applies to crimes that require proof of a particular mental state or knowledge.

Associated with specific intent is the requirement of scienter, the knowledge that makes a person criminally liable for his or her physical acts. Also associated with specific intent is willfulness, which means intentional behavior, or else causing social harm with a bad motive. Generally, one is not criminally liable for negligence. To establish criminal liability, the negligence must amount to criminal negligence, which has no single meaning at common law. In most cases, it is a gross deviation from the standard of care required of an individual.

Transferred intent applies when one intends to harm one person and instead harms another. The law assumes intent to harm the actual victim.

In the Model Penal Code, the traditional terms *willfully* and *maliciously* have been replaced by four types of culpability: purposely, knowingly, recklessly, and negligently. Knowingly means voluntarily and intentionally, not by accident or mistake.

Actus reus and *mens rea* must exist together at the time a crime is committed. Causation is also an element of a crime's *actus reus*. The defendant's act must have been the cause of the harm to society. Most causation issues arise in criminal homicide cases when the act causes an unintended death.

Additional Assignments

1. Read the selected cases and associated material for Chapter 3 posted at www.mycrimekit.com.
2. Complete the online study guide material for Chapter 3 posted at www.mycrimekit.com.
3. Discussion and thought questions:
   a. What are the basic requirements for criminal liability?
   b. Under what circumstances may an individual be guilty of a crime by failing to act?
   c. What is meant by voluntary actions?
   d. Distinguish between intent and causation.
   e. How does the Model Penal Code differ from common law regarding the mens rea requirement?

Notes

1. Joshua Dressler, *Understanding Criminal Law*, 2nd ed. (New York: Matthew Bender, 1995), 69.
2. See the discussion in Wayne R. LaFave and Austin W. Scott, Jr., *Criminal Law*, 2nd ed. (St. Paul, MN: West, 1986).
3. *Martin v. State,* 17 So. 2d 427 (Ala. 1944).
4. *Knox v. Commonwealth*, 735 S.E. 2d 711 (Ky. 1987).
5. *New York Times*, March 17, 1964, 1.

6. As quoted from Joshua Dressler, *Understanding Criminal Law*, 2nd ed. (New York: Matthew Bender, 1995), 101.

7. Oliver Wendell Holmes, *The Common Law* (Boston: Little, Brown, 1881), 63.

8. Ronald Perkins, "A Rationale of Mens Rea," 52 Harv. L. Rev. 905 (1939).

9. *Thacker v. Commonwealth*, 134 Va. 767 (Va. 1922).

10. Arnold H. Loewy, *Criminal Law,* 2nd ed. (St. Paul, MN: West, 1987), 118.

11. *Morissette v. United States*, 342 U.S. 246 (1952).

12. *United States v. Murdock*, 284 U.S. 141 (1931).

13. *State v. Rocker*, 475 P. 2d 684 (Haw. 1970).

14. *State v. Peterson*, 522 P. 2d 912 (Crt. of Appeals of Oregon 1974).

15. William Blackstone, IV *Commentaries* at 200. Posted at web site http://ebooks.adelaide.edu.au/b/blackstone/william/comment/book2.10.html and accessed August 12, 2010.

16. *Commonwealth v. Shea*, 316 A. 2d 319 (Mass. 1984).

17. Phillip E. Johnson*, Criminal Law*, 4th ed. (St. Paul, MN: West, 1990) 66.

18. Robert M. A. Johnson, "Is It a Crime?" 21 *Criminal Justice* 1 (Fall 2006).

CHAPTER 4

Inchoate or Anticipatory Crimes and Criminal Liability

Chapter Outline

Attempt
   Model Penal Code (MPC 5.01)
   The Elements of Attempt
   Special Problems in Attempt

Solicitation
   Model Penal Code (MPC 5.02)
   The Elements of Solicitation
   Special Problems in Solicitation

Conspiracy
   Model Penal Code (MPC 5.03)
   The Elements of Conspiracy
   Special Problems in Conspiracy

Accomplices and Accessories
   Model Penal Code
   The Elements of the Crime of Accomplice
   The Elements of the Crime of Accessory
   Special Problems with Accomplices
   Special Problems with Accessories
   Summary of Accomplices and Accessories

Comparing and Contrasting Inchoate Crimes
   Attempt
   Solicitation
   Conspiracy
   Accomplices/Accessories

What you should know about inchoate or anticipatory crimes and criminal liability. After reading this chapter, you should know

- Why society punishes inchoate crimes.
- What constitutes attempt, solicitation, and conspiracy.
- Why accomplices and accessories are held liable for their acts.

- The elements for each of the crimes discussed.
- The differences between each of the inchoate crimes.

Key Terms

After reading this chapter, you should understand the following key terms:

accessory: One who, after an offense has been committed, aids, conceals, or warns a principal with the intent that the principal avoid arrest, prosecution, conviction, or punishment for the crime.

accessory after the fact: A person who did not participate in the crime but furnished postcrime assistance to keep the offender from being detected or from being captured.

accessory before the fact: A person who aids and abets in preparation for crime commission but who was not present at the crime scene.

accomplice: One who, with the purpose of promoting or assisting in the commission of the offense, aids, agrees to aid, or attempts to aid in planning or committing the offense; or, having a duty to prevent the offense, fails to do so.

accomplice liability: The degree of criminal blameworthiness of one who aids, abets, encourages, or assists another person in the commission of a crime.

attempt: A specific intent to commit a substantive crime, coupled with an act in furtherance of that intent that goes beyond mere preparation.

complicity: Refers to the degree of involvement in a crime as either a principal or as an accomplice.

conspiracy: An agreement between two or more parties for the purpose of achieving an unlawful objective or a lawful objective by an unlawful means, where one of the parties to the agreement commits an overt act.

inchoate crime: A criminal act that goes beyond mere thought but occurs before the substantive criminal act is completed. Also called preparatory crime.

parties to a crime: All those who take part in the commission of a crime and those who aid and abet and are therefore criminally liable for the crime.

plurality requirement: The legal requirement that a conspiracy must involve two or more parties.

preparatory act: Act committed by the offender in preparation or prior to the commission of the substantive crime.

principal(s): Person(s) who commit the substantive crime.

solicitation: Asking, encouraging, or soliciting another person to commit a crime, with the intent that the substantive crime will be committed by the other person.

Wharton's rule: A rule applicable to conspiracy cases that holds that when the targeted crime by its very nature takes more than one party to commit, there can be no conspiracy when no more than the number of parties required to commit the offense participated in it.

The basketball principle "no harm, no foul" does not apply to incomplete or **inchoate crimes**. Failed or incomplete efforts to commit criminal misconduct are considered to be dangerous conduct warranting prohibition before harm to others or property can occur. In this chapter, we will examine the law of inchoate or anticipatory crimes. This is one of the most confusing areas of criminal law. At the same time, it is one of the most critical.

These inchoate or anticipatory crimes can attach to each of the substantive crimes that are discussed elsewhere in this text.

As we will see, any discussion of these crimes may involve gray areas of the law. Picture yourself on a path. If you take three steps down that path, you have not committed a crime. However, if you take another step, society proclaims you are a criminal. The issue to be considered when dealing with inchoate crimes is the stage at which mere preparation changes to active participation. Questions such as how far a person has to go down the path toward the commission of a substantive crime have played havoc with the criminal justice system for years.[1]

Inchoate crimes, also called preparatory or anticipatory crimes, are those acts that go beyond mere thought but occur before the substantive criminal act is completed.[2] These acts are punished as crimes even though no major physical injury takes place. The most common inchoate or anticipatory crimes are attempts, solicitation, and conspiracy. There are other anticipatory crimes that are considered "hidden" in that they are not commonly considered anticipatory crimes even though they have all the attributes of an anticipatory crime. The most common of the hidden anticipatory crimes are burglary and the possession of burglary tools or counterfeit dies. As will be discussed in Chapter 11, burglary is the entry into a building with the intent to commit a crime, which makes it a crime committed while preparing to commit another crime. Possession of burglary tools or counterfeit dies are similar in nature.

The purpose of these laws prohibiting certain preparatory crimes is to prevent a defendant from committing the substantive crime that is the objective of the inchoate act. Society has determined that certain acts should be punished so that specific injuries caused by substantive crimes can be avoided. Statutes therefore define certain preparatory conduct as criminal and punish this conduct before the commission of the substantive offense. These crimes are attempt, solicitation, and conspiracy.

The Model Penal Code (MPC) lists three basic reasons for making these actions criminal:

1. Law enforcement agencies must be able to intervene prior to the commission of a substantive crime. By making these acts criminal in nature, the courts have jurisdiction.
2. **Preparatory acts** indicate that the defendant is inclined to commit a crime. There must be a basis for intervention to stop this process.
3. Such acts should not go unpunished simply because the defendant was unable to finish the act. This would be an injustice to society.[3]

ATTEMPT

One who has a purpose and intention to slay another and he merely wounds him should be regarded as a murderer.

PLATO, LAWS[4]

One who is taken in the act of robbery or burglary, even though he does not carry it out, will be hanged.

ENGLISH JUSTICE WILLIAM SHARDLOW[5]

One of the best known anticipatory offenses is the crime of **attempt**. Unlike solicitation or conspiracy, the crime of attempt occurs in the open and may involve serious injury to another person. We have all read newspaper accounts of someone shooting a storeowner one or more times during a robbery. If the victim dies, the offender will be charged with murder. However, if the victim lives, the defendant will be charged with robbery and attempted murder. The next section will discuss this very serious inchoate offense.

While the definition and elements of the crime of attempt seem simple, courts and scholars have encountered trouble in defining its various parts. Most authorities agree on the basic definition of the crime, but subtle differences appear when they discuss how far a person must go beyond mere thought and into the realm of action to constitute an attempt. The Model Penal Code focuses on the defendant's conduct in defining the crime of attempt.

Case on Point

Merging of Inchoate Crimes: Commonwealth v. Welch

Defendant appeals from the judgment of sentence following his conviction of criminal conspiracy (robbery) and criminal attempt (homicide). The court noted that a person may not be convicted of more than one of the inchoate crimes of criminal attempt, criminal solicitation or criminal conspiracy for conduct designed to commit or to culminate in the commission of the same crime (18 Pa.C.S. § 906). Section 906 was designed to prevent multiple inchoate charges that carry with them the same criminal intent.

Inchoate crimes merge only when directed to the commission of the same crime, not merely because they arise out of the same incident. A defendant's sentences for attempted burglary and conspiracy to commit burglary merge because they arise from conduct directed to the commission of the same crime.

The court noted that the record established that the conspiracy to steal an all-terrain vehicle (ATV) was not designed to commit or culminate into the attempted murder of the owner of the ATV. Defendant and his co-conspirators were in the process of stealing an ATV and did not develop the intent to commit murder until the owner disrupted the robbery and chased him on foot. When defendant stopped running, aimed his firearm and shot at the owner, his conduct exceeded the scope of his conspiratorial agreement to steal an ATV. As such, the attempt to commit murder and conspiracy to commit robbery are independent crimes, each with their own separate factual basis and criminal purpose. Defendant's convictions for both the conspiracy to commit robbery and attempted murder were correct.

2006 PA Super 339, 912 A.2d 857 (Pa. Super. Ct. 2006).

Model Penal Code (MPC 5.01)

The MPC states:

   1. *Definition of Attempt.* A person is guilty of attempt if he:
      a. purposely engages in conduct that would constitute the crime if the attendant circumstances were as he believes them to be; or

     b. when causing a particular result is an element of the crime, he does or omits to do anything with the purpose of causing or with the belief that it will cause such result without further conduct on his part; or

     c. purposely does or omits to do anything that, under the circumstances as he believes them to be, is an act or omission constituting a substantial step in a course of conduct planned to culminate in his commission of the crime.

2. *Conduct That May Be Held Substantial Step Under Subsection (1)(c).* Conduct that may be a substantial step under Section (1)(c) must be strongly corroborative of the defendant's criminal purpose. Each of the following acts may be considered a substantial step as a matter of law:

     a. lying in wait, searching for, or following the victim,

     b. enticing or seeking to entice the victim to go to the place where the crime is to be committed,

     c. reconnoitering the place where the crime is to occur,

     d. unlawfully entering a structure, vehicle, or enclosure that is the contemplated scene of the crime,

     e. possessing materials to be used in a crime that were designed for the crime or that under the circumstances serve no lawful purpose,

     f. possessing, collecting, or fabricating material to be used in the commission of a crime at or near the scene of the crime, where such possession, collection, or fabrication serves no lawful purpose, and

     g. soliciting an innocent agent to engage in conduct constituting an element of the crime.[6]

Attempt

Defined

Attempt consists of a specific intent to commit a substantive crime, coupled with an act in furtherance of that intent that goes beyond mere preparation.

Elements

The crime of attempt has two basic elements:

1. The specific intent to commit a crime.
2. An act or conduct to carry out the intent to commit the specific crime that goes beyond mere preparation.

     The drafters of the MPC divide the crime of attempt into two categories: (1) The crime of attempt occurs when the defendant has completed all planned acts but has failed to accomplish the substantive crime,[7] and (2) the crime of attempt occurs when the defendant has not completed all planned acts and for that reason has failed to accomplish the substantive crime.[8]

The first category involves situations in which the defendant cannot complete the substantive crime. The MPC also relies on these sections to reject the concept of impossibility, which has been utilized successfully as a defense in attempt prosecutions. The second category involves the preparatory acts necessary before the commission of the crime. These preparatory acts involve the defendants taking action in the form of embarking on any of the substantial steps listed in the code.

In summary, the MPC expands the scope of liability for attempt in a manner consistent with the purpose of punishing dangerous persons by (1) placing the emphasis on what the defendant has already done rather than on what remains to be accomplished, (2) ensuring that liability will be imposed only if some definite purpose of a criminal act is shown, and (3) evaluating the conduct in light of the defendant's statements.

Every U.S. jurisdiction punishes the crime of attempt.[9] Although composed of only two elements, this offense is more complex than it appears. The next section will discuss each of those elements.

The Elements of Attempt

The crime of attempt can be divided into two elements:

THE SPECIFIC INTENT TO COMMIT A CRIME The intent element in the crime of attempt requires the defendant to possess simultaneously two types of intent: (1) the intent to commit the acts or cause the result constituting the crime of attempt; and (2) the intent necessary to commit the substantive offense.

Practicum 4.1

Defendants were armed and planning to rob a payroll carrier. They were searching for the contemplated victim when they were arrested by the police.

ISSUE: Did the defendants commit the crime of attempted robbery?

Early court decisions would have found the defendants not guilty, as they had not proceeded beyond the preparation stage.[10] However, under the MPC, the defendants would be found guilty under the "lying in wait" or "searching" provisions of the code.

The element of intent in the crime of attempt does not exist in the abstract. Rather, the intent necessary for attempt must be wrapped into the substantive offense the defendant is trying to commit. For example, if the charge is attempted theft, and theft is defined as requiring a specific intent to permanently deprive another of her property, then the same intent must be proven in the crime of attempted theft. It is not sufficient to show that the defendant intended simply to commit an unspecified criminal act.

Many notable scholars have criticized the rule that there can be no attempt without specific intent. For example, Supreme Court Justice Oliver Wendell Holmes stated in his *Common Law*:

Acts should be judged by their tendency, under the known circumstances, not by the actual intent which accompanies them. It may be true that in the region of attempts, as elsewhere, the law began with cases of actual intent, as these cases were the most obvious ones. But it cannot stop with them, unless it attaches more importance to the etymological meaning of the word attempt than to the general principles of punishment.[11]

Despite the influence of Justice Holmes, specific intent remains a necessary element of the modern crime of attempt.

AN ACT OR CONDUCT IN FURTHERANCE OF THE INTENT TO COMMIT THE CRIME THAT GOES BEYOND MERE PREPARATION The defendant must undertake some substantial step in furtherance of the commission of the substantive crime.[12] Numerous authorities have spent a considerable amount of time examining to what extent the defendant must act to be found guilty of attempt. There are two main approaches to this issue: (1) Preparation versus perpetration: Some jurisdictions will find the offender guilty if his acts show he was preparing to commit the substantive offense. Other courts have required the defendant's acts to go beyond mere preparation and into the perpetration of the crime.[13] (2) The probable distance test: This test focuses on what acts the defendant has completed. The question is: "Would the defendant have stopped his conduct in committing the crime, given the actions he has already completed, absent outside intervening factors?"[14]

The better view seems to be that of the MPC. It focuses on what has been done (e.g., lying in wait to kill the victim), rather than on what is left undone (the actual killing of the victim). The essence of the offense, according to the MPC, is dangerous people rather than dangerous acts.

Special Problems in Attempt

LEGAL IMPOSSIBILITY A defendant cannot be punished for attempting to do something that is not a crime, even if she misunderstands the law and believes it is a crime. Since she has not committed an act that violates the law, society holds that she has not completed a dangerous act. The defendant therefore could raise the defense of legal impossibility. Under a different scenario, the defendant in order to avoid the payment of customs taxes sneaks an antique book past customs. The defendant did not realize that there were no customs on antique books. Has he committed an attempt to evade customs? No. It is another example of a legal impossibility.

FACTUAL IMPOSSIBILITY A defendant will be found guilty of the crime of attempt even if it was factually impossible for her to commit the crime. The issue is not a misunderstanding of the law but a mistake as to the facts surrounding the crime.

When the defendant has illustrated her dangerousness to society, she will not be excused simply because it was factually impossible for her to finish the crime. For example, Ralph

Damms is charged with attempted murder. Ralph Damms's wife Marjory filed for divorce. One evening Ralph went to Marjory's house, and they got into a quarrel. She ran for help and he chased her. She fell down. Ralph crouched over her and held a pistol at her head. Two officers testified that Ralph pointed the pistol directly at her head and pulled the trigger twice. The officers checked the pistol and found that it was unloaded. Ralph contended that he stated, "It won't fire," at which time, to show her that it would not fire, he pointed the gun at the ground and pulled the trigger twice. The jury believed the police officers' version and convicted Ralph of attempted murder in the first degree. The appellate court upheld the jury's finding that Ralph intended to kill his wife. The court stated that a "factual impossibility" is not a defense to crime. The question as to whether the gun was loaded was a factual, not a legal, question.[15]

The issue of legal and factual impossibility adds to the confusion surrounding the crime of attempt. Unfortunately, in the real world, criminals very seldom commit crimes according to textbook definitions. Therefore, we must examine all the facts involved in any incident to determine what, if any, crime has been committed.

The crime of attempt is determined by examining the defendant's state of mind, reviewing the acts he or she has undertaken, and comparing both of these with the elements of the substantive crime. Attempt is a crime that society has determined should be punished simply because the defendant has undertaken certain physical preparatory acts.

A defendant's attempt to hire an undercover police detective, who was posing as a hired assassin, supported a charge of attempted murder because there was a direct but ineffectual act toward accomplishing the intended killings, as required under *Pen C § 21a*. The defendant secured an agreement with the detective, provided necessary information, and paid a $5,000 down payment. *People v. Superior Court (Decker) (2007) 41 Cal 4th 1, 58 Cal Rptr 3d 421, 157 P3d 1017, 2007 Cal LEXIS 5099.*

Practicum 4.2

Defendant tampered with a draft for $2.50 by writing in the figure 1 so as to make what read $2 50/100 appear as $12 50/100. She did not change the written sum of Two Dollars and Fifty Cents, nor did she attempt to modify the stamped words, "Ten Dollars or Less," that were on the draft.

ISSUE: Does the defense of legal impossibility apply?

The court held that the defendant was not guilty of attempted forgery, although she had accomplished everything she intended to do. This was not a crime, since forgery requires the alteration of a material part of a document, and the figures were not a material part of the draft.[16]

Practicum 4.3

Defendant received property from A, believing that he was committing the offense of receiving stolen property. However, the property was not stolen. It was being used by A in a sting operation to catch the defendant in possession of stolen property. Defendant was charged with receiving stolen property and attempting to receive stolen property.

ISSUE: Can the defendant use the defense of impossibility?

Under the traditional approach, he would have the defense of legal impossibility and therefore be entitled to an acquittal as to both charges. The property was not stolen, so the defendant cannot be convicted of receiving stolen property. Since it was legally impossible for him to be convicted of the substantive crime, he cannot be convicted of attempting to commit that crime.[17]

Practicum 4.4

Defendant reached into the victim's pocket, intending to steal money he believed the victim had in his pocket. The victim had removed the money before the defendant acted, and therefore it was factually impossible for the defendant to steal from the victim.

ISSUE: Is factual impossibility a defense to the crime of attempted larceny?

The courts can find the defendant guilty of attempted larceny. The law will punish the defendant for his acts even though he failed to commit a crime. His actions displayed a dangerousness and willingness to violate the mores of society.[18]

The crime of solicitation, on the other hand, is based upon verbal statements by the defendant.

SOLICITATION

*The solicitation to another to a crime is as a rule far more dangerous to
society than the attempt to commit the same crime. For the solicitation
has behind it an evil purpose, coupled with the pressure of a stronger
intellect upon the weak and criminally inclined.*

STATE V. SCHLIEFER, 121 A. 805 (1923), JUDGE C.J. WHEELER.

Case on Point

United States v. Resendiz-Ponce

The respondent, a Mexican citizen, was charged with violating 8 U.S.C. § 1326(a) by attempting to reenter the United States after having been deported. The district court denied his motion to have the indictment dismissed because it did not allege a specific overt act that he committed in seeking reentry.

Justice Stevens:

> At common law, the attempt to commit a crime was itself a crime if the perpetrator not only intended to commit the completed offense, but also performed some open deed tending to the execution of his intent. More recently, the requisite "open deed" has been described as an "overt act" that constitutes a "substantial step" toward completing the offense. "Criminal attempt" is defined to include an act or omission constituting a substantial step in a course of conduct planned to culminate in his commission of the crime. As was true at common law, the mere intent to violate a federal criminal statute is not punishable as an attempt unless it is also accompanied by significant conduct.
>
> Not only does the word "attempt" as used in common parlance connote action rather than mere intent, but more importantly, as used in the law for centuries, it encompasses both the overt act and intent elements. Consequently, an indictment alleging attempted illegal reentry under 8 U.S.C.S. § 1326(a) need not specifically allege a particular overt act or any other "component part" of the offense. For indictment purposes, use of the word "attempt" is sufficient to incorporate the substantial step element. The word "attempt" necessarily means taking a substantial step.

127 S. Ct. 782 (U.S. 2007).

The crime of **solicitation** was originally called "incitement" in its antecedent form in England. Basically, the crime of solicitation punishes spoken words coupled with a criminal intent. The crime has its roots in the early nineteenth century, when the English courts determined that words urging the commission of a crime should be punished. In *Rex v. Higgins*, the defendant was charged with soliciting a servant to steal his master's goods. The servant did not carry out Higgins's request. The attorney representing Higgins argued that there was no case or precedent upon which to convict the defendant. The court found Higgins guilty, relying more upon the policy of finding the acts to be an offense than upon whether the offense previously existed in the common law.[19] We have progressed quite far since the time Higgins was convicted. Today there are laws setting forth the crime of solicitation. The MPC establishes a clear statutory framework that defines the elements of this crime.

Solicitation

Defined

Solicitation consists of asking, encouraging, or soliciting another person to commit a crime, with the intent that the substantive crime will be committed by the other person.

Elements

The crime of solicitation has two elements:

1. The intent that another party commit the crime
2. Asking, encouraging, or requesting another party to commit a crime

Solicitation statutes have historically been directed at specific offenses, such as the solicitation to commit prostitution. Despite the widespread use of solicitation laws, many jurisdictions still do not have a general solicitation statute. Others have a general statute and numerous solicitation statutes directed as specific offenses, a condition that frequently provides the prosecutor with a choice as to which statute she may charge the defendant under.

Model Penal Code (MPC 5.02)

The MPC states that a person is guilty of solicitation if he,

> with the purpose of promoting or facilitating a crime, commands, encourages, or requests another to engage in specific conduct which would constitute the crime or an attempt to commit the crime.

Court opinions have differed on whether a real social danger exists in solicitation to commit a crime. Some courts hold that such conduct is not a threat to society because the person solicited can refuse.[20] Other courts have stated that solicitation is a very dangerous act, in that it encourages cooperation among criminals.[21]

The MPC takes the position that purposeful solicitation presents dangers calling for preventive intervention and that the art of solicitation indicates a disposition toward criminal activity to call for liability. Moreover, the fortuity that the person solicited may not agree to commit or attempt to commit the incited crime plainly should not relieve the solicitor of liability, when otherwise she would be a conspirator or an accomplice.[22]

Under the MPC, solicitation of any crime—misdemeanor or felony—is sufficient for the crime of solicitation. If A solicits B to commit theft, it does not matter if it is grand theft or petty theft. The independent crime of solicitation has occurred. If the act solicited is serious enough to be classified as a crime, its solicitation should be punished.

The majority of states make it a criminal offense to encourage another person to commit a crime. This encouragement is punishable even if the other person fails to accomplish the solicited act. These states follow the MPC view that solicitation applies to the request to commit any crime (felony or misdemeanor).[23] However, some states, while making solicitation a crime, limit the offense to the more serious crimes.[24]

The Elements of Solicitation

The crime of solicitation can be divided into two elements:

THE INTENT THAT ANOTHER PARTY COMMIT A CRIME Solicitation is a specific intent crime. The defendant must intend that another person commit a crime. He must act on this intent by attempting to communicate in some form to another person. This communication must inform the other person that the defendant desires the other party to engage in illegal conduct.

ASKING, ENCOURAGING, OR REQUESTING ANOTHER TO COMMIT A CRIME The defendant has completed the crime when, with the necessary intent, she asks, counsels, urges, requests, or commands another to commit the crime. Only the spoken words or communicated thoughts are necessary. The other party does not have to act to make the crime complete.

Special Problems in Solicitation

COMMUNICATION TO THE OTHER PARTY The crime is complete even if the defendant fails to communicate the solicitation to another party effectively.[25] In other words, the other party does not have to hear, understand, or receive the communication for the crime to be complete. Once the defendant has spoken, written, or otherwise attempted to communicate the words asking the other party to commit the underlying offense, the crime of solicitation has occurred. For example, if a person sends an e-mail to another party asking the other party to commit a crime, the crime is complete when the e-mail is sent even though the other party never received the e-mail.

REQUEST TO COMMIT A LEGAL ACT A person may not be convicted of the crime of solicitation if he is asking the other party to commit a legal act, even though he mistakenly believes it to be a crime. If such conduct is legal, the theory of legal impossibility comes into play.

Under "innocent instrumentality" the individual being solicited must be told or made aware of the fact that he or she is being asked to engage in criminal conduct and not merely to perform an act that appears to be lawful. For example, if John wished to kill Mary, gives Steve some poisoned cookies, and requests that Steve take the cookies to Mary, John is not guilty of solicitation. He is probably guilty of at least attempted murder, but not solicitation. A similar situation exists if John asks Steve to build a secret compartment in John's automobile. John tells Steve that he needs the secret compartment to keep his valuables. John, however, wants the compartment built to smuggle drugs into the United States. While this may be an attempt to smuggle drugs, it is not solicitation to commit a crime.

WITHDRAWAL OF THE SOLICITATION The MPC allows such a withdrawal as a defense, if it is complete and voluntary. However, the courts are split as to whether this is a defense to the crime. The crime of solicitation basically involves spoken or written words. The crime is complete if the defendant expresses his or her thoughts with the specific intent that the other party commit the offense.

Certain acts are punished as criminal without requiring specific harm to an individual. Society has determined that the injury occurs when a defendant attempts to persuade another to commit the criminal act.

The third type of inchoate crime is conspiracy. Unlike attempt and solicitation, conspiracy requires two actively involved parties.

CONSPIRACY

Conspiracy is a complex crime that involves many different theories of criminal liability. The crime of conspiracy was unknown in early common law. The offense came into being as a result of the enactment of three statutes by King Edward I of England. Conspiracy is a crime that occurs in secret. The critical part of this crime is the agreement between two or more persons to commit a crime or to achieve a lawful objective in an unlawful manner. There have been conspiracies to overthrow governments, to defraud shareholders of corporations, and to commit other high-profile crimes. Society has determined that, since conspiracy occurs behind closed doors or in secret, the acts leading up to the substantive crime should be punished as a crime.

As noted by one appellate court, conspiracy is an inchoate crime. It does not require the commission of the substantive offense that is the object of the conspiracy. As an inchoate crime, conspiracy fixes the point of legal intervention at the time of agreement to commit a crime, and thus reaches further back into preparatory conduct than attempt. *People v. Swain (1996) 12 Cal 4th 593, 49 Cal Rptr 2d 390, 909 P2d 994, 1996 Cal LEXIS 198.*

Conspiracy applies to all crimes. As noted by an early court case; the words "any crime" are intended to include all crimes, whether felonies or misdemeanors, known to the law of this state and whether defined and made punishable by the Penal Code or by any other statute. *Doble v. Superior Court of San Francisco (1925) 197 Cal 556, 241 P 852, 1925 Cal LEXIS 267.* Conspiracy is not synonymous with aiding and abetting or participating; it implies agreement to commit crime, while to aid and abet requires actual participation in act constituting offense. *People v. Malotte (1956) 46 Cal 2d 59, 292 P2d 517, 1956 Cal LEXIS 153.*

Model Penal Code (MPC 5.03)

1. A person is guilty of conspiracy if he:
   a. enters into an agreement with another person,
   b.
      i. to engage in criminal conduct or attempts or solicits another to commit a crime, or
      ii. agrees to aid such person in planning or committing a crime or an attempt or solicitation of such crime. . . .
5. No person may be convicted of conspiracy, except for felonies of the first and second degree, unless an overt act in furtherance of the conspiracy has occurred.

The MPC defines conspiracy as an agreement to engage in or to bring about a criminal offense, entered into with the purpose of promoting or facilitating the crime's accomplishment. The code rejects the older common law position that punished agreements to commit any act violating public health or morals. The code also departs from the common law position in the area of merger. In certain situations, it allows punishment for both the conspiracy and the unlawful act that was the object of the conspiracy.[26] The MPC also applies a stricter standard for imposition of criminal liability under the conspiracy offense: Defendants can be found guilty of conspiracy only if they meet the tests set forth in the section dealing with accomplice liability.

Conspiracy

Defined

Conspiracy is an agreement between two or more parties for the purpose of achieving an unlawful objective or a lawful objective by an unlawful means where one of the parties to the conspiracy commits an overt act.

Elements

The crime of conspiracy has four basic elements:

1. An agreement between two or more persons
2. With specific intent (for the purpose of)
3. Achieving an unlawful objective or achieving a lawful objective in an unlawful manner, and
4. The commission of an overt act in furtherance of the conspiracy

---

Federal courts have encountered difficulty in defining conspiracy.[27] In *Krulewitch v. United States*, Justice Robert H. Jackson, in his dissenting opinion, discussed the nature and elements of the crime:

> This case illustrates a present drift in the federal law of conspiracy which warrants some further comment because it is characteristic of the long evolution of that elastic, sprawling and pervasive offense . . .

> The modern crime of conspiracy is so vague that it almost defies definition. Despite certain elementary and essential elements, it also, chameleon-like, takes on a special coloration, from each of the many independent offenses on which it may be overlaid. It is always "predominantly mental in composition" because it consists primarily of a meeting of minds and an intent.[28]

There are numerous variations of the crime of conspiracy. Some states require an overt act, other states have degrees of conspiracies, while others require an unlawful objective or an attempt to commit a substantive crime.

In California, the courts use the following definition of conspiracy when instructing juries: A conspiracy is an agreement between two or more persons with the specific intent to agree to commit a public offense . . . , and with the further specific intent to commit such offense, followed by an overt act committed in this state by one or more of the parties for the purpose of accomplishing the object of the agreement.[29]

This jury instruction is based upon the California Penal Code definition of conspiracy. California Penal Code Section 182 is in many ways similar to the MPC and can be considered an example of a modern statute representing the majority position.

The Elements of Conspiracy

The crime of conspiracy can be divided into four elements:

AN AGREEMENT BETWEEN TWO OR MORE PERSONS The essence of the crime of conspiracy is an agreement between two or more persons. Scholars have argued over the extent of proof necessary to find an agreement.[30] The MPC allows conviction of a person based upon a unilateral agreement. This may occur where (1) the defendant thinks an agreement has been reached or (2) for some reason the other party is not convicted of the crime of conspiracy. This conclusion is reached by reading sections 503(1)(a), 503(1)(b), and 504(1)(b).

Courts have addressed the issue of whether the defendant's presence at the scene of a meeting where the agreement is reached is sufficient to indicate involvement in the conspiracy. They have held that mere attendance at a meeting where an agreement is reached does not prove that the defendant entered into the agreement.

On occasion, courts will infer that there was an agreement, even though there are no independent facts supporting this conclusion. The Supreme Court explained the rational for this rule in *Blumenthal v. United States*, when it held:

Secrecy and concealment are essential features of successful conspiracy. The more completely they are achieved, the more successful the crime. Hence the law rightly gives room for allowing the conviction of those discovered upon showing sufficiently the essential nature of the plan and their connections with it, without requiring evidence of knowledge of all its details or of the participation of others. Otherwise the difficulties, not only of discovery, but of certainty in proof and of correlating proof with pleading would become insuperable, and conspirators would go free by their very ingenuity.[33]

Practicum 4.5

The defendant was present during a number of conversations with other charged conspirators. During these meetings, the other defendants planned to commit a burglary. While defendant was present, he did not participate in the planning or the commission of the burglary.

Mere knowledge of, approval of, or acquiescence in the object or purpose of the conspiracy, without an intention and agreement to cooperate in the crime, is insufficient to make one a conspirator.[31]

> *ISSUE: Is mere presence at a meeting where a conspiracy is formed sufficient involvement to hold a person criminally liable?*

Practicum 4.6

The victim was walking down the street when she was stopped and restrained by the first defendant. The second defendant took the victim's wallet from her pocket.

> *ISSUE: Do the defendants' acts establish a conspiracy?*

There are no facts showing that the defendants entered into an agreement to commit a robbery. However, courts will not require direct evidence that the co-conspirators had an express plan to commit the offense in order to charge and convict the defendants of conspiracy and robbery. An agreement may be implied from the fact that the defendants acted jointly in carrying out the substantive crime.[32]

SPECIFIC INTENT The element of specific intent is a gray area, with scholars and courts reaching different positions.[34] However, the very definition of conspiracy seems to require two distinct patterns of thought or intent: (1) Since the definition of conspiracy requires an agreement, each party must have intended to enter into the agreement to commit the same crime. (2) All parties must have the same intent as it relates to the crime in question. In essence, there must be a meeting of the minds to satisfy the intent requirement of conspiracy.[35]

ACHIEVING AN UNLAWFUL OBJECTIVE OR ACHIEVING A LAWFUL PURPOSE IN AN UNLAWFUL MANNER This element is very similar to the first element requiring that the parties reach an agreement. However, it sharpens the focus of the agreement mandate by requiring proof that the parties intended to commit a crime. While this element requires the defendant to agree to commit an unlawful act, it allows for two alternative methods by which this requirement can be satisfied.

One approach or method requires an agreement to achieve an unlawful object. This is the traditional view of conspiracy. The second alternative requires the conspirators to have an unlawful purpose as the objective of the conspiracy.

THE COMMISSION OF AN OVERT ACT IN FURTHERANCE OF THE CONSPIRACY Authorities further disagree as to the requirement of an overt act. The MPC requires an overt act only if the conspiracy is to commit a felony of the third degree or a misdemeanor.[36] The federal rule in most situations requires an overt act.[37] Some jurisdictions argue that the agreement itself is the necessary act, while others require an additional overt act.

It is not necessary that the overt act be the substantive crime or the object of the conspiracy. Neither does the overt act, standing by itself, have to be unlawful. The purpose of requiring an overt act is to show "that the conspiracy is at work."[38]

Special Problems in Conspiracy

THE REQUIREMENT OF AN AGREEMENT BY AT LEAST TWO PERSONS If all the other co-conspirators are acquitted or the charges are dismissed against them, some jurisdictions have held that the defendant alone cannot be convicted, since there is only one person, and conspiracy, by its definition, requires an agreement. Because a person cannot enter into an agreement with himself or herself, there can be no conspiracy.[39] However, the MPC allows conviction of a single defendant, no matter what happens to the other co-conspirators, since conspiracy requires an agreement by the defendant, not with the defendant.[40]

Most states do not follow the MPC rule but instead adhere to the Wharton's rule, which states that when the targeted crime by its very nature takes more than one party to commit, there can be no conspiracy when no more than the number of parties required to commit the offense participated in it. For example, in cases where only two persons are involved and one is a government agent or informer, the other cannot be convicted of conspiracy. This is because the crime of conspiracy requires at least two people to have the requisite criminal specific intent, and a government agent by definition cannot be a co-conspirator. The evidence was sufficient to support defendant's convictions of conspiracy to commit murder and kidnapping for ransom, even though one of the three conspirators became a government informer (*People v. Liu (1996, Cal App 1st Dist) 54 Cal Rptr 2d 578*).

WITHDRAWAL The general rule is that withdrawal from the conspiracy after an overt act has been committed is no defense.[41] The rationale for holding an offender liable once the overt act is completed seems to be society's determination to punish the crime of conspiracy, not necessarily its ultimate goal. However, the MPC would allow withdrawal as a defense if the defendant's withdrawal caused the conspiracy to fail.[42]

LIABILITY FOR CRIMES OF CO-CONSPIRATORS The general rule is that the defendant and each member of the conspiracy are liable for all crimes committed by each member of the conspiracy, where it was a reasonably foreseeable result of the conspiracy and done in furtherance of it.[43] Some authorities would argue that this position imposes a strict liability standard on co-conspirators for acts of their fellow conspirators.[44]

DURATION OF THE CONSPIRACY The conspiracy lasts until all the objectives of the conspiracy are completed. The objectives of the conspiracy may include lawful acts after the commission of the substantive crime, and when this is the case, the conspiracy continues until those acts are accomplished.

Conspiracy is a crime that requires more acts than solicitation does, but it does not require the defendant to come as close to the commission of the substantive crime as attempt does. The offense imposes liability on the defendant for crimes committed by co-conspirators. Conspiracy combines spoken words with an overt act but does not require the commission of the planned unlawful object.

ACCOMPLICES AND ACCESSORIES

An individual is guilty of a crime when he or she commits certain acts that meet all the elements of a particular offense. In addition, other persons may be guilty of the same crime if their conduct satisfies certain requirements, even though they did not actually engage in the conduct that is prohibited under the substantive crime.

Society has determined that certain acts that assist in the commission of a crime should be prohibited even though they do not directly contribute to satisfying the individual elements of the offense. In order to hold persons liable for these acts, we have established the concept of aiding and abetting. Over the years, this concept has been modified and codified into two separate forms of liability: An **accomplice** is one who promotes another to commit a crime, and an **accessory** is one who, after the offense has been committed, assists the perpetrator in escaping justice. Persons who "aid and abet" others in the commission of crimes will be held liable and punished as if they directly participated in those crimes.

Some states and the MPC take the position that accomplices should be held liable only for those crimes that are contemplated or planned.[45] The majority position imposes liability for all foreseeable acts that result from the accomplice's activity. In *People v. Croy*, the California Supreme Court upheld a conviction of an accomplice, imposing liability for reasonably foreseeable crimes committed by the perpetrator.[46]

Model Penal Code

ACCOMPLICE (MPC 2.06)

3. A person is an accomplice when she:
   a. with the purpose of promoting or facilitating the commission of the crime,
      i. solicits another person to commit it, or
      ii. aids or agrees or attempts to aid such person in planning or committing it, or
      iii. having a legal duty to prevent the offense, fails to take reasonable efforts to do so, or
   b. her conduct is expressly declared by law to establish her complicity.

The MPC does away with the common law distinction between **principal** and accessory before the fact. It combines all the acts constituting these offenses into the definition of **accomplice**. Subsection (3) of the code lists the instances in which a party can be an accomplice of another. Paragraph (a) requires that the actor have the purpose of promoting or facilitating the commission of the offense, and that one of three other conditions be present. Paragraph (b) provides that a party can also be declared an accomplice if his conduct is expressly covered by the law to establish his complicity. The code begins with a reaffirmation of the general principle that criminal liability is based upon conduct, but it applies this principle to situations in which the conduct involved may be that of another. An accomplice is punished the same as a principal under the MPC.

Scope of Liability—Accomplices and Accessories

Defined

Accomplice

One who, with the purpose of promoting or assisting in the commission of the offense,

1. Solicits another to commit the crime.
2. Aids, agrees to aid, or attempts to aid in planning or committing the offense.
3. Having a duty to prevent the offense, fails to do so.

Accessory

One who, after an offense has been committed, aids, conceals, or warns a **principal** with the intent that the principal avoid arrest, prosecution, conviction, or punishment for the crime.

Elements

Accomplice

One will be convicted as an accomplice when he or she,

1. With the intent of assisting in the commission of a crime,
2. Solicits, aids, or assists another in committing the crime or, having a duty to prevent the crime, fails to use reasonable efforts to do so.

Accessory

One will be convicted as an accessory when he or she,

1. After a crime has been committed,
2. Aids, conceals, or warns a principal,
3. With the intent that the principal avoid arrest, prosecution, conviction, or punishment.

ACCESSORY (MPC 242.3)

3. A person is an accessory if he, with the purpose to hinder the arrest or other legal process against a person:
   a. harbors or conceals the other, or
   b. provides aid or other means of avoiding arrest, or
   c. conceals or destroys evidence or other information, or
   d. warns the other party, or
   e. supplies false information to a police officer.

This section applies to specific efforts to hinder the apprehension, prosecution, conviction, or punishment of another. This provision of the code covers the common law offense of being an accessory after the fact but breaks with tradition as it relates to that crime.[47] Punishment under the MPC is less than the punishment for the substantive offense that the accessory attempted to cover up.

The federal rule is very similar to the MPC in that it has abolished the distinction between the accessory after the fact and the perpetrator and now holds both liable. The federal rule makes this an offense separate from the substantive crime.[48] Under common law, an accessory could not be convicted without the prior conviction of the principal. The Supreme Court has ruled that the legislative history of Title 18 U.S. Code, Section 2, indicated a congressional intention to permit prosecution of one who aids and abets a federal crime despite prior acquittal of the actual perpetrator of that offense.[49]

The majority of states hold that those who aid and abet are principals and therefore guilty of the same crime committed by the perpetrator. The distinction that existed under the common law regarding accessory before the fact and principal has for the most part disappeared. New Hampshire has a representative statute, which reads as follows:

A person is an accomplice of another person in the commission of an offense if:
(a) with the purpose of promoting or facilitating the commission of the offense, he solicits such other person in committing it, or aids or agrees or attempts to aid such other person in planning or committing it . . .[50]

Under common law, accessories after the fact were considered parties to the substantive crime. However, most states now consider an accessory's acts separate from the major crime and impose a distinct, if somewhat lesser, punishment for the accessory's actions.

The state of Colorado provides:

(1) A person is an accessory to crime if, with intent to hinder, delay, or prevent the discovery, detection, apprehension, prosecution, conviction, or punishment of another for the commission of a crime, he renders assistance to such person. . . .

. . .

(3) Being an accessory to crime is a class 4 felony if the offender knows that the person being assisted has committed, . . . a crime, and if that crime is designated by this code as a class 1 or class 2 felony.[51]

The common law tradition of establishing separate offenses for different phases of criminal conduct was modified by the majority of states when they addressed the issue of accomplice or accessory liability.

Practicum 4.7

The defendant, at the suggestion of another, agreed to participate in a robbery and traveled with the others to the scene of the crime. However, fearing she might be recognized by the neighbors, she departed the scene without participating in the offense.

ISSUE: *Did the defendant's actions make her an accomplice to the crime of robbery?*

The court (without considering the defense of withdrawal) reversed her conviction as an accomplice on the grounds that her acts did not come within the definition of one who "aids" in the commission of a crime, nor did she counsel, hire, or otherwise procure the crime.[52]

The Elements of the Crime of Accomplice

WITH THE INTENT OF ASSISTING IN THE COMMISSION OF A CRIME There are two types of intent the accomplice must possess: (1) the same intent to commit the substantive crime that the perpetrator must have, and (2) a purpose or affirmative knowledge that his acts would further the commission of the crime.

Early court decisions conflicted on whether innocent aid to another with knowledge of his criminal intent was sufficient for conviction. It has been argued that holding such a person responsible is consistent with the preventive nature of criminal law.[53] However, the modern trend, which has been adopted by the MPC and some jurisdictions, is to require the accomplice to act with a purpose to substantially facilitate the commission of the crime.[54]

SOLICITS, AIDS, OR ASSISTS ANOTHER IN COMMITTING THE CRIME OR, HAVING A DUTY TO PREVENT THE CRIME, FAILS TO USE REASONABLE EFFORTS TO DO SO The defendant must solicit, aid, encourage, or otherwise promote in any significant manner the commission of the crime. Simple encouragement without physical assistance is sufficient to establish criminal liability. If the defendant had a legal obligation to prevent the commission of a crime and failed to exercise reasonable efforts to do so, she will be considered an accomplice.

The Elements of the Crime of Accessory

AFTER A CRIME HAS BEEN COMMITTED It must be proved that a crime in fact has occurred; however, many statutes do not require finding the perpetrator guilty as a condition of holding the accessory liable.

AIDS, CONCEALS, OR WARNS A PRINCIPAL Such acts must occur after all the elements necessary to complete the substantive crime have been completed. It is sometimes difficult to determine if the defendant aided, concealed, or warned a principal at a time that would make him a participant or if his actions occurred after the crime was finished. If the defendant provides assistance during the commission of a crime, he is guilty as a principal. However, if he provides assistance after the crime was complete, he is guilty as an accessory. If a person provides assistance to someone he knows has committed an offense by assisting her in her escape, he will be guilty as an accessory after the fact.[55]

WITH THE INTENT THAT THE PRINCIPAL AVOID ARREST, PROSECUTION, CONVICTION, OR PUNISHMENT There are two intent requirements in this element: (1) The defendant knew she was assisting someone who had committed a crime, and (2) she rendered aid for the purpose of assisting the perpetrator to avoid the justice system.

Special Problems with Accomplices

WITHDRAWAL One who withdraws after encouraging or assisting in the commission of a crime may escape liability, if he withdraws before the crime is complete. Under the MPC, to escape liability the defendant must do certain acts that render his prior assistance useless, provide timely warning, or attempt to prevent the crime.[56] The majority of states are in accord with the code's position.[57]

Special Problems with Accessories

FAILURE TO REPORT A CRIME There are many reasons why citizens will not report a crime. Some of us are afraid to get involved, others fear retaliation by the offenders, and a few are so busy that they simply believe they do not have the time to make a phone call and discuss the matter with the police. If a person knows a crime has been committed and does not have a duty to report it, failure to report does not make her an accessory.

LACK OF PURPOSE TO IMPEDE LAW ENFORCEMENT Prosecution of a person as an accessory will not be affirmed if the defendant's motive was one of charity. In *State v. Jett*, the defendant's conviction as an accessory was reversed. The court found his intent in taking a rape victim out of the state to have her child was to protect the girl's reputation rather than to conceal the rapist's crime.[58]

Summary of Accomplices and Accessories

Accomplice or accessory liability is based upon the principle that persons who assist, before or after, in the commission of a crime should not escape punishment merely because they did not actually commit the substantive crime. Accomplices or accessories, to be held criminally liable, must render aid for the purpose of assisting the perpetrator in either committing the crime or escaping liability.

COMPARING AND CONTRASTING INCHOATE CRIMES

Attempt

1. *The substantive offense* (the object of the attempt, the crime that the defendant is trying to commit). If the defendant completes all the elements of the substantive crime, he may be charged with that offense, but not with the crime of attempt. However, if the jury finds that the defendant did not complete all the elements of the substantive crime, it may still convict him of the crime of attempting to commit the substantive crime. Unlike solicitation and conspiracy, the defendant does not have to disclose his thoughts to another person.
2. *Solicitation.* The crime of attempt requires the defendant to go far enough down the path of criminal conduct so as to progress beyond mere preparation. Solicitation, however, may occur so early in the conduct of criminal activity that the defendant has not done enough to be convicted of the crime of attempt.
3. *Conspiracy.* The crime of attempt can be committed by one person, while conspiracy requires at least two persons.
4. *Accomplices/accessories.* Such parties may be guilty of a crime committed by another person. The defendant charged with attempt will be held accountable for her own actions.

Solicitation

1. *The substantive offense.* The defendant is asking someone to commit this separate crime.
2. *Attempt.* If the party solicited by the defendant tries to commit the substantive offense and fails, the defendant may be charged with attempting to commit the substantive offense.
3. *Conspiracy.* The crime of solicitation does not require that an agreement be reached, while an agreement is an essential element of conspiracy. However, solicitation may precede a series of actions that become a conspiracy.
4. *Accomplices/accessories.* If the other party commits the crime the defendant solicited her for, the defendant will be held liable as an accomplice to the substantive offense. Since solicitation occurs before a crime is committed, the defendant could not be charged as an accessory.

Conspiracy

1. *The substantive offense.* There is no separate substantive crime in conspiracy.
2. *Attempt.* Conspiracy requires an agreement between two persons, while attempt requires only the defendant to act.
3. *Solicitation.* Conspiracy requires acts beyond words, while solicitation is complete once the necessary thoughts are communicated.
4. *Accomplices/accessories.* A defendant charged with conspiracy is liable for acts of co-conspirators without a showing that he intended to commit the crimes that the

co-conspirators committed. Accomplice and accessory liability attach only upon knowledge of the nature of the crimes committed.

Accomplices/Accessories

1. *The substantive offense.* The defendant tries to encourage someone else to commit this crime or attempts to assist the perpetrator in avoiding capture after it has occurred.
2. *Attempt.* Accomplice and accessory liability require actions by another party, while attempt can be committed by the defendant.
3. *Solicitation.* While accomplice and accessory liability attach for spoken words, there must be some action on the part of the perpetrator in acting on their words. Solicitation occurs upon the communication of the thought, without any requirement that anyone act upon those words.
4. *Conspiracy.* Criminal liability for conspiracy attaches absent the commission of any other substantive criminal violation. For accomplice or accessory liability to attach, the underlying crime must have occurred.
5. *Accomplice versus accessory.* An accomplice is one who is involved before or during the commission of the substantive offense, while an accessory becomes a player after the offense has been committed.

HOW WOULD YOU RULE?

The owner of a jewelry store conspired with defendant and gave him permission to rob her store. During the sham robbery, the property taken was in the possession of the owner's innocent employees and the employees were forced to open the safes. Was the defendant properly convicted for conspiracy to commit robbery?

SEE: *PEOPLE V. SMITH (2009, 1ST DIST) 2009 CAL APP LEXIS 1607.*

Summary

Inchoate or anticipatory crimes are those offenses that are preparatory to the completion of the underlying substantive offense. Society has enacted laws to punish persons when they start down the path toward the commission of a substantive offense.

Attempt involves a defendant's intent to commit a substantive offense. Intent alone is insufficient, however, and the defendant must undertake some action to carry out her intent that is a substantial step toward completion of the underlying crime. Solicitation punishes spoken words that request the other party to commit the underlying offense. This crime is considered dangerous even in the absence of specific physical action. The defendant must possess the necessary intent and communicate with another party. Conspiracy is a crime that occurs in secret or "behind closed doors." The law punishes a person for entering into an agreement with others to commit a crime or to commit a lawful act in an unlawful manner. The crime requires that one of the co-conspirators perform some overt act in furtherance of the conspiracy.

Accomplices are those persons who assist the perpetrator before or during the commission of a crime, while accessories render aid after the offense has been committed. We have imposed liability on these parties because their assistance either before or after the commission of the substantive offense encourages others to commit crimes.

Depending on the parties' intent, an act may be an innocent gesture or a serious step toward the commission of an offense. Since criminals usually do not announce their state of mind, we must examine their acts to determine if the necessary intent is present. We can do that only by reviewing the facts surrounding each offense. The laws concerning inchoate offenses require a close examination of the parties' intent, their acts, and the facts surrounding the criminal act.

Additional Assignments

1. Read the selected cases and associated material for Chapter 4 posted at www.mycrimekit.com.
2. Complete the online study guide material for Chapter 4 posted at www.mycrimekit.com.
3. Discussion and thought questions:
   a. Should the crime of attempt carry the same punishment as the substantive offense?
   b. Is the criminal conduct and motive involved in a crime of attempted murder any less serious than the commission of the crime of murder?
   c. Should the crime of attempt be limited to only serious offenses?
   d. Should a person be convicted of the crime of solicitation for simply speaking certain words?
   e. Is the crime of conspiracy more serious than the crimes of attempt and solicitation?

Notes

1. For a dated but excellent article discussing this dispute, see Thomas Sayre, "Criminal Attempts," 41 *Harv. L. Rev.* 821, 822–837 (1929).
2. Inchoate is used to describe something just begun or incomplete.
3. American Law Institute, Model Penal Code (hereafter referred to as MPC), Part I, Article 5 (1985), p. 293.
4. Plato, *Laws,* trans. Trevor J. Saunders (Middlesex, England: Penguin Books, 1975), 397.
5. As reported in Jerome Hall, *General Principles of Criminal Law,* 2nd ed. (Indianapolis: Bobbs-Merrill, 1960), 564.
6. This statement from the MPC has been simplified for easier understanding.
7. MPC 5.01(1)(a) and (b).
8. MPC 5.01(1)(c).
9. For example: "A person is guilty of an attempt to commit a crime when, with intent to commit a crime, he engages in conduct which tends to effect the commission of such crime." N.Y. Penal Law 110.00.
10. See *People v. Risso,* 246 N.Y. 334, 158 N.E. 888 (1927).
11. Oliver Wendell Holmes, The *Common Law* (Boston: Little, Brown, 1963), 612.
12. Lawrence Crocker, "Justice in Criminal Liability: Decriminalizing Harmless Attempts," *Ohio State Law Journal* 53 (1992):1057.
13. *State v. Breman,* 276 P. 2d 364 (Kan. 1954).
14. *Boyles v. State,* 175 N.W. 2d 277 (Wis. 1970).
15. *State v. Damms,* 9 Wis. 2d 183 (1960).

16. *Wilson v. State*, 85 Miss. 678, 38 So. 46 (1905).

17. *See People v. Jaffee*, 185 N.Y. 497 (1906). However, scholars have criticized Jaffee's result as a twisted ruling involving a mixture of legal and factual impossibility. See John Keedy, "Criminal Attempts at Common Law," 102 U. Pa. L. Rev. 464, 477 (1954) and *Booth v. State*, 398 P. 2d 863 (Okla. Crim. App. 1964).

18. See *People v. Morgan*, 123 N.Y. 254, 54 N.E. 412 (1890).

19. *Rex v. Higgins*, 102 Eng. Rep. 269, 274 (1801).

20. *Hicks v. Commonwealth*, 86 Va. 223, 9 S.E. 1024 (1889).

21. *State v. Schleifer*, 99 Conn. 432, 121 A. 805, 809 (1932).

22. MPC and Commentaries, Part I, p. 366.

23. MPC and Commentaries, Part I, 5.02, p. 370.

24. See Cal. Penal Code 653f, which falls into this classification.

25. MPC 5.02(2).

26. MPC and Commentaries, Part I, 5.02, p. 390.

27. See 18 U.S.C. 371, which reads: "If two or more persons conspire to commit any offense against the United States, or to defraud the United States . . . in any manner or for any purpose, and one or more of such persons do any act to effect the object of the conspiracy. . . ."

28. *Krulewitch v. United States*, 336 U.S. 440 (1947), at 445–454.

29. See California Jury Instructions, Criminal (CALJIC) No. 6.10 and 6.10.5.

30. "Developments in the Law—Criminal Conspiracy," 72 Harv. L. Rev. 920, 948 (1959).

31. *Cleavor v. United States*, 238 F. 2d 766, 771 (10th Cir. 1956).

32. *Bender v. State*, 253 A. 2d 686 (1969).

33. *Blumenthal v. United States*, 332 U.S. 539 (1947) at 556.

34. William Harno, "Intent in Criminal Conspiracy," *University of Pennsylvania Law Review* 89 (1941): 624.

35. *United States v. United States Gypsum* Co., 438 U.S. 422, 433 n.20 (1978).

36. MPC 5.03(5).

37. 18 U.S.C. 371.

38. *Yates v. United States*, 354 U.S. 298, 334 (1957).

39. *Eymon v. Deutsch*, 373 P. 2d 716 (Ariz. 1962).

40. MPC 5.03(1).

41. *Orear v. United States*, 261 F. 257 (5th Cir. 1919).

42. MPC 5.03(6).

43. *Pinkerton v. United States*, 328 U.S. 640 (1946).

44. Wayne R. LaFave, Modern *Criminal Law* (St. Paul, MN: West, 1978), pp. 647–648.

45. MPC 2.06(3)(a).

46. *People v. Croy,* 41 Cal. 3d 1 (1985).

47. See Rollin Perkins, "Parties to Crime," 89 *U. Pa. L. Rev.* 581 (1941).

48. 8 U.S.C. 2 reads as follows:

ACCOMPLICE [PRINCIPAL]

(a) Whoever commits an offense, or aids, abets, counsels, commands, induces or procures its commission. . . .

(b) Whoever willfully causes an act to be done which if directly performed by him or another would be an offense.

18 U.S.C. 3 READS AS FOLLOWS:

ACCESSORY [AFTER THE FACT]

Whoever, knowing that an offense has been committed, receives, comforts, or assists the offender in order to hinder or prevent his apprehension, trial or punishment.

49. *Standefer v. United States*, 447 U.S. 10, 18–20 (1980).

50. N.H. Rev. Stat. Ann. 626:8.

51. Col. Rev. Stat. § 18-8-105.

52. *Commonwealth v. Perry*, 149 Mass. 357, 256 N.E.2d 745 (1970).

53. *Backum v. United States*, 112 F. 2d 635 (4th Cir. 1940).

54. MPC and Commentaries, Part I, 2.06, pp. 316–319.

55. *United States v. Balano*, 618 F. 2d 624 (10th Cir. 1979).

56. MPC 2.06(6)(c).

57. MPC and Commentaries, Part I, 2.06, p. 326.

58. 69 Kan. 788, 77 P. 546 (1904).

Defenses

Chapter Outline

What you should know about defenses. After reading this chapter, you should know

- The differences between criminal responsibility, justification and excuse defenses, and procedural defenses.

- The difference between the various types of insanity tests.

- The various syndrome defenses such as the premenstrual, posttraumatic, and battered woman syndromes.

- The situations when use of deadly force is permitted in self-defense or defense of others.

- The rationale for use of duress as a defense.

- The various procedural defenses.

Key Terms

After reading this chapter, you should understand the following key terms:

battered woman syndrome: A condition that affects women who have been continually abused by their spouses to the degree that their mental functioning is impaired.

battered women: Women who have experienced physically or psychologically injurious behavior at the hands of men with whom they once had, or are continuing to have, an intimate relationship.

defense: A justification or excuse presented by the perpetrator to reduce or eliminate his or her criminal liability.

entrapment: A government agent's actions that induce a person to commit a crime.

imperfect self-defense: One's use of force against another with the purpose of injuring or killing the victim in the mistaken belief that force was necessary to defend oneself.

insanity: A legal concept that excuses the defendant's conduct based upon his or her lack of a required mental state.

posttraumatic stress disorder: The development of characteristic symptoms following an extremely traumatic direct personal experience of an event that involves actual or threatened death or to serious injury.

premenstrual syndrome (PMS)/premenstrual tension (PMT): Symptoms that many women face that begin ten to fourteen days prior to the menstrual period and become progressively worse until the onset of menstruation. Women suffering with PMS/PMT are often irritable and under stress.

statute of limitations: Requirement that criminal prosecutions commence within a certain period of time after the crime occurred.

syndrome: A complex of signs and symptoms presenting a clinical picture of a disease or disorder.

syndrome-based defenses: Defenses that are predicated on, or substantially enhanced by, the acceptability of syndrome-related crimes.

S imply understanding that a person has committed a criminal act does not stop the inquiry process. Society has established certain bars or defenses to acts that would normally be considered criminal in nature. These defenses are an integral part of criminal law theory and practice. These are not obscure technical theories that are rarely encountered. In many criminal trials, defenses play an important and critical role.

As Focus 5.1 illustrates, defenses can take what appears to be a clear criminal offense and allow the perpetrator to walk away a free person or, in the case of an insanity verdict, to be placed in a mental hospital instead of a prison. A defense is a justification or excuse presented by the perpetrator to reduce or eliminate his or her criminal liability. While there are many different ways to classify defenses, for ease of understanding, we have grouped them into three categories: defenses based on the lack of criminal responsibility, justification and excuse, and procedural defenses.

CRIMINAL RESPONSIBILITY

Most **defenses** raise issues that involve the defendant's state of mind. However, certain criminal responsibility defenses arise from the defendant's mental status. Defenses that go to the mental capacity of the accused are infancy, insanity, diminished capacity, intoxication, premenstrual and battered spouse syndromes, and posttraumatic stress disorder. The legal concepts regarding how criminal responsibility is determined and who has the capacity to commit a crime have undergone extensive changes since the concepts were first introduced. In the Middle Ages, even animals were held criminally responsible for harm they had caused. Domestic animals were tried in secular courts in the same manner as human beings. Wild animals were required to be tried before the religious courts. The common belief was that criminals and animals who committed wrongs were possessed of the devil. For example, in 1499, a bear was tried and convicted of murder. It is reported that the attorney appointed to represent the bear argued that the bear had a right to be judged by his peers (other bears). In the 1700s, a dog was tied to a marketplace pillory for a period of one year for biting a man on the leg.

Focus 5.1

- Wanting to impress actress Jodie Foster, John Hinckley, Jr., stalked, shot, and wounded President Ronald Reagan. He was tried for attempted murder and found to be insane.
- A young man engaged in sexual relations with a woman whom he had just met. After the act was completed, she reported the incident to the police. The offender claimed the defense of consent. In the William Smith rape case, the jury acquitted the male; in the Mike Tyson case, the jury found the offender guilty of rape.
- A woman was raped by her husband. While he was sleeping, she took a knife and cut off his penis. The man was charged with sexual battery and the woman was charged with assault with great bodily injury. The man was acquitted and the woman was found not guilty by reason of insanity. The Bobbitts' trials raised our awareness of defenses such as the battered woman syndrome and the insanity defense.
- Two brothers claimed they were sexually abused by their father for years. They testified that their mother knew of the abuse and did not stop it. Finally, fearing for their lives, they killed both parents. The Menendez brothers used a form of self-defense in their trials.

Criminal responsibility defenses attempt to show that the defendant did not have the mental ability to form the necessary intent to commit the criminal act. This defense is a form of excuse. In other words, the defendant will admit to committing the criminal act but claim he is excused from criminal liability because he lacked the capacity to form the necessary intent that goes along with the act.

Infancy

At civil law, a person reaches his or her majority in most states at the chronological age of eighteen years. The age at which children become criminally responsible for their conduct is not as clear. States have adopted statutes that establish when a minor may be held criminally liable.

The general rule is that children under the age of seven years are not held criminally responsible for their conduct.[1] There is generally a presumption that between the ages of seven and fourteen, the child does not have the required mental capacity. Evidence, however, may be introduced by the state to show that a child between the ages of seven and fourteen is mature enough. Often, in these cases, testimony of medical persons and other experts is used to show that the child has emotionally, physically, and mentally reached the level of capacity at which the child should be held accountable for his or her conduct.

Children fourteen years and older are presumed to have the mental capacity to commit criminal offenses. In the majority of states, they normally will be under the jurisdiction of juvenile rather than adult criminal court if they are under the age of seventeen. It is the chronological age, not the mental age, that is used to determine the capacity of the child.[2]

As Practicum 5.1 (on page 85) indicates, the presence or absence of certain facts may change how we view the competency of a minor. Infancy is a mental status that society has determined should be evaluated when addressing the guilt of children. In some situations, it is not an easy chore. However, determining competency in minors is a relatively simple task in comparison to understanding the next personal defense: insanity.

Insanity

Insanity is a controversial defense. It is the subject of numerous articles and news stories each year. One study, however, indicated that the public may not be too concerned about the frequency with which the defense is used. That study concluded that the insanity defense was used in fewer than 2 percent of all trials involving serious crimes.[3] Because of the complexity of this form of defense, it is normally raised only in the most serious cases, such as murder or attempted murder. The question of insanity may arise at the time of the criminal conduct, at the time of trial (referred to as incompetency), during incarceration, and just prior to execution.

Practicum 5.1

Age, Crime, and the Burden of Proof

From birth to age seven: The child is not held liable for criminal acts.

Age seven to fourteen: The child is presumed to be unable to form the necessary intent. However, proof may be introduced to show otherwise.

Age fourteen and older: The child is presumed to have the mental capacity to commit criminal offenses.

Apply the above presumptions to the following factual patterns and discuss the results.

1. A six-year-old child was caught leaving a local supermarket with three pieces of candy in his pocket. Should the child be charged with shoplifting (petty theft)? Does the fact that the child hid the candy right before he left the store indicate he knew it was wrong?

2. A thirteen-year-old child was arrested for joyriding (a form of auto theft in some jurisdictions). Should the child be charged with theft? What if the car was his father's car and the parents were separated? What if it was a stranger's car and the child was a member of a local gang that specialized in stealing cars?

3. A fifteen-year-old male child engaged in sexual relations with a seventeen-year-old female. The female admitted to initiating the encounter but claimed that at the last moment she did not want to complete the act of intercourse and the child forced her by holding her down. The child admitted to the act, stating that this was his first sexual experience and he lost control of himself.

Insanity, at the time the act was committed, negates the required mental state of the actor, and therefore, the individual has not committed the crime. For example, battery requires a general intent to commit the offense. If, however, the individual does not have the ability to formulate the required intent, one of the essential elements of the crime is missing, and the individual has not committed the crime.

Insanity at trial time is referred to as incompetency to stand trial. The accused must have a sufficient mental state in order to assist her attorney in the defense of the case. If the accused is not sufficiently competent, the trial must be delayed. Unlike the question of mental state at the time of the act, which negates the guilt, incompetency to stand trial refers only to the ability of the accused to assist her counsel and does not negate the commission of the offense. If the accused is determined to be incompetent to stand trial, the state is required to delay the trial until the individual is competent. The practical effect of this requirement is that in most cases the trial can never be held, because the accused's mental state either does not change or gets worse.

At common law, if the individual is insane at the time he is scheduled to be executed, the execution is delayed. One theory regarding the delay is that the individual should understand the gravity of the punishment being inflicted on him. A second theory is that the individual, if sane, might offer some reason for the execution to be stayed.

Execution is stayed if the person is insane. In *Billiot v. Epps, 2009 U.S. Dist. LEXIS 104153 (S.D. Miss. Nov. 3, 2009)*, an appellate court noted that the prohibition against execution of the mentally ill is based on ancient traditions of English common law. When *Ford v. Wainwright, 477 U.S. 399, 106 S. Ct. 2595, 91 L. Ed. 2d 335 (1986)*, was decided, no state permitted the execution of the insane. Prior to *Ford*, however, the United States Constitution provided only procedural due process protection for the exemption from execution that was provided by state law. *Ford* recognized that the Eighth Amendment also provides a restriction on a state's substantive power to execute the mentally incompetent. Associate Supreme Court Justice Powell stated in *Ford v. Wainwright*:

If the defendant perceives the connection between his crime and his punishment, the retributive goal of the criminal law is satisfied. And only if the defendant is aware that his death is approaching can he prepare himself for his passing. Accordingly, I would hold that the Eighth Amendment forbids the execution only of those who are unaware of the punishment they are about to suffer and why they are to suffer it. *Ford v. Wainwright, 477 U.S. 399, 412 (1986)*.

Insanity during incarceration may result in the criminal's transfer to a mental institution. The individual's prison time, however, continues to be counted off during this period. If the individual's insanity still exists on the completion of the term of incarceration, she may be involuntarily detained in a mental institution under civil proceedings. There are, however, certain procedural and hearing rights that must be observed before the individual may be involuntarily confined to the mental institution.

TESTS FOR INSANITY Insanity is a complex area of the law that is often misunderstood by both the general public and even some professionals in the field of criminal justice. Insanity in its legal sense excuses the defendant's conduct based upon lack of required mental state. Insanity is a legal concept that uses medical knowledge to come to a determination regarding the defendant's mental status. Five basic tests for insanity have been used in the American court system: (1) the M'Naghten test, (2) the irresistible impulse test, (3) the Durham rule, (4) the federal test, and (5) the Model Penal Code (MPC) or American Law Institute (ALI) test.

The oldest rule used to determine the sanity of the accused is the M'Naghten test. This rule was first used in 1843 in a famous English trial.[4] In that case, Daniel M'Naghten was suffering from a delusion that the prime minister, Sir Robert Peel, was conspiring to kill him. He fired at Peel but missed him and killed Peel's personal secretary. The jury found him guilty of murder, but the House of Lords reversed that decision and established the M'Naghten test for insanity. This rule, also referred to as the "right and wrong" test, is as follows:

> Individuals are presumed to be sane and to possess a sufficient degree of reason to be responsible for their crimes, until the contrary be proven. For individuals not to be legally responsible for their acts, they must be laboring under such a defect of reason, from diseases of the mind, as not to know the nature and quality of the acts that they were doing, or, if they did know it, that they did not know that it was wrong.

The M'Naghten test was criticized because of the vagueness of the terms "disease of the mind" and "know." Various authorities and psychiatrists testified in different ways as to whether a particular defendant was suffering from a disease of the mind so as not to know the acts were wrong. For a modern example of a M'Naghten insanity plea, suppose that the defendant was suffering from such a disease of the mind that he believed that the next-door neighbor was an alien who was trying to kill him, so he picked up a shotgun that he believed to be a stun gun and fired it at the neighbor. Therefore, he had a disease (delusions regarding the neighbor and the idea that the shotgun was a stun gun), and he did not know that what he was doing was wrong.

Owing to the confusion surrounding the M'Naghten test, in 1887 some jurisdictions adopted the irresistible impulse test. The landmark case in this area was *Parsons v. State*, where an Alabama court set forth the modern version of the irresistible impulse test.[5] Basically, this test holds that a person will be considered insane if as a result of a disease of the mind she was unable to control her behavior. Just as the name of this test implies, if the defendant could prove that she was suffering from a disease of the mind so that she could not control an impulse to commit criminal acts, then she would be considered insane.

This test also was controversial, and in 1954 the U.S. Court of Appeals in Washington, DC, decided the case of *Durham v. United States*.[6] Although this decision also caused debate, some jurisdictions adopted its rationale as their test for insanity. The Durham test does away with the right or wrong requirement of the M'Naghten rule and states that a person is insane if he committed a criminal act that was a product of a mental disease or defect. The same problem inherent in the M'Naghten test regarding mental disease or defect afflicted the Durham rule.

This patchwork of insanity defenses was very confusing. Adding to this confusion was the enactment of the federal Insanity Defense Reform Act of 1984, which established a fourth type of insanity test.[7] The federal test, also known as the severe mental disease test, requires that the defendant, as a result of severe mental disease or defect, be unable to appreciate the nature and quality of the wrongfulness of his act or acts.

Approximately one year after the Durham decision, the ALI's Model Penal Code (MPC) established the substantial capacity test. In an effort to clarify these conflicting and vague rules regarding insanity, many states began to adopt the ALI test. It is being used in a growing number of states. The test is found in Section 4.01 of the MPC and reads as follows:

1. A person is not responsible for criminal conduct if at the time of such conduct as a result of mental disease or defect he lacks substantial capacity either to appreciate the criminality (wrongfulness) of his conduct or to conform his conduct to the requirements of the law.
2. As used in this Article, the terms mental disease or defect do not include abnormality manifested only by repeated criminal or otherwise antisocial conduct.

The primary difference between the M'Naghten and the ALI tests is that the M'Naghten test requires the defendant to show total mental impairment, whereas the ALI test requires only that the defendant show that she lacked the "substantial capacity" to conform her conduct to the requirements of law, that is, lack of self-control.

Understanding the various insanity tests can be confusing, to say the least. Table 5.1 sets forth the basic standards of each of the insanity rules or tests.

TABLE 5.1 Standards for the Various Insanity Tests

Test	Legal Standard	Burden of Proof	Who Bears the Burden of Proof
M'Naghten	Didn't know what he was doing or didn't know it was wrong	Varies from jurisdiction to jurisdiction	Varies from jurisdiction to jurisdiction
Irresistible Impulse	Could not control his behavior to jurisdiction	Varies from jurisdiction to jurisdiction	Varies by jurisdiction
Durham	The criminal act was caused by his mental illness	Beyond a reasonable doubt	Prosecutor
ALI/MPC	Lacks substantial capacity to appreciate the wrongfulness of his conduct or to control it	Beyond a reasonable doubt	Prosecutor
Federal Position	Lacks capacity to appreciate the wrongfulness of his conduct	Clear and convincing evidence	Defense

Source: Adapted from Norvill Morris, "Insanity Defense," Crime File, National Institute of Justice, U.S. Department of Justice (Washington, DC, undated).

When John Hinckley, Jr., shot and wounded former President Ronald Reagan, he claimed he was insane at the time of the incident. The jury found him not guilty by reason of insanity. Although Hinckley remains at a secure mental hospital, this incident caused the general public to become enraged at the use of the insanity defense in criminal cases. Some jurisdictions shifted the burden of proof, from requiring the government to prove that the defendant was sane at the time of the crime to requiring the defendant to prove that he was insane at the time. Other states adopted a more strict definition of insanity. California voters passed what some authorities refer to as the "wild beast" test for insanity. This test requires the defendant to prove that he was suffering from a mental disease or defect that totally destroyed his ability to know right from wrong and to exercise any control over his actions. The California Supreme Court later interpreted this referendum to mean that the voters were rejecting the substantial capacity test and returning to the M'Naghten test.

Focus 5.2

Insane, but for How Long?

The insanity defense is also complicated by the fact that a person may be considered temporarily insane. Under this concept, a person may be insane at the time of the crime and regain his or her sanity by the time the criminal trial starts. This is the defense used by Mrs. Bobbitt when she cut off her husband's penis after he raped her. Expert testimony at the trial convinced the jury that Mrs. Bobbitt was insane at the time of the act. She was found not guilty by reason of insanity and, after a short stay in a mental institution, was released.

The confusion over the insanity defense continues today. Other personal defenses also raise issues regarding the mental status of the defendant, such as the diminished responsibility defense.

Diminished Responsibility

Some defendants suffer from mental diseases or stresses that, while they do not completely impair their reasoning ability, do affect their reasoning. The concept of diminished responsibility is similar to the insanity defense, except that it is a partial defense. It tends to diminish the responsibility of the defendant, for example, to reduce first-degree murder to a lesser offense.

Many states reject this personal defense, and those that allow it limit its use to specific intent crimes, permitting evidence to prove that the defendant lacked the mental state to commit an element of the offense. For example, in some jurisdictions the accused could have a premeditated murder offense reduced to second-degree murder by establishing that, because of her mental state, she could not have formed the specific intent to commit murder.

Diminished responsibility is distinct from insanity. If a defendant is found not guilty by reason of insanity, he or she is normally committed to a mental hospital instead of prison. If a defendant claims to have been suffering from diminished responsibility, that claim may negate the specific intent necessary for a certain crime but will not absolve the defendant of all guilt. Juries will return a verdict of guilty to a lesser offense.

Diminished Responsibility under U.S. Insanity Defense Reform Act

In 1984, the federal government passed the U.S. Insanity Defense Reform Act (18 U.S.C.S. § 17). The act, however, applies only to federal cases. One provision of the act required a trial judge to exclude evidence of a mental condition that does not support a legally acceptable theory of a lack of mens rea. The U.S. Court of Appeals for the Third Circuit held in *United*

States v. Askari, 2007 (U.S. App. LEXIS 8420 [3d Cir. Pa., April 11, 2007]) that the act prohibits defenses such as diminished responsibility and diminished capacity when those defenses do not negate mens rea. The same court, in an earlier decision, *United States v. Pohlot* (827 F.2d 889, 1987 U.S. App. LEXIS 11347, 23 Fed. R. Evid. Serv. [CBC] 1121 [3d Cir. Pa. 1987]), held that Congress did not intend to bar all evidence of mental abnormality from the jury's consideration of mens rea, but it did restrict the use of the diminished responsibility defense.

Focus 5.3

Determining Insanity Tests

Kwoset v. State

The problems involved in determining what test for insanity should be used are demonstrated by the Supreme Court of Wisconsin's struggle with the issue.

Excerpt from the Supreme Court of Wisconsin Decision (8 Wis. 2D 640)

The appellant has urged upon this court a need to re-examine the test of insanity in criminal cases in the interest of justice. There is merit to this argument. The M'Naghten rule as applied in Wisconsin should be modified and changed.

This court has been committed to the M'Naghten rule, commonly called the right-and-wrong test, which was formulated over 100 years ago in M'Naghten's Case (1843), 10 Clark & F. 200, 209, 8 Eng. Reprint 718. As originally stated, the accused was not legally responsible if he was "laboring under such a defective reason, from disease of the mind, as not to know the nature and quality of the act he was doing; or, if he did know it, that he did not know he was doing what was wrong." This test applied to the accused's lack of knowledge of right and wrong in respect to the specific act challenged and of its nature and quality, but in practice the test has sometimes been stated to the jury in the abstract and conversely in the affirmative as a test of sanity. Although the M'Naghten rule has been subject to much criticism, it is still the test in the majority of states, but in several of them the rule has been modified or supplemented by the irresistible-impulse test. The M'Naghten Case was an attempt to state a legal standard in terms of the nature of man, of his mental process, and of his moral responsibility. It is considered defective in that it emphasizes only the cognitive and omits the volitional aspect of man's nature and is not in keeping with present-day thinking of medical science.

In *Oborn v. State (1910), 143 Wis. 249, 272, 126 N. W. 737,* after a review of the earlier Wisconsin cases, this court reaffirmed the M'Naghten rule and rejected the irresistible-impulse modification of it saying: "This court is not committed to the doctrine that one can successfully claim immunity from punishment for his wrongful act, consciously committed with consciousness of its wrongful character, upon the ground that, through an abnormal mental condition, he did the act under an uncontrollable impulse rendering him legally insane. One, at his peril of punishment, commits an act while capable of distinguishing between right and wrong, and conscious of the nature of his act. He is legally bound, in such circumstances, to exercise such self-control as to preclude his escaping altogether from the consequences of his act on the plea of insanity, though his condition may affect the grade of the offense. Thus far the charity of the law goes and no farther." This reasoning assumes that one who has knowledge of right and wrong and of the nature of the act necessarily has the power or capacity of choice or self-control.

In *Jessner v. State (1930), 202 Wis. 184, 231 N. W. 634,* the original M'Naghten rule was somewhat modified and, so far as the inability to distinguish between right and wrong in respect to the specific act, was affirmed, but doubt was expressed as to the correctness of the additional element of the rule referring to the lack of knowledge of the nature and the quality of the act. Oehler v. State (1930), 202 Wis. 530, 535, 232 N. W. 866, stated the rule to be "such a perverted condition of the mental and moral faculties as to render the person incapable of distinguishing between right and wrong." In *State v. Johnson (1940), 233 Wis. 668, 290 N. W. 159,* in answering the argument that the right-and-wrong test was abolished by ch. 620, Laws of 1917, when "or feeble-minded" was added to sec. 357.11, Stats., now sec. 957.11, governing pleas of insanity, this court again reaffirmed the right-and-wrong test, including the element relating to the nature and quality of the act, stating (p. 670): "It does not follow, however, that one of less mental caliber than another but still knowing the nature of his act and whether it is right or wrong is to be excused from responsibility therefore." In Simecek v. State (1943), 243 Wis. 439, 447, 10 N. W. (2d) 161, this court said: "One may be medically insane and yet be criminally responsible for his acts."

In the latest expression of this court in *State v. Carlson (1958), 5 Wis. (2d) 595, 93 N. W. (2d) 354,* it was stated that some members of the court were of the opinion that the M'Naghten rule should be modified, but since the question was not raised, it should not be decided in that opinion. However, the court, in passing upon the admissibility of evidence, stated (p. 607): "We are of the opinion, however, that if the offered testimony, together with other expert testimony, had sufficiently tended to prove that at the time of the offense defendant was subject to a compulsion or irresistible impulse by reason of the abnormality of his brain, the testimony should have been admitted. Even under the right-wrong test, no evidence should be excluded which reasonably tends to show the mental condition of the defendant at the time of the offense." By the language in the Carlson case we did not adopt the irresistible-impulse test, but the case does cast doubt upon the Johnson and Oborn decisions.

It is important and necessary that the law of criminal responsibility in this state should be clarified in keeping with such present medical and psychiatric knowledge as is in accord with basic principles of criminal responsibility and with the respective duties of the court and jury. No test should require the court or the jury to abdicate its functions by allowing medical witnesses and psychiatrists to determine the ultimate fact on theories and standards unrecognized and unapproved by law.

In 1953, a royal commission in England in its report on capital punishment, 1949–1953, reported that the M'Naghten rule was so defective that the law on the subject ought to be changed. The majority was in favor of total abrogation of the rule, leaving the jury to determine whether at the time of the act the accused was suffering from a disease of the mind (or mental deficiency) to such a degree that he ought not to be held responsible. The difficulty with this test is a lack of the definition of the word "ought" to guide the jury. Three members of the commission believed the rule should be extended to add that if at the time of the act as a result of a disease of the mind (or mental deficiency) the accused was incapable of preventing himself from committing it, he was not responsible.

In 1954, the old New Hampshire test was rephrased in *Durham v. United States (1954), 94 U.S. App. D. C. 228, 241, 242, 214 Fed. (2d) 862, 874, 45 A. L. R. (2d) 1430.* This rule is "simply that an accused is not criminally responsible if his unlawful act was the product of mental disease or mental defect." This decision in suggesting instructions under the rule stated that an accused suffering from a mental disease or defect would still be responsible for his unlawful act if there was no causal connection between such mental abnormality and the act. Perhaps causation is what is meant by the ambiguous word "product" in the test. If it is, the formulation of the rule ought to state it expressly and to what required degree. Moreover, the decision expressly contemplates leaving the ultimate question of fact to the jury to apply its ideas of moral responsibility in each case to the individual prosecuted for the crime. "The jury's range of inquiry will not be limited" and would "be guided by wider horizons of knowledge concerning mental life. The question will be simply whether the accused acted because of mental disorder."

The Durham rule, while paying lip service to "freedom of the will," is so broad that it ceases to be a practical and workable test under the jury system. While the subject of much discussion and hailed by some psychiatrists (generally those of the psychoanalytical school), the Durham rule has not been followed by some eight state and two federal circuit courts that have had the occasion to re-examine this question. Over fifty years before the Durham Case, this court rejected the "product test" in *Eckert v. State (1902), 114 Wis. 160, 89 N. W. 826.*

The Durham rule's great weakness is that it provides no legal standard by which a jury can test conflicting medical and psychiatric testimony or by which the jury can evaluate such opinions. Psychiatrists differ radically in their theories of mental illness, of the nature of man, and of the mental process. They range from those who contend all criminals are insane in some sense of the word and no one is responsible for his acts, to those who believe people are endowed with the power of self-control that may be destroyed or impaired by a mental disease or defect through no fault of their own. The determinists and some psychoanalysts consider human actions to be so influenced or controlled by urges, impulses, and the subconscious as to be caused or determined without any power within people to control or choose their course of conduct in any situation. Other psychiatrists believe that people have a highly complex, integrated personality with the power of self-choice and determination, and whose mental process has a unity of perceiving, apprehending, judging, and willing that may be interfered with by a disease or defect of the mental order through no fault of theirs.

Criminal law and responsibility are based upon the fact that an individual human being is mentally free to exercise a choice between possible courses of conduct in respect to those acts condemned by the law and therefore morally and legally responsible. A human being has inherently and within him- or herself a free will—the power of self-control. In those situations when the volitional power is impaired to such a degree, is totally destroyed, or the requisite psychological conditions are not present for the exercise of a free choice, because of mental disorder or defect, responsibility for such act should not be imputed to that person. The original M'Naghten rule deals with two requirements for the free exercise of the will—knowledge and reason. Lacking either, the will is not free. But there are other conditions of the mind that affect the freedom of choice. The mind does not function in departments but as an integrated whole. The various steps involved in the mental process that produces a physical act are affected differently by various mental diseases and defects, and differently in many individuals. A test of legal insanity must include the essence of insanity. No one-sentence definition has been devised that is entirely satisfactory. But for legal purposes, the standard should include those effects on the mental process caused by mental disease or defect that have a direct relation to the justice of the conviction.

One who has the power in a given situation to choose between the doing or the not-doing of an unlawful act and freely chooses to do the unlawful act must be held criminally responsible in our society. And, conversely, if the accused did not have such volitional capacity because of its total or substantial destruction or of its inability to function freely in a given situation, either in the light of knowledge or because of the lack of it, and such incapacity was caused by and was the result of a mental disease or defect, such individual is not criminally responsible for such act and is legally insane. However, in cases when the normal functioning of the will is affected temporarily because of the overpowering influence of passion or emotion that the accused might have and ought to have controlled, such person should be criminally liable. A person cannot knowingly allow his or her emotions, urges, and passions to take control. Such so-called irresistible impulses are merely unresisted urges.

The concept of man's freedom of self-control is in accord with the basic theory of criminal law to punish those who ought to be punished. This test is not based on any new idea, but it enlarges the present concept of insanity in criminal cases in this state by including and emphasizing the volitional factor in human conduct expressly as a part of the test of insanity. It acknowledges that the volitional faculty in man is a prime element of criminal responsibility and the lack of it or the inability to exercise it freely is the essence of legal insanity when caused by a mental disease, or defect, and not self-induced by emotions or impulses that the accused might have controlled.

Somewhat similar tests, but perhaps broader in their wording stressing the volitional aspect of criminal responsibility, are stated in *Parsons v. State (1886), 81 Ala. 577, 585, 2 So. 854, 859,* as follows: "No one can deny that there must be two constituent elements of legal responsibility in the commission of every crime, and no rule can be just and reasonable which fails to recognize either of them: (1) Capacity of intellectual discrimination; and (2) freedom of will," citing many cases, and in *State v. White (1954), 58 N. M. 324, 330, 270 Pac. (2d) 727, 731,* which followed the minority view of the royal commission on capital punishment and added to the M'Naghten rule the following: "(c) Was incapable of preventing himself from committing it." See 22 University of Chicago Law Review, 317–404, for a series of articles by law professors and psychiatrists under the caption, "Insanity and the Criminal Law—A Critique of Durham v. United States." There is also a collection of the cases and a discussion of the problem in 45 A. L. R. (2d) 1447.

> The most satisfactory statement of our views in rule form and the one that should be adopted is formulated in the Model Penal Code of the American Law Institute and favored by a substantial majority of its council. Draft 4, sec. 4.01 of the Model Penal Code provides (p. 27):
>
> "(1) A person is not responsible for criminal conduct if at the time of such conduct as a result of mental disease or defect he lacks substantial capacity either to appreciate the criminality of his conduct or to conform his conduct to the requirements of law."
>
> "(2) The terms 'mental disease or defect' do not include an abnormality manifested only by repeated criminal or otherwise antisocial conduct."

The Insanity Defense Reform Act also shifted the burden of proof to the defendant to prove the affirmative defense of insanity by clear and convincing evidence. Congress shifted this burden because of testimony that proving a defendant sane beyond a reasonable doubt was virtually impossible.

Intoxication

Another criminal responsibility defense that involves negating intent is intoxication. One who is charged with a crime may raise the issue of intoxication as a defense. However, the result depends on whether the intoxication was voluntary or involuntary.

Involuntary intoxication may provide a complete excuse for criminal liability under some circumstances. The MPC allows involuntary intoxication as a defense, "[i]f by reason of such intoxication, the actor, at the time of his conduct, lacks substantial capacity either to appreciate its criminality or to conform his conduct to the requirements of law."[8] The problem involves exactly what is considered involuntary. The case law recognizes several situations in which involuntary intoxication is a complete defense. The first and most obvious case is that in which the defendant was tricked into drinking or ingesting alcohol or drugs that rendered her incapable of forming the necessary intent for the crime that was committed.[9]

The second instance of involuntary intoxication as a defense occurs when the defendant claims he was forced to consume the substance. The courts have been very restrictive in allowing this intoxication by duress defense. The MPC requires that the substance be consumed under circumstances that would afford a defense to a criminal charge,[10] thus incorporating the duress defense requirement in the intoxication by duress defense.

Voluntary intoxication is considered a defense only if, as a result of the intoxication, the defendant is unable to form the necessary intent required for the specific criminal act. For example, if a person consumed several drinks at a local bar and, in a drunken stupor, attempted to enter the wrong house, she would not be guilty of attempted burglary. Some court cases hold that voluntary intoxication may negate specific intent crimes but will not provide a defense to general intent crimes. Some jurisdictions have enacted statutes that remove voluntary intoxication as a defense, since the perpetrator knowingly ingested the alcohol or drugs prior to commission of the crime.

Syndromes/Disorders

Two syndromes and a disorder have been used as defenses, and each of these mental conditions is surrounded by controversy. They are the premenstrual and battered women syndromes and posttraumatic stress disorder.

Premenstrual syndrome (PMS)/premenstrual tension (PMT) is believed to affect approximately 40 percent of American women between the ages of twenty and forty.[11] Normally, the symptoms begin ten to fourteen days prior to the menstrual period and become progressively worse until the onset of menstruation. In some women, it continues for several days after the onset. Common symptoms include the following:

irritability

anxiety

mood swings

depression

migraine headaches

fainting

dizziness

allergies

As one woman stated, "There is a pervasive sense of things always falling apart." Susan Lark states that severely afflicted women are most vulnerable to extreme behavior during this period.[12] Katherine Dalton, an English physician, reports an increase in the likelihood of accidents, alcohol abuse, suicide attempts, and crimes committed by some women suffering from premenstrual tension. Dalton states that, in many cases, the affected women have Dr. Jekyll and Mr. Hyde personality splits—they are "mean," "witchy," and "irritable" during the PMT period. They often yell at their children, pick fights with their husbands, and snap at friends and coworkers. After the symptoms leave, they often spend the rest of the month trying to repair the damage done to the relationships.[13]

Posttraumatic stress disorder came to our consciousness as a result of Vietnam veterans suffering flashbacks and other mental disorders because of their service during the war. While some authorities also call this disease the Vietnam vet syndrome, its existence is not limited to those who served in Vietnam.[14]

The posttraumatic stress disorder is the development of characteristic symptoms following exposure to an extreme traumatic stressor involving direct personal experience of an event that involves actual or threatened death or serious injury.[15]

Examples of such experiences include military combat, violent personal assault such as rape or robbery, or other extraordinary life-threatening events. The traumatic event can be re-experienced in various ways such as flashbacks, dreams, and, occasionally, dissociative states that last from a few seconds to several days.

If the defendant is suffering from posttraumatic stress syndrome to the extent that he either cannot form the necessary intent or, as a result of the syndrome, meets the requirements of insanity, courts may find no criminal liability. This is an emerging area in criminal law, and we will see this concept developing as we learn more about this specific disorder.

The last of the **syndrome-based defenses** is **battered woman syndrome**. In order to understand this defense, it is necessary to discuss briefly the history and development of the concept of **battered women**. We have come a long way in understanding the dynamics that are involved in spousal abuse. Even with these advances in knowledge, there are still those who believe that a woman can simply leave an abusive relationship any time and that if she stays she must enjoy the beatings or instigate them.

Practicum 5.2

PMS as a Defense—The Case of Sandie Smith

Sandie Smith, an English barmaid, was convicted of carrying a knife and threatening a police officer. At the time of her final offense, she was on probation for stabbing another barmaid to death. Smith's background included nearly thirty convictions for assault and battery and eighteen attempted suicides. A review of her background established that her outbursts of erratic behavior always occurred several days prior to her menstrual period. Her attorney was successful in getting the British court to accept PMS as a mitigating factor. Since the trial, Smith has received a daily injection of progesterone. It appears that she has not been involved in any violent criminal behavior since she has been on the progesterone treatment.

ISSUE: What are the problems with allowing the use of PMS as a defense to violent criminal behavior?[16]

There are numerous definitions of battered women. One of the most inclusive defines battered women as follows:

> Battered women [are] those who have experienced physical or psychological injurious behavior at the hands of men with whom they once had, or were continuing to have, an intimate relationship.[17]

This definition does not require that the couple be married or even living together. There are situations in which the wife has left the abusive spouse only to be tracked down and beaten or worse. Nor does this definition establish a "minimum" level or amount of force to be exerted by the battering partner. Any form of physical or psychological violence qualifies under this definition.

Lenore E. A. Walker is one of the leading experts in the area of spousal abuse and is credited with advancing the knowledge and research on battered women.[18] Dr. Walker's original research established that battering is not a random act. It occurs in a "cycle of violence" that involves three distinct patterns of behavior.[19] The three phases in the cycle of violence are tension-building period, acute battering incident, and loving-contrition or absence-of-tension phase.

All these dynamics establish a situation that precludes a battered woman from leaving her spouse. This phenomenon has been entitled learned helplessness. This concept attempts to explain why an outwardly normal woman loses the ability to make decisions that would protect her from the abuser.

As a result of these forces, women are bound to abusive partners more tightly than if they were handcuffed to them. They believe their spouses are all-powerful. They have truly been brainwashed to believe they can never prevail against them. Women who are battered develop what Walker has identified as the battered woman syndrome, which can therefore be defined as a condition that affects women who have been continually abused by their spouses to the degree that their mental functioning is impaired. This disorder is not classified as a mental illness. However, there is authority for the position that it should be considered a subcategory of the posttraumatic stress disorder.[20]

The constant terror that battered women live with may finally place them in a position of believing they must attempt to kill the abuser or face death themselves. Because of this terror, some battered women may strike when the abusing partner least expects the attack, such as when he is sleeping, passed out, or returning home.[21] When these women kill, they do not attempt to flee the jurisdiction or hide the fact of the killing; on the contrary, they may call the police and report the crime themselves. This report normally leads to an investigation and charges against the battered spouse. These women many times will claim that they suffered from battered woman syndrome and attempt to use the concept of self-defense to justify their acts. The theory will be discussed in more detail later in this chapter.

JUSTIFICATION AND EXCUSE

The section above has discussed limitations on criminal responsibility because of a lack of mental capacity, whether that lack resulted from infancy, insanity, diminished responsibility, intoxication, or impairment as a result of a number of syndromes. The common law and modern statutes recognize other defenses independent of the actor's mental state. These defenses are classified as justifications and excuses.

Justification defenses arise when the defendant has engaged in conduct that is not punished under criminal law. The conduct might be desirable from society's perspective, such as when a police officer arrests a suspect. Without justification, such actions might constitute assault, false imprisonment, kidnapping, and other "crimes." Other conduct, while not desired or encouraged by society, may still fall under justification, as when a person kills another in self-defense. Without justification, the killing of another might be classified as murder or manslaughter.

Excuse defenses occur when the defendant is not considered at fault for having committed a crime. Some authorities state that lack of mental capacity falls within the excuse defense. However, for purposes of clarity, we have separated lack of mental capacity from this area and addressed it above. Excuse defenses include actions such as stealing under duress or necessity. The justification and excuse defenses include self-defense, defense of others, defense of property, duress, necessity, use of force in making arrests, resisting unlawful arrests, mistake, consent, and entrapment.

Practicum 5.3

Nutrition and Criminal Defenses—The "Twinkie" Defense

When you consider nutrition and criminal behavior, realize that Americans buy seven hundred million Twinkies a year, 80 percent of them on impulse. Over fifty billion Twinkies have been sold in the past sixty years. On May 22, 1979, Dan White, a former San Francisco county supervisor, was convicted of voluntary manslaughter for the November 1978 killing of San Francisco Mayor George Moscone and Supervisor Harvey Milk. White was originally charged with first-degree murder (a capital offense). The prosecutor argued to the jury that White was guilty of cold-blooded murder. It was established that White had gone to City Hall to talk to the mayor. He had entered through a window to avoid the metal detector at the main entrance (he was carrying a snub-nosed revolver). He shot Mayor Moscone and Harvey Milk with the weapon nine times, killing both of them. White readily admitted killing the mayor and Supervisor Milk, who was his most vocal opponent on the San Francisco Board of Supervisors.

White's defense attorney, Douglas Schmidt, presented evidence to establish that White had suffered from diminished capacity caused by a "biochemical change" in his brain. According to to the defense's theory of the case, White was incapable of the premeditation, deliberation, and malice required to obtain a murder conviction. Evidence at trial indicated that White was a manic-depressive with a high degree of stress caused by financial and other personal problems. A defense medical expert testified that White suffered from a "genetically caused melancholia" and, at the time, he was "discombobulated." Defense witnesses, who included family members, friends, and experts, testified about Wshite's moods and his diet. One defense psychiatrist testified that White's compulsive diet of candy bars, Twinkies, and Coke was evidence of a deep depression and resulted in excessive sugar intake, which either caused or aggravated a chemical imbalance in his brain.

QUESTION: Should the diet of the defendant be considered in determining his or her accountability for criminal misconduct?

Self-Defense

In understanding the concept of self-defense, it is important to distinguish between deadly force and nondeadly force. Normally, a person is justified in using deadly force only to protect himself or others with what he reasonably believes is necessary to combat imminent, unlawful deadly force. Self-defense contains the components of "proportionality" and "necessity." Proportionality requires that the force used must not be out of proportion to the force necessary to protect. A person is not privileged to use force that is disproportional to the threat that the actor reasonably believes that he is facing.

There must also be a necessity to use the force to prevent imminent, unlawful deadly force. For example, if a person threatens to attack the victim at some future date, the victim has other alternatives than the use of force to protect herself. Deadly force is generally defined as force likely to cause death or grievous bodily injury. In most cases, the identification of force as deadly is based on the objective likelihood of the outcome.

The use of force is based on what appears to be reasonably necessary. Accordingly, self-defense is permitted if the actor makes a reasonable mistake of fact regarding the need to use deadly force. For example, if a stranger points a weapon at the victim, the victim can reasonably assume that the weapon is loaded and act accordingly to protect himself. It would not matter if later it was determined that the stranger's weapon was unloaded.

Generally, the use of deadly force in self-defense is limited to those situations in which the actor is not the aggressor. In most jurisdictions, a person may not start a fight and then use deadly force to protect herself. There are exceptions to this general rule. For example, suppose D mildly insults A. A becomes unreasonably outraged and attempts to kill D. In this case, D probably could use self-defense to protect herself. In addition, in most jurisdictions, if an aggressor starts a fight and then clearly tries to retreat, deadly force may be justified if retreat is unsuccessful. An aggressor is one whose affirmative unlawful conduct is reasonably calculated to produce a fight that may cause injurious or fatal consequences. In determining whether a person is an aggressor, the courts look only at her conduct at the time that she used the deadly force. For example, suppose A starts a fight with V. The fight is broken up. The next day, without warning, V attacks A. In this situation, V would be considered the aggressor.

The general rule is that a nonaggressor has no duty to retreat prior to using deadly force. A significant number of jurisdictions, however, reject this rule and hold that if the actor can safely retreat, he must do so prior to resorting to deadly force. Even those jurisdictions that require the nonaggressor to retreat prior to use of deadly force generally recognize the "castle" exception. While there is some conflict among scholars, most legal authorities in criminal law argue that a person does not have to retreat from his home or business (castle) before using deadly force.[22]

Some jurisdictions recognize the "imperfect" form of self-defense. Imperfect self-defense occurs when the one using force against another does so with the purpose of injuring or killing the victim in the mistaken belief that use of the force was necessary to defend herself. Under this concept the imperfect defense, while not a complete justification for the use of deadly force, will reduce the offense of murder to the lesser one of manslaughter. There is some authority for the position that courts should accept **imperfect self-defense** arguments and allow the victim to go free.

This is the position that battered women who kill their abusers have taken during several court hearings.[23]

Typical self-defense jury instructions require the trier of fact to judge the defendant's action by the "reasonable person" standard. In essence, what would the average or reasonable person do if he or she encountered the same or a similar situation? This standard poses problems for battered women, since it does not allow the jury to judge her actions by her reality—that of living with a deadly and unpredictable assailant. Although some courts are beginning to allow jurors to place themselves in the battered woman's shoes and view her actions from her perspective, others still hold to the reasonable, objective standard of self-defense. One of the most famous uses of the imperfect self-defense concept occurred in California, where the Menendez brothers claimed they feared for their safety and it was necessary to kill their parents, even though at the time the parents were not engaged in any assaultive acts.

Focus 5.4

Lack of Self-Defense

One movement is to consider the lack of self-defense as an element of the crime that the prosecution must establish. An example of this is contained in the *State v. Bellany* case decided by the Supreme Court of South Carolina [359 S.E.2d 63; 1987 S.C. LEXIS 304]. Excerpts of that case are set forth below.

> Appellant was convicted of murder and criminal conspiracy. He received the death penalty and five years, respectively. This case consolidates appellant's direct appeal and our mandatory review of the death sentence, pursuant to S.C. Code Ann. § 16-3-25 (1976, as amended). We reverse and remand.
>
> On February 11, 1986, appellant bought a .38 caliber pistol at a pawn shop. On February 28, 1986, appellant killed the victim by shooting him five times in the head at close range. At trial, the state contended that this was a contract killing or murder for hire. The state attempted to prove that appellant's co-defendant, Von Ceil Lewis (Lewis), hired him to kill the victim, Roland Vereen (Vereen). Lewis's alleged motive was to prevent Vereen from continuing to steal items from her home as she believed he had been doing since she had refused to continue selling drugs for him. Appellant contended that while his co-defendant had repeatedly asked him to kill Vereen, he had refused to do so. He claims that he shot Vereen in self-defense after Vereen pulled a gun on him.
>
> Appellant contends that the trial court's charge failed to comply with the self-defense charge suggested in State v. Davis, 282 S.C. 45, 317 S.E. (2d) 452 (1984) and made mandatory in State v. Glover, 284 S.C. 152, 326 S.E. (2d) 150 (1985). We agree.
>
> In its charge, the trial court properly set forth the four elements of self-defense. The trial court erred, however, in the subsequent portion of its charge dealing with the burden of proof in self-defense cases. The jury was instructed that the accused is required to establish the plea of self-defense by the preponderance or the greater weight of the evidence. After explaining what is meant by "a preponderance of the evidence," the trial court stated, "and that's the standard, that's the burden that the defendant must carry in order to prove the defense of self-defense in this case."

This charge is in direct contravention of the model charge given in Davis, supra, and made mandatory in Glover, supra. The relevant portion of the self-defense charge as set forth in Davis states, "If you have a reasonable doubt of the defendant's guilt after considering all the evidence including the evidence of self-defense, then you must find him not guilty. On the other hand, if you have no reasonable doubt of the defendant's guilt after considering all the evidence including the evidence of self-defense, then you must find him guilty." It is clear that the defendant need not establish self-defense by a preponderance of the evidence but must merely produce evidence that causes the jury to have a reasonable doubt regarding his guilt.

Reversed and remanded.

[COURT'S FOOTNOTE: As Professor McAninch observed, "The clear implication of the proposed instruction is that self-defense is no longer to be considered an affirmative defense which must be established by the defendant by a preponderance of the evidence. [I]f any reasonable doubt remains as to self-defense, the jury must acquit."]

The rules regarding the use of nondeadly force are similar to those for the use of deadly force. The actor must reasonably believe that the force used is necessary to prevent an imminent unlawful force. There is no duty, however, for a nonaggressor to retreat prior to using nondeadly force.

Defense of Others

As a general rule, a person is justified in using force to prevent unlawful attack upon another person when the one using force reasonably believes that the one under attack is in imminent danger of harm and the use of force is necessary to avoid the danger. Some early English and American cases required the one being defended to be related to the defender. However, the modern view does not retain this requirement, and a person can use force to defend a stranger. In most jurisdictions, the actor has the same rights to use force as the person being attacked. It is often stated that, when you use force to save a third person, you step into the shoes of the third person with whatever rights that third person had to defend himself. Some jurisdictions, however, allow a person to defend a third person based on reasonable appearances, that is, what a reasonable person would believe was appropriate.

Defense of Property

Generally, deadly force is never permitted to protect property. At common law, however, deadly force was allowed to protect one's home. The use of nondeadly force to protect property is limited only to property in a person's possession. One is not permitted to use any force to reclaim property that is not in her possession. Forcible self-help is not favored by the law. Common law did allow for the use of nondeadly force to recapture property immediately if it was retaken as the result of hot pursuit.

The use of mechanical devices to protect one's property is also prohibited under the rules establishing the use of deadly force and defense of property. One cannot use a spring gun or other deadly device to protect his property from theft or trespass. While some jurisdictions allow for use of these devices if the owner could have used deadly force, the better view and the one adopted by the drafters of the MPC is that the use of deadly devices to protect property is never justified.[24]

As Practicum 5.4 (on page 103) illustrates, the use of deadly force will vary depending on the facts presented. It is always easy after the fact to second-guess what the user of force should have done. Self-defense, defense of others, and defense of property all require that the person using the force act reasonably and that the use of force was necessary to prevent injury or death to the person using force. Another defense that requires reasonableness and necessity is duress.

CASTLE DOCTRINE Many states have enacted "castle doctrine" statutes. Under common law, a person generally had an obligation to retreat before using deadly force if the person could safely retreat unless he or she was in his or her home. Under the castle doctrine, there is no legal duty to retreat as long as the person is in a place where he or she has a right to be. The building or vehicle must be occupied at the time for the deadly force provision to apply, and the person using the force cannot provoke the attacker or be involved in criminal activity at the time. It is referred to as the "castle doctrine" drawing from the idea that a person's home is his or her castle and he or she should have a right to defend it. Note, however, that, unlike common law, it applies to locations other than the home.

Florida's "castle doctrine": A typical statute involving the castle doctrine is that enacted in Florida in 2005.

Fla. Stat. § 776.013. Home protection; use of deadly force; presumption of fear of death or great bodily harm

(1) A person is presumed to have held a reasonable fear of imminent peril of death or great bodily harm to himself or herself or another when using defensive force that is intended or likely to cause death or great bodily harm to another if:

(a) The person against whom the defensive force was used was in the process of unlawfully and forcefully entering, or had unlawfully and forcibly entered, a dwelling, residence, or occupied vehicle, or if that person had removed or was attempting to remove another against that person's will from the dwelling, residence, or occupied vehicle; and

(b) The person who uses defensive force knew or had reason to believe that an unlawful and forcible entry or unlawful and forcible act was occurring or had occurred.

Prior to the enactment of the statute, the law in Florida concerning self-defense could be divided into two parts: First, there were the rules that governed when deadly force could be used if one was attacked in one's own home. Second, there were the rules that governed when deadly force could be used if one were attacked outside of one's own home. When outside of the home, an individual had a duty to retreat if possible.

Duress

Sometimes people are forced to do what they do. When what they are forced to do is wrong it seems that compulsion ought to count in their favor. After all, we say, such a person was not free to do otherwise . . . he couldn't help himself, not really. No claim to avoid blame appeals more urgently to our moral institutions, yet none presents more problems of detail. There are times, after all, when we ought to stand firm and run the risk of harm to our selves instead of taking a way out that means harm to others.[25]

If a defendant commits a criminal act under duress, the duress may be a complete defense. There are four major issues involving the defense of duress: (1) Which crimes does duress excuse? (2) What constitutes duress? (3) When must the duress occur? and (4) Is a threat sufficient to constitute duress?[26]

Duress is not a defense to homicide or crimes involving serious bodily injury. The theory behind this rule is that, when the choice is between killing an innocent person or oneself, one ought to die rather than escape by the murder of an innocent. If duress is not a complete defense to aggravated assault or battery, it may still reduce the crime to one of simple assault or battery.

To constitute duress, there must be an immediate threat to injure or kill. Some states, like Minnesota, recognize only threats of immediate death as a defense. Most states are less restrictive, accepting immediate or imminent threats of injury or death. Threats of future harm and threats to damage reputation or profession are insufficient to constitute duress. For example, a threat to break a person's arm if he did not steal a car was sufficient to constitute duress. However, a threat to damage one's car if one did not commit perjury was held insufficient to constitute duress. There must also be a belief that the threat will be carried out. Most states require that the belief must be both reasonable and honest. Other states require only that the belief must be an honest one.

In *McMaugh v. State*, the Rhode Island Supreme Court addressed the issue of battered women and duress.[27] Ann McMaugh suffered a long pattern of abuse by her husband. This included beating, pulling out large chunks of her hair, and threatening her with various weapons he kept about the house. This cycle of violence increased in intensity and continued during their trial for murder.

On the evening of the murder, the husband and another male had an altercation at a local bar. The husband left with Ann, returned a short time later with two handguns, and waited in the parking lot for the victim to exit the lounge. After another argument, the husband fired two shots, resulting in the victim's death. The police arrived and arrested Ann and her husband. They were charged with first-degree murder, conspiracy, and a weapons charge. They were subsequently released on bail, and it was during this period that Ann's husband increased his psychological and physical pressure on Ann. The husband convinced her to testify that she

---

Practicum 5.4

When Is Deadly Force Authorized?

A female college student awakened to the sound of glass being smashed. She grabbed her trusty 12-gauge sawed-off shotgun and fired one round through the front door, killing the intruder. Was she justified in using deadly force?

1. Suppose the "intruder" was a drunken neighbor who mistook her apartment for his own?
2. What if the college student had just heard the local radio station advising people to stay off the streets at night because a serial killer was murdering young females in her part of the city?
3. What if the intruder was the student's former spouse, and she had been physically abused by him in the past and had obtained a temporary restraining order?

Would your answers be any different if the intruder were inside the house when the student fired her shotgun?

1. Would it be okay if she fired as he climbed through a window?
2. What if he were inside, appeared unarmed, and stated, "I just want to talk to you"?
3. What if he had a knife and was advancing toward her, but she could leave by the back door?

caused the death by throwing one of the weapons into the backseat where it accidentally discharged, killing the victim. He ordered her to repeat the story over and over and beat her when she did not perform to his satisfaction. Despite objections by her attorney, Ann testified as directed by her husband. However, during this time, no one was aware of the mental hold that Ann's husband had over her, nor was her attorney aware that Ann's husband had ordered her to testify in the manner she did.

The jury found Ann guilty of murder, conspiracy, and the weapons charge, and she was sentenced to state prison. It was only after she had been separated from her husband for a period of months while serving her sentence that she agreed to tell others about the abuse she suffered and the fact that her husband forced her to testify as she did during the trial.

The motion for new trial clearly established that Ann McMaugh was suffering from battered woman syndrome and that her husband's influence over her was so great as to prevent her from cooperating with her own attorney. The Supreme Court of Rhode Island held that the focused pattern of extreme physical and mental abuse by her codefendant husband prevented her from assisting her attorney. It thus ordered a new trial.

In *People v. Romero*, another court examined the issue of duress and the commission of crimes by battered women.[28] Debra and Terrance Romero were not married, but they began living together in March 1989. About six weeks after Debra moved in, Terrance began hitting her, and he continued to do so every day. She left him several times, but he found her and persuaded her to return. He also stated that, if he couldn't have her, nobody else would. In May 1989, Debra and Terrance began a robbery spree that ended in July. They were arrested and charged with one count of robbery and four counts of attempted robbery. Debra admitted to committing all the acts but claimed she did so out of fear of Terrance. Terrance testified that he never committed any of the acts, loved Debra, and had never threatened or hit her. Debra's defense attorney never investigated or presented any evidence that she was a battered woman. Debra was convicted of all the crimes and sentenced to state prison for a term of five years, eight months.

In reversing the conviction, the *Romero* court held:

> BWS evidence would have deflected the prosecutor's [and Terrance's] challenge to [Debra's] credibility. Such evidence would have assisted the jury in objectively analyzing [Debra's] claim of [duress] by dispelling many of the commonly held misconceptions about battered women. As the record reflects, the prosecutor [and Terrance] exploited several of these misconceptions in urging the jury to reject [Debra's duress] claim. . . . [brackets in original quote][29]

The court reversed the conviction and ordered a new trial, holding that duress is very similar to self-defense and that evidence of the battered woman syndrome would have educated the jury regarding the myths surrounding battered women. This, in turn, would have allowed them to find Debra not guilty because she acted under duress.

In summary, for duress to be a complete defense, there must be a reasonable and actual belief that a life is in danger or serious bodily injury is threatened, and that the danger is present and immediate. Recent cases dealing with battered women and duress may signal a change in the traditional requirement of reasonableness in this defense.

Necessity

The defense of necessity is similar to the defense of duress in that it is based upon a balancing of the evils a person faces. On occasion, a person may confront natural circumstances such as being trapped on a mountainside during a snowstorm. He understands that if he breaks into a cabin and eats the food inside he may be committing a burglary, but he also knows that to stay outside unprotected may result in his death. While the person has committed the crime of burglary, the defense of necessity will allow him to escape punishment.

The common law view was that the forces had to arise as a result of nature rather than other human beings. However, the modern view, including that of the MPC, is to establish a broad range of "choice of evils" that does not limit the danger to any particular source or type. There is authority for the position that you cannot cause or contribute to the disaster or circumstances that cause the evils to arise, thereby requiring you to use the defense of necessity. Some legal experts take the position that this defense would even allow the killing of another if done to avoid a greater harm.[30] As Practicum 5.5 indicates, this is a controversial issue in the defense of necessity.

Practicum 5.5

How Hungry Must You Be to Kill Another?

In 1884, four people were cast away on the high seas during a storm 1,600 miles from the Cape of Good Hope. Three of them, Dudley, Brooks, and Stevens, were able-bodied seamen, and Parker was a seventeen-year-old boy. Their lifeboat was open to the elements and had no food or water. For the first three days they had nothing to eat or drink. On the fourth day they caught a turtle, on which they subsisted for several days. They had no fresh water except for occasional rain.

On the eighteenth day, when they had been without food or water for seven days, Dudley proposed that they draw lots and decide who should be put to death so that the other three could eat his remains and continue to live. They could not agree to this plan. On the next day, after Dudley and Stevens discussed the matter, they decided the boy should die since he had no relatives and they did. Dudley then killed the boy with a knife, and the remaining three fed upon the boy's body for three days, until they were rescued on the fourth day.

> **ISSUE:** *Should the survivors be convicted of murder? Why?*

The court found them guilty of murder and sentenced them to death, holding that necessity did not constitute a defense to killing another. However, their sentences were commuted to six months in prison by the Crown.[31] Was this a proper holding? What do you think should be the punishment, if any, for this factual pattern today?

Individuals cannot simply claim that "Mother Nature made me do it" and walk away from any criminal charges. Like other defenses, the defense of necessity requires the harm done to be as little as possible, considering the threat. Additionally, the threatened harm must be imminent. A person cannot steal food from a store, saying that a snowstorm may arrive sometime in the next week or so. In some situations, if the person claiming the defense of necessity caused or contributed to the threatened harm, she may not be able to use the defense.

Use of Force in Making Arrests

Unfortunately, some persons resist arrest. Thus, the officer may need to use force to effect the arrest. Society has authorized this force, and therefore, the officer is justified in using reasonable force to carry out his or her duties. The issue surrounding use of force in making an arrest really involves how much force is reasonable under the circumstances.

The videotape of Rodney King being repeatedly struck by members of the Los Angeles Police Department led to a national debate on the proper use of force in making an arrest. The beating of Rodney King was not the first time police have been accused of using excessive force, nor unfortunately will it be the last time that officers may lose control of their emotions and respond with aggression.

If a suspect is armed and firing his weapon at the officers, few of us would deny them the right to respond with equal or greater force in an effort to arrest him. The proper amount of force to be used in any situation will vary depending on a number of factors. The force being overcome by the officer, whether other officers are present, the training the officer has received, and the law enforcement agency's policy on the use of force are just a few of the factors that will determine when and how an officer exerts force in effecting an arrest.

The U.S. Supreme Court has examined the use of force and arrests on several occasions. The landmark case in this area is *Tennessee v. Garner*.[32] In that case, two Memphis, Tennessee, police officers responded at 10:45 in the evening to answer a report of a prowler inside a house. Upon arriving at the scene, a neighbor told them that she had heard breaking glass and "they" or "someone" was breaking in next door. Officer Hymon went to the back of the house and saw someone running across the backyard. Hymon observed Garner crouching at the base of a chain-link fence. The officer was reasonably certain that Garner was unarmed. The officer identified himself and observed Garner begin to climb over the fence. The officer was convinced that if Garner made it over the fence he would escape, and therefore, he fired one round that struck and killed Garner. The Supreme Court held that an arrest is, in fact, a seizure of the person and therefore subject to the reasonableness requirement of the Fourth Amendment. It went on to say that the use of deadly force to prevent the escape of all felony suspects, whatever the circumstances, is constitutionally unreasonable.

The decision to use deadly force is a complex issue that cannot be fully addressed in this text. However, the principle of using force to make an arrest is accepted in our society. When an officer uses force correctly to arrest a high-profile violent criminal, that officer is a hero. However, if she makes a mistake or intentionally uses excessive force, she may face criminal charges.

Up to this point, we have been discussing the amount of force that may be used by an officer when making a lawful arrest. What happens if the officer is making an unlawful arrest? Can the average citizen resist that unlawful arrest? That issue is the next type of defense to be examined.

Resisting Unlawful Arrest

It is generally stated that at common law a person had a right to resist an unlawful arrest. Today, jurisdictions differ in their positions on whether a person can use nondeadly force to resist an unlawful arrest. However, legal scholars argue that no one should be authorized to use even nondeadly force in resisting an unlawful arrest. There are remedies for an unlawful arrest today that were not available in early England. These remedies include legal action against the officer and the others involved in the unlawful arrest. The MPC has adopted this position and prohibits the use of any force to resist an unlawful arrest by a known peace officer.[33] Accordingly, the better-reasoned position is that an individual generally does not have the right to resist an arrest by a peace officer.

Practicum 5.6

Instant Decisions and Deadly Force

In view of Garner, under which of the following situations would you fire your weapon at the suspect? Assume for the moment that your departmental policy is not to fire warning shots or attempt to wound suspects. At 3:30 a.m. you are responding to a report of shots fired and observe a person standing in the middle of the road with a .45-caliber handgun in his hand. You exit your marked police vehicle, identify yourself as a police officer, and order him to drop the weapon.

1. The suspect puts his hands up in the air, still holding his weapon, and yells, "Come and take it away from me!"
2. He begins to raise the weapon and points it at you, stating that unless you leave he will kill you.
3. He fires one round in the air and yells that the next one has your name on it.
4. He states that he has one round left and fires it at you but misses.
5. He fires several rounds at you.

Mistake

There is probably no substantive area of criminal law that is more confusing than mistake or ignorance of fact or law. Some scholars examine the nature of the mistake while others compare the totality of circumstances. Ignorance of the law has been used in situations in which the defendant was completely unaware of any statute prohibiting his conduct, as well as situations in which the defendant was mistaken regarding the law when he acted.

The drafters of the MPC attempted to simplify this complex area by viewing it from the intent or mens rea requirement of all criminal acts.[34] Therefore, the easy way to approach this complex issue is to remember that if the mistake of fact negates the existence of the necessary intent on the part of the defendant, there is a defense. The critical question becomes what type of intent was required for the act to be criminal. Once this is determined, the rules regarding mistake of fact or law are relatively easy to apply.

Mistake of fact cases involve three forms of liability: specific intent crimes, general intent crimes, and strict liability crimes. In specific intent crimes, it is easy to understand that, if a defendant was mistaken regarding an aspect of the offense, she would not have the necessary specific intent to commit the crime. Therefore, mistake of fact operates as a defense. In general intent crimes, mistake of fact will be a defense if the mistake relates directly to the general intent required for the commission of the crime. In strict liability crimes, a mistake of fact is not a defense if it relates to an element for which strict liability applies.

Mistakes or ignorance of law also may operate as a defense. We have all heard the adage, "Ignorance of the law is no excuse." Unfortunately, this statement is a simplification of a series of rules that apply to criminal conduct. Ignorance or mistake of the law as to whether certain conduct is a crime is not a defense. Society assumes its members will know and obey the law. To do otherwise would allow anyone accused of a crime to claim ignorance and thereby avoid prosecution. Mistake of law may be a defense if the crime is a specific intent offense. Other instances of mistakes of law are not so clear. Some states allow mistake of law as a defense if the defendant relied on the advice of government prosecutors. Others allow mistake of law as a defense in situations in which new statutes have been enacted and subsequent court decisions hold that the statute was unconstitutional and therefore the acts under it were criminal in nature. In these limited situations, courts allow mistake of law to act as a defense. As the above discussion indicates, mistake as a defense is a complex and often confusing area of the law. The MPC approach of analyzing mistake from the mens rea perspective is the preferred method of examining this defense.

Consent

The general rule is that the consent of the victim is not a defense to criminal prosecution. The rationale behind this rule is that a criminal act harms society, and consent by the victim does not remove this harm. For example, *People v. Lenti* held that it is no defense to the crime of hazing fraternity pledges that they may have consented to undergo these acts. The harm is said to be to society as a whole and not to the individual.[35] Certain crimes such as rape have as an element the lack of consent of the victim. As to these crimes, consent by the victim does away with one of the necessary elements of the offense and would be a bar to prosecution.

Entrapment

Entrapment occurs when a government agent induces a person to commit a crime. The defense of **entrapment** is based on the concept that the government should not entice innocent people into committing criminal acts. Encouraging people to commit crime breeds public resentment of the police and undermines the effectiveness of our law enforcement system. Entrapment does not justify criminal behavior; it merely excuses the behavior. Unlike most other defenses, this defense's primary objective is not to protect innocent persons but to discourage certain police misconduct.

Entrapment is a defense that is available only for the less serious offenses. It is never considered an excuse for criminal homicide, rape, or aggravated assault or battery. It is mainly used in cases involving consensual crimes such as buying narcotics, prostitution, illegal sales of alcohol, and gambling.

The subjective test asks whether the government agent created or manufactured the intent to commit a crime in the mind of an innocent person. Accordingly, entrapment depends on how the specific defendant was involved and whether the defendant was predisposed to commit the crime. This test, used by the federal government and most states, assumes that it is unfair to make criminals out of people whom the government induced to commit crimes. Note that it limits the defense to those defendants who were not predisposed to commit an offense.

The other major test used in the area is the objective test. It asks whether the government did more than provide the defendant with an opportunity to commit a crime. This test focuses on the government's activity, not the defendant's. Another way of stating the objective test is that it finds entrapment whenever law enforcement activity causes a reasonable person to commit a crime although he was not predisposed to do so.

Entrapment has not occurred where police activity (1) has as its end the interruption of a specific ongoing criminal activity, and (2) utilizes means reasonably tailored to apprehend those involved in the ongoing criminal activity.

Practicum 5.7

Decoy Operations and Entrapment

The Tampa Police Department set up a decoy operation in a high-crime area. An officer posed as a drunken bum drinking wine. The officer leaned against a building near an alleyway with money plainly sticking out of his pants pocket. The defendant, with a woman friend, passed the officer. About fifteen minutes later, the defendant returned to the alley and took the money from the officer's pants. The defendant did not attempt to injure the officer in any manner. At trial, it appeared that the police were not seeking any particular individual, nor were they aware of any prior criminal acts by the defendant.

ISSUE: Do the actions of the police in setting up a decoy constitute entrapment in this case?

The court, using the objective standard, held that the officer's conduct constituted entrapment. The court stated that entrapment occurs where the "decoy simply provided the opportunity to commit a crime to anyone who succumbed to the lure of the bait." The court also stated that, even if the police were seeking to catch persons who had been rolling drunks in the area, the criminal scenario here, with money clipped to the pocket of the officer, carried with it the "substantial risk that such an offense will be committed by persons other than those who are ready to commit it." The court stated that the police must fight crime, not engage in the manufacture of new crimes.[36]

One of defense counsel's major problems with the entrapment defense is that the accused must admit that she committed the crime before she can claim that the police induced the commission of the offense. For example, you cannot deny buying cocaine and then claim that the police caused you to buy it. A few states and the federal government will allow the defendant to deny guilt and then plead entrapment. From a practical point of view, it is difficult to persuade the judge or the jury that the police enticed the defendant to commit the crime after the defendant has denied committing the offense.

To constitute entrapment, the individual who is doing the encouraging must be a government agent. Entrapment does not occur when a private individual induces another to commit an offense. Paid informers and other civilians who are working with the police are considered government agents, the same as police officers.

PROCEDURAL DEFENSES

Procedural defenses are traditionally examined in courses that focus on criminal procedure and/or constitutional law. However, some of the more common procedural defenses are included in this text because many legal scholars and the MPC discuss them under the broad heading of criminal law defenses rather than criminal procedure. This is not a text on constitutional law, so only the highlights and major aspects of these defenses are examined.

Practicum 5.8

How Many Requests Are Too Many?

An informant working for the police contacted the defendant and asked to buy LSD from him. The defendant said no. Over the next few weeks, the informant called the defendant as many as fifteen times a day and would leave messages on his answering machine if no one answered. The defendant finally agreed to sell LSD to the informant and was arrested for selling illegal drugs. The defendant was convicted of selling a controlled substance.

ISSUE: Do the actions of the informant constitute entrapment in this case?

Under the objective test for entrapment, once the defendant can show he has been the target of persuasive police conduct, regardless of whether he was in fact persuaded to commit the offense, focus is directed to police conduct itself, and the question becomes whether persuasion by the law enforcement agent was such as to cause an ordinarily law-abiding person of average resistance to commit the offense, not whether it was such as to cause the defendant himself, given his proclivities, to commit it. Conviction of the defendant was upheld by the Texas Court of Criminal Appeals.[37]

How do you justify the results in Practicums 5.7 and 5.8? What is different in the fact patterns? Do you agree with the court's decision in the LSD case? Why? Why not?

Double Jeopardy

The Fifth Amendment states: "No person . . . shall . . . be subject for the same offense to be twice put in jeopardy of life or limb . . . ." This amendment protects individuals from repeated governmental efforts to convict them of the same crime. The right attaches as soon as the defendant is put to trial. This normally occurs with the impaneling and swearing of the jury.

The prohibition against double jeopardy prevents the government from prosecuting the defendant for the same crime after a conviction or an acquittal. It also prohibits multiple punishments for the same offense. However, it does not prevent the government from retrying the case if the jury cannot agree on the guilt or innocence of the defendant. This is called a *hung jury*, and the case may be set for a new trial.

Statute of Limitations

The **statute of limitations** requires that criminal prosecutions commence within a certain period of time after the crime occurred. It is a jurisdictional requirement. Accordingly, failure to commence prosecution within the required period bars the state or federal government from prosecuting the accused. The statute is designed to ensure that an individual is not accountable indefinitely for the commission of an offense. For example, in some states most felonies have a four-year statute of limitations, which means that the state must initiate criminal proceedings against the defendant within four years from the date the offense was discovered or should have been discovered. In other states, the time limit starts on the date of the commission of the crime. Serious offenses such as murder, rape, and kidnapping generally do not have a statute of limitations. The statute is tolled (does not run) while the accused is outside the jurisdiction of the state (or federal government, in the case of federal crimes). For example, suppose the crime of forgery has a four-year statute of limitations. The defendant commits forgery and then leaves the state for two years. In determining whether the statute of limitations has run (expired), the two years that the defendant was beyond the jurisdiction of the court would be excluded in computing the period.

The statute of limitations is an affirmative defense and must be raised by the accused. Normally, this is accomplished at pretrial hearings. Once it has been raised by the defendant, the prosecution must then establish that the statute has not run. The statute of limitations differs from a speedy trial problem. The statute of limitations starts running when the crime is discovered or should have been discovered and stops when prosecution is initiated, which in most cases is the filing of the formal complaint. Time is computed by excluding the first day (date crime was committed or should have been discovered) and including the last day (when the prosecution begins). The requirements of speedy trial start when the accused is charged or arrested.

Focus 5.5

Two Trials: Different Results—Double Jeopardy?

Rodney King

Most Americans are familiar with the videotaped beating of Rodney King. In 1992, the officers were charged and tried in a California state superior court. Koon and two other Los Angles police officers were acquitted on all charges filed by the L.A. District Attorney's Office. Powell was acquitted on all but one count. The officers were subsequently charged with a federal criminal statute that makes it a federal crime to violate another person's federal civil rights. The basis for the federal criminal charge was the exact acts that the officers had been charged with and acquitted in state court. In that case, they were convicted and sentenced to federal prison.

ISSUE: Was it double jeopardy to try the officers a second time?

What are the benefits of being able to charge a person twice—once in state court and once in federal court? Are there any potential problems with this approach?

O. J. Simpson

What about the O. J. Simpson trials? He was tried and acquitted for the murder of his wife and her friend. The victim's family filed a civil lawsuit against O. J. Simpson, and he was found liable for their deaths.

ISSUE: Was it double jeopardy to file the civil lawsuit?

Why could the victim's family file the civil action? Does double jeopardy apply in these types of cases?

Are there any similarities between the Rodney King cases and the O. J. Simpson cases?

HOW WOULD YOU RULE?

Daniel and Cynthia had an intimate relationship while students at the University of Iowa in 2005. They continued dating that spring, spent the summer in their respective hometowns, and then resumed their relationship in the fall of 2005, but with more "ups and downs." In late January 2006, Cynthia decided to end the relationship. Daniel's sadness over the breakup turned to anger toward Cynthia. He would contact her by e-mail, telephone, and text message hundreds of times a day. She told him repeatedly that she did not want to have contact with him, to no avail.

On September 14, 2006, Cynthia was leaving a class and encountered Daniel, who brought out two sandwiches and insisted that they eat dinner together. After first telling him "no," Cynthia finally gave in "under the condition that he leave me alone for good after we had dinner." However, after they ate together on the riverbank, Cynthia tried to leave, but Jason grabbed her arm and started dragging her away. Cynthia was able to place a cell phone call to her mother, who in turn contacted the Iowa City police.

The police arrested Daniel and charged him with assault. On November 4, 2006, the court issued a protective order in conjunction with the criminal charge. Daniel contacted Cynthia the very day he was released from jail.

The district court held a competency hearing on November 27, 2007, at which a doctor opined that Daniel was competent to stand trial. The doctor diagnosed Daniel as suffering from Asperger's syndrome. The doctor stated that the syndrome does not include delusions or hallucinations. Although Asperger's syndrome affects a person's ability to interact socially, the doctor explained that it does not affect cognitive understanding. He noted that many people with Asperger's hold jobs.

As trial judge in this case, would you hold that Daniel had a defense to his criminal acts?

SEE: *STATE V. JASON, 2009 IOWA APP. LEXIS 1634 (IOWA CT. APP. DEC. 17, 2009)*

Summary

Except for strict liability crimes, all crimes contain an actus reus and a mens rea. The term defense is used to indicate those matters that, if successfully presented by the defense, will negate the existence of either the actus reus or the mens rea. Even if the government can prove the essential elements of the offense, the defense may raise one or more defenses to the criminal prosecution that could result in acquittal. Defenses to criminal conduct can normally be grouped in three categories: criminal responsibility, justification and excuse, and procedural defenses.

Defenses that go to the criminal responsibility of the accused are infancy, insanity, diminished responsibility, intoxication, and the various syndromes. The general rule is that children under the age of seven years are not held criminally responsible for their conduct. Between seven and fourteen, there is generally a presumption that the child lacks the required mental capacity, but the state may introduce evidence to show that the child is mature enough to be held criminally accountable for the conduct in question.

Insanity is a controversial defense. It is the subject of numerous articles and news stories each year. Insanity at the time the act was committed negates the required mental state of the actor; therefore, the individual has not committed the crime. Insanity at trial is referred to as incompetency to stand trial. The accused must have a sufficient mental state in order to assist his or her attorney in the defense of the case. If not, the trial must be delayed.

The most widely used test to determine the sanity of the accused is the M'Naghten test, also referred to as the "right-and-wrong" test. The concept of diminished responsibility is similar to the insanity defense, except that it is a partial defense. It tends to diminish the responsibility of the defendant, for example, to reduce first-degree murder to a lesser offense. It is often used in mercy killings and disappointed lover cases.

The primary defense that justifies the use of force is self-defense. Others include the right of a police officer to use force to make an arrest and the right to protect others from illegal harm. Normally, a person is justified in using deadly force only to protect himself or others from what he reasonably believes is imminent, unlawful deadly force. Self-defense contains the components of "proportionality" and "necessity." It is generally stated that at common law a person had a right to resist an unlawful arrest. Since an arrest may be unlawful for a number of reasons, however, the common law right applied only to those that occurred in provocative circumstances. The statutes in most states have abolished this common law right to resist an unlawful arrest.

Generally, deadly force is never permitted to protect property. At common law, however, deadly force was allowed to protect one's home. The use of nondeadly force to protect property is limited only to property in a person's possession. A person is not permitted to use any force to reclaim property that is not in her possession.

Procedural defenses such as double jeopardy and the statute of limitations require that the government act properly when bringing charges against a person suspected of committing a crime. While technical in nature, these types of defenses ensure that the government will not use its power in a prejudicial manner.

Defenses are a controversial subject within criminal law. On one hand, no one should be unfairly charged with a crime if he acted properly. However, criminals should not walk free simply because the government made a technical mistake. This is a fine line that constantly shifts as society changes its values, and those values are reflected in changing criminal codes.

Additional Assignments

1. Read the selected cases and associated material for Chapter 5 posted at www.mycrimekit.com.
2. Complete the online study guide material for Chapter 5 posted at www.mycrimekit.com.
3. Discussion and thought questions:
   a. Which is the most comprehensive test for insanity? Why?
   b. Why is insanity a legal issue and not a medical issue?
   c. Suppose a person suffering from posttraumatic stress syndrome experiences a flashback that causes him to believe that he is back in Vietnam in combat. Should the individual be excused from criminal liability if he kills ten children at a schoolyard during the flashback?
   d. Is the enactment of a "castle doctrine" similar to Florida's a wise decision? Justify your opinion.
   e. Should we have the defense of entrapment? Why?

Practicum

Give factual examples in which defendants could use the defenses listed below:
1. consent
2. entrapment
3. necessity
4. insanity

Notes

1. Application of Gault, 387 U.S. 1 (1967).
2. *State v. Dillon,* 93 Idaho 698, 471 P. 2d 553 (1970).
3. "Insanity Plea Seldom Used," *Milwaukee Journal,* June 20, 1990, p. A-1.
4. *M'Naghten's* Case, 8 Eng. Rep. 718 (1843).
5. 81 Ala. 577, 2 So. 854 (1887). It should be noted that the irresistible impulse test actually predated the *M'Naghten rule.* For an excellent historical discussion of the evolution of these early insanity rules, see John Keedy, "Irresistible Impulse as a Defense in Criminal Law," 100 U. *Pa. L. Rev.* 956, 961 (1952).
6. *Durham v. United States*, 214 F. 2d 862 (D.C. Cir. 1954).
7. 18 U.S.C. § 401 (1984).
8. MPC § 2.08(4).
9. *People v. Scott*, 146 Cal. App. 3d 823 (1983), involved a defendant who became involuntarily intoxicated when he drank punch laced with PCP and subsequently committed a crime.
10. MPC § 2.08(5)(b).
11. J. H. Morton, et al., "A Clinical Study of Premenstrual Tension," 65 *Amer. J. of Obstetrics and Gynecology* 1182 (1953).
12. Susan Lark, *Premenstrual Syndrome* Self-Help Book (Los Angeles: Forman, 1984), 19.
13. Katherine Dalton, "Menstruation and Crime," *British Medical Journal*, vol. 2 (1961): 1752–1753.
14. John R. Ford, "In Defense of the Defenders: The Vietnam Vet Syndrome," 19 *Crim. L. Bull.* 434 (1983).
15. See *Diagnostic and Statistical Manual of Mental Disorders,* 4th ed. (DSM-IV) (Washington, DC: American Psychological Association, 1994), section 309.81, pp. 424–428, for a complete discussion of this disorder.
16. *Regina v. Smith*, No. 1/A/82, [C. A. Crim. Div. Apr. 27, 1982]. "Premenstrual Syndrome: A Criminal Defense," 59 *Notre Dame L. Rev.* 263 (1983).
17. Gayla Margolin et al., "Wife Battering," in *Handbook of Family Violence*, Vincent B. Van Hasselt et al., eds. (New York: Plenum, 1988), 93.

18. Lenore E. A. Walker, *The Battered Women* (New York: HarperCollins, 1979).

19. Id.

20. See *People v. Aris*, 215 Cal. App. 1178 (1989).

21. Contrary to popular belief, not all battered spouses kill their abusive partners when they are asleep. See Holly Maguigan, "Battered Women and Self-Defense: Myths and Misconceptions in Current Reform Proposals," 14 U. Pa. L. Rev. 379 (1992), in which 223 cases of battered women who killed their partners were analyzed. Of the 223 incidents, 75 percent involved confrontation, 20 percent were nonconfrontational cases, 8 percent were "sleeping" cases, 8 percent involved the defendant as the initial aggressor during a lull in the violence, and the remaining 5 percent were unknown because the court opinions did not discuss the incident facts. (Percentages total over 100 due to incidents involving more than one category.)

22. Wayne R. LaFave and Austin W. Scott, Jr., *Criminal Law*, 2nd ed. (St. Paul, MN: West, 1986), 454, and Rollin M. Perkins and Ronald N. Boyce, *Criminal Law*, 3rd ed. (Mineola, NY: Foundation Press, 1988), 1138, for an analysis of the no-retreat doctrine in a person's castle.

23. Harvey Wallace, "The Battered Women Syndrome: Self-Defence and Duress as Mandatory Defences?" *Police* J. (April–June 1994), p. 133.

24. MPC § 3.06(5) and (i), 12 Cal. 3d 470 (1974), the leading case in this area, holding that use of mechanical devices is not permitted even in the absence of statutory language permitting or prohibiting their use.

25. Hyman Gross, *A Theory of Criminal Justice* (New York: Oxford University Press, 1978), 275–276.

26. American Law Institute, *Model Penal Code and Commentaries,* Part I (Philadelphia: American Law Institute, 1978) 368–380.

27. 612 A. 2d 725 (1992).

28. *People v. Romero,* 15 Cal. App. 4th 1519 (1992).

29. Id. at 1560.

30. LaFave and Scott, supra note 22, at 442–443.

31. *Regina v. Dudley and Stevens,* Queen's Bench (1884).

32. 471 U.S. 1 (1985).

33. MPC § 3.04(2)(a)(i).

34. MPC § 2.04(1)(a).

35. 260 N.Y.S. 2d 284 (1965).

36. *Cruz v. State,* 465 So. 2d 516 (Fla. 1985).

37. *England v. State of Texas,* 887 S.W. 2d 902; 1994 Tex. Crim. App. Lexis 91 (1994).

Homicide

Chapter Outline

What you should know about homicide. After reading this chapter, you should know

- The elements of each of the types of homicide.
- The reasons for the felony-murder rule.
- The differences between each of the types of homicide.

- The justification for the establishment of the negligent homicide classification.
- The difference between suicide and euthanasia.

Key Terms

After reading this chapter, you should understand the following key terms:

criminal homicide: Killing that involves unlawful conduct and evil intent on the part of the killer.

euthanasia: Another name for mercy killing.

excusable homicide: Killing another by mistake or in self-defense. A killing conducted in a manner that criminal law does not prohibit.

felony-murder rule: Liability for murder when a death results during, and as a result of, any dangerous felony committed by the defendant.

homicide: The killing of a human being by another human being.

involuntary manslaughter: The unintentional killing of another human being caused during the commission of an unlawful act not amounting to a felony or as the result of criminal negligence.

justifiable homicide: Killing under circumstances sanctioned by the sovereign.

manslaughter: The unlawful killing of a human being, carried out without malice. Differs from murder in that malice and premeditation are lacking.

mass murderer: One who kills several victims at the same time in one location.

murder: The purposeful, knowing, or reckless unlawful killing of another human being.

negligent manslaughter: The unintentional killing of another human being caused by the negligence of the defendant.

serial murderer: One who kills several persons over a period of time, which can range from weeks to years.

suicide: The taking of one's own life.

voluntary manslaughter: The intentional and unlawful killing of another person in response to adequate provocation.

The word homicide brings to mind such infamous killers as Charles Whitman (University of Texas tower murderer), Charles Manson, and other cold-blooded murderers including Coral Eugene Watts, a serial killer who murdered more than a dozen women. However, homicide encompasses much more than premeditated murder. It is a generic term meaning the killing of one human being by another.[1] While the killing of another human being has been recognized for centuries as prohibited conduct, the exact nature of the crime was not clearly defined during early historical times.

The English common law established three forms of homicide: justifiable homicide, excusable homicide, and criminal homicide. All three of these were the killing of another human being. The distinction between them involved the circumstances surrounding the killing.

Justifiable homicide is killing under circumstances sanctioned by the sovereign. Killing during war or acting as an executioner for the state are examples of justifiable homicide. In this form of homicide, the person doing the killing does not harbor any evil intent and acts under "color of law."

Excusable homicide occurs when one kills another by mistake or in self-defense. When one kills another as a result of an unprovoked attack, the law would deem this to be an act of self-defense and thus the killing is "excused." If a person were driving his car through a neighborhood at ten miles per hour and struck and killed a child who darted out from behind a bush, the law may hold that the driver was not at fault, and therefore, the killing was excusable homicide.

Criminal homicide is the most serious type of homicide. This type of killing involves unlawful conduct and evil intent on the part of the killer. Criminal homicide is not sanctioned by the state and is considered one of the most serious crimes in our society.

Homicide is a common law crime created by English judges rather than the English legislature.[2] The early common law decisions have, in some instances, been translated into statutes in many of our states. These statutes have broken down the crime of homicide into graded levels—murder, voluntary and involuntary manslaughter, and negligent manslaughter. The most serious type of homicide is murder. Those who have watched television believe they understand what is involved in murder. However, the laws surrounding murder can be confusing and complex. The crime of murder involves more than a sniper shooting, an axe slaying, or a revenge killing—it requires a specific set of circumstances to establish the elements of murder.

MURDER

Murder is a crime in all major legal systems. It is considered as the most serious of the homicide classifications. According to the Federal Bureau of Investigation (FBI), one murder is committed, on average, every thirty-one minutes.[3] When we think of homicide, we automatically recall the April 2007 mass shooting at Virginia Tech University, when Cho Seung-Hui, a mentally deranged student, killed thirty-two individuals in the largest mass shooting in U.S. history. Before that shooting, the deadliest mass shooting in the United States occurred in 1991, when George Hennard drove a pickup truck into a Killeen, Texas, cafeteria and fatally shot twenty-three people before shooting and killing himself. Early history tells of Cain killing his brother, Abel, what many claim was the first murder. John Wilkes Booth earned his place in history by assassinating President Abraham Lincoln. The name Charles Whitman may not sound familiar until the description "Texas Tower Killer" is used. Then we remember the story of Whitman, a former Eagle Scout who, after murdering his mother and wife, climbed to top of a tower at the University of Texas and murdered sixteen people and wounded thirty more before he died.

Murder

Defined

Murder is the purposeful, knowing, or reckless unlawful killing of another human being.

Elements

The crime of murder has two distinct elements:

1. The defendant must have acted with the necessary—express or implied—specific intent to kill.

2. The defendant's conduct must have caused the death of another human being.

While there have been and will continue to be sensational murderers such as the Manson Family Cult that killed pregnant actress Sharon Tate and several others, most homicides are not the stuff of movies or television. They range from killings stemming from arguments with family or acquaintances to deaths that occur as a result of simply not following the rules of the road when driving a car. Since early times, there has been controversy over the definition, classification, and types of murder. The following discussion of the elements of murder attempts to clarify this controversy. The classification of murder will be addressed in subsequent sections, and the types or degrees of murder will be examined later in this chapter.

The Elements of Murder

The crime of murder can be divided into two basic elements:

THE DEFENDANT MUST ACT WITH THE NECESSARY SPECIFIC INTENT TO KILL OR ENGAGE IN CONDUCT SO OUTRAGEOUS THAT THE SPECIFIC INTENT TO KILL WILL BE INFERRED Over the years, courts and scholars have debated the proper name to use when describing the intent, or mens rea, necessary for murder.[4] Malice aforethought was at one time the favored term to describe the defendant's intent in a murder case. Many states have moved away from using malice aforethought and have substituted other terms to define the necessary specific intent. For example, Pennsylvania uses the terms poison, lying in wait, willful, deliberate, or premeditated to establish the necessary specific intent.[5] New York uses phrases such as "with the intent to cause the death of another" and "a depraved indifference to human life," and "recklessly engages" in conduct causing a great risk of death.

Contrary to how they are portrayed on popular television shows, murderers seldom announce their state of mind before or during the commission of the crime. Courts are, therefore, required to review the facts of the case to determine if the defendant exhibited, via her actions, the necessary intent for murder. By whatever term or name it is called, the mens rea necessary for murder is a specific intent to kill or conduct so outrageous that the specific intent to kill will be inferred.

Practicums 6.1 to 6.4 set forth a series of fact patterns that the courts have addressed when discussing the intent requirement of the crime of murder.

Practicum 6.1

Russian Roulette

The defendant was playing a game of Russian roulette. He pointed a revolver loaded with a single cartridge at the victim. The weapon fired on the third try, and the victim died.

ISSUE: Did the defendant have the necessary intent for the crime of murder?

The court upheld the defendant's conviction for murder, stating that his action evidenced the necessary intent for murder despite evidence that the defendant had not desired to kill his friend.[6]

THE DEFENDANT'S CONDUCT MUST HAVE CAUSED THE DEATH OF ANOTHER HUMAN BEING This element requires a death as a result of the defendant's acts or failure to act. Any behavior by the defendant will suffice. This element also includes the term another human being. This term presumes a living person. As we will examine under Special Problems with Homicide, this issue can run the gamut from "Is the person still alive?" (euthanasia) to "Has the person gained life?" (killing of a fetus). Similarly, the definition of murder precludes suicide, since that is the taking of one's own life.

Practicum 6.2

Criminal Negligence as a Substitute for Criminal Intent

The defendant had loaded three rounds of live ammunition into a revolver and left it unattended in the kitchen of his friend's house. His friend, unaware that the cylinder in this weapon rotates to the left, before firing turned the cylinder to the adjacent empty chamber to make the weapon safer. Defendant returned and picked up the weapon and pointed at a friend without inspecting it and pulled the trigger. It did not fire. Still expecting the next chamber to be empty, he pulled the trigger again and it fired a live round, hitting his friend in the head and killing him instantly.

ISSUE: Does the defendant's criminal negligence substitute for the lack of his criminal intent?

The court said the criminal negligence cannot substitute for criminal intent. But they did find the evidence sufficient to authorize a rational trier of fact to find beyond a reasonable doubt that the defendant was guilty of felony-murder based on the underlying felony of aggravated assault and possession of a firearm during the commission of a felony.[7]

Practicum 6.3

Reckless Disregard for Life?

Defendant claimed she was attempting to shoot over the victim's head in order to scare him. The bullet struck the victim and he died.

ISSUE: Was the defendant's conduct of such a nature as to allow a court to presume she intended to kill the victim?

The court found the defendant guilty of murder, stating that, even if her assertion was true, the conduct of the defendant showed such a reckless disregard for life as to be the equivalent of a specific intent to kill.[8]

Practicum 6.4

Intent to Kill?

The defendant fired several shots into a house that he knew was occupied by several persons. His actions caused the death of the victim.

> **ISSUE:** Did the defendant's conduct evidence an intent to kill?

The court upheld the defendant's murder conviction, stating that his conduct was imminently dangerous and evinced a wicked and depraved heart.[9]

Model Penal Code (MPC 210.2)

The Model Penal Code (MPC) attempted to solve problems inherent in the various statutory definitions of murder. The code separates homicide into three basic categories: murder, manslaughter, and negligent manslaughter. The MPC traces the history of murder from its common law background up to the adoption of the code. It points out that the common law definition of murder included the term *malice aforethought*.[10] The drafters of the code then reviewed the legislative background involving the use of malice aforethought in the United States and concluded that use of the term should be abolished because it was too imprecise.[11]

The MPC states that the crime of murder occurs when

1. the defendant causes the death of another human being, and
2. a. it is committed purposely or knowingly, or
    b. it is committed recklessly under circumstances manifesting extreme indifference to the value of human life. Such recklessness is presumed if the defendant is an actor or an accomplice in the attempt or commission or flight after commission of the crimes of robbery, rape, deviate sexual intercourse by force or fear, arson, burglary, kidnapping, or felonious escape.

The code establishes that murder may be committed in either of two ways: (1) purposeful or knowing homicide or (2) reckless homicide manifesting extreme indifference.

PURPOSEFUL OR KNOWING HOMICIDE Purposefully and knowingly refer to the defendant's subjective state of mind. Liability for homicide under this section requires that the defendant engage in conduct with the conscious goal of causing the death of the victim or at least that the defendant was aware that death would result from his actions.[12]

RECKLESS HOMICIDE MANIFESTING EXTREME INDIFFERENCE Recklessness, under the code, assumes that the defendant is aware that her actions are creating a substantial risk of death. This risk must be too great to be deemed justified for any valid purpose that the defendant's actions serve.

Under the MPC, the question is whether the defendant's conscious disregard of the risk, considering the circumstances of the case, so far departs from acceptable behavior that it constitutes a "gross deviation from the standard of conduct that a law-abiding person would observe in the actor's situation."[13]

While the MPC attempted to solve the problem of conflicting statutory definitions of murder, the drafters of the code were not successful in presenting a definition that the U.S. Congress would accept. The federal government uses a definition of murder that is different from that in the MPC.[14] In *United States v. Fleming*, a federal court discussed malice aforethought. The defendant was charged with murder that arose from an automobile collision. He was driving his car at seventy to one hundred miles an hour on a parkway where speed limits from thirty to a maximum of forty-five miles an hour were clearly posted. Additionally, he was found to have a blood alcohol level of .315. The defendant crossed over into the oncoming traffic lane, struck the victim's car, which was traveling in the opposite direction, and killed her. The federal court held:

> Malice Aforethought, as provided in 18 U.S.C. § 1111(a), is the distinguishing characteristic which, when present, makes a homicide murder rather than manslaughter.
>
> . . .
>
> . . . , in addition to being intoxicated while driving, defendant drove in a manner that could be taken to indicate depraved disregard of human life, particularly in light of the fact that because he was drunk his reckless behavior was all the more dangerous.[15]

Sidebar on Murder: Why Did the Defendant Do It?

While motive is not an element of any form of homicide, prosecutors and jurors will want to know why the defendant killed the victim. Thus motive, while not necessary to proving the crime of murder, helps convince jurors of the reasons for the defendant's acts. Who can definitively explain why "Son of Sam" or Lizzie Borden committed such heinous crimes? The reasons for the crime of murder are as varied as the myriad emotions that drive a person to act. What we do know about those "types" who commit murder is based upon statistics gathered by law enforcement agencies when they investigate and arrest persons for murder. In 1997, criminal activity was the cause of murder 19 percent of the time. Arguments were the motivation for murder 28 percent of the time, and arguments about money added another 1 percent. Juvenile gang-related killings accounted for 5 percent of all homicides, while fights due to the influence of alcohol and arguments over money each involved 1 percent of murders. Other nonspecified activity accounted for 9 percent of homicides. While the FBI may keep extremely accurate statistics and the police may conduct thorough investigations of all murder cases, in 31 percent of all murders in 1997 no motive could be established. The figures do not add up to 100 percent, since there were other miscellaneous homicides, including babysitters killing the children they were watching, sniper shootings, gangland killings, and institutional homicides, that account for the remaining murders.[16]

This is a classic example of a factual pattern whereby the courts will imply malice when circumstances show an "abandoned and malignant heart."

The majority of states have failed to adopt the MPC's definition of murder and continue to use terms such as willful, deliberate, or premeditated killing of another. Other states continue to use the term malice aforethought to encompass the terms *intentionally*, *knowingly*, or *recklessly*.

Simply knowing the definition of murder is only the first step in understanding this crime. When someone kills another in a premeditated or reckless way, the courts and society must examine the killing to determine how serious or heinous the act was. This determination assists in defining the degree of murder.

Degrees of Murder

In early English common law, there were no degrees of murder. However, the United States developed the "first degree" and "second degree" concept of murder in Pennsylvania as early as 1794. This law contained a preamble that explained the rationale behind establishing different degrees of murder: "And whereas the several offenses, which are included under the general denomination of murder, differ so greatly from each other in the degree of their atrociousness, that it is unjust to involve them in the same punishment."[17]

The two forms or degrees of murder are based upon the seriousness of the type of homicide. First-degree murder is normally classified as a killing that is premeditated. This type of killing occurs when the defendant had time to reflect on the act and to form the intent to kill.[18] Examples of premeditated murders include those in which the defendant carries out the killing by using explosives, lying in wait to ambush the victim, using poison, or killing by torture. Most states have very simple second-degree murder statutes that hold all other murders to be of the second degree. The establishment of degrees of murder is society's attempt to divide this type of homicide into two classifications based on the seriousness of this crime. All murders are serious, but some are more terrifying than others.

Serial Murder

While any murder is the killing of a human being and is certainly frightening to think about, one type of murderer in particular sends chills down the spine of any normal person. The serial killer is the night stalker of murderers. While there is some debate over the definition of a **serial murderer**, most authorities agree that a serial murderer is one who kills several persons over a period that can range from weeks to years.[19]

One of the best-known serial murderers was Jack the Ripper, who killed several women over a period in London. He was never caught, and these crimes were never solved, although there have been a number of theories and articles written about his acts. Other well-known serial murderers are the Green River Killer, who is believed to have killed more than fifty female hitchhikers, transients, and prostitutes near the Seattle area; the "Witch" Sarah Aldrete, who sacrificed victims in order to provide an aura of protection for members of a Mexican drug-smuggling ring; Dorothea Puente, who poisoned renters at her boardinghouse and then cashed their Social Security checks; and the infamous Hillside Strangler in Los Angeles.

In an effort to understand crime and criminals, researchers create typologies. These are classifications based upon certain characteristics. By studying these characteristics, scholars, researchers, law enforcement officials, and others hope to understand why particular individuals commit certain types of crimes. There have been several noteworthy typologies of serial murders. Ronald M. Holmes and John DeBurger identified four types of serial killers:

Visionary serial killers murder in response to commands or directions from a voice or vision. Many are suffering from some form of psychosis.

Mission-oriented serial killers believe their mission or goal in life is to rid society of certain types of people, such as prostitutes.

Hedonistic serial killers are perhaps the most chilling of the lot, in that they seek thrills during the murders. Many of these killers become sexually involved with their victims either prior to or after killing them. They may also engage in sexual mutilation of their victims.

Power-control-oriented serial killers seek power over their victims. They report getting enjoyment from watching their victims plead, beg, and cower before them.[20]

Sidebar on Murder: Do You Know a Killer When You See One?

Wouldn't life be simpler and much safer if all murderers resembled large, ugly, and deformed Neanderthals? Unfortunately, this is not the case, even though our fears may conjure up such images. In reality, a murderer may be any good-looking, all-American male standing in a college campus parking lot with a cast on his arm asking young women if they could help him put his bike up on his car's bike rack. This is how Ted Bundy, convicted of three murders and implicated in as many as thirty more, chose some of his victims.

While there are no specific physical types that can be classified as murderers, recent statistics drawn from arrest records may shed some light on the average characteristics of those who kill.

Age	20–24 years
Sex	64% male
	8% female
	28% unknown
Race	32% white
	37% black
	2% other
	29% unknown

Source: U.S. Department of Justice, *Uniform Crime Report 2007* (Washington, DC: Government Printing Office, 2008).

Eric W. Hickey has conducted several studies on serial killers and is considered one of the nationally recognized experts in this area. In an early work, he classified serial killers into three distinct groups based upon mobility:

Traveling serial killers often travel to different locations seeking victims to kill.

Local serial killers stay in one area and commit their crimes in that location.

Serial killers who never leave their home or place of employment lure their victims into their residence or place of employment and kill them within these areas.[21]

As we learn more about serial murderers, there are certain to be more typologies of this most dangerous of all killers. There is both a repulsion and attraction to studying this type of murderer, whose crimes boggle the imagination. Hickey has pointed out that between 1800 and 1995, sixty-two female and 337 male serial killers were responsible for a minimum of 2,526 and a maximum of 3,860 deaths.[22]

Serial murderers, those who kill one victim at a time, should be distinguished from **mass murderers**, who kill several victims at the same time in one location. Mass murderers have been with us since our nation was formed, and until the discovery and in-depth study of serial killers, mass murderers were considered the most dangerous killers in our society. In 1989, a deranged welder by the name of Patrick Edward Purdy entered a Stockton, California, schoolyard armed with an AK-47 assault rifle and began a killing spree that ended with five dead children and thirty wounded victims. The Stockton schoolyard massacre is a chilling example of mass murder.

To summarize this discussion, murder is the killing of another human being with the necessary specific intent. States have used terms such as malice aforethought, a depraved heart, or the willful, deliberate, or intentional intent to kill to describe the intent necessary for murder. Additionally, this intent must be coupled with an act, or failure to act when required to do so, that causes the death of another human being. Finally, legislatures have divided murder into two classes or degrees: first and second degree. The next section will examine another aspect of the crime of murder—those murders that are committed during the commission of a felony.

FELONY-MURDER

The felony-murder rule is a statutory formulation that holds a person liable for murder if a death results during his commission of certain felonies. The rationale behind the rule is that when a person commits a felony that is inherently dangerous, and someone dies during that crime, the intent to kill will be inferred. Thus the defendant may be charged with the crime of murder even though there are no facts supporting the specific intent requirement that is normally required to convict a person of murder. This rule has generated controversy since its inception. Proponents of the **felony-murder rule** argue that it is a deterrent. If criminals may be charged with murder during the commission of certain dangerous felonies, they may not be as eager to commit these crimes. Others believe that this rule is a form of "strict liability" and should not be applied to the crime of murder. Some scholars argue that it leads to unjust results because the defendant may not have intended to kill anyone.

The Elements of Felony-Murder

The crime of felony-murder is divided into two elements:

THE DEFENDANT MUST COMMIT OR ATTEMPT TO COMMIT A DANGEROUS FELONY

This element includes the requirement that the defendant intend to commit the underlying dangerous felony. Once this unstated but necessary aspect is satisfied, the next issue to be examined is the type or character of the felony.

Felony-Murder

Defined

The felony-murder rule applies when a death results during, and as a result of, any dangerous felony committed by the defendant.

Elements

The felony-murder rule or doctrine has two elements:

1. The defendant must have committed or attempted to commit a dangerous felony.
2. Death must have resulted during the commission of a felony.

The majority of states require the felony to be dangerous to life. While no single list of dangerous felonies applies in all states, most states consider the following felonies to be sufficiently dangerous to human life to trigger application of the felony-murder rule: arson, rape, robbery, burglary of an inhabited dwelling, and kidnapping.

Some jurisdictions require the felony to be mala in se instead of mala prohibita. All jurisdictions have some sort of limiting criterion on application of the rule to any and all felonies. The court system in many jurisdictions places judicial limitations on application of the doctrine. Some courts require that the felony be independent of the murder. Under this limitation, an assault with a deadly weapon could not support a conviction of murder using the felony-murder rule.[23] Other courts have inquired into the facts surrounding each case to determine if the commission of the felony involved a foreseeable risk to life.[24]

Practicum 6.5 sets forth a case that examines a factual pattern involving the felony-murder rule and the distinction between the underlying crime and a charge of murder based upon the felony-murder rule.

DEATH MUST HAVE RESULTED DURING THE ATTEMPT OR COMMISSION OF THE DANGEROUS FELONY The fact that someone died is relatively easy to prove. The complex issue in this element deals with the question of who did the killing. Practicums 6.5 through 6.9 set forth cases in which the courts have discussed who may be charged with murder by using the felony-murder rule when someone dies during the commission of a felony.

These five practicums point out that certain types of felonies are considered inherently dangerous, and if a death results during the commission of these felonies, the defendant will be held liable under the felony-murder rule. The defendant will be charged with murder even if the intended victim reacts and kills one of the attackers. Such a reaction by victims is considered probable or possible; therefore, any death occurring during these felonies will be considered foreseeable.

Practicum 6.5

The defendant operated her car recklessly, and as a result she killed the victim. The killing in this situation was involuntary manslaughter, a felony.

ISSUE: Does the felony-murder rule apply to the crime of manslaughter?

The court held that the same act cannot be the basis of a charge of manslaughter, a felony, and then be used to establish an element of murder. If this were the case, manslaughter would cease to exist as a separate crime, and all manslaughters would automatically become felony-murders.[25]

Model Penal Code (MPC 210.2)

The MPC has abolished the felony-murder rule. The drafters of the code believed that the rule produced too large a discrepancy between the defendant's culpability for commission of a dangerous felony and the culpability necessary for murder.[26]

However, the code's definition of murder is broad enough to allow a person to be charged with murder under certain circumstances when a death results during the commission of a felony. Thus, persons who cause death during the commission of a felony will be convicted of murder if they (1) intended to kill, or (2) knew that a death would result, or (3) manifested a certain level of indifference to human life.[27]

Practicum 6.6

Two people stopped the victim while she was walking down the street and attempted to rob her. The first robber stood in front of the victim and held a knife to her ribs. The second robber stood behind the victim and struck her over the head with the butt of a loaded pistol. The impact caused the pistol to discharge, killing the first robber.

ISSUE: Does the felony-murder rule apply in this type of situation?

The court upheld the second robber's conviction of murder under the felony-murder rule, indicating that armed robberies are very likely to result in unintended deaths.[28]

Practicum 6.7

The victim and defendant began kissing on the side of the road in the defendant's truck. When the defendant tried to take off the victim's pants, she said "no." The defendant then slapped her several times across the face. He then pulled off her pants and tried to get on top of her. The victim pushed the defendant off her. He then threw her out of the truck and drove away. She was found the next day dead of hypothermia.

ISSUE: *Is the defendant guilty of felony-murder?*

The Wyoming Supreme Court upheld the trial court's ruling that since the defendant was guilty of sexual assault and the evidence in this case established that because the defendant shoved her out of the pickup after she resisted him, the victim died of hypothermia. Given this evidence, it is obvious the victim's death occurred as part of a continuous transaction involving the perpetration of the sexual assault. The defendant is, therefore, guilty of felony-murder. The court stated that killing amounts to felony-murder when it occurs within an unbroken chain of events that comprise felony, such that homicide and underlying felony must be part of one continuous transaction. The court concluded that the homicide was part of a continuous transaction involving the attempted rape.[29]

Additionally, the code does allow the felony-murder concept to come into play in one area. The code establishes a presumption that the necessary degree of recklessness exists for a conviction of murder when a death occurs during the commission or attempted commission of certain specified felonies. These felonies are robbery, sexual attack, arson, burglary, kidnapping, or felonious escape. This presumption also arises if the defendant is in flight after committing one of these felonies when a death has resulted during that felony.[30]

Practicum 6.8

The defendant attempted to rob two people. The first victim reached for his gun in an attempt to stop the robbery. The defendant fired her weapon at him, and he returned the fire, aiming at the defendant but accidentally hitting and killing the other victim.

ISSUE: *If a victim kills another person during a felony, can the defendant be charged with murder under the felony-murder rule?*

The court held that defendant was guilty of murder under the felony-murder rule on the theory that the attempted robbery set in motion a chain of events that resulted in a death and that the defendant should have been aware of this possibility.[31]

Practicum 6.9

The defendant and his two accomplices decided to rob a Uni-Mart store. The robbery commenced shortly after midnight. One of the accomplices fatally shot the store clerk, and all three boys ran out the store without taking any money.

ISSUE: *If the killing is not in furtherance of the crime and only committed by one of the accomplices, can the others be charged under the felony-murder rule?*

The appellate court upheld the jury finding and found that evidence that all three men ran out after the shooting establishes that the killing was in furtherance of the robbery and the defendant is guilty of felony-murder.[32]

The MPC has had very little impact on the abolition of the felony-murder rule. Most states, as well as the federal government, have retained the rule even when revising their criminal statutes. The federal government allows a person to be charged with murder if death results during the commission of certain listed federal crimes.[33] A majority of states hold that a killing will be classified as murder if it was caused by the defendant when she attempted or committed a dangerous felony.

There are two justifications for the continued use of the felony-murder rule: (1) The rule deters dangerous felonies by adding a charge of murder if a person dies during the attempt or commission of these types of felonies, and (2) the rule cuts down on the use of violence during the commission of felonies by imposing the threat of a murder charge if someone dies during the felony.[34]

The modern trend is to uphold the felony-murder rule but limit its application to those situations in which there is a direct or proximate causal relationship between the felony and the killing. The felony-murder rule has its foundations in the theory of deterrence. It is believed that imposition of the charge of murder for the killing of another during the commission of a felony will stop criminals from committing crimes. While the MPC has abolished the use of the term felony-murder, its definition of murder includes many situations in which the application of the rule would apply. A majority of states have limited the applicability of the felony-murder rule both as to the type of felony it applies to as well as the duration of its application. The felony-murder rule is a complex criminal law doctrine that requires careful factual analysis. This analysis must consider the dangerousness of the underlying felony as well as the possible consequences of both the defendant's and victim's acts.

VOLUNTARY MANSLAUGHTER

Voluntary manslaughter is considered the second-most serious form of homicide. While it requires the same type of intent that is necessary for murder, the crime is "downgraded" to voluntary manslaughter if there was a factual pattern that provoked the defendant into killing a person. This provocation does not excuse the defendant's acts; rather, society has made a determination that some facts inflame the passions of a reasonable person to the point that he will react by killing the instigator. This killing, while intended, is not in the same class as murder, and therefore, should be treated differently.

The Elements of Voluntary Manslaughter

The elements of voluntary manslaughter are as follows:

THE DEFENDANT MUST HAVE ACTED WITH THE SAME INTENT REQUIRED FOR THE CRIME OF MURDER (EXPRESSED OR IMPLIED INTENT TO KILL) Voluntary manslaughter is an intentional killing of another. However, a majority of states downgrade a killing from murder to manslaughter when the defendant was provoked into killing the victim.

In order to reduce murder to voluntary manslaughter, the provocation must be of such a nature as to cause a reasonable person to kill. Yet reasonable people, no matter what the provocation, do not kill. The law recognizes this fact by holding that one who kills upon provocation is guilty of manslaughter, and one who acts in a reasonable manner in killing another, such as in self-defense, is not guilty of any crime. The use of reasonable force in defending oneself is discussed in more detail in Chapter 5.

Voluntary Manslaughter

Defined

Voluntary manslaughter is the intentional and unlawful killing of another person in response to adequate provocation.

Elements

The crime of voluntary manslaughter has three elements:

1. The defendant must have acted with the same intent required for the crime of murder (express or implied intent to kill).
2. There must be adequate provocation for the defendant's actions.
3. His conduct must have caused the death of another human being.

THERE MUST HAVE BEEN ADEQUATE PROVOCATION FOR THE DEFENDANT'S ACTS For the defendant to claim adequate provocation, two requirements must be satisfied: first, the provocation must be adequate. While the MPC dispenses with this requirement, a majority of the states still use it.[35] Second, the killing must be in the heat of passion. The provocation must be so extreme that the defendant acted in a murderous rage. The defendant's passion must be sudden and with no cooling-off period. The MPC also eliminates this requirement. The drafters of the code reasoned that, if the defendant was not under the influence of extreme mental or emotional distress at the time of the killing, no cooling-off period had occurred. The majority of states retain this requirement and use the reasonable person standard to determine if sufficient time has elapsed to enable a reasonable person to gain control of his passion.

Practicum 6.10 sets forth a factual pattern dealing with provocation.

Practicum 6.10

Adequate Provocation?

Approximately seven weeks prior to the killing, the defendant found his wife in bed with the victim. Six weeks later, the defendant and the victim were involved in a fight. During that same period, the defendant and his wife had an argument, and the wife left their home and went to live with her parents. On the afternoon of the killing, the victim and the defendant's wife returned to the defendant's home.

The defendant walked up to the victim's car, pulled out a gun, and killed him.

The court held that it was a well-settled principle that the "preceding event" may have a "final accumulation" that when taken together may provide adequate provocation.[36] Thus, while the defendant may have had a cooling-off period of seven weeks, the sight of the victim at his own home was sufficient to provide the "final accumulation" that again ignited his passions.

ISSUE: Was the killing the result of adequate provocation?

THE DEFENDANT'S CONDUCT MUST HAVE CAUSED THE DEATH OF ANOTHER HUMAN BEING The traditional view requires a causal relationship between the defendant's act and another's death. Refer to Chapter 3 for a more detailed discussion of causation.

Model Penal Code (MPC 210.3)

The MPC does away with use of the terms voluntary or involuntary manslaughter. It defines manslaughter as:

1. The unlawful killing of another human being
2. a. committed in a reckless manner, or
   b. committed under the influence of extreme mental or emotional disturbance for which there is a reasonable explanation or excuse.

The drafters of the code did not believe that the law of manslaughter was well developed by the states. This section of the code was founded on the belief that the pattern of statutory treatment of manslaughter by the states was substantially deficient for failing to confront the major policy questions raised by this offense.[37] New York has accepted the MPC view in its definition of manslaughter in the first degree.[38]

While some states accepted the MPC position, the federal government still classifies manslaughter into two separate crimes—voluntary and involuntary manslaughter.[39] In *United States v. Collins*, the court discussed the facts necessary to support a finding that the defendant was acting upon a sudden quarrel or in the heat of passion. Collins, who was convicted of first-degree murder, had been a probationary employee of the New Orleans post office. On November 24, 1980, he entered the post office, inquired about the location of the intended victim, stalked the victim while concealing his weapon, and, upon finding her, shot and killed her with a .30-caliber carbine. The defendant had been informed four days earlier that his personnel evaluation rating had been changed by the victim, and he believed that as a result he would lose his job. The court held:

> None of this evidence amounts to provocation adequate to reduce a charge of murder to voluntary manslaughter. While the crime of manslaughter is in some sense "irrational" by definition in that it arises out of a person's passions, the provocation must be such as would arouse a reasonable and ordinary person to kill someone.
>
> . . .
>
> The incidents described by the defendant as the cause of his rage are not of the sort that would cause an ordinary, reasonable person to act rashly, without deliberation and from passion.[40]

A majority of states as well as the federal government retain the concept of voluntary manslaughter. Our society seems to be reluctant to punish a person by charging her with murder when there were objective facts to support the position that she was provoked into killing another human being.

Voluntary manslaughter is based upon the concept that a killing that would ordinarily be classified as murder may be downgraded to voluntary manslaughter if adequate provocation exists. While the MPC has eliminated the term "voluntary manslaughter," a majority of states retain this classification of homicide. Adequate provocation requires that the defendant be provoked and that the provocation be so grievous that he or she acted in the heat of passion and without his or her rage cooling off. While voluntary manslaughter requires intentional acts as part of the killing, the next form of homicide requires only an act that results in a death.

INVOLUNTARY MANSLAUGHTER

Involuntary manslaughter is one of the most confusing forms of homicide in that it involves the death of another person under factual situations that do not establish a wicked and depraved mind. Rather, in some cases, the death results from activities that many persons in society engage in on a daily basis—drinking and driving, speeding in a school zone, cleaning a handgun, or playing with a weapon without checking to ensure that it is unloaded.

Involuntary Manslaughter

Defined

Involuntary manslaughter is the unintentional killing of another human being caused during the commission of an unlawful act not amounting to a felony or as the result of criminal negligence.

Elements

The crime of involuntary manslaughter is composed of three elements:

1. The killing of another human being was unintentional.
2. The death occurred either
   a. during the commission of an unlawful act not amounting to a felony, or
   b. as the result of criminal negligence
3. The defendant's unlawful act or negligence caused the death.

The Elements of Involuntary Manslaughter

The elements of involuntary manslaughter are the following:

THE KILLING OF ANOTHER HUMAN BEING WAS UNINTENTIONAL The defendant need not intend to kill the victim to be found guilty of involuntary manslaughter. He or she need only have the general intent to commit the act or acts that caused the death.

DEATH OCCURRED AS A RESULT OF AN UNLAWFUL ACT OR THE DEFENDANT'S CRIMINAL NEGLIGENCE If the defendant commits a misdemeanor and death results, she may be charged with involuntary manslaughter. This type of unlawful act is sometimes referred to as the "misdemeanor-manslaughter doctrine."[41] The most common form of misdemeanor is a traffic offense, but other misdemeanors will meet this requirement. For example, a simple battery may suffice. An unintentional killing caused by any criminally negligent act of the defendant is involuntary manslaughter. The courts require more than simple "civil negligence." The criminal negligence standard involves a high and unreasonable risk of death to another.

The handling of firearms calls for a higher degree of care than normal, and criminal negligence will be found in the unintended killing by the defendant when he was handling or using a weapon.[42] The MPC deals with these situations under negligent manslaughter, which will be discussed later.

In addition to the causal link between the defendant's act and the death, some courts require a close connection between the time and place of the act and the death.[43] Additionally, for the defendant's conduct to be unlawful, it is not necessary that he knows that some law forbids his conduct.[44] There is no requirement that the defendant has any specific intent to violate the law that makes his conduct unlawful.

THE DEFENDANT'S UNLAWFUL ACT OR NEGLIGENCE CAUSED THE DEATH The defendant may violate a statute or act in a criminally negligent manner, but unless her conduct causes the victim's death, the courts will not hold her criminally liable. For example, a person who is required to have a license to perform services might perform those services, and the victim might die. Unless the failure to obtain a license was the condition that caused the death, the courts will not hold the defendant liable.[45]

Model Penal Code (MPC 2.02[2][d])

The MPC does not classify unintentional killing as involuntary manslaughter. Rather, it classes homicides that are committed recklessly as manslaughter.

The code defines recklessly as follows:

> A person acts recklessly with respect to a material element of an offense when he consciously disregards a substantial and unjustifiable risk that the material element exists or will result from his conduct. The risk must be of such a nature and degree that the actor's failure to perceive it, considering the nature and purpose of his conduct and the circumstances known to him, involves a gross deviation from the standard of care that a reasonable person would observe in the actor's situation.

Practicum 6.11 illustrates the degree of recklessness that would support a conviction for involuntary manslaughter.

The federal system defines involuntary manslaughter as killing during the commission of an unlawful act not amounting to a felony or killing that results from the commission of a lawful act without due caution.[46] A majority of states retain the involuntary manslaughter classification. These states define this crime in much the same terms as the federal government.

Practicum 6.11

Reckless Conduct

The defendant was home watching television. The victim arrived and appeared to be under the influence of drugs. The defendant assisted the victim in injecting heroin into her arm. The victim died, and the defendant summoned the police.

ISSUE: Did the defendant act recklessly?

The court found that the defendant acted recklessly and was guilty of involuntary manslaughter.[47]

Involuntary manslaughter is the unintended killing of another person. The law will hold the defendant accountable in either of two situations: (1) a death resulted when the defendant was committing an unlawful act not amounting to a felony, or (2) the defendant acted with criminal negligence that caused the death of another. The same facts may constitute murder in some states under the felony-murder rule because the act of injecting heroin into the victim's arm could be considered as a dangerous felony and a death resulted.

NEGLIGENT MANSLAUGHTER

Negligent manslaughter did not exist at common law and is generally considered a statutory crime. It is based upon the MPC position that voluntary and involuntary manslaughter are difficult concepts to apply in some instances. As a result, the drafters of the MPC established the concept of negligent manslaughter.

The Elements of Negligent Manslaughter

The elements of negligent manslaughter are the following:

THE KILLING OF ANOTHER HUMAN BEING WAS UNINTENTIONAL As with involuntary manslaughter, the defendant does not have to intend to kill another person. The death of the person may be unintentional.

THE DEATH RESULTED FROM A NEGLIGENT ACT BY THE DEFENDANT The MPC and those states that have adopted its position require more than civil negligence to hold a defendant liable for negligent homicide. The courts usually require gross negligence. This is a higher standard than mere civil negligence but does not reach the level of recklessness necessary for voluntary manslaughter.

In those states, such as California, that have adopted a separate vehicular manslaughter statute, mere negligence may be sufficient to charge a defendant with vehicular manslaughter.

The different degrees of negligence are the following:

simple negligence	civil liability
gross negligence	negligent or voluntary manslaughter
recklessness	involuntary manslaughter

Criminal negligence involves the failure of the defendant to perceive the risk in a situation in which he has a legal duty of awareness. The defendant's negligence caused the death. This is the traditional causation requirement. The negligent act or actions of the defendant must cause the death of the victim.

Negligent Manslaughter

Defined

Negligent manslaughter is the unintentional killing of another human being caused by the negligence of the defendant.

Elements

The crime of negligent manslaughter is composed of three elements:

1. The killing of another human being was unintentional.
2. The death resulted from a negligent act by the defendant.
3. The defendant's negligence caused the death.

Model Penal Code (MPC 210.4)

As we stated earlier, the MPC has abolished the distinction between voluntary and involuntary manslaughter. It classifies manslaughter into two crimes: manslaughter and negligent manslaughter. The manslaughter classification was discussed in the section Voluntary Manslaughter.

Under the MPC, negligent manslaughter is defined as follows:

> Criminal homicide constitutes negligent homicide when it is committed negligently.

The code's definition of negligence requires proof of substantial fault and limits criminal sanctions to cases in which "the significance of the circumstances of fact would be apparent to one who shares the community's general sense of right and wrong."[48] The code imposes criminal liability for inadvertent risk situations only in those cases in which the defendant is grossly insensitive to the interests and claims of another person in society.

A majority of the states and the federal government have not adopted the MPC view. These states retain the voluntary/involuntary classification. However, many of these states use criminal negligence as a ground for conviction under their involuntary manslaughter statutes.[49]

Negligent manslaughter is a relatively new crime. The line between gross negligence and recklessness is thin, yet courts and legislatures use the distinction as a method of classifying homicides by degree of seriousness. The negligent manslaughter statutes are attempts by the states to hold persons accountable when they violate society's norms beyond mere negligence but below the standard of recklessness.

SPECIAL PROBLEMS IN HOMICIDE

The Victim Must Be a Living Human Being

What is the defendant charged with if he injures a pregnant woman, and the child she is carrying dies as a result of the defendant's actions? The traditional common law rule was that a fetus is not a human being until it is born alive—when it is independent of the mother.[50] The

California legislature has enlarged its homicide statute to include killing of a fetus without consent of the mother.[51] New York has also modified the common law rule by providing that it is homicide to kill an unborn child with which a female has been pregnant for more than twenty-four weeks.[52]

Death Must Occur within a Year and a Day

The traditional view was that death must occur within a year and a day from the defendant's act. The justification for this rule was that any longer period would lead to proof problems in the causation element of homicide.[53] Because of advancing medical techniques, it seems questionable that this traditional rule will survive much longer. The year-and-a-day rule is now the exception rather than the rule.[54]

Case on Point

Rogers v. Tennessee

Justice O'Connor:

Turning to the particular facts of the instant case, the Tennessee court's abolition of the year and a day rule was not unexpected and indefensible. The year and a day rule is widely viewed as an outdated relic of the common law. Petitioner does not even so much as hint that good reasons exist for retaining the rule, and so we need not delve too deeply into the rule and its history here. Suffice it to say that the rule is generally believed to date back to the 13th century, when it served as a statute of limitations governing the time in which an individual might initiate a private action for murder known as an "appeal of death"; that by the 18th century the rule had been extended to the law governing public prosecutions for murder; that the primary and most frequently cited justification for the rule is that 13th century medical science was incapable of establishing causation beyond a reasonable doubt when a great deal of time had elapsed between the injury to the victim and his death; and that, as practically every court recently to have considered the rule has noted, advances in medical and related science have so undermined the usefulness of the rule as to render it without question obsolete.

532 U.S. 451, 121 S. Ct. 1693 (2001).

Suicide

Homicide is the killing of another human being. It is not homicide to kill yourself. However, the common law view was that **suicide** was murder and that one who assisted the victim was a party to the crime and could be charged with homicide.[55] The modern trend is not to classify suicide as homicide but to establish a separate crime for those persons who aid another to commit suicide.[56]

SUICIDE STATUTES Oregon was the first state to enact a statute permitting physicians to assist others in committing suicide. The statute, referred to as the "Death With Dignity Act," permits physicians to prescribe lethal drugs to persons who are expected to live less than six months, provided the person who requests the drugs is making an informed decision. The statute, Ore. Rev. stat. 127.880 et. seq., states in part that actions taken in accordance with ". . . [the act] . . . shall not, for any purpose, constitute suicide, assisted suicide, mercy killing or homicide, under any law." The act in subsequent sections defines in detail the provisions under which physician-assisted suicide is permitted.

Compare the above Oregon statute with those of New York, Washington, and Oklahoma. New York Penal Code Section 125.15 (1999) provides that a person is guilty of manslaughter in the degree when ". . . he intentionally causes or aids another person to commit suicide." Washington Revised Code 9A.36.060 (1999) provides that a person is guilty of promoting a suicide when he knowingly causes or aids another person to attempt suicide.

In *Baxter v. State, 2009 MT 449, P50 (Mont. 2009)*, the Montana Supreme Court noted that the Montana Rights of the Terminally Ill Act indicates legislative respect for a patient's autonomous right to decide if and how he or she will receive medical treatment at the end of his or her life. The Terminally Ill Act explicitly shields physicians from liability for acting in accordance with a patient's end-of-life wishes, even if the physician must actively pull the plug on a patient's ventilator or withhold treatment that will keep the patient alive. There is no statutory indication that lesser end-of-life physician involvement, in which the patient himself commits the final act, is against public policy. The court held that under § 45-2-211, MCA, a terminally ill patient's consent to physician aid in dying constitutes a statutory defense to a charge of homicide against the aiding physician when no other consent exceptions apply.

Robert Baxter referred to in the *Baxter v. State* cases was a retired truck driver from Billings. He was terminally ill with lymphocytic leukemia with diffuse lymphadenopathy. At the time of the district court's decision, Mr. Baxter was being treated with multiple rounds of chemotherapy, which typically become less effective over time. As a result of the disease and treatment, Mr. Baxter suffered from a variety of debilitating symptoms, including infections, chronic fatigue and weakness, anemia, night sweats, nausea, massively swollen glands, significant ongoing digestive problems, and generalized pain and discomfort. The symptoms were expected to increase in frequency and intensity as the chemotherapy lost its effectiveness. There was no cure for Mr. Baxter's disease and no prospect of recovery. Mr. Baxter wanted the option of ingesting a lethal dose of medication prescribed by his physician and self-administered at the time of Mr. Baxter's own choosing.

The United States Supreme Court has issued decisions on the subject of whether there is a right to assisted suicide under the United States Constitution. In *Washington v. Glucksberg, 138 L. Ed. 2d 772, (U.S. June 26, 1997)*, the Court reversed a decision of the Ninth Circuit Court of Appeals which had held that the State of Washington's prohibition against assisted suicide violated the Due Process Clause. Like the trial court's decision in the instant case, the Court reasoned that the asserted "right" to assistance in committing suicide was not a fundamental liberty interest protected by the Due Process Clause.

The United States Constitution does not prohibit a state from imposing criminal penalties on one who assists another in committing suicide. For example, Cal. Pen Code § 401 provides that every person who deliberately aids, or advises, or encourages another to commit suicide, is guilty of a felony.

Oklahoma is one of the states that have enacted the Assisted Suicide Prevention Act (63 Okl. St. § 3141.1 (2009)), which provides that it is the intent of the Oklahoma legislature to protect vulnerable persons from suicide. The act makes it a crime to knowingly assist another person to commit suicide or to attempt to commit suicide.

Focus 6.1

Euthanasia

In April 1999, a physician named Jack Kevorkian was sentenced to prison for assisting a man suffering from an incurable illness to kill himself. Dr. Kevorkian has publicly acknowledged that he has assisted at least 130 other persons to die by assisted suicide. On three other occasions when Dr. Kevorkian was charged with assisted suicide, juries acquitted him. Dr. Kevorkian and those who believe in euthanasia have established websites where people may order books, review laws, and learn more about mercy killing. Derek Humphry, the president of the Euthanasia Research and Guidance Organization, stated that:

> The severity of the sentence on Kevorkian will drive the practice of voluntary euthanasia and assisted suicide even further underground. It will not stop it. Kevorkian is by no means the only doctor who helps people die—just the one who does and also openly campaigns for societal acceptance of the practice.[57]

Euthanasia

Euthanasia is more commonly known as mercy killing. Courts and society have wrestled with this complex issue for many years. An example of euthanasia is the killing of a loved one to prevent further suffering. Under existing statutes, this killing would be classified as a homicide. Even though one who commits euthanasia bears no ill will toward the victim and believes his act is morally justified, he nevertheless acts with an intent to kill if he is able to comprehend that society prohibits his act regardless of his personal belief.

In murder or voluntary manslaughter cases, it is not necessary for the defendant to hate her victim; it is simply necessary that she intend to kill or act recklessly. Euthanasia is a complex legal and moral issue, one that we will see more of as medical science advances.

COMPARING AND CONTRASTING HOMICIDES

Murder

Murder is the most serious of the homicide crimes. The crime of murder requires a specific intent (express or implied) to kill another. This intent can be classified as willful, premeditated, or reckless. While voluntary manslaughter involves the same type of specific intent to kill, the intent in voluntary manslaughter must arise suddenly in a heat of passion.

Voluntary Manslaughter

Voluntary manslaughter is the second-most serious form of homicide. It is very similar to murder in that the defendant must have intended to kill the victim. However, society will downgrade this act from murder to voluntary manslaughter if there was adequate provocation.

Involuntary Manslaughter

While murder and voluntary manslaughter both require specific intent—express or implied—to kill another human being, involuntary manslaughter does not require any such intent. The defendant need only have the intent necessary to commit the unlawful act or do any act in a criminally negligent manner. If death results from this act, he may be charged with involuntary manslaughter.

Negligent Manslaughter

In a relatively new classification of homicide, the MPC and a minority of states have established a definition of homicide for deaths that result from the gross negligence of the defendant.

HOW WOULD YOU DECIDE?

Judy Onesavanh and Sophal Ouch were planning a party for their son's birthday. Around 9:00 p.m. on September 13, 2003, they and a friend, Bounthavy Onethavong, were driving to the store in Stockton in a blue Mitsubishi that Onesavanh's father owned. Onesavanh's brother, George, also drives the car. The police consider George to be highly ranked in the Asian Boys street gang (Asian Boys).

That evening Ouch was driving, with Onesavanh in the front passenger seat and Onethavong behind Ouch. While they were stopped in the left turn lane at a traffic light, a blue Honda with tinted windows pulled up beside them. When the light changed, gunfire erupted from the Honda, hitting all three occupants of the Mitsubishi. Onethavong was killed, having received two bullet wounds in the head. Onesavanh was hit in the back and seriously wounded. Ouch was shot in the cheek and suffered a fractured jaw.

Ouch and Onesavanh identified the Honda's driver as "T-Bird," known to the police to be Rathana Chan, a member of the Tiny Rascals Gangsters (Tiny Rascals), a criminal street gang. The Tiny Rascals do not get along with the Asian Boys. Chan was never found. The forensic evidence showed that three different guns were used in the shooting, a .22, a .38, and a .44, and at least six bullets were fired. Both the .38 and the .44 struck Onethavong; both shots were lethal. Only the .44 was recovered. It was found at the residence of Sokha and Mao Bun, brothers believed to be members of a gang.

Two months after the shooting, the police stopped a van while investigating another suspected gang shooting. The defendant was a passenger in the van. He was arrested and subsequently made two statements regarding the shooting in this case. He admitted he was in the backseat of the Honda at the time; T-Bird was the driver and there were two other passengers. Later, he also admitted he fired a .38-caliber firearm. He said he did not point the gun at anyone; he just wanted to scare them.

If you were an associate justice on the state supreme court, would you uphold the defendant's conviction for murder? Justify your decision.

SEE: *PEOPLE V. CHUN, 45 CAL. 4TH 1172, 1179 (CAL. 2009)*

Summary

Homicide is one of the oldest acts that society has classified as criminal. All homicides involve the death of another human being. The distinction between the various classifications of homicide lies with the mens rea of the defendant.

If the defendant specifically intended to kill the victim, and he either carefully formulated the plans or acted with a high degree of recklessness, he may be charged with murder. Depending on the facts surrounding the murder, he might face murder in the first or second degree.

Society has established the felony-murder rule to deter persons from committing dangerous felonies. If someone dies during the commission of this type of felony, the defendant will face murder charges, even though she did not intend to kill the victim or intend that anyone die.

Voluntary manslaughter is very similar to murder, but society has downgraded the seriousness of this homicide—if adequate provocation is present. There are three requirements for adequate provocation: (1) the provocation must be legally adequate, (2) the killing must occur during the heat of passion, and (3) there must not have been a cooling-off period.

Involuntary manslaughter and negligent manslaughter are the least serious homicides. These killings are not intentional and result from, in the case of involuntary manslaughter, an unlawful act or a criminally negligent act. Negligent manslaughter results from a criminally negligent act by the defendant, resulting in the victim's death.

The distinction between the various forms of homicide is sometimes blurred. An examination of the defendant's intent or state of mind coupled with a review of the facts surrounding the killing will assist in determining the proper classification of the homicide.

Additional Assignments

1. Read the selected cases and associated material for Chapter 6 posted at www.mycrimekit.com.
2. Complete the online study guide material for Chapter 6 posted at www.mycrimekit.com.
3. Discussion and thought questions:
   a. The intentional killing of another human being is a serious act. We have established degrees of murder—first degree and second degree. Should we have degrees of murder? Why? Why not?
   b. What is the key distinction between murder and felony-murder?
   c. If a person in her home at night sees someone breaking in through the window and shoots and kills him, what form of homicide has occurred? Would it make any difference if the deceased was a neighbor youth who was drunk and appeared to have entered the home by mistake? What if the homeowner was a young mother alone with her one-year-old baby?
   d. If a person drinks a quart of gin and then attempts to drive home and kills someone on the road, which form of homicide should that person be charged with? What if the defendant had two previous convictions for driving under the influence? What if the accident would have occurred even if the defendant was not intoxicated?
   e. Is negligent manslaughter a realistic classification for homicide? Justify your answer.

Practicum

1. How does your home state classify homicides? Degrees of murder?
2. Has your home state adopted the Model Penal Code's classification of homicides?
3. Develop a fact scenario that involves the crime of voluntary manslaughter.
4. Develop a fact scenario that involves the felony-murder rule.

Notes

1. See *Commonwealth v. Carroll*, 412 Pa. 525, 194 A.2d 911 (1963).
2. Wayne R. LaFave and Austin W. Scott, Jr., *Criminal Law*, 2nd ed. (St. Paul, MN: West, 1986).
3. U.S. Department of Justice, BJS, *Uniform Crime Reports–1998* (Washington, DC: Government Printing Office, 1999), 4.
4. LaFave and Scott, supra note 2, at 528–545.
5. 18 Pa. Cons. Stat. §§ 2501–2502.
6. See *Commonwealth v. Malone*, 354 Pa. 180, 47 A.2d 445 (1946).
7. *Dunagan v. The State*, 269 Ga. 590; 502 S.E. 2d 726 1998 Ga. LEXIS 751.
8. See *Myrick v. State*, 199 Ga. 244, 34 S.E. 2d 36 (1945).
9. See *People v. Jernatowski*, 238 N.Y. 188, 144 N.E. 497 (1924).
10. American Law Institute, *Model Penal Code and Commentaries, Part II*, § 2.10.2, pp. 14–15.
11. Id. at pp. 15–20.
12. Id. at pp. 20–21.
13. American Law Institute, *Model Penal Code and Commentaries, Part II*, § 2.10.2, p. 21.
14. 18 U.S.C. 1111 states: "Murder is the unlawful killing of a human being with malice aforethought. Every murder perpetrated by poison, lying in wait, or any other kind of willful, deliberate, malicious, and premeditated killing; . . . [see the discussion of the felony-murder rule] . . . is murder in the first degree. Any other murder is murder in the second degree."
15. U.S. Department of Justice, *Uniform Crime Reports–1997* (Washington, DC: Government Printing Office, 1998), 23.
16. 739 F.2d 945 (4th Cir. 1984), at 948.
17. Pennsylvania Laws of 1794, Chapter 257, Sections 1 and 2 (1794).
18. See State v. Snowden, 313 P.2d 706 (Idaho 1957).
19. See Eric W. Hickey, *Serial Murderers and Their Victims*, 2nd ed. (Belmont, CA: Wadsworth Publishing Company, 1997), 12.
20. Ronald M. Holmes and John DeBurger, *Serial Murder* (Newbury Park, CA: Sage, 1988), 55–60.
21. Eric W. Hickey, "The Female Serial Murderer," 2 J. Police and Crim. Psychol. (October 1986), 72–81.
22. Hickey, supra note 18, at p. 27.
23. See Note, "The California Supreme Court Assaults the Felony Murder Rule," 22 Stan. L. Rev. 1059 (1970).
24. For a classic discussion of this issue, see Rollin Perkins, "Malice Aforethought," 43 Yale L. J. 537 (1934).
25. See *State v. Fisher*, 120 Kan. 226, 243 P. 291 (1926).
26. MPC and Commentaries, Part II, § 210.2, pp. 29–42.
27. MPC, §§ 210.2(1)(b) and 210.3(1).
28. See *Robbins v. People*, 142 Colo. 254, 350 P.2d 818 (1960).
29. *Daniel Lee Harris v. The State of Wyoming*, 933 p. 2d 1114; 1997 Wyo.LEXI548.
30. MPC, § 210.2(1)(b).
31. *Commonwealth v. Moyer*, 357 Pa. 181, 53 A.2d 736 (1947).
32. *Commonwealth of Pennsylvania v. Clarence Lauden Berger*, 715 A.2d 1156; 1998 Pa. Super LEXIS 836.
33. 18 U.S.C. 1111 reads: "Every murder . . . committed in the perpetration of, or attempt to perpetrate, any arson, escape, murder, kidnapping, treason, espionage, sabotage, aggravated sexual abuse or sexual abuse, burglary, or robbery; or perpetrated from a premeditated design unlawfully and maliciously to effect the death of any human being other than him who is killed, is murder in the first degree."

34. See *State v. Goodseal*, 220 Kan. 487, 493, 553 P.2d 279, 286 (1976).

35. For a discussion of provocation and adultery, see Note, 86 J.P. 617 (1922) [English Cases], and for a discussion of provocation and mutual combat, see Comment, "Manslaughter and the Adequacy of Provocation: The Reasonable Man," 106 U. Pa. L. Rev. 1021 (1958).

36. *Commonwealth v. Voytko*, 349 Pa. Super. 320, 530 A.2d 20 (1986).

37. See *People v. Velez,* 144 Cal. 3d 588 (1983).

38. See N.Y. Penal Law § 125.20(2) and § 125.25(a).

39. 18 U.S.C. 1112 defines this crime as follows:
(a) Manslaughter is the unlawful killing of a human being without malice. It is of two kinds:

. . .

Voluntary—Upon sudden quarrel or heat of passion.

40. *United States v. Collins*, 690 F.2d 431 (5th Cir. 1982), at 437.

41. See LaFave and Scott, *Criminal Law*, supra n. 2, at p. 594.

42. See *People v. Velez*, supra note 34.

43. See *People v. Mulcahy*, 318 Ill. 332, 149 N.E. 266 (1925).

44. People v. Nelson, 309 N.Y. 231, 128 N.E.2d 391 (1955).

45. *People v. Penny*, 44 Cal. 2d 861, 285 P.2d 926 (1965).

46. 18 U.S.C. 1112 defines involuntary manslaughter this way:
(a) Manslaughter is the unlawful killing of a human being without malice. It is of two kinds:

. . .

Involuntary—In the commission of an unlawful act not amounting to a felony, or in the commission in an unlawful manner, or without due caution and circumspection, of a lawful act which might produce death.

47. *People v. Crucoani*, 70 Misc. 2d 528, 334 N.Y.2d 515 (1972).

48. See Wechsler and Michael, supra note 1, at 701, 747–751.

49. See, for example, 18 Pa. Cons. Stat. § 2504.

50. See *Keefer v. Superior Court*, 2 Cal. 3d 619, 470 P.2d 617 (1970).

51. Cal. Penal Code § 187(a).

52. N.Y. Penal Law §125.00.

53. See *Commonwealth v. Ladd*, 166 A.2d 501 (Pa. 1960) (Musmanno dissenting).

54. See Cal. Penal Code § 194, which allows three years and one day.

55. See *Burnett v. People*, 204 Ill. 208, 68 N.E. 505 (1905). For a review of state and federal law in this area, see Note, "Legal Murder: The Intentional Killing of the Unborn," Crim. Law Journal 23 (1989).

56. Cal. Penal Code § 401.

57. www.finalexit.org/drkframe.html (October 3, 1999).

CHAPTER 7

Sex Offenses

Chapter Outline

Rape
The Elements of Rape
Model Penal Code (MPC 213)
Summary of Rape

Sodomy and Oral Copulation
The Elements of Sodomy
The Elements of Oral Copulation
Model Penal Code (MPC 213.2)
Summary of Sodomy and Oral Copulation

Other Sexual Acts and Offenses
Criminal Offenses
Other Sexual Behavior
Sexual Predator Statutes
Sex Offender Registration and
    Notification Act (SORNA)
Summary of Other Sexual Acts and
    Offenses

Sexual Assault

What you should know about sex offenses. After reading this chapter, you should know

- The nature of the crime of rape.
- What constitutes the crimes of sodomy and oral copulation.
- The various types of sexual offenses.
- The rationale behind sexual predator statues.
- Purpose of rape shield laws.

Key Terms

After reading this chapter, you should understand the following key terms:

bestiality: Sexual activity with animals. Also known as zoophilia.

criminal sexual conduct: A gender-neutral term used in some states and applied to a wide variety of sex offenses, including rape, sodomy, criminal sexual conduct with underage individuals, and deviate sexual conduct.

cunnilingus: Consensual oral stimulation of the female sex organs.

date rape: Cohesive sexual advances by an acquaintance that conclude in intercourse.

deviate sexual intercourse: Any contact between any part of the genitals of one person and the mouth or anus of another person.

exhibitionism: Repeated intentional acts of exposing the genitals to an unsuspecting stranger for the purpose of achieving sexual excitement.

fellatio: Consensual oral stimulation of the male sex organs.

forcible rape: Rape that is accomplished against another person's will by means of force, violence, duress, menace, or fear of immediate and unlawful bodily injury.

homosexuality: Exclusive sexual relations with members of the same sex.

necrophilia: Sexual activity with a corpse.

oral copulation: The unlawful act of copulating the mouth of one person with the sexual organs or anus of another by use of force or fear.

pedophilia: The act or fantasy of engaging in sexual activity with prepubertal children.

rape: The unlawful act of sexual intercourse with another person against that person's will by force, fear, or trick.

rape shield law: A statute that is intended to protect victims of rape by limiting a defendant's in-court use of the victim's prior sexual history.

sexual assault: A statutory crime that combines all sexual offenses into one offense.

sexual contact: Any touching of the anus, breast, or any part of the genitals of another person done with the intent to arouse or gratify the sexual desire of any person.

sodomy: The unlawful sexual penetration of the anus of one person by the penis of another, committed by use of force or fear.

spousal rape: The rape of one's spouse.

statutory rape: Sexual intercourse, whether consensual or not, with a person under the legal age of consent as specified by state statute.

transsexual: An individual who feels trapped in the body of the wrong sex.

transvestism: The act of a heterosexual male dressing in female attire.

voyeurism: Repeatedly observing unsuspecting people who are naked, in the act of disrobing, or engaging in sexual activity.

The discussion of sex offenses is a necessity in any examination of criminal law. This chapter is not intended to cause anyone displeasure or discomfort. For some students, this will be their first exposure to physical acts that are not considered normal or even talked about in polite company. Some of the acts discussed in this chapter will show a twisted and sick mind. Sex crimes or offenses are repulsive to modern society, and they range from violent and gross behavior to simply a seamy side of modern life.

Many of these crimes, while they involve acts that could be classified as having sexual connotations, are considered by many experts to be nothing more than violent acts of aggression against women. Some authorities have placed rape under the heading of violent crime and reserved discussion of other sex offenses for general public disorder chapters.[1] We have elected to place all serious sex-related offenses in one chapter for purposes of discussion and comparison.

Chapter 12 discusses obscenity, prostitution, and games of chance under the general heading of Crimes against Public Morals. This is in accord with the treatment of these offenses by the drafters of the Model Penal Code (MPC).[2] In addition, many states group these offenses in one section in their criminal law statutes.

One of the best-known and publicized sex offenses is rape.

RAPE

Rape is one of the most feared, misunderstood, and repulsive crimes in the United States. Until the trial of Senator Ted Kennedy's nephew, William Kennedy Smith, many Americans had unrealistic images of rapists. They believed a rapist was a low-life animal who prowled the night and looked like a Neanderthal, with a sloping brow and beady eyes. While William Kennedy Smith was acquitted of all charges, the publicity surrounding the trial in Florida exposed millions of people to the courtroom drama of a rape case. The "experts" hired by the various media discussed all aspects surrounding the crime of rape. A rapist looks just like the neighborhood boy or the man who delivers the morning paper. He can be anywhere and strike any time. While many scholars have researched the issue, no one has yet come forward with a single acceptable reason for why men engage in the crime of rape. There is no known cause or genetic factor that predisposes some men to engage in this type of assaultive sexual behavior. However, several theories have been advanced to explain the reasons why certain persons carry out these acts against women.

Donald Symons suggests that man's biological sex drive is behind his aggressive assault. Rape is viewed as an instinctive drive associated with the need to perpetuate the species. Symons's theory holds that men still have this primitive sex drive that mandates having sex with as many women as possible. His position holds that rape is intertwined with sexuality as well as violence.[3] Paul Gebhard sets forth the position that rapists are suffering from psychotic tendencies or have sadistic feelings toward women.[4] In addition, A. Nicholas Groth and Jean Birnbaum suggest that every rapist exhibits anger, power, and sadism.[5] These three scholars accept the psychological explanation for rape.

Diana Russell, in her book *The Politics of Rape*, advances the theory that rape is part of the masculine qualities accepted in U.S. society. Russell's position is that in our society young boys are taught to be aggressive and dominant. Men learn to separate their sexual desire from other intimate feelings such as love and respect. Rape is viewed as a form of domination over women.[6]

There are numerous other theories on why men engage in this assaultive behavior toward women. At present there does not appear to be one generally accepted cause for this crime. What most authorities will agree upon is that rape is a violent crime, it is a crime involving the sexual organs of both the offender and the victim, and it is a crime that subjects women to psychological duress and pain.[7] The crime of rape may appear at first glance to be a relatively simple crime with two basic elements; however, these elements contain numerous complex legal and emotional issues.

The Elements of Rape

The crime of rape can be divided into two basic elements:

UNLAWFUL SEXUAL INTERCOURSE This element is specifically gender neutral in its approach. Traditional common law and early statutes authorized prosecution of men for rape. As we will discuss, this is the view of the MPC. Early courts and legislators took the position that a man cannot be raped, either by another man or by a woman. In fact, many of the existing statutes hold to this position. Michigan has an example of a more progressive statute that defines rape in gender-neutral language.[8] To assume that men can rape women and not to accept the possibility that a woman can rape a man is to perpetuate a position that women are the weaker sex and naturally submissive to the demands of men.

For purposes of rape, sexual intercourse requires penetration of the penis into the vagina. Penetration does not have to result in a completed act of sexual intercourse. There is no requirement for ejaculation or emission by the male for the crime to be complete. This position allows for a virgin to be raped and still retain her hymen.

In early court cases, the prior sexual history of the victim was admitted. There were a variety of theories upon which the victim could be cross-examined regarding her previous sexual activity: to show that, since she had intercourse with another person, she was more likely to have consented to intercourse with the defendant; or to illustrate that she was a person of loose morals and therefore would have intercourse with anyone, including the defendant. Modern statutes prevent introduction of this kind of evidence. These statutes, called **rape shield laws**, prohibit the defendant or his attorney from questioning the victim regarding her previous sexual activity or introducing other evidence surrounding her past sexual practices.[9]

Closely related to the victim's past sexual history, but separate from it, is the issue of consent. This is one of the most complex and emotional issues in the crime of rape. The classic defense in most rape cases is that the victim consented to sexual intercourse. Of course, defendants do not raise this issue if physical force was involved or the victim was underage, and therefore, incapable of granting consent. However, many rapes involve the use of threats or slight force that result in overcoming the victim's initial resistance. In these cases, the defendant will argue that the victim consented, and therefore, it was not rape but consensual sexual activity between adults. Tied to the issue of consent is society's position that minors cannot knowingly give consent to certain acts. One of these acts is sexual intercourse. Issues regarding intercourse with minors, unconscious persons, and incompetents will be discussed in more detail in the following section.

Rape

Defined

Rape is the unlawful act of sexual intercourse with another person against that person's will by force, fear, or trick.

Elements

The crime of rape has two elements:

1. Unlawful sexual intercourse.
2. Committed by use of force, fear, or trick.

Committed by Use of Force, Fear, or Trick Three distinct situations are covered by this element of the crime. Rape may occur when the victim's resistance is overcome by force, when the victim is placed in a situation in which she fears for her safety, and therefore, submits to the act, or when the victim is tricked and becomes incapable of giving consent.

Sidebar on Rape: Rape Trauma Syndrome

Rape trauma syndrome is a type of posttraumatic stress disorder. The essential feature of this disorder is the development of characteristic symptoms after the sexual assault that are usually beyond the range of ordinary human experience. Often the victim will have recurrent painful memories of the incident or recurring dreams or nightmares in which the incident is re-experienced.

Diminished responsiveness to the external world, called "psychic numbing," usually starts after the rape. A victim may feel detached from others and complain that she has lost the ability to become interested in activities that were previously meaningful to her—particularly those associated with intimacy, tenderness, and sexuality.

The courts are divided on whether to admit expert testimony on rape trauma syndrome or the emotional or psychological stress symptoms suffered by victims of **forcible rape**. Some courts have held such evidence is irrelevant, others have stated that its prejudicial effect outweighs its probative value, and others argue that it lacks any scientific acceptability.

Should evidence of the victim's mental state after the rape be admitted into evidence? Why? Why not?

In the first situation, the defendant uses brute force to require the victim to submit to the sexual acts. This force may take the form of a physical beating with fists, clubs, or other objects. The victim is left battered, with physical marks on her body, as a result of the violent assault by the perpetrator. Her clothing may be ripped from her body, and she may be in a state of physical and emotional shock as a result of her encounter.

A second situation is very similar to the first but occurs when the victim fears for her safety and no longer resists the attacker's advances. This fear may be caused by the defendant's brandishing of a weapon, whether it be a knife, gun, or club. Another situation is where the victim submits to an attacker who threatens her with the use of force if she resists. In these situations, the victim may comply with the attacker's demands and not have any marks on her as a result of the incident. A third form of this "consent" occurs where the victim initially tries to resist but becomes frightened and then complies with the attacker's demands. In the beginning, she may attempt to pull away from him or resist his efforts to disrobe her, but as the act progresses, she becomes frightened and discontinues her resistance.

The third situation involves the defendant's "tricking" the victim. This is a very broad category that includes sex with minors and incompetents as well as use of alcohol or drugs to render the victim incapable of giving informed consent. As we briefly discussed above, our society has determined that persons under a certain age cannot legally give consent for purposes of engaging in sexual intercourse.

Focus 7.1

Consent and the Rape Shield Law

A woman was raped by two men. In the sixteen-day period between when she was raped and when she reported the act to the police, she went to the alleged rapists' house and had consensual sex with the men. The defendants raised these facts at the trial.

ISSUE: *Is evidence of consensual sex after an alleged rape admissible to prove that the rape was consensual?*

The appellate court held that the rape shield statute refers not only to sexual acts occurring before the incident charged, but to any sexual conduct by the victim. However, in this case, the court held that the trial court did not abuse its discretion in finding that the evidence was admissible regarding the question of consent.

State of Arkansas v. David W. Babbs and Russell C. Conger, 334 Ark 105; 971 S.W.2d 774; 1998 Ark Lexis 439.

Practicum 7.1

Great Bodily Injury

Some rape statutes enhance the penalty for the crime if the victim suffers great bodily injury. The defendant attacked the victim and beat her until she submitted to the sexual assault. As a result, her injured teeth eventually died and fell out. In addition, she suffered impairment of the functioning of the jaw.

ISSUE: *Were the injuries sufficient to constitute great bodily injury?*

The court relied upon medical testimony that the victim did and would continue to suffer physical pain as a result of the beating in finding there was great bodily injury.[10]

The common law held consensual intercourse with a minor under the age of ten was rape.[11] In modern society, the general rule is that when a female reaches the age of eighteen, she is considered an adult and capable of entering into binding contracts and giving consent for purposes of engaging in lawful sexual intercourse. The issue does not normally arise at this age, however. Consent becomes important when the defendant engages in sexual intercourse with a minor between the ages of three and sixteen. There are numerous incidents of child sexual abuse where the defendant has engaged in a course of sexual intercourse with a minor over a period of years. Since the victim cannot legally agree to intercourse, the defendant may be charged with rape. There are wide variations among the states regarding the age at which a minor can give consent. Many jurisdictions have special statutes that prohibit sexual relations with young children. Some of these statutes call this type of sexual intercourse "**statutory rape**," and some impose penalties as severe as for forcible rape.

Practicum 7.2

Rape Charges Enhancement

The victim was a four-year-old child who was beaten before and during the rape by the defendants. The child's anal opening had been stretched as a result of the forceful rape.

ISSUE: Do the wounds suffered by the child constitute an enhancement on the rape charges?

The Tennessee court stated that all forcible rapes involve a degree of trauma. In this case, the injuries inflicted upon the victim exceed the trauma apart of the forcible rape, and therefore, are a proper enhancement factor.[12]

Practicum 7.3

Great Bodily Injury

The defendant attacked the victim, held a weapon to her body, and forced her to engage in sexual intercourse. After penetration had occurred, the defendant stabbed her with a knife.

ISSUE: Were the injuries sufficient to constitute great bodily injury?

The court indicated that the attack was a vicious assault but could not find great bodily injury, as the defendant stabbed the victim after the act had occurred. The statute required the injury to occur before intercourse.[13] Great bodily injury was rejected only as an aggravating factor in the rape, and the defendant could be charged with a separate count of assault.

Practicum 7.4

Consent

The victim was alone in her home when the rapist broke in through a window. He threatened her with a knife and stated he was going to take her. Fearing that the offender might have AIDS, the victim asked if he would wear a condom. The assailant agreed, and she placed the condom on his penis. He then proceeded to have intercourse with her.

ISSUE: Did she consent?

A Texas grand jury refused to indict the defendant for rape, believing that the "victim" had consented to the act of intercourse by asking the offender to use a condom and assisting him in placing it on his penis. The case was referred to a second grand jury, which indicted the defendant. He was tried, found guilty of rape, and sentenced to confinement.

What is your opinion? Should the victim have resisted more? Could the defendant have believed she was consenting?

A person who is classified as mentally incompetent cannot legally give consent to sexual relations. When a person takes advantage of these types of victims and has intercourse, the law allows him to be charged with rape. The issue with this type of situation is defining what constitutes mental incompetence. States have approached this issue in a variety of ways: Some states hold a person to be incompetent if she is incapable of expressing any judgment on the matter.[14] Other states impose a requirement that the woman lack the ability to comprehend the moral nature of the act.[15] A third group of states addresses the issue of incompetence by asking if the woman had the capacity to understand the character and probable consequences of sexual intercourse.[16] The first approach is too restrictive and would protect only those women suffering from an extreme form of mental retardation. The second alternative is vague in that the courts would have to examine the victim's moral values. The last approach seems to allow the most latitude and protects both the defendant and victim. The drafters of the MPC have adopted this approach with a slight variation that requires the defendant to know that the victim is suffering from a mental condition that renders her incapable of appraising the nature of her conduct.[17]

The third category involves "tricking" the victim by causing her to use alcohol or drugs to the point that she is unconscious or so impaired that she cannot consent to the act of sexual intercourse. The test in this area is similar to the approach used when dealing with incompetent victims.

The states have adopted various laws regarding the crime of rape. At present there is no single definition that is accepted by all jurisdictions. Because of this confusion, the drafters of the MPC studied this crime in detail and adopted a proposal that attempts to address the many diverse issues surrounding the crime of rape.

Sidebar on Rape: Acquaintance Rape

The crime of acquaintance rape—or, as it is sometimes called, "**date rape**"—was newly defined in the 1980s and 1990s. Acquaintance rape involves cohesive sexual advances that conclude in intercourse. It normally occurs between persons who are dating or have a social relationship. It may involve threats or actual force that causes the victim to submit to the act. Many victims do not report such incidents because they not involve a stranger "jumping out of the bushes."[18]

Three out of four rapes or sexual assaults involve offenders who had a prior relationship with the victim as either a family member, intimate, or acquaintance.[19] What is more startling is the fact that 22 percent of all females raped by nonstrangers did not report the crime because they were afraid of reprisals by the offender or his family or friends.[20]

Authorities in the field are split regarding the actual percentage of rapes involving nonstrangers. Some believe the actual number of date rapes is very low in comparison to violent rapes by strangers.[21] Others accept the Department of Justice statistics regarding the percentage of rapes by nonstrangers and attribute the low numbers to a reluctance on the part of the victim to report these sexual advances.[22] One survey reported that on a Midwestern college campus, 100 percent of the victims knew the rapist.[23]

Model Penal Code (MPC 213)

The MPC was concerned with the divergent listing of acts involved with the crime of rape and attempted to establish a single definition with different grading schemes by dividing the crime into three felony levels. The code reserves the most serious category for those acts of aggression resulting in serious bodily injury or where there is no voluntary social or sexual relationship between the parties.

The MPC defines rape as follows:

A male who has sexual intercourse with a female not his wife is guilty of rape if:

(a) he compels her to submit by force or by threat of imminent death, serious bodily injury, extreme pain, or kidnapping to be inflicted on anyone, or

(b) he has substantially impaired her power to appraise or control her conduct by administering or employing without her knowledge drugs, intoxicants, or other means for the purpose of preventing resistance; or

(c) the female is unconscious; or

(d) the female is less than ten years old.

Rape is a felony of the second degree unless (i) in the course thereof the actor inflicts serious bodily injury upon anyone, or (ii) the victim was not a voluntary social companion of the actor upon the occasion of the crime and had not previously permitted him sexual liberties, in which case the offense is a felony of the first degree.[24]

Practicum 7.5

A husband (the defendant) and his wife had been separated for a period of time. She had obtained a judgment of divorce, but prior to the entry of the final decree, the defendant attacked and raped her. She was maintaining a separate residence. He broke into her apartment, told her to be quiet or he would kill her, and engaged in sexual intercourse with her.

ISSUE: Can a husband who is legally separated from his wife be convicted of the crime of rape?

The court held that the defendant could be convicted of rape, since the state statute did not exempt a spouse as a potential victim of rape.[25]

The MPC does not classify unlawful sexual intercourse between a husband and his wife as rape. This would be the case if the husband physically assaulted his wife and forced her to submit to the act. Today, many states have statutes that authorize the prosecution of a husband for the rape of his wife.[26] In addition, the code specifies that rape involves only a man assaulting a woman and not vice versa. Both of these positions are out of date in modern society. Today we understand the dynamics of spousal abuse and can accept that a husband may in fact rape his wife in what is called **spousal rape**. As we discussed above, modern-thinking legislators have made the crime gender neutral and thereby allow a female to be charged with raping a male.

The drafters of the code seemed to be concerned with the burden of proof in the crime of rape and required that the victim suffer bodily injury or be raped by a stranger to constitute the most serious form of this crime. This flies in the face of modern society and imposes a stigma on a person who is raped by an acquaintance and does not resist to the point that she is physically injured. In addition, the drafters ignore the realities of modern life and the fear that a woman may experience when dragged from a street and raped. The drafters of the MPC would either require her to resist to the point that she is physically injured or require the assailant to beat her before the crime is considered one of the more serious felonies. The more acceptable view, set forth in the earlier discussion, does not require bodily injury for the crime of rape. The federal statutes are in accord with this position. The MPC attempted to define the crime of rape very narrowly and in the process imposed an additional burden of proof on the victim of this crime. As the earlier discussion indicates, rape is not a simple crime.

Summary of Rape

Rape is an emotional and complex crime that is not restricted to one economic segment of our society. Rich and poor alike can and do suffer the consequences of this assaultive act. The crime involves unlawful sexual intercourse by means of force, fear, or trick. It is usually a crime that occurs in secret, and there are no witnesses except the victim.

Practicum 7.6

Husband (the defendant) and his wife were legally married. He forced her to engage in sexual intercourse even though she protested and did not at any time give verbal consent.

ISSUE: Was the husband guilty of rape?

This court reached a contrary result by stating that marriage presumes consent to sexual relations, and therefore, the crime of rape cannot occur.[27] It should be noted that many states have amended their laws, and in those states, a spouse can be convicted of raping his wife. In addition, in some states the husband could be prosecuted for assault and battery on the wife or sexual assault.

Should There Be a Time Limit after Consent Is Withdrawn?

When a woman consents to sex and then changes her mind, how fast must the man stop? Courts in seven states have ruled that during the sex act, the woman may withdraw her consent. If the male does not stop, then the act amounts to rape. In many states, once the sex act has begun, if the woman withdraws her consent and the man does not stop, it is not rape, based on the concept that the act of rape is completed with penetration and the initial act of penetration was consensual. Note: However, continuing to have sex is several states may be a form of assault. Victims' rights advocates are pushing for state laws giving the woman a right to withdraw her consent. However, even those advocates concede that it's hard to set a time frame within which sex must cease after consent is withdrawn.

The MPC adopts a definition of rape that is graded by its seriousness. The most serious form of rape, according to the drafters of the code, involves rape with great bodily injury to a woman or rape by a stranger. Other rapes are considered less serious felonies. In addition, the MPC does not define rape to include a sexual assault by a husband against his wife.

Modern statutes address the crime in a gender-neutral manner. This allows a woman to be charged with raping a man. In addition, these statutes prohibit a husband from raping his wife.

SODOMY AND ORAL COPULATION

According to the Bible, the ancient city of Sodom was destroyed by God because of its residents' unspeakable sexual acts. The term **sodomy** was derived from this biblical description of a city and its citizens who engaged in certain deviant sexual acts.[28] In early England, sodomy was considered so vile that the famous legal commentator William Blackstone refused to name it. He referred to the act as "the infamous crime against nature."[29] This early revulsion continued in America, and some statutes still refer to the crime by the term coined by Blackstone. One state charges sodomy as "the abominable and detestable crime against nature."[30]

Similar to those for rape, the definition and elements of sodomy include the requirement that force or fear be used to overcome resistance. While numerous states have modified their earlier position regarding acts between consenting adults, some states still punish the act whether it is homosexual or heterosexual in nature. These states do not require that any physical coercion be used by the perpetrator for the statute to apply. In other words, some states punish sodomy even if it is a consensual act between consenting adults in the privacy of their own bedroom.

Sodomy

Defined

Sodomy is the unlawful sexual penetration of the anus of one person by the penis of another, committed by use of force or fear.

Elements

The crime of sodomy has three elements:

1. Unlawful sexual penetration of the anus of one person.
2. By the penis of another.
3. By use of force or fear.

In *Bowers v. Hardwick*, 1986 (478 U.S. 186), the United States Supreme Court held that the due process clause of the federal Constitution's Fourteenth Amendment did not (1) confer a fundamental right upon homosexuals to engage in consensual sodomy or (2) invalidate a Georgia statute that criminalized acts of consensual sodomy—regardless of whether the participants were of the same sex—even when the acts in question occurred in the privacy of the home. In so holding, the Supreme Court noted that (1) the laws of many states made such conduct legal, and (2) proscriptions against such conduct had "ancient roots." In 2003, in the case of *Lawrence v. Garner*, the Supreme Court revisited their rulings set forth in *Bowers* and reversed *Bowers*.

Justice Kennedy stated in *Lawrence* [539 U.S. 558] that the liberty interest in the Constitution protects a person from unwarranted government intrusions into a dwelling or other private places. In our tradition, the State is not omnipresent in the home. And there are other spheres of our lives and existence, outside the home, where the State should not be a dominant presence. Freedom extends beyond spatial bounds. Liberty presumes an autonomy of self that includes freedom of thought, belief, expression, and certain intimate conduct. The instant case involves liberty of the person both in its spatial and more transcendent dimensions.

The question before the Court was the validity of a Texas statute making it a crime for two persons of the same sex to engage in certain intimate sexual conduct. In Houston, Texas, officers of the Harris County Police Department were dispatched to a private residence in response to a reported weapons disturbance. They entered an apartment where one of the petitioners, John Geddes Lawrence, resided. The right of the police to enter does not seem to have been questioned. The officers observed Lawrence and another man, Tyron Garner, engaging in a sexual act. The two petitioners were arrested, held in custody overnight, and charged and convicted before a justice of the peace.

The Court concluded that the petitioners were free as adults to engage in the private conduct in the exercise of their liberty under the Due Process Clause of the Fourteenth Amendment to the Constitution. The Court reversed the decision.

The Elements of Sodomy

The crime of sodomy can be divided into three basic elements:

UNLAWFUL SEXUAL PENETRATION OF THE ANUS OF ONE PERSON Early English law punished the act with an animal or another human. However, U.S. statutes have divided these acts into two separate crimes, and to be convicted of the crime of sodomy, the offender must penetrate another human's anal cavity. The crime as written applies to both female and male partners.

BY THE PENIS OF ANOTHER At one time, the law in England required not only penetration but an emission or ejaculation to make the crime complete.[31] However, the modern view is that any penetration by the penis is sufficient to establish this element of the crime. The crime is complete upon any penetration.

BY USE OF FORCE OR FEAR As with the crime of rape, knowing voluntary consent is a defense to the crime of sodomy. Thus, sodomy between consenting adults would not be a crime. This is the case whether the act is homosexual or heterosexual in nature. The same type or amount of force or imposition of fear that is required in rape is necessary in sodomy.

The Elements of Oral Copulation

The crime of oral copulation has three elements:

THE UNLAWFUL ACT OF COPULATING IN OR WITH THE MOUTH OF ONE PERSON This element of oral copulation requires that either the offender or the victim use his or her mouth during the commission of the crime. Penetration is not required. Any form of contact, such as kissing or other actions, is sufficient.

WITH THE SEXUAL ORGANS OR ANUS OF ANOTHER The crime traditionally punished copulation with another's sexual organs or anus. It is immaterial whether the act is committed by the offender on the victim or the victim is forced to commit the act on the assailant. In either situation, the crime is complete with the touching of the mouth to another's sexual organs or anus.

A distinction must be made between consensual sexual acts between adults and oral copulation that is criminal in nature. Consensual acts of this nature are called *fellatio* and *cunnilingus*. **Fellatio** is the consensual oral stimulation of male sex organs and **cunnilingus** is the consensual oral stimulation of female sex organs. The crime of **oral copulation** may be committed by a woman on another woman, by a man on another man, by a woman on a man, or by a man on a woman.

Oral Copulation

Defined

Oral copulation is the unlawful act of copulating the mouth of one person with the sexual organs or anus of another by use of force or fear.

Elements

The crime of oral copulation has three elements:

1. The unlawful act of copulating the mouth of one person.
2. With the sexual organs or anus of another.
3. By use of force or fear.

BY USE OF FORCE OR FEAR The act, to be punished as a crime, must not be consensual. Force or fear must be used to overcome resistance. The amount of force or fear necessary for the charge is the same for rape, sodomy, and oral copulation.

Model Penal Code (MPC 213.2)

At the time of the adoption of the MPC, most states did not limit "crimes against nature" to only sodomy. The states punished fellatio and cunnilingus as well as anal intercourse and bestiality. States enacted specific criminal statutes prohibiting these acts. These state statutes punished consensual as well as forced deviant sexual acts. The drafters of the code made a determination that private sexual acts between consenting adults should not be viewed as criminal in nature and therefore excluded them from coverage of deviate sexual intercourse.

The MPC defines **deviate sexual intercourse** as sexual intercourse with some penetration, however slight; emission is not required.[32] The code defines deviate sexual intercourse by force or imposition as follows:

1. ***By Force or Its Equivalent.*** A person who engages in deviate sexual intercourse with another person, or who causes another to engage in deviate sexual intercourse, commits a felony of the second degree, if:
   a. he compels the other person to participate by force or threat of imminent death, serious bodily injury, extreme pain, or kidnapping, to be inflicted upon anyone; or
   b. he has substantially impaired the other person's power to appraise or control his conduct, by administering or employing without the knowledge of the other person drugs, intoxicants, or other means for the purpose of preventing resistance; or
   c. the other person is unconscious; or
   d. the other person is less than ten years old.

Practicum 7.7

Oral Copulation

The defendant was the live-in boyfriend of the mother of one of the victims. The six-year-old victim and her seven-year-old girlfriend were home with the defendant after the victim's mother left for work. The defendant, nude, went into the bedroom where the victims slept. He then rubbed Vaseline between the girls' legs and on himself. He referred to the Vaseline as "love jelly" or "love cream." He then lay on his back and had both girls touch his penis. The defendant also had both girls put their mouths on his penis, and he kissed one of the victims between her legs.

ISSUE: Is the defendant guilty of oral copulation?

The court held that contact with the mouth or vagina by the sexual organ of an aggressor is sufficient, and there is no requirement of penetration. The crime is complete with an act or instance of uniting or joining two or more separate and independent parts or units, a coming together, combination, or junction. There is no requirement of penetration within the definition of oral copulation.[33]

---

2. ***By Other Imposition.*** A person who engages in deviate sexual intercourse with another person, or who causes another person to engage in deviate sexual intercourse, commits a felony of the third degree if:
   a. he compels the other person to participate by any threat that would prevent resistance by a person of ordinary resolution; or
   b. he knows that the other person suffers from a mental disease or defect that renders him incapable of appraising the nature of his conduct; or
   c. he knows that the other person submits because he is unaware that a sexual act is being committed upon him.

The drafters of the code were attempting to establish a uniform set of rules that would apply to offenses that society as a rule did not care to discuss or in some instances even acknowledge. They were able to bring uniformity to this area of the law and yet accept that certain consensual acts performed by adults in the privacy of their own home should not be considered criminal.

Summary of Sodomy and Oral Copulation

Sodomy and oral copulation are crimes that were referred to in biblical times. They continue to this date to be known as crimes against nature. The U.S. Supreme Court has ruled that homosexual sodomy is not protected by any fundamental right to privacy. However, the drafters of the MPC and many states have decriminalized consensual acts of this nature between consenting adults. This is the case even if the adults are of the same sex. These acts, when forced upon an unconsenting adult or child, are considered by many to be some of the most serious sex offenses in our society.

OTHER SEXUAL ACTS AND OFFENSES

Numerous other sexual acts and offenses are of interest to those involved in the criminal justice system. Some of these acts involve sexual activity between consenting adults that is carried out in the privacy of their own home. Other sexual acts are bizarre and, many would argue, are the mark of a sick and twisted mind. In order to present a well-rounded discussion of this area of criminal law, this section will briefly examine these acts and offenses.

Criminal Offenses

There are separate texts dealing with deviant sexual behavior. The purpose of this section is to make the reader aware that there is an entire field of sex crimes outside the norm even to the hardened law enforcement officer. These crimes involve sexual activity that society has condemned and outlawed.

In 1992, the world watched, listened, and read with rapt attention and revulsion the horrors detailed by confessed sex killer Jeffrey Dahmer. Dahmer, thirty-one, was arrested and tried in a Milwaukee court on charges of killing, mutilating, and engaging in sex with up to fifteen young male victims.

Dahmer's tales were both repulsive and staggering. He admitted to attempting to perform lobotomies on some of his victims while they were drugged, in the hopes of controlling them by making them zombielike. When these efforts failed, he then strangled them and dissected the corpses.[34] In addition, Dahmer confessed to engaging in sex with the bodies. While Dahmer readily admitted to all of his acts, he claimed he was insane at the time he committed the offenses. A jury listened to all the horrid details and found Dahmer sane.

Dahmer claimed he was suffering from necrophilia and was therefore insane and should be placed in a mental institution instead of state prison. Samuel Friedman, a psychologist who testified at Dahmer's sanity trial, indicated that, while Dahmer had symptoms of necrophilia, his diagnosis was a severe personality disorder, and that Dahmer was fully able to appreciate right from wrong and to conform his conduct to the dictates of the law. Friedman testified that he believed Dahmer when he told police that he engaged in cannibalism and experienced uncontrolled feelings of lust as he killed the victims.[35]

Dahmer's tale illustrates that there are certain individuals in our society who will act in ways that are repugnant to all normal people. The following discussion focuses on some of the more common sexual offenses in this area.

Pedophilia is the act or fantasy of engaging in sexual activity with prepubertal children. Prepubescent children are generally thirteen years old or younger. This type of sexual activity is the person's preferred or exclusive method of achieving sexual excitement. As adults, these individuals generally prefer sexual activities with children of the same sex. Most states have specific statutes that make sexual activity with a minor, usually under the age of sixteen, a crime. Some statutes classify this as a misdemeanor and others as a felony.

Bestiality, also known as zoophilia, is the act of engaging in sexual activity with animals. There are as many different offenses as there are animals, although law enforcement officials have indicated that chickens, dogs, and sheep appear to be the most common animals used in this type of sex offense.

Necrophilia consists of engaging in sexual activity with a corpse. This offense is prohibited by 250.10 of the MPC, which makes it a misdemeanor to treat a corpse in a way that the offender knows would outrage ordinary family sensibilities. Conduct such as dissection, mutilation, disinterment, sale, and sex with a corpse are indictable acts. This is not an act that last occurred in the Middle Ages and still rests upon the books. During the Dahmer sanity trial, it was revealed that Dahmer used a condom while having sex with some of the bodies. The prosecution cited his desire to avoid sexually transmitted disease from the dead body as evidence of his sanity.

Exhibitionism is the repeated intentional act of exposing one's genitals to an unsuspecting stranger for the purpose of achieving sexual excitement. This definition excludes the occasional lapse that most normal people experience when they undress in their own home and forget to close the blinds. In addition, it does not include the male who sometimes forgets to button or zip up his pants. Exhibitionists are very deliberate in their acts. Many times, young children will be the victims of this type of offense. Many states have specific statutes dealing with exhibitionism, while others classify it as disorderly conduct.

Voyeurism involves the offender's repeatedly observing unsuspecting people who are naked, in the act of disrobing, or engaging in sexual activity. The voyeur does not desire to engage actively in sexual relations with the person or persons he is observing. The viewing by itself is the preferred or exclusive method of achieving sexual excitement. These offenders are known as "peeping Toms" by law enforcement agencies.[36]

This section has examined deviant sexual offenders who can pose either a simple nuisance or a serious danger to members of the public. Some would argue that they are mentally ill and need treatment, while others would opt for confinement for anyone who engages in these offenses.[37] Our society has made all of the above acts criminal in nature and punishes the offender with jail or prison, depending on the nature of the crime.

Other sexual acts, while they may still be technically viewed as a crime in some states, are becoming more accepted in our society. The following section will examine these acts.

Other Sexual Behavior

There is a broad range of sexual acts and activities that may be considered erotic and unusual. A vast majority of Americans may not participate in these acts, but so long as they are conducted between consenting adults, our society has made a determination not to attach a criminal stigma to them. Two of the better-known and well-researched areas of sexual behavior that are of interest to members of the criminal justice system are homosexuality and transvestism.

Homosexuality is defined as exclusive sexual relations with members of the same sex. Women who engage in this type of sexual activity are known as lesbians. Men who select only males as their sexual partners are known as homosexuals.

Homosexual behavior has been traced back to ancient Greece, where homosexuality was viewed as natural in many segments of Greek society. Plato's Symposium extolled the virtues of homosexual behavior and indicated that homosexual lovers would make the best soldiers.[38] One scholar indicates that homosexuality was not considered socially deviant behavior until the time of Thomas Aquinas and St. Augustine, who argued that it is unnatural because it does not lead to conception.[39] In 1980, the DSM-II classified homosexual behavior as an alternative sexual lifestyle rather than deviant behavior. Unfortunately, even in the medical community, there remains a core of opinion that homosexuality is an unnatural sexual behavior.

The problems and misunderstandings occur when a person solicits or commits homosexual acts on an unwilling victim. Unfortunately, a segment of our society will become outraged at all homosexual activity. This response is no more rational than becoming angry with all heterosexuals because an offender has raped a helpless victim.

A **transsexual** is an individual who feels trapped in the body of the wrong sex. In 1953, Christine Jorgensen gained worldwide attention when he underwent a sex change operation that transformed him from a male to a female. Since that time thousands of transsexuals have undergone sex changes.[40]

Transvestism is the act of a heterosexual male dressing in female attire. Transvestism is often linked with and confused with homosexuality. Some transvestites will act as prostitutes and lure an unsuspecting john (customer) to a motel. The surprise that accompanies the discovery can result in violence to either the john or the transvestite. However, it must be underscored that cross-dressing itself is not a crime.

Sexual Predator Statutes

Many states have adopted sexual predator statutes that provide for institutionalization, treatment, registration, or all three, of individuals convicted of certain sex crimes. The state of Florida has adopted one of the common statutes. An interesting case that reflects how the statute works and some of the problems with the statutes is the *Florida v. Robinson* case [873 So. 2d 1205, 2004].

When the vehicle in which appellee Leon Robinson and a companion were riding ran out of gas, they began to walk. Shortly thereafter, Robinson's companion saw an opportunity to steal a car, and he did so—even though he saw a baby in the back seat. When Robinson entered the car moments later, he noticed the baby. Shortly after stealing the car, Robinson left the child, still sitting in her car seat, in front of a doctor's office. Robinson was convicted of carjacking and kidnapping. He received two life sentences, which were not at issue in the appeal.

The trial court ruled that, pursuant to Florida Statute Chapter 775.21(4)(c), Robinson was a "sexual predator" because he had been convicted of kidnapping a minor that was not his child, even though there had been no sexual component to the crime. The Florida Court of Appeals reversed the designation as a sexual predator. The Florida Supreme Court affirmed. The court noted that because of the stigma attached to sexual predator status, the lifelong registration requirements, and the attendant adverse employment affects, the designation as a sexual predator was a deprivation of a protected liberty interest, triggering a substantive due process analysis. The Supreme Court held that as the predicate crimes of carjacking and kidnapping had no sexual element and there was no sexual motive for them, the designation of defendant as a sexual predator based solely on his conviction for kidnapping a minor who was not his child violated his right to due process of law.

The court stated that where a defendant does not contest the classification of some individuals as sexual predators but simply argues that he does not belong within the classification, his argument raises a due process claim and that the Equal Protection Clause is only concerned with whether the classification pursuant to a particular legislative enactment is properly drawn. Procedural due process is the constitutional guarantee involved with a determination of whether a specific individual is placed within a classification. It is the Due Process Clause that protects the individual against the arbitrary and unreasonable exercise of governmental power.

The court pointed out that a sexual predator not in the custody or supervision of the Florida Department of Corrections must register in person within forty-eight hours of establishing temporary or permanent residence, or any time he or she moves, with both the Florida Department of Law Enforcement or the local sheriff and with the Department of Highway Safety and Motor Vehicles. Under the Florida Sexual Predators Act, the sole criterion for determining whether a defendant must be designated a "sexual predator" is whether the defendant was convicted of a qualifying offense. Based on the unambiguous language of the Act and the clearly stated legislative intent, the act is mandatory and affords no discretion to the trial judge to designate an individual a sexual predator if the statutory criteria are established. Both the United States and Florida constitutions protect individuals from arbitrary and unreasonable governmental interference with a person's right to life, liberty, and property.

Sex Offender Registration and Notification Act (SORNA)

In 2006, the U.S. Congress enacted the Adam Walsh Child Protection and Safety Act, *42 U.S.C. § 16901 et seq.,* which includes the Sex Offender Registration and Notification Act (SORNA). SORNA was enacted in order to protect the public from sex offenders and offenders against children, and in response to the vicious attacks by violent predators against seventeen named victims of sex crimes. *42 U.S.C. § 16901.* SORNA establishes a comprehensive national system for the registration of sex offenders and requires anyone convicted of specified crimes, including aggravated sexual abuse, to register with the national sex offender registry. *42 U.S.C. § 16911(4)(A)(i).* SORNA defines convictions to include juvenile delinquency adjudications of aggravated sexual abuse if the offender is fourteen years of age or older at the time of the offense. *42 U.S.C. § 16911(8).*

Summary of Other Sexual Acts and Offenses

The law criminalizes certain types of deviant sexual activity. These crimes cause members of society both disgust and outrage. They range from the very dangerous, like pedophilia, to the mere nuisance, like voyeurism. Homosexuality has become accepted in our society and is no longer viewed as a disease. Transvestism is the act of cross-dressing. This act by itself is not a crime, but when the transvestite acts in violation of other laws, it becomes an item for the front page of national newspapers.

SEXUAL ASSAULT

The current trend in the United States is to combine all nonconsensual sexual offenses into one statutory crime of **sexual assault**. For example, Texas Penal Code 22.011 describes the offense of sexual assault in the State of Texas.

> TEX. PENAL CODE § 22.011 (2009)
>
> § 22.011. SEXUAL ASSAULT
>
> (a) A person commits an offense if the person:
>   (1) intentionally or knowingly:
>   (A) causes the penetration of the anus or sexual organ of another person by any means, without that person's consent;
>   (B) causes the penetration of the mouth of another person by the sexual organ of the actor, without that person's consent; or
>   (C) causes the sexual organ of another person, without that person's consent, to contact or penetrate the mouth, anus, or sexual organ of another person, including the actor; or
>   (2) intentionally or knowingly:
>   (A) causes the penetration of the anus or sexual organ of a child by any means;
>   (B) causes the penetration of the mouth of a child by the sexual organ of the actor;
>   (C) causes the sexual organ of a child to contact or penetrate the mouth, anus, or sexual organ of another person, including the actor;
>   (D) causes the anus of a child to contact the mouth, anus, or sexual organ of another person, including the actor; or
>   (E) causes the mouth of a child to contact the anus or sexual organ of another person, including the actor.

HOW WOULD YOU DECIDE?

*Convicted of sexual assault for having **sexual contact** with a person under the age of sixteen, the defendant appealed, arguing insufficiency of the evidence to support the conviction. The victim, who was sixteen at trial, she stated she did not know how old she was when defendant touched her and could not recall what grade she was in then.*

How would you rule on defendant's appeal on the issue of sufficiency of evidence?

SEE: UNITED STATES V. ESPINOSA, 585 F.3D 418 (8TH CIR. S.D. 2009)

Summary

An entire class of criminal offenses centers on sexual activity. These range from violent physical assaults such as rape to nuisance offenses such as voyeurism. There is a great deal of controversy surrounding crimes such as rape because they occur in secret without witnesses. The traditional rape occurs when an offender requires the victim to submit to sexual acts by using physical force or fear. The 1980s and 1990s spawned an awareness of the phenomenon of unwanted sexual advances by acquaintances, resulting in acceptance of the term *date rape*.

Sodomy is the penetration of the anus by the penis of another. Many states still make consensual sodomy a crime. The U.S. Supreme Court has upheld the authority of states to regulate this type of conduct as a crime, even among consenting adults.

There is another group of sexual offenders who are of concern to police. These range from those who sexually molest young children to the peeping Toms who lurk in the darkness. The former receive prison terms, while the latter are considered a low priority by many law enforcement agencies.

Additional Assignments

1. Read the selected cases and associated material for Chapter 7 posted at www.mycrimekit.com.
2. Complete the online study guide material for Chapter 7 posted at www.mycrimekit.com.
3. Discussion and thought questions:
   a. Should rape be classified as a violent assault against a person or as a sex offense? Justify your position.
   b. Should forcible sodomy and oral copulation be punished the same as rape? Why?
   c. Discuss the implications of the Supreme Court's ruling in the Lawrence case. Does the ruling have any impact on heterosexual relations?
   d. Are the acts listed in the last section of the chapter (pedophilia, bestiality, and so forth) the acts of a criminal or a mentally ill person?
   e. Why has society accepted homosexuality?

Practicum

1. How does your home state classify rape and other sexual crimes?
2. Does your home state have a rape-shield statute?
3. Develop a definition of a rape that is gender-neutral and includes the various classifications of rape.
4. How do your state statutes on sexual crimes differ from the Model Penal Code?

Notes

1. See, for example, Joel Samaha, *Criminal Law*, 6th ed. (St. Paul, MN: West, 1999), where the author has a chapter titled "Crimes Against Persons: Criminal Sexual Conduct and Others," which includes rape, battery, assault, and kidnapping.
2. The drafters of the code did not classify rape with other violent crimes. See MPC §§ 213–213.6, which discusses a wide variety of sexual offenses. The MPC includes another article dealing with public indecency (Article 251).
3. Donald Symons, *The Evolution of Human Sexuality* (London: Oxford University Press, 1979).
4. Paul Gebhard et al., *Sex Offenders: An Analysis of Types* (New York: Harper & Row, 1965) 198–205.
5. A. Nicholas Groth and Jean Birnbaum, *Men Who Rape* (New York: Plenum, 1979) 101.
6. Diana Russell, *The Politics of Rape* (New York: Stein and Day, 1975). For a more modern article that supports Russell's position, see Donald Mosher and Ronald Anderson, "Macho Personality, Sexual Aggression and Reactions to Guided Imagery of Realistic Rape," J. Res. Personality 77 (1987).
7. For a survey of literature in the field, see "New Research Examines Psychology of Sexual Violence," *Law Enforcement News* (John Jay College of Criminal Justice, New York), January 15, 1992, 1.
8. Michigan does not use the term "rape" and substitutes instead the term "criminal sexual conduct." In addition, the statute is gender neutral and refers to the "actor" as the person who is accused of criminal conduct. See Mich. Comp. Laws §§ 750.520a–750.520i.
9. Vermont's statute is an example of such a rape-shield law. See Vt. Stat. Ann. tit. 13, §3255(3) (A) (B).
10. See *State v. Roberts*, 293 N.C. 1, 235 S.E.2d 203 (1977).
11. William Blackstone, 4 *Commentaries* 212.
12. See *State of Tennessee v. Phillip Ray Griffis and Mellissa Faith Rogers*, 9645. W.2d. 577; 1997 Tenn. Crim. App. LEXIS 427.
13. See *State v. Gray*, 292 N.C. 270, 233 S.E.2d 905 (1977). Great bodily injury was rejected only as an aggravating factor in rape, and the defendant could be charged with a separate count of assault.
14. For an early case taking this position, see *Whitaker v. State*, 199 Ga. 344, 34 S.E.2d 499 (1945).
15. *State v. Dombroski*, 145 Minn. 278, 176 N.W. 985 (1920).
16. *State v. Meyers*, 37 Wash. 2d 759, 226 P.2d 204 (1951).
17. MPC §213.1(2)(b).
18. Ruth Masters and Cliff Roberson, *Inside Criminology* (Englewood Cliffs, NJ: Prentice-Hall, 1990), 380.
19. *Sex Offenses and Offenders, An Analysis of Data on Rape and Sexual Assault*, Office of Justice Programs, U.S. Department of Justice, Washington, DC, February 1997.
20. *Sourcebook of Criminal Justice Statistics – 1992*, U.S. Department of Justice, *Uniform Crime Report – 1997* (Washington, DC: Government Printing Office, 1998), Table 3.31, p. 271.
21. For a survey supporting this position, see Joan M. McDermott, *Rape Victimization in 26 American Cities* (Washington, DC: Government Printing Office, 1979).

22. Clifford Kirkpatrick and Eugene J. Kanin, "Male Sex Aggression on a University Campus," 22 Am. Soc. Rev. (February 1957), 52.

23. Thomas Meyer, "Date Rape: A Serious Campus Problem That Few Talk About," *Chronicle of Higher Education*, December 5, 1984, A15.

24. MPC §213.1.

25. See *Commonwealth v. Chretien*, 417 N.E.2d 1203 (1981).

26. Va. Code Ann. §18.2-61 is an example of such a statute. For an excellent discussion of marital rape, see Robert T. Sigler and Donna Haywood, "The Criminalization of Forced Marital Intercourse," in *Deviance and the Family*, Frank E. Hagen and Marvin B. Sussman, eds. (New York: Haworth, 1988), 71–85.

27. See *State v. Bell*, 90 N.M. 134, 560 P.2d 925 (1977).

28. See *Commonwealth v. Poindexter*, 133 Ky. 720, 118 S.W. 943 (1909).

29. William Blackstone, 4 *Commentaries* 215.

30. See *Phillips v. State*, 248 Ind. 150, 222 N.E. 2d 821 (1967) for a case upholding the filing of an indictment using this language for the crime of sodomy.

31. 1 East P.C. 480 (1803).

32. MPC §213.2.

33. See *Dorch v. State*, 458 So. 2d 357 (1984).

34. "Dahmer Reportedly Lobotomized His Victims Before Killing Them," *Boston Globe*, January 20, 1992, 4.

35. "Dahmer Was Not Psychotic, Expert Says," *Boston Globe*, February 8, 1992, 6.

36. The term "peeping Tom" is derived from the fable of a man who allegedly stole a peep at Lady Godiva on her famous ride through Coventry.

37. For authority supporting the position that these acts represent mental illness, see American Psychiatric Association, *Diagnostic and Statistical Manual of Mental Disorders*, 4th ed., revised (DSM-IV) (Washington, DC: American Psychiatric Association, 1994), "Sexual Disorders," 266 et seq.

38. W. Masters, V. Johnson, and R. Kolodny, *Masters and Johnson on Sex and Human Loving* (Boston: Little, Brown, 1968).

39. J. Boswell, *Christianity, Social Tolerance, and Homosexuality* (Chicago: University of Chicago Press, 1980).

40. Masters, Johnson, and Kolodny, supra note 38.

CHAPTER 8

Other Crimes against Persons

Chapter Outline

Kidnapping
    Model Penal Code (MPC 212.1)
    Types of Kidnapping
    Kidnapping as a Federal Crime

False Imprisonment
    Model Penal Code

Trafficking in Humans
    Victims of Trafficking and Violence
        Protection Act of 2000

Stalking
    Extent of Stalking
    High-Tech Stalkers

Assault and Battery
    Battery
    Assault

Aggravated Assault and Battery
    Intent
    Transferred Intent

Mayhem

Terrorism

What you should know about other crimes against persons. After reading this chapter, you should know

- The elements for the crimes of kidnapping, false imprisonment, assault, battery, and mayhem.
- The movement requirement necessary to constitute the crime of kidnapping.
- The various types of kidnapping.

- The violations of personal liberty involved in both kidnapping and false imprisonment.
- What constitutes the crime of stalking.
- The two types of assault.
- The difference between simple and felonious assaults.

Key Terms

After reading this chapter, you should understand the following key terms:

asportation: Carrying away another's person or property.

aggravated assault: An assault that is committed with the intention of committing an additional crime such as assault with the intent to commit rape or murder. Also refers to assault committed in a manner likely to cause great bodily harm or under circumstances as specified by a statute.

assault: An attempt to commit battery, or intentionally putting another in fear of unlawful contact.

battery: An offensive body contact.

bodily injury: Physical harm to a human being. In assault or battery cases the term refers to the unlawful application of physical force on the person of the victim even when no actual physical harm results.

false imprisonment: Unlawful violation of the personal liberty of another. A lesser included offense of kidnapping.

felonious assault: Assault or battery with aggravating factors—for example, assault with the intent to commit rape, assault with a motor vehicle, assault on a peace officer, and assault with a dangerous weapon.

mayhem: Malicious deprivation of a member of the body or disfigurement of the body.

present ability: As used in assault statutes, a term meaning that the person attempting the assault is physically capable of immediately carrying it out.

stalking: A course of conduct that causes a reasonable person to fear bodily injury or death for himself or herself or members of his or her family.

transferred intent: Situation in which the offender intends to injure one person and by mistake or accident injures another.

This chapter discusses the traditional crimes against persons: kidnapping, false imprisonment, assault and battery, and mayhem.

KIDNAPPING

Kidnapping is one of those crimes that invade the privacy of a person and take away his or her liberty. It is essentially an aggravated form of false imprisonment. Under early common law, when kidnapping meant stealing away women or children from their country, it was only a misdemeanor. It was still only a misdemeanor in New Jersey in 1932 when Charles Lindbergh's son was taken in probably the most famous kidnapping case of all time.[1] Because of the emotional reaction and sympathy that were generated by Lindbergh's status of hero, states quickly enacted harsh new kidnapping statutes. Prior to that case, however, kidnapping was not considered a serious offense.[2] Most of the statutes enacted as a result of the Lindbergh case are still in force today. Kidnapping is now considered a serious felony.

Under common law and in most states, movement of the victim is required to constitute the crime of kidnapping. Movement is also referred to as **asportation**. The movement must be unlawful, meaning only that the victim has not given consent and the movement is not pursuant to a valid legal order or court process.

Under common law, the movement element required that the victim be taken to another county. The modern requirement is only that the movement be substantial as opposed to slight movement. For example, the movement of a victim across a room was not considered substantial by one court.[3] Forcing a victim to walk approximately four hundred yards at gunpoint was, however, considered substantial.[4] In the famous case involving Caryl Chessman, who was known as the "red light bandit," Chessman forced a young woman to leave her car and get into his, a distance of approximately twenty feet. His conviction for kidnapping was upheld by the appellate court, which stated that the movement in this case was substantial because the victim was forced to move from the safety of her car to his car. The court stated that distance was only one of the factors examined in determining whether the movement was substantial.[5] Since many violent crimes involve some movement of the victim, many jurisdictions require movement to be substantially greater than that which would normally occur incident to the underlying crime. Most states use a two-pronged test to determine if the movement requirement has been established:

1. Was the movement by compulsion?
2. Was the movement substantial?

A few states have eliminated or reduced the need for a substantial movement to constitute the crime of kidnapping. The supreme courts of Florida and New Jersey have stated that there is a trend toward upholding kidnapping convictions in situations in which the distance the victim moved was slight (from one side of the room to the other) but the purpose in confining the victim was for use as a hostage. In addition, in 1990, a New Jersey court upheld a kidnapping conviction where the victim was tied up while the defendant raped his wife.[6] Normally, kidnapping is committed by forcing the victim to move to a different location. The force may be by direct physical force or by threat of physical force. The force necessary to constitute the crime is sufficient as long as the victim fears some kind of harm will occur if the force is used. No actual physical force or express threats are necessary to effectuate the movement.

The Lindbergh Kidnapping

During the evening of March 1, 1932, the son of Charles A. Lindbergh was kidnapped from the Lindbergh home in East Amwell, New Jersey. A ransom note demanding $50,000, with instructions for payment, was found in the baby's room. The ransom was paid on April 2, 1932, but the baby was never returned. His body was found on May 12 in a cemetery in the Bronx, New York. Autopsy revealed that the child had died as the result of three violent blows to the skull. Many researchers believe that the fractures were suffered when the child was dropped during the kidnapping. The baby's room was on the second story of the home, and it appeared that a ladder used by the kidnappers had broken during the commission of the crime.

Six years prior to the crime, Charles Lindbergh had become an American hero by being the first person to fly across the Atlantic Ocean alone. The Lindbergh case was widely followed in the newspapers and on the radio.

On October 8, 1934, one Bruno Hauptmann was arrested. He was tried and convicted of causing the death of a child in the course of a burglary and was executed. In 1982, Hauptmann's widow unsuccessfully sued the State of New Jersey, claiming that her husband was innocent of any involvement in the case.

In certain situations, fraudulently getting the victim to move may be sufficient. There is some confusion, however, regarding movement by fraud. One court held that there was a kidnapping with taking by fraud where the offender induced a girl to get into his car for the purpose of going to his house for a babysitting job.[7] In this case, the offender did not take the girl to his house but to a different location. Had he taken the girl to his home and then raped her, it would have been rape but might not have been kidnapping. The general rule is that if the victim consents to the movement, even if the consent was obtained by fraud, there is no kidnapping. If, however, the movement is to a different location or goes beyond the limits of the consent, the conduct may constitute kidnapping.

Kidnapping

Defined

Kidnapping is the willful and unlawful seizing, confining, and carrying away of another person by either force, threat of force, fraud, or deception.

Elements

The crime of kidnapping in most states has five distinct elements:

1. The seizing of a person.
2. The confining or restraining of the person.
3. The unlawful carrying away (asporting) of the person.
4. The use of force, threat of force, or, in certain cases, fraud or deception.
5. The knowledge that the movement of the victim was unlawful.

Kidnapping requires an intent to act without the authority of the law. Accordingly, a person who takes another from one place to another believing that the taking is authorized by law is not guilty of kidnapping in most states.[8]

The motive for the unlawful taking is immaterial. For example, a police officer who arrests an individual in one state and illegally takes the individual into another state where the individual can be prosecuted for murder has committed the crime of kidnapping even though her motive, bringing a criminal to justice, was honorable.

Model Penal Code (MPC 212.1)

A person is guilty of kidnapping if he unlawfully removes another from his place of residence or business, or a substantial distance from the vicinity where he is found, or if he unlawfully confines another for a substantial period in a place of isolation, with any of the following purposes:

a. to hold for ransom or reward, or as a shield or hostage; or
b. to facilitate the commission of any felony or flight thereafter; or
c. to inflict bodily injury on or to terrorize the victim or another; or
d. to interfere with the performance of any governmental or political function.

Kidnapping is a felony of the first degree unless the actor voluntarily releases the victim alive and in a safe place prior to trial, in which case it is a felony of the second degree. A removal or confinement is unlawful within the meaning of this section if it is accomplished by force, threat, or deception, or, in the case of a person who is under the age of fourteen or incompetent, if it is accomplished without the consent of the parent, guardian, or other person responsible for general supervision of that person's welfare.

Types of Kidnapping

There are several different types of kidnapping. The most common kinds are forcible kidnapping, kidnapping with the intent to commit a lewd and lascivious act with the person kidnapped, kidnapping with the intent to take out of state, kidnapping by the noncustodial parent of his or her children, and kidnapping for the purpose of bringing a person into the state.

Under common law, a parent could not be guilty of kidnapping his or her own children. Presently, with the increasing number of separated families, states have passed statutes to provide that the taking of the child by the noncustodial parent in violation of a valid court order constitutes the crime of kidnapping. In 1981, Congress passed the Parental Kidnapping Prevention Act, which facilitates interstate enforcement of custody and visitation orders. This act gives the Federal Bureau of Investigation (FBI) jurisdiction when a noncustodial parent who kidnaps his or her child crosses state lines. One of the debates in this area is whether the crime is simple kidnapping or a form of aggravated kidnapping. Many argue that the offense is less serious when parents kidnap their own children. Others contend that the crime is more serious because it is a violation of a court order, and therefore, also a direct attack on the ability of our judicial system to resolve family conflicts.

Kidnapping for the purpose of bringing a person into the state is a relatively new form of kidnapping and is not recognized in all states. It is designed primarily to prevent law enforcement officers from circumventing the extradition process when a wanted individual is discovered in another state or country; or to prevent noncustodial parents from bringing their children into the state in violation of a court order. For example, suppose the police in California find a person wanted in California living in Mexico. Several police officers, on their own time, go to Mexico, capture the individual, and bring him back to California. This would constitute the California crime of kidnapping for the purpose of bringing an individual into the state.

Many states make it a crime to pose as a kidnapper in order to obtain any ransom or reward or to extort any thing of value from another.

Kidnapping as a Federal Crime

Kidnapping is one of the few crimes that are routinely investigated by the federal government. Federal authority is based on the assumption that the victim will be taken across state boundaries. Federal law prohibits kidnapping or abduction of any person for reward or ransom, when willful interstate transportation of the victim or use of the special maritime or territorial jurisdiction of the United States is involved.[9] Federal kidnapping statutes provide for life imprisonment as the maximum punishment. One of the underlying goals in establishing a federal kidnapping statute is to empower the FBI to investigate kidnapping cases. The FBI normally cannot investigate conduct unless it constitutes a federal crime.

FALSE IMPRISONMENT

False imprisonment is a lesser included offense to kidnapping. It also involves the unlawful violation of the personal liberty of another. The critical difference between kidnapping and false imprisonment is that kidnapping requires the movement (asportation) of the victim. In those states that have eliminated the movement requirement, the crimes of kidnapping and false imprisonment have essentially merged into the same crime.

As we noted earlier, the essential difference between kidnapping and false imprisonment is that no movement or asportation is required for the crime of false imprisonment. In several states, if the length of the restraint is substantial and it is secret, the crime is kidnapping. In most states, false imprisonment is a misdemeanor unless committed by violence or menace. False imprisonment, like kidnapping, is a specific intent crime. To establish false imprisonment, the prosecutor must prove not only that the victim's liberty was forcibly and unlawfully restrained but that the defendant was aware his or her actions were unlawful. Like kidnapping, motive is normally not material except to help establish specific intent.

The Model Penal Code (MPC) requires that the restraint substantially interfere with the victim's liberty. The force used may be physical force or threat of physical force to the victim or another. False imprisonment may be established if a police officer orders a person to get into a police car (and the person obeys) when the officer knows that he does not have the right to so order the person. The MPC also establishes the crime of "felonious restraint" for aggravated false imprisonment.

SECTION 212.2 FELONIOUS RESTRAINT A person commits a felony of the third degree if he knowingly:

    a. restrains another unlawfully in circumstances exposing him to risk of serious bodily injury; or
    b. holds another in a condition of involuntary servitude.

SECTION 212.3 FALSE IMPRISONMENT A person commits a misdemeanor if he knowingly restrains another unlawfully so as to interfere substantially with his liberty.

False Imprisonment

Defined

False imprisonment is the unlawful violation of the personal liberty of another.

Elements

False imprisonment has four distinct elements:

    1. The seizing of a person.
    2. The confining or restraining of the person.
    3. The use of force or threat of force and, in some cases, fraud or deception.
    4. The knowledge that the restraint is unlawful.

TRAFFICKING IN HUMANS

In 2003, FBI agents raided a brothel in South Texas. They found an eleven-year-old girl on a cot in a room of about thirty-six square feet. A threadbare sheet covered the bed. There were two items on a small bedside table: a teddy bear and a roll of paper towels. It was later determined that the girl had been brought illegally into the United States, held captive, and forced to have sex with up to thirty men per day.

Sara Elizabeth Dill, a lawyer with Catholic Legal Services in Miami, Florida, contends that this phenomenon is occurring every day in the United States and throughout the world. Women and children are trafficked internationally to become slaves in the constantly growing sex trade. She notes that the United Nations estimates that 700,000 to one million persons are trafficked annually. According to Dill, although nations and international organizations are beginning to take measures to combat trafficking, the problem continues to escalate and spread to new countries. She states that international crime syndicates benefit from trafficking because it is a less risky yet more profitable form of organized crime. Prostitution and trafficking produce the third-highest source of illegal income, only slightly less than narcotics and illegal arms sales. Dill noted that in recent years the United States has adopted comprehensive crime control legislation, including special sectors of law enforcement and other agencies to specifically combat human trafficking.[10]

Victims of Trafficking and Violence Protection Act of 2000

The United States Congress adopted the Victims of Trafficking and Violence Protection Act of 2000 to prevent trafficking in humans and in part to further protection to immigrant women and children victimized by domestic violence. Title V of the act was designed to improve battered immigrant women's access to the immigration protections initially established by the Violence Against Women Act of 1994, specifically the cancellation of removal and suspension of deportation provisions of that act. The goal was to protect battered immigrant women and children against deportation and to encourage their cooperation with law enforcement authorities against their abusers. The act provides for financial grants to give them access to services and legal representation. In addition, the act creates a new nonimmigrant visa classification to facilitate the reporting of crimes to law enforcement officials by trafficked, exploited, victimized, and abused aliens who do not have lawful immigration status. The act also grants the attorney general discretion to convert the status of a nonimmigrant to that of a permanent resident based on humanitarian grounds, preservation of the family unit, or other public interest justification. Two sections of the U.S. Code involving criminal provisions are set forth below:

> 18 USCS § 1590. Trafficking with respect to peonage, slavery, involuntary servitude, or forced labor
>
> Whoever knowingly recruits, harbors, transports, provides, or obtains by any means, any person for labor or services in violation of this chapter shall be fined under this title or imprisoned not more than 20 years, or both. If death results from the violation of this section, or if the violation includes kidnapping or an attempt to kidnap, aggravated sexual abuse, or the attempt to commit aggravated sexual abuse, or an attempt to kill, the defendant shall be fined under this title or imprisoned for any term of years or life, or both.

18 USCS §1591(a). Sex trafficking of children or by force, fraud, or coercion

(a) Whoever knowingly—

    (1) in or affecting interstate or foreign commerce, or within the special maritime and territorial jurisdiction of the United States, recruits, entices, harbors, transports, provides, or obtains by any means a person; or

    (2) benefits, financially or by receiving anything of value, from participation in a venture which has engaged in an act described in violation of paragraph (1), knowing that force, fraud, or coercion described in subsection (c)(2) will be used to cause the person to engage in a commercial sex act, or that the person has not attained the age of 18 years and will be caused to engage in a commercial sex act, shall be punished as provided in subsection (b).

STALKING

Although **stalking** behavior in general has been around for many years, sometimes resulting in the tragic deaths of the stalker's victims, it is only recently that specific acts of stalking have been criminalized by state legislation.

Historically, much of the information contained in current journal articles dealing with stalking was culled from news reports and television shows. Unfortunately, this did not provide the hard scientific data or other significant information needed to inform and support the general public about this type of violence. Consequently, it is not clearly understood why individuals engage in stalking or what measures can be taken to prevent this behavior.

The stalking and subsequent death of Rebecca Schaeffer, the co-star of the television series *My Sister Sam* in 1989 provided the impetus for the adoption of the nation's first stalking law. That law was enacted in 1990 in California and at this time all but two states have followed with their own legislation.[11] The remaining two states, Arizona and Maine, utilize their harassment and terrorizing statutes to combat stalking.[12]

Some state statutes are in a continual state of amendment in an effort to provide more protection to victims of stalking with the result that some states prohibit certain acts. For example, in some states but not all states, a suspect may not be allowed to do some or any of the following: be present, approach, pursue or follow, trespass onto property, lay in wait, intimidate, vandalize, conduct surveillance, harass, display a weapon, restrain, or commit bodily injury upon the victim. Because of this varied patchwork of statutes, The National Institute of Justice was tasked by Congress in 1993 to develop a model antistalking law.[13] From this model act, stalking can be defined as shown in the box on the next page.

This definition covers most situations involving the behavior discussed earlier and at the same time is not unduly broad or ambiguous. One of the key elements in the above definition is the course of conduct requirement. This element mandates that the stalker carry out a series of acts to complete the stalk, but it does not require two or more specific acts of stalking.

Stalking

Defined

Stalking is a course of conduct that causes a reasonable person to fear bodily injury or death for himself or herself or members of his or her family.

Elements

1. A course of conduct directed at a person that would cause a reasonable person to fear bodily injury to himself or a member of his or her immediate family or to fear the death of himself or herself or a member of his or her immediate family.
2. Knowledge that the victim or his or her family will be placed in fear of injury or death.
3. Acts inducing fear in the victim of injury to himself or herself or a member of his or her immediate family or induce fear in the specific person of the death of himself or herself or a member of his or her immediate family.

Source: National Institute of Justice, U.S. Department of Justice, *Project to Develop a Model Anti-Stalking Code for States* (1993), 43.

Congress has responded to this growing awareness of the crime of stalking by including a section titled "National Stalker and Domestic Violence Reduction" (28 USC 534 et seq. and 42 USC 14031 et seq.) within the Violent Crime Control and Law Enforcement Act of 1994.[14] This subsection of President Clinton's crime bill authorized federal and state agencies to enter information regarding stalking into the National Crime Information Center and its incorporated criminal history databases. This bill also appropriated $6 million for grants to states and local governmental units to improve processes for entering data regarding stalking and domestic violence into local, state, and national crime information databases.

In September 1996, Congress added a series of laws aimed at criminalizing stalking. Title 18 U.S. Code, Section 2261A, makes it a federal crime to cross state lines with the intent to injure or harass another where such travel places the victim in reasonable fear of death or great bodily injury to himself or herself or a member of that person's immediate family.[15] Title 18 U.S. Code, Section 2262, makes it a federal crime to cross a state line or enter or leave Indian country with the intent to violate a protective order that was issued to prevent stalking.[16]

As we indicated earlier, there is a great deal still to be learned about stalking. However, the inclusion of grant funds in the new crime bill allowing states and local agencies to upgrade processes and procedures for entering data regarding this offense will allow professionals to conduct in-depth studies to deepen their understanding of stalking dynamics.

Extent of Stalking

As with new phenomena, estimates on stalking vary greatly depending on the source used. The National Institute of Justice and the Centers for Disease Control recently published research based upon the results of a nationally representative telephone survey of 8,000 men and 8,000 women.[17] This survey provides one of the first national databases on stalking activity in the United States. The authors used a modified version of the National Model Code in their research. According to this survey, stalking is more common than previously thought. For example, 8 percent of all women and 2 percent of all men surveyed reported being stalked at some time during their life. When asked if they had been stalked within the past year, 1 percent of all women and 0.4 percent of all men responded that they had been stalked within the past twelve months. Using U.S. Census statistical information of the number of men and women in the United States, this translates into an estimated 1,006,970 women and an estimated 370,900 men who were victimized by stalkers on a yearly basis. Although stalking may be committed by either sex, females are the victim 78 percent of the time. Women are also more at risk of being stalked by intimate partners than by strangers (59 percent of women compared with 30 percent of men are stalked by intimates). This study establishes a strong link between stalking and other forms of violence in intimate relationships. Eighty-one percent of all the women stalked were stalked by a current or former intimate. Even with the high rate of stalking and the continuing publicity surrounding these cases, only half of the victims report their stalking to law enforcement. According to this study, the average stalk lasts approximately two years (1.8 years). Almost one-fifth of all the victims move to a new location in an attempt to evade or stop the victimization.

Some states have amended their stalking laws to expressly include stalking via the Internet. For example, under the California Penal Code 646.9, a person commits stalking if he or she "willfully, maliciously, and repeatedly follows or harasses another person and . . . makes a credible threat with the intent to place that person in reasonable fear of his or her safety, or the safety of his or her immediate family." "Credible threat" includes that performed through the use of an electronic communication device, or a threat implied by a pattern of conduct or a combination of verbal, written, or electronically communicated statements. "Electronic communication device" includes telephones, cellular phones, computers, video recorders, fax machines, or pagers. Florida has recently added cyberstalking as an additional means of stalking (Fla. Stat. 784.048 [2003]).

Many other state stalking statutes are broad enough to encompass stalking by e-mail or other electronic devices, including computers. Some state stalking statutes define prohibited conduct to include the communication of threats and harassment without specifying the means of delivery; therefore, they include electronically communicated threats and harassment by those devices.

High-Tech Stalkers

In California, when one woman ended her dating relationship with her boyfriend, the boyfriend went online and posted her name, phone number, and address in chat rooms and stated that she fantasized about being raped. At least six times, men showed up at her door in the middle of the night prepared to rape her to carry out her "rape fantasy." In Colorado, when a wife refused to drop divorce proceedings, her husband used global positioning satellite (GPS) technology to track her every move in her car.

When the first edition of the Principles of Criminal Law was published, states were just passing stalking laws. At that time, little was known of stalkers and their behaviors. As noted by Mary Boland, when most state stalking statutes were enacted, no one could envision how the technology revolution and the information superhighway could be used by stalkers. She points out that technology is opening doors to new ways for stalkers to frighten, harass, surveil, and terrify their victims. She also notes that cell phones and digital cameras are now a significant part of a stalker's "toolkit." Boland contends that the law is scrambling to keep up, and despite obvious stalking behaviors, in some jurisdictions the law does not consider these behaviors stalking.

Boland sees stalking as about control or domination through harassing or frightening conduct that intrudes on the privacy of the victim and is often designed to produce fear in the victim. She notes that the conduct ranges from the annoying to the predatory to the homicidal. Boland states that no single profile of a stalker has emerged from research, but studies have shown that stalkers range from former partners who refuse to accept a breakup and feel rejected or angry, to persons who seek revenge, to those obsessed with the idea that they are "in love" with a person they may not even know or may hardly know, to those who seek some "connection" with a high-profile or celebrity target. According to Boland, without intervention, stalkers will continue their conduct for about two years on average. Boland explains that technology allows a stalker to remain anonymous or at least avoid the risk of being discovered lurking outside the victim's home or work. Stalkers can be anywhere from the next room to another continent and engage in their threats or harassment at any hour of the day or night.[18]

For additional information on stalking, contact the Stalking Resource Center at the National Center for Victims of Crime: www.ncvc.org/src or 202-467-9700 (technical assistance to practitioners; maintains a database of current legislation on stalking; publishes a stalking newsletter). Crime victims can call 1-800-FYI-CALL for assistance.

For additional information on computer, crime visit www.cybercrime.gov (U.S. Department of Justice website with specialized information for law enforcement, lawyers, teachers, media, victims, and other members of the public—including parents).

ASSAULT AND BATTERY

Assault and **battery** are frequently considered the same offense, although they are separate and distinct. A battery consists of the unjustified offensive touching of another. An assault is either an attempted or a threatened battery. The critical difference between assault and battery is that battery requires an actual or constructive touching of the person. In some aggravated assault crimes, the "assaults" actually refer to batteries. For example, the crime of assault, causing serious **bodily injury**, is actually a battery rather than an assault (see the discussion on aggravated assaults).

Battery

The unjustified offensive touching is the actus reus of the crime of battery. In most states, no actual bodily injury is necessary to constitute battery. The MPC, however, requires at least a slight bodily injury to constitute the crime of battery. It is not necessary that the victim actually fear physical harm as the result of the touching. For example, offensively touching the breasts of a woman or kissing her may be a battery.

In many cases, it is unclear whether the touching should be considered offensive. For example, a hug or kiss from an elderly aunt may be offensive to a young child, but it is certainly not criminal. The test generally used is whether a reasonable person would consider the touching offensive.

It is immaterial how the offender causes the offensive touching. For example, it can be firing a weapon or hitting with the fist. There is no requirement to actually touch the person—a constructive touching is sufficient. In one famous case, the accused was convicted of battery when he hit the horse that the victim was riding. In another case, a defendant was convicted of battery when he convinced a six-year-old girl to touch his sexual organs.[19, 20]

Battery

Defined

Elements

Battery has three distinct elements:

1. The willful and unlawful.
2. Use of force or violence.
3. Against the person of another.

DEFENSES TO BATTERY Consent may be a defense to battery as long as the contact is not unlawful. For example, a person may consent to being kissed or fondled, and the consent would be a defense to a battery charge. Participation in sporting events is a common example of consent to battery (the quarterback of a football team cannot claim he was unlawfully struck by the charging linebacker). If, however, the contact is unlawful, consent is no defense. A person cannot legally consent to being shot with a pistol, nor can a minor legally consent to sexual contact.

Assault

There are two standard types of assault: (1) the attempted battery and (2) placing a person in fear of a battery by menacing behavior. In several states, like California, the second type of behavior is not an assault. In those states, assault is only an attempted battery. Since an assault is in many cases an attempted battery, a defendant may be convicted of an assault even though a battery was actually committed.

Case on Point

State v. Fransua

Facts: The defendant and victim were drinking in a bar in Albuquerque and got into an argument. The defendant told the victim that he would shoot him (the victim) if he (the defendant) had a gun. The victim then went to his car, removed a loaded pistol from the car, and returned to the bar. The victim handed the pistol to the defendant. The defendant then shot the victim with the pistol.

Question: Did the actions of the victim in procuring the weapon and inviting the defendant to shoot him constitute a defense to the charge of battery?

Holding: The actions of the victim did not amount to a valid consent to the shooting. The court held that a state makes certain violent acts crimes for at least two reasons: (1) to protect the persons of its citizens and (2) to prevent a breach of the public peace. Even if the victim has so little regard for his person as to request injury, the public has a stronger, overriding interest in preventing and prohibiting acts such as these.

510 P.2d 106 (1973).

AGGRAVATED ASSAULT AND BATTERY

Aggravated assaults or batteries are assaults and batteries with aggravating factors—for example, assault with the intent to commit rape, assault with a motor vehicle, assault on a peace officer, and assault with a dangerous weapon.

In most cases, an assault unaccompanied by a battery is only a misdemeanor. We often describe those as "simple assaults." The aggravated assaults, which are felonies, are often referred to as "**felonious assaults**."

For purposes of aggravated assaults, a dangerous weapon is generally defined as an instrument likely to cause serious bodily injury.

Intent

In most states, the courts have extended battery not only to intentional conduct but to those situations where the defendant has acted in a criminally negligent fashion. Normally, criminal negligence is conduct that the accused knew or should have known would result in harm to others. Several states have limited battery to situations where the accused acted in a willful, wanton, or reckless manner.

Transferred Intent

The doctrine of **transferred intent** is applied to those cases where the offender intends to injure one person and by mistake or accident injures another. The intent to injure is transferred to the actual victim. The intent may still be used to establish an assault on the intended victim.

For example, suppose the defendant shoots at X, intending to kill her. He misses and hits V. Defendant is guilty of assault on X and battery on V. The battery of V is based on the doctrine of transferred attempt.

Assault

Defined

An assault is an attempt to injure the person of another or to frighten without actual injury.

Elements

Assault ("attempted" battery type) has three distinct elements:

1. An unlawful attempt.
2. With apparent **present ability**.
3. To commit an injury to the person of another.

   Assault ("threatened" battery type) has three distinct elements:

1. A threat.
2. With apparent present ability.
3. To commit an injury to the person of another.

Unaware Victim

The defendant, in an attempt to kill the victim, fires a rifle in the general area where the victim is sleeping. The victim is unaware of the shooting. Has an assault occurred?

In most states, an assault occurs in the above factual situation even if the victim is unaware of the attempted battery. Knowledge of the attempt is not an element of assault (attempted battery). For the threat type of assault, however, most states require the victim's awareness of the threat.

MAYHEM

In early law, **mayhem** was the malicious deprivation of a member of the body in order to render a person less able to defend himself. It was later expanded to include the disfigurement of the body. In most states, mayhem is a specific intent crime. Some states also include reckless conduct where there is an obvious indifference to the likelihood of disfigurement or maiming.

Mayhem

When It Is as Plain as the Nose on Your Face

Kim Smith was the manager of a local bar in Idaho Falls, Idaho. Smith claimed that Willie Woods attacked him at one in the morning in the bar because of a previous fight that Woods had lost to Smith. Woods came to the bar looking for Smith, hit him twice, and was holding him down on a bar table when Smith fought back. Woods lost this fight and a thumb-sized piece of his nose when Smith bit off his nose. Smith put his trophy in a rum-filled shot glass and left it on a cooler at the end of the bar.

Smith claimed it was self-defense and he was merely keeping the nose until someone came to the bar and claimed it. However, other witnesses stated Smith was keeping it as a trophy. Local police charged Smith with mayhem, and the victim, Woods, stated that his nose is now in evidence instead of on his face.

Idaho Council on Domestic Violence, "Man Bites Off Piece of Nose in Bar Fight," *Idaho Press Tribune*, February 23, 1998.

Mayhem is an aggravated form of battery. It is considered a serious crime in that it results in the loss of use of a part of the body or disfigures a person. In 1993, a young man returned home and allegedly assaulted his spouse sexually. After the act of intercourse, the wife picked up a knife and cut off her sleeping husband's penis. She then left the house and threw the penis into a field. Both parties were charged with crimes: the husband with sexual battery and the wife with maiming her husband. The Bobbitts' name became a household word, and men and women still debate the validity of the wife's response to the alleged sexual assault.

Mayhem

Defined

Mayhem is unlawfully and maliciously depriving a human being of a member of his or her body, or disabling, disfiguring, or rendering useless a member of the body.

Elements

There are three elements to the crime of mayhem:

1. An unlawful battery.
2. With malicious infliction of or attempt to inflict violent injury.
3. Resulting in depriving a person of a member of his body, or disabling, disfiguring, or rendering it useless, or cutting or disabling the tongue, or putting out an eye, or slitting the nose, ear, or lip.

Several years ago, in California, Terry Singleton kidnapped a young girl, drove to a deserted area, sexually assaulted her, then cut off both her arms and left her for dead. She survived and lived to testify against her assailant, with the result that he was sentenced to a long term in the state prison. Unfortunately, this crime still occurs in our society and can have long-term emotional and physical consequences for the victim.

TERRORISM

Terrorism constitutes the commission of a traditional crime but with the intent to coercing a population or influencing a government course of action through fear or intimidation. Defining what constitutes an act of terrorism is difficult. For example, Schmalleger describes terrorism as a crime against the public. *[Frank Schmalleger, Daniel Hall and John J. Dolatowski,* Criminal Law Today, *4th ed. (Columbus, OH: Pearson), 342].* But aren't all crimes considered as a crime against the public or the state? Others look at intent, that is, the intent to influence a government course of action through fear or intimidation, but as will be noted in the discussion on extortion, such an intent is also the central element of the crime of extortion.

The federal government, rather than defining what constitutes terrorism, merely lists actions that constitute the crime. A close look at the statute indicates that many traditional criminal acts that would not normally be considered as terrorist acts are included with the coverage of the statute.

18 U.S. CODE § 2332B§ 2332B. ACTS OF TERRORISM

(a) Prohibited acts.
   (1) Offenses. Whoever, involving conduct transcending national boundaries and in a circumstance described in subsection (b).
      (A) kills, kidnaps, maims, commits an assault resulting in serious bodily injury, or assaults with a dangerous weapon any person within the United States; or
      (B) creates a substantial risk of serious bodily injury to any other person by destroying or damaging any structure, conveyance, or other real or personal property within the United States or by attempting or conspiring to destroy or damage any structure, conveyance, or other real or personal property within the United States; in violation of the laws of any State, or the United States, shall be punished as prescribed in subsection (c).
   (2) Treatment of threats, attempts and conspiracies. Whoever threatens to commit an offense under paragraph (1), or attempts or conspires to do so, shall be punished under subsection (c).

While there are state statues that attempt to define a terrorist criminal act, the statutes also fail to adequately define how the crime differs from traditional crimes. One key factor that distinguishes a terrorist act from traditional crime is the selection of the victims. In terrorist acts, the identity of the victims is not important to the criminal. For example, in the destruction of an airplane, the identity of the passengers is not important to the terrorist. What is important is the message the terrorist is sending to a political group or nation by destroying the airplane.

HOW WOULD YOU RULE?

The evidence presented at trial indicated that the defendant, a complete stranger, hugged two young girls on first seeing them at an apartment complex. He then picked up the younger girl and carried her to a location just beyond the security gate of the apartment building, a distance of up to seventy feet. Is the evidence sufficient to convict the defendant of false imprisonment?

SEE: PEOPLE V. DOMINGUEZ, 2010 CAL. APP. LEXIS 12 (CAL. APP. 2D DIST. JAN. 11, 2010)

Summary

Kidnapping invades the victim's privacy and takes away his or her liberty. It is essentially an aggravated form of false imprisonment. Kidnapping is the willful and unlawful seizing, confining, and carrying away of another person by either force, threat of force, fraud, or deception. Movement of the victim, also referred to as asportation, is a necessary element of the crime. The movement must be unlawful, meaning without the victim's consent and not pursuant to a valid legal order. A few states have eliminated or reduced the need for substantial movement.

False imprisonment is a lesser included offense to kidnapping that also violates the personal liberty of the victim. Unlike kidnapping, it does not require movement (asportation) of the victim. Where the movement requirement for kidnapping has been eliminated, kidnapping and false imprisonment have essentially merged into the same crime.

Assault and battery are separate and distinct offenses. A battery is the unjustified offensive touching of another. An assault is an attempted or threatened battery. The critical difference between assault and battery is that battery requires an actual touching of the person. The two standard types of assault are (1) attempted battery and (2) placing a person in fear of a battery by menacing behavior. Aggravated assaults or batteries involve factors that make the crime more dangerous. Mayhem means unlawfully and maliciously depriving a human being of a member of his or her body, or disabling, disfiguring, or rendering a member of the body useless.

Additional Assignments

1. Read the selected cases and associated material for Chapter 8 posted at www.mycrimekit.com.
2. Complete the online study guide material for Chapter 8 posted at www.mycrimekit.com.
3. Discussion and thought questions:
   a. Explain the differences between assault and battery.
   b. What are the two types of assaults?
   c. Describe a course of conduct that would meet the definition of stalking.
   d. What is the essential difference between kidnapping and false imprisonment?

Practicum

1. How does your home state classify the various assault and battery crimes?
2. In your home state, can a parent be guilty of kidnapping his or her child? If so, explain under what circumstances.
3. How does your home state define "assaults"?

Notes

1. See *State v. Hauptmann*, 180 A. 809 (1935).
2. In the Hauptmann case, the prosecution charged the defendant with stealing the clothes that the kidnapped baby was wearing. The prosecution also charged the defendant with burglary of the residence of Charles Lindbergh based on the contention that the defendant broke into and entered the residence with the intent to commit a theft therein (of the clothes). Kidnapping was only a minor crime compared to the others. Hauptmann was convicted of burglary, theft, kidnapping, and felony-murder and was later executed. See *State v. Hauptmann*, 180 A. 809 (1935).
3. *People v. Maxwell*, 94 Cal. 3rd 562 (1978).
4. *People v. Stanworth*, 1 Cal. 3rd 601 (1974).
5. *People v. Chessman*, 38 Cal. 2d 166 (1951).
6. *State v. LaFrance*, 569 A.2d 1308 (1990).
7. *State v. Missner*, 435 P.2d 638 (1967).
8. *People v. Weiss*, 276 N.Y. 384, 12 N.E.2d 514 (1938).
9. 18 U.S.C. §201.
10. S. Dill, "Old Crimes in New Times: Human Trafficking and the Modern Justice Systems," 21 *Crim. Just.* 12 (Spring 2006).
11. Public Law 106-386, Sec. 2002(d)(s), 114 Stat. 1,464 (2002).
12. K. L. Attinello, "Anti-Stalking Legislation: A Comparison of Traditional Remedies Available for Victims of Harassment Versus California Penal Code Section 646.9," 24 *Pac. L. J.* 945 (1993).
13. K. S. Morin, "The Phenomenon of Stalking: Do Existing State Statutes Provide Adequate Protection?" 1 *San Diego Just. J.* 123 (1993).
14. U.S. Departments of Commerce, Justice, and State, and the Judiciary and Related Appropriations Act for Fiscal Year 1993, Public Law 103-395, Section 109(b).
15. Public Law 103-322, September 13, 1994.
16. Public Law 104-201, Div. A., Title X, Sec. 1096(a), Sept. 23, 1996, 110 Stat. 2655.
17. Public Law 10104-201, Div. A, Title X, Sec. 1069(b)(2), Sept. 23, 1996, 110 Stat. 2656.
18. P. Tjaden and N. Thoennes, *Stalking in America: Findings from the National Violence Against Women Survey*, U.S. Department of Justice (April 1998).
19. Mary L. Boland, "Taking Aim at the High-Tech Stalker," 20 *Crim. Just.* 40 (Spring 2008).
20. *Beausoleil v. United States*, 107 F.2d 292 (1957).

CHAPTER 9

Robbery, Extortion, and Bribery

Chapter Outline

Robbery

The Elements of Robbery
Model Penal Code (MPC 222.1)
Summary of Robbery

Extortion

The Elements of Extortion
Model Penal Code (MPC 223.4)
Summary of Extortion

Special Problems in Robbery and Extortion

Distinguishing Robbery from Extortion
Distinguishing Extortion from Other Theft Crimes

Bribery

Commercial Bribery

What you should know about robbery, extortion, and bribery. After reading this chapter, you should know

- Why robbery is considered a distinct type of larceny.

- The differences between the various types of robbers.

- The difference between robbery and extortion.

- How extortion is different from other theft crimes.

- What constitutes the crime of bribery.

- What constitutes commercial bribery.

Key Terms

After reading this chapter, you should understand the following key terms:

addict robber: Offender who is addicted to a controlled substance and robs to support a habit.

alcoholic robber: Offender who engages in robberies to support an addiction to alcohol. May commit the crime while intoxicated and as a result get caught more often than the other classes.

blackmail: A form of extortion in which a threat is made to disclose a crime or other social disgrace.

bribery: An agreement to give a public official money or property of any value in exchange for the official to do or refrain from doing something that is against or contrary to an official duty.

extortion: A common law crime that deals with official misconduct. The crime prohibits officials from collecting money from citizens in return for the officials' performing their public duties.

force or fear: The physical act necessary for the crime of robbery.

home-invasion robbery: Any robbery that occurs when an offender enters a dwelling with the intent to commit robbery and does commit robbery of the occupant therein.

opportunist robber: Offender who will commit all types of larceny offenses, including robbery. The most common type of robber.

presence of another: An element of robbery that is broadly interpreted to include any place within the sight, hearing, or even smell of another person.

professional robber: A career criminal who plans and executes robberies very carefully and operates in a group.

robbery: The theft of property from the person or immediate presence of another by the use of force.

Robbery is one of the most serious forms of theft crime in the United States. It is one of four major violent crimes grouped together by the Federal Bureau of Investigation (FBI) for purposes of comparison (the other three are rape, assault, and murder). Some authorities include robbery and extortion in chapters that deal with property crimes,[1] where they are discussed together.[2] We have decided to place robbery and extortion in a separate chapter for several reasons: First and foremost, the scholars who drafted the Model Penal Code (MPC) believed that robbery was of such a distinctive nature that it deserved a separate article. The drafters explained that this crime was being defined as a distinct offense because of the special danger associated with the commission of the crime against the victim. Extortion is included because of its similarity to robbery. In some penal codes, statutory extortion is included in the chapter on robbery.[3] Examining these crimes together allows for better understanding of each individual crime. The second reason that robbery deserves special attention is that it combines both theft and assault into one menacing act. The specter of an armed robber lurking nearby in the darkness is in the mind of every person who walks to a car late at night. Since 1992, the rate of robbery in the United States has declined. Regionally, the Southern states accounted for 34 percent of all the robberies, followed by the Western states with 24 percent, the Northeastern states with 22 percent, and the Midwestern states with 19 percent.[4] Even though robbery is down in numbers, it is still a violent and feared crime. Citizens are afraid to leave their homes to go shopping for fear of being robbed, even in broad daylight. We are turning our homes into individual armed fortresses. Any student of criminology, criminal justice, or sociology needs to understand the dynamics of this violent theft crime on our law enforcement agencies, our cities, and our society.

ROBBERY

Over and over, we read of persons being robbed as they leave work. Stores both large and small have been the target of armed robberies. Daily news reports cover the drama of bank and armored car robberies. It is no wonder that the average citizen is frightened by the prospect of facing a street mugger.

Statistics validate this fear. Fifty-five percent of all robberies take place between 6 p.m. and 6 a.m. One in every three involves injury to the victim. Seventeen percent occur at or near the victim's home, and 10 percent occur in a parking lot or garage.[5] Fewer than 1 percent of the victims suffered no monetary loss. Over 28 percent lost less than $50, and at the other extreme, 18 percent were robbed of $500 or more.[6]

There have been numerous studies and reports concerning the crime of robbery. These range from statistical analysis of the crime to attempts to classify robbery by patterns. One classic typology was constructed by F. H. McClintock and Evelyn Gibson, who categorized robberies in five distinct areas:

Robbery of persons who control money or goods includes robberies of commercial establishments such as jewelry stores, banks, and offices.

Robbery in an open area includes street muggings, purse snatches, and other attacks on streets, in parking lots, and in open garages.

Robbery in private residences normally occurs after the offender has broken into the victim's home.

Robbery by a short-term acquaintance includes robbery that occurs after a chance encounter, such as a meeting at a party or a bar or a brief sexual encounter.

Robbery by a long-term acquaintance is relatively rare but does occur on a regular basis. It may include robbery from someone who has been romantically involved with the offender for a short period.[7]

Robbery

Defined
Robbery is the theft of property from the person or immediate presence of another by use of force or fear.

Elements
The crime of robbery has three distinct elements:

1. Theft of property.
2. From the person or presence of another.
3. By use of force or fear.

Another well-known typology was offered by John Conklin. He classified robberies by identifying the type of offender rather than the location of the robbery. Conklin classified robbers in four major categories:

Professional robbers are career criminals who pursue robbery as a way of life. They plan and execute these robberies very carefully, operating in groups with specific tasks assigned to each member. They may plan and carry out three to four major robberies in any given year.

Opportunist robbers are the most common type. They do not specialize in robbery but will commit all types of larceny offenses, with robbery just one of many. They normally do not plan their crimes but act when the opportunity presents itself.

Addict robbers are addicted to a controlled substance and rob to support their habit. However, most drug abusers are interested in quick and safe crimes and will commit burglary or other theft crimes before turning to robbery. The addict robber does not plan the robbery in the same detail as the professional robber but is more cautious than the opportunist robber.

Alcoholic robbers have little interest in planning their offenses and engage in robberies to support their addiction. Many of them commit the crime while intoxicated, and as a result they are caught more often than the other classes.[8]

These and other scholars have attempted to classify various aspects of the crime of robbery in an effort to explain why or how it occurs. This information assists society in understanding this dangerous and personal crime. Robbery is a personal crime in that the victim comes into contact with the offender for a period sufficient to cause fear or fright. How long the contact must be and the level of fear necessary to constitute robbery is explained in the next section.

The Elements of Robbery

The crime of robbery has three distinct elements:

THEFT OF PROPERTY The theft element of robbery is very similar to the element contained in the discussion of larceny. One of the distinctions between larceny and robbery is that many larceny statutes establish a value that determines whether the theft will be treated as a misdemeanor or felony. This is not the case when dealing with robbery. The value of the item taken is immaterial to establishing the seriousness of the crime. It will be considered robbery if the mugger on the street demands and receives one dollar or five thousand. The offender must intend to keep the property. Thus robbery is a specific intent crime. As with larceny, there must be specific intent to deprive the owner of the property. In robbery, this is fairly easy to prove by looking at the defendant's words or actions or both. The defendant does not have to retain the property for any length of time to establish this intent. For example, if an offender pulls a gun on a citizen, demands money, and then flees the scene with the money, the fact that a police officer arrests the offender one block from the scene does not allow the defendant to claim he did not intend to keep the money. The courts will infer the specific intent to keep the property.

The property may be anything and of any value. An empty wallet is property for purposes of robbery. If a victim is required to part with the wallet, this element is complete. It does not matter that the fair market value of the wallet may be two dollars. The legislatures and courts have taken this position because of the second and third elements of the crime—robbery is a personal crime involving danger to the victim.

FROM THE PERSON OR PRESENCE OF ANOTHER The taking of the property must be from the "person or presence" of another. The term presence is broadly interpreted to include any place within sight or hearing, or even smell. In one famous case, a cow was stolen from a large herd of cattle that was scattered across a mile or more on a plain. The herd was being watched by a cowboy. The court held that the cow was taken from the immediate presence of the cowboy.[9] Someone may commit a burglary, and the victim will not find out until she discovers the property is missing from her home or business. Robbery, however, requires that the property be taken from the person or from that person's immediate presence. The term **presence of another** requires that the offender must take property that he does not own. However, this element of robbery does not mandate that the victim have physical possession of the item that is taken. The property does not have to be attached to the victim by a string, belt, or other item. It is sufficient if the victim has control over the item. For example, if the victim was sitting on a park bench with his package lying next to him and the offender approached him, pulled a gun, and stated, "I'm taking your package, don't try to stop me," a robbery was committed, even though the victim was not holding the package at the time the offense occurred.

Practicum 9.1 points out the breadth of this element of the crime of robbery. If a person has physical control over property and is prevented from stopping the crime because of force or fear created by the actions of the offender, this element has been satisfied. A different problem arises if the victim has control over the property but is unaware that the offender has taken it. This issue is addressed in the final element of the crime.

Practicum 9.1

In Presence of the Victim?

The defendants entered the victim's home, pointed weapons at him, tied him up, and left him in the bathroom. They then ransacked the bedroom and made off with the victim's personal property.

ISSUE: Was the taking from the person or presence of the victim?

The court held the elements of robbery had been satisfied because the victim was prevented from interfering by the weapons employed by the defendants.[10]

BY USE OF FORCE OR FEAR The traditional robbery occurs when the offender confronts the victim, brandishes a weapon of some sort, and demands money. This is clearly an act that places the victim in fear for his or her safety. The second situation arises when the robber physically assaults the victim, and, as a result, the victim surrenders his or her property or is prevented from resisting.

Other situations are not so clear as they relate to this element of the crime. Is a pickpocket guilty of robbery? The offender removes property from the person of another. However, the victim is unaware of the act, and therefore, the final element of robbery—**force or fear**—is missing. Accordingly, a pickpocket is guilty of larceny, not robbery. What if force is added to the situation? Is the mugger who approaches from behind and quickly snatches an old lady's purse from her hand without giving her a chance to resist guilty of robbery? Property is removed from the presence of another and force is used to accomplish the crime. The courts are divided on this issue. Some hold that since the victim was unaware of the act until after it was completed, the final element of robbery is missing and the crime is larceny.[11] The rationale for this position is that the victim was not touched or placed in fear of bodily harm. Other states specifically include this type of act as robbery.[12] The better position is that, since the victim may be harmed as the purse is jerked from her possession, the element of robbery—specific harm to the victim during a taking of property—has been satisfied, and this type of act should fall under the definition of robbery.

Another issue that arises under this element is the question of when the victim must be physically assaulted or placed in fear. Is it robbery if the force or fear occurs before the taking? During the taking? After the taking? The easiest answer is that the victim must be aware of the incident before the taking occurs. If the victim becomes aware of the incident during the taking, the courts are divided. This is the purse-snatcher situation just discussed. A more complex fact pattern arises when the taking occurs and then the victim is prevented from reclaiming the property by force or fear. In this case, should the defendant be charged with two crimes (simple larceny and assault) or one crime (robbery)? Practicums 9.2 and 9.3 on pages 190, 191 address this issue.

Sidebar on Robbery: Is the Gun Loaded? Is It Real?

The U.S. Supreme Court put to rest the question of whether a defendant could be convicted of armed robbery with an unloaded gun in *McLaughlin v. United States*.[13] In that case the defendant was charged with armed robbery, and the question arose as to whether he could be convicted if the gun was unloaded. The court gave three justifications for upholding the conviction: (1) A gun is an inherently dangerous instrument, and the law may presume that it is always dangerous, (2) the display of a gun instills fear in the average citizen, and (3) it may be used as a club.

The second question has been addressed by numerous court decisions. Typically, these robberies involve "toy guns." Toy guns may be made of rubber, plastic, or metal and typically appear to be real weapons. The distinction between toy guns and real weapons is that toy guns cannot propel any harmful projectile toward the victim. Most jurisdictions appear to agree that a defendant who puts the victim in fear by using a toy gun may be convicted of unarmed robbery. The issue arises when the defendant is charged with armed robbery and raises the defense that the weapon was a toy gun.

Some jurisdictions apply an objective standard and require that the defendant be armed with a weapon that, under the circumstances of the crime of robbery, was deadly or dangerous. This approach attempts to determine if the weapon could be used as a club against the victim. This standard ignores the feelings and fear of the victim. The subjective standard relies on the victim's state of mind. If the victim believed the robber was using a gun, that evidence is sufficient for a conviction. In *State v. Felix*, the defendant was convicted of armed robbery when the weapon was a nasal inhaler pressed against the victim's back, simulating a deadly weapon.[14]

The force or fear necessary for the commission of robbery is a complex factual determination. Questions such as where the property is located, when the victim became aware of the crime, and whether physical force or intimidation was used must be answered when addressing this element. As the above discussion indicates, robbery is both a dangerous and a personal crime. This combination of larceny and assault is considered so distinctive that the drafters of the Model Penal Code (MPC) set it apart from other theft crimes by including the offense as a separate article in the code.

Model Penal Code (MPC 222.1)

The drafters of the MPC examined the history of the crime of robbery and pointed out that the average citizen is especially frightened by the violent petty theft that occurs in the streets and alleys of almost every city. The ordinary citizen may become angry at surreptitious larceny, embezzlement, or fraud, but the specter of a street mugger committing a robbery late at night on a deserted street raises terror in the minds of almost everyone.

Focus 9.1

Armed Robbery: Level of Proof

1. Since armed robbery traditionally carries a more severe sentence, should the state be required to prove the weapon was real? In the alternative, should the state be required to prove that the defendant used the "weapon" in a dangerous manner?
2. Which standard should apply, the objective or subjective one? Why? Justify your answer.

Practicum 9.2

Was Robbery Committed?

During a chance meeting, the defendant indicated an interest in purchasing the gun that was in the victim's possession. The defendant asked for the victim's consent to examine the weapon, and after obtaining consent he was given the weapon. He examined the gun and, upon finding it was loaded, pointed it at the victim and told him to run for his life. After the victim left the scene of the crime, the defendant fled with the weapon.

ISSUE: Was a robbery committed?

The court held that the force or fear occurred after the defendant was in possession of the property. Since force was a necessary element of the crime, this was not robbery.[15] This early case overlooks the distinction between possession and custody. The modern view and the MPC would hold that the defendant was guilty of robbery because he used force to prevent the victim from reclaiming property that was under his control or in his immediate presence.

The MPC defines robbery as follows:

A person is guilty of robbery if, in the course of committing a theft, he:

a. inflicts serious bodily injury upon another; or
b. threatens another with or purposely puts him in fear of immediate serious bodily injury; or
c. commits or threatens immediately to commit any felony of the first or second degree.

An act shall be deemed "in the course of committing a theft" if it occurs in an attempt to commit theft or in flight after the attempt or commission.

Practicum 9.3

Robbery?

The victim returned home and discovered that her jewelry was missing from the bedroom. Suspecting that her former boyfriend had taken the property, she drove over to his house and, upon entering, discovered him and his friends admiring her jewelry at the kitchen table. When the victim demanded its return, defendant pulled out a handgun and threatened to kill her unless she left the apartment.

ISSUE: Was a robbery committed?

In this situation, the courts will look at the incident to determine whether the force used against the victim was part of the original transaction. Since the taking was complete, and the defendant had made his getaway, the courts would hold that the defendant could be charged with burglary and assault for threatening to kill her but not with robbery.[16]

Practicum 9.4

Armed Robbery?

The defendant suddenly appeared behind the victim in a parking lot one night. He slipped a bag over her head and punched her. He took her keys, opened the door of her car, and pushed her into the car and onto the passenger side floorboard. At this point the bag came off of her head; the defendant then showed the victim a hatchet and told her to shut up.

ISSUE: Did the defendant commit armed robbery?

The court said it was not armed robbery because he was in complete control of the car before he threatened her with the hatchet. She did not know he had a weapon until he had already taken possession of the car, so the robbery was over. The weapon was used to prevent her escape.[17]

The drafters of the MPC examined the question of whether robbery should continue to be treated as a separate offense since the core of the crime is the combination of theft and the fact or threat of immediate harm. One argument is that the offense could be treated as two separate crimes and punished accordingly. However, this course was not adopted by the drafters of the code for two reasons: First, the combination of some types of assault with theft is properly regarded as a more serious offense and should receive a punishment greater than the sum of the penalties for the two offenses viewed separately. Second, long tradition reinforces the judgment that robbery be considered a separate crime.[18]

One of the special problems addressed by the MPC concerns whether a person should be charged with robbery if he does not succeed in obtaining any of the victim's property. The drafters believed that the danger to the victim was present even if the perpetrator did not complete the act of carrying away any property. Thus, they would punish the crime even if the defendant did not actually obtain any property from the victim. This issue is addressed in the language of the code that states, "If it occurs in an attempt to commit theft . . ." Under the code, once the victim is placed in danger, the penalty attaches even if the robber has picked a victim with no money.

Another issue revolves around the issue of culpability after the robber has obtained the victim's property. The code punishes the perpetrator who, after having obtained the property, threatens or uses force to retain the property, to escape, or to prevent pursuit. Under this definition, a defendant may lawfully obtain property from a victim then commit the crime of robbery by threatening the victim with force when the victim attempts to regain possession or control of the property. A typical fact pattern that would be considered robbery under this definition would involve the perpetrator who fills up her automobile with gas and draws a gun to prevent the service station attendant from receiving any money as payment for the gas or stopping the robber from leaving the station.

The MPC modernizes the common law rules regarding robbery by punishing the act as a crime even if the robber does not obtain anything of value. In addition, the code makes it a crime to lawfully obtain property, then use force or fear to prevent the owner from reclaiming it. At the same time, the code retains the essence of the common law crime—a theft committed by force or fear.

Carjacking is an old crime with a new name. When we speak of carjacking, we refer to the theft of an auto by use of force. It is a form of robbery. The separate crime of carjacking was created because of the escalation of robberies where the object of the robbery was to obtain the victim's automobile has led many states and the federal government to enact statutes to cover carjacking.

HOME INVASION ROBBERY Many states have created an aggravated form of robbery for those robberies that take place in an inhabited dwelling. For example, Florida's statutes define **home-invasion robbery** as "any robbery that occurs when an offender enters a dwelling with the intent to commit robbery and does commit robbery of the occupant therein." Other states have similar legislation.

FLA. STAT. § 812.135§ 812.135. HOME-INVASION ROBBERY

(1) "Home-invasion robbery" means any robbery that occurs when the offender enters a dwelling with the intent to commit a robbery, and does commit a robbery of the occupants therein.

(2) (a) If in the course of committing the home-invasion robbery the person carries a firearm or other deadly weapon, the person commits a felony of

the first degree, punishable by imprisonment for a term of years not exceeding life imprisonment as provided in s. 775.082, s. 775.083, or s. 775.084.

(b) If in the course of committing the home-invasion robbery the person carries a weapon, the person commits a felony of the first degree, punishable as provided in s. 775.082, s. 775.083, or s. 775.084.

(c) If in the course of committing the home-invasion robbery the person carries no firearm, deadly weapon, or other weapon, the person commits a felony of the first degree, punishable as provided in s. 775.082, s. 775.083, or s. 775.084.

In *Bowers v. State,* 679 So. 2d 340, (Fla. Dist. Ct. App. 1st Dist. 1996), a Florida appellate court held that the defendant could not be convicted of two counts of home-invasion robbery based on one entry of a single dwelling that was occupied by two owners. Defendant had assaulted both owners. The court noted that the statute establishing the crime of home-invasion robbery clearly contemplates a single entry into a dwelling and the ensuing robbery of one or more occupants. Accordingly, only one count of home-invasion robbery properly could be charged where there was only one entry into the single dwelling.

The court also held that because the defendant was also convicted of the crime of burglary with assault based on the same entry into the home, that the offense of home-invasion robbery was merged into the burglary charge, which in Florida was a greater offense. The court then vacated the conviction for home-invasion robbery and noted that defendant's conviction for burglary with assault was a first-degree felony punishable by life. § 810.02(2)(a), Fla. Stat. (1995).

Summary of Robbery

Robbery is a distinct crime that combines two other serious offenses—theft and assault. It is considered one of the four major violent crimes in the United States. Every state has a specific statute that punishes conduct meeting the definition of robbery.

The modern view and the MPC have addressed issues regarding whether robbery can be committed if the offender fails to actually obtain anything of value from the victim and whether a robbery is committed when the offender lawfully obtains property but uses force or fear to prevent the owner from reclaiming the property. The majority of states and the code both define these acts as robbery.

EXTORTION

Extortion was a common law crime that dealt with official misconduct. It prohibited officials from collecting money from citizens in return for the officials' performing their public duties. As such it concerned the administration of governmental functions and duties. The common law and early statutory prohibitions of extortion focused on the unlawful collection of any fee by a government official. It did not require proof of threat, force, or duress by the official. The act was complete if the fee was collected under color of the office.[19] This unlawful collection of a fee under color of office was complete in any of the following situations: (1) if a fee was collected when the law did not authorize one; (2) if the fee collected was more than that authorized; and (3) if a fee was authorized, but none was due at the time one was collected. Blackstone defined extortion as an abuse of public justice, which consists in any officer's unlawfully taking, by color of his office, from any man, any money or thing of value that is not due to him, or more than is due or before it is due.[20]

While there are still statutes prohibiting such conduct on both the state and federal levels, the modern crime of extortion focuses more on theft by use of threats of future violence or exposure of secrets. The best known of these modern crimes of extortion is **blackmail**. However, extortion is broader than the specific crime of blackmail. In some situations, it is very close to robbery. That is why, this offense is included in this chapter. Discussion of extortion at this time allows for a comparison with the crime of robbery. The elements of extortion are similar to those of robbery but contain significant differences.

The Elements of Extortion

The crime of extortion consists of three elements:

THEFT OF PROPERTY Like robbery, extortion is a theft crime. However, unlike robbery, extortion requires the offender to obtain something of value. Therefore, if the offender does not receive anything of value, the crime will be attempted extortion.

Extortion

Defined

Extortion is the theft of property from another person by means of threats of future violence, exposure of secrets, or taking or withholding official action.

Elements

The crime of extortion has three elements:

1. Theft of property.
2. From another person.
3. By means of threats of future violence, exposure of secrets, or taking or withholding official action.

FROM THE PERSON OF ANOTHER Extortion is a theft crime; therefore, the property must come from another person. One cannot steal from oneself. This element of the crime is similar to robbery in that the property may be taken from the person or presence of the victim. The victim does not have to own the property for the crime to be complete. If the victim has custody or control over the property and is induced to part with it because of acts of the offender, the crime is complete.

BY MEANS OF THREATS OF FUTURE VIOLENCE, EXPOSURE OF SECRETS, OR TAKING OR WITHHOLDING OFFICIAL ACTION This is the heart of the crime and what distinguishes it from both robbery and other theft crimes. One of the key distinctions between robbery and extortion is that robbery requires a threat of immediate injury while extortion is accomplished by threatening the victim with injury in the future. The majority of states make it a crime to threaten future physical injury in order to obtain another's property. If the defendant were to threaten to kill the victim in the future unless she pays a monthly stipend to the defendant, the crime of extortion has occurred. Some states prohibit threatening economic harm in exchange for money. For example, if the defendant threatens to destroy the victim's business in the future unless the victim pays the defendant money, the courts have held this type of activity to be extortion.[21] Practicum 9.5 examines the issue of threats and economic harm.

Extortion may also occur when the offender threatens to expose a secret held by the victim. This is the classic case of blackmail. The secret may be that the victim has committed a crime sometime in the past or has engaged in other acts that would bring discredit upon himself or his family. It is not a defense to extortion that the victim is in fact guilty of the crime or has in fact committed the acts that are the subject of the threat. The MPC discusses extortion and defines it very broadly.

Model Penal Code (MPC 223.4)

The drafters of the code examined the history of the crime and discussed the scope of the extortion section, which covers threats, rather than force, deception, or stealth. They pointed out that related offenses include blackmail and, in some instances, robbery. The MPC defines extortion as follows:

A person is guilty of theft if he purposely obtains property of another by threatening to:

1. inflict bodily injury on anyone or commit any other criminal offense; or
2. accuse anyone of a criminal offense; or
3. expose any secret tending to subject any person to hatred, contempt, or ridicule, or to impair his credit or business repute; or
4. take or withhold action as an official, or cause an official to take or withhold action; or
5. bring about or continue a strike, boycott, or other collective unofficial action, if the property is not demanded or received for the benefit of the group in whose interest the actor purports to act; or
6. testify or provide information or withhold testimony or information with respect to another's legal claim or defense, or
7. inflict any other harm which would not benefit the actor. It is an affirmative defense to prosecution on paragraphs (2), (3), or (4) that the property

obtained by threat of accusation, exposure, lawsuit, or other invocation of official action was honestly claimed as restitution or indemnification for harm done in the circumstances to which such accusation, exposure, lawsuit or other official action relates, or as compensation for property or lawful services.

Case on Point

People v. Ge Zhang

Ge Zhang was convicted after a jury trial of extortion, second-degree commercial burglary, and shooting at an uninhabited building. On appeal, Zhang contended the evidence was insufficient to support his convictions for attempted extortion and also challenged the sufficiency of the evidence as to several other counts.

Facts: Zhang telephoned Ching Mong Loo, who worked in the City of Industry, to collect a debt Zhang claimed Loo owed to Mu-Chun Chen, a businessman in Taiwan. Loo denied he owed Chen any money and hung up the telephone after Zhang, in a threatening tone, told Loo he was going to collect the money. Several days later, Loo and his coworkers discovered three bullet holes in a glass window of the store where he worked, which faced the street. When the Los Angeles County Sheriff's Department investigated the shooting, Loo told them about Zhang's demand for money. Based on the discovery of bullets inside the building and the configuration of the bullet holes, a deputy testified the shooter had fired from outside the building.

Several days after the shooting, Zhang spoke to Loo on the telephone and insisted once again in a threatening tone that Loo owed Chen money, which Zhang was going to collect. After Zhang demanded that Loo meet him in person, Loo agreed to meet Zhang at a store where Loo believed he would be safer. Zhang arrived at the store to meet Loo; a codefendant accompanied Zhang. The three men went into a conference room. For the next thirty minutes, Zhang and Loo spoke in Chinese while the codefendant, who was seated directly across the table from Loo, stared at Loo with a menacing expression; Loo testified he was scared by the codefendant's demeanor. Zhang gave Loo one week to collect $5,000 in cash. Loo agreed to collect as much as he could.

Court's opinion: Extortion, a specific intent crime, is the obtaining of property from another, with his consent induced by a wrongful use of force or fear. The force or fear induced by a threat must be the operating or controlling cause compelling the victim's consent to surrender the thing to the extortionist. Attempted extortion is an attempt, by means of any threat, to extort money or other property from another. The elements of attempted extortion are (1) a specific intent to commit extortion and (2) a direct, ineffectual act done toward its commission. The jury was properly instructed on both extortion and attempted extortion as a lesser included offense of the crime charged.

2006 Cal. App. LEXIS 8490 (2006).

Practicum 9.5

Threat Sufficient to Constitute Extortion?

A union representative went to the office of the general manager of a cement company and told him that the cement trucks that had just left the plant were sitting down the road, and the drums wouldn't turn until the manager signed a union contract. The manager testified that the reference to the drums indicated that cement would harden in the trucks and the company would have to spend a considerable amount of money repairing the trucks unless the manager signed the agreement.

ISSUE: Was this type of threat extortion?

The court held the union representative had committed extortion by attempting to threaten the general manager with economic injury. The representative's statements were not protected by the First Amendment to the Constitution or by federal labor law. The court pointed out that, under federal labor laws, the union representative had clear authority to put economic pressure on the employer. However, the union representative also had a duty to bargain collectively with the goal of reaching an agreement. The statements were an unequivocal threat rather than a statement that the employees were going to strike.[22]

The threats listed in subsections (1) through (7) do not have to be expressed. They may be implied from the nature of the conversation. For example, the defendant may ask for money in exchange for protection from future injury where she conveys the impression that unless she is paid she will in some manner cause the victim to suffer harm. The lawful union strike or other action based upon a claim of right is specifically excluded under the language at the end of the section. The behavior prohibited by the extortion section is closely analogous to the conduct that is proscribed as criminal coercion under Section 212.5. The MPC defines criminal coercion as follows:

A person is guilty of criminal coercion if, with purpose unlawfully to restrict another's freedom of action to his detriment, he threatens to:

a. commit any criminal offense; or
b. accuse anyone of a criminal offense; or
c. expose any secret tending to subject any person to hatred, contempt, or ridicule, or to impair his credit or business repute; or
d. take or withhold action as an official, or cause an official to take or withhold action.

The criminal coercion section was intended to cover those situations that were not specifically addressed by other sections of the MPC. For example, physical menacing is prohibited by Section 211.1 (assault), and threat of violence by Section 211.3 (terroristic threats), while obtaining property of another by means of threats is covered by Section 222.1 (robbery). The code requires the threat to be for an improper purpose.

This means the defendant must intend to coerce conduct that he has no legal right to require. Thus, threats to require another to pay a lawful debt do not fall under this section. Practicum 9.6 addresses the issue of whether a threat to expose past activities can be considered coercion. As Practicum 9.6 indicates, obtaining sexual favors as a result of threatening to tell others of past sexual activity would be covered under this section.

The MPC prohibits threats of future injury in exchange for money or other items of value. The extortion section is complemented by another section dealing with criminal coercion. Both sections cover a wide spectrum of activities yet establish affirmative defenses for claims of right.

Summary of Extortion

Extortion is a common law crime that was aimed at preventing acts of misconduct by public officials. While these prohibitions still remain, the crime has been broadened to include acts that threaten another with future harm or exposure to hate, contempt, or ridicule. The modern crime of blackmail is a classic example of extortion. The MPC has retained this crime and classifies it as a form of theft.

Extortion and robbery are similar in that both involve taking the property of another. The major distinction between these crimes involves the timing of the threats. In robbery, it is an immediate threat of physical harm, whereas in extortion a threat to commit an injury in the future is required.

Practicum 9.6

Threats to Expose True Facts

During mid-1982, the defendant and the victim, a married woman, carried on a sexual liaison. After September, they remained just friends. In early December, the victim advised the defendant in a telephone conversation that her husband and daughter would be away on vacation at the end of the month. At 1:30 a.m. on December 29, the defendant appeared at her home, desiring to resume the sexual aspects of their relationship. The victim declined, stating she wanted to make her marriage work. The defendant replied that he would tell her husband of the past sexual activities with him and would bring over friends in support of the revelations. The victim then agreed to sexual intercourse with the defendant. The next day, the victim reported the incident to the police.

ISSUE: Is the defendant guilty of criminal coercion?

The court found that the defendant's threat to reveal the victim's past sexual relationship was of such a nature as to expose her to hatred, contempt, or ridicule. In response to the defendant's allegation that the statute was vague, the court found the statute constitutional in that it specifically described the prohibited conduct. The court further held that the fact the acts threatened to be exposed were true was not a defense.[23]

SPECIAL PROBLEMS IN ROBBERY AND EXTORTION

Both robbery and extortion are common law crimes that have a long history in both England and the United States. Each crime on the surface is relatively easy to define and understand. However, certain issues need to be addressed in more detail. This section will examine two of the major issues dealing with these crimes: distinguishing robbery from extortion and distinguishing extortion from other theft crimes.

Distinguishing Robbery from Extortion

Both crimes are based upon the concept of taking the property of another without permission. In addition, as with all theft crimes, there must be a specific intent to permanently deprive the owner of the use and enjoyment of the property. However, there are significant differences between these crimes:

- There is a threat to inflict immediate harm (robbery) rather than a future harm (extortion).
- The nature of the harm threatened is different: In robbery, physical force is used to compel the victim to part with the property. In extortion, the threat may be future physical harm, but it can also include threats to economic interests, accusations of crime, and exposing a personal or family secret.
- Except for certain limited federal bank robbery statutes, robbery must be committed in person, while extortion may be committed over the phone or by mail.
- The victim must comply immediately with the demands in a robbery, while under extortion, the demands require future compliance.

As this discussion indicates, the crimes are similar in many ways, yet they have individual characteristics that make them distinct crimes. Both are crimes to be feared. However, the fear is different in each crime. In robbery, the fear relates to immediate physical injury, while extortion raises fears of future injury or embarrassment. The fear of physical injury relates to the amount of force used during a robbery. Just as extortion may be distinguished from robbery, so may extortion be distinguished from other theft crimes.

Distinguishing Extortion from Other Theft Crimes

The crime of extortion is one of theft based upon threats to the victim. It is distinct from other theft crimes in that the victim is placed in fear of either future physical harm or other economic or personal injury. This element of fear is the major characteristic that distinguishes extortion from other crimes of larceny.

Theft by false pretenses requires that the property be obtained as a result of the offender's misrepresentations or lies. Theft by false pretenses does not involve any threat of physical danger to the victim, nor is the victim threatened with exposure of secrets or ruin of any business enterprise.

Embezzlement involves a person who has possession of an employer's goods. If the defendant had custody of goods, the crime becomes larceny rather than embezzlement. In extortion, the defendant does not have either custody or possession of the property that is the object of the threat. The purpose of the threat is to obtain the property from the victim or from the victim's custody, control, or possession.

Extortion and other theft crimes all involve the wrongful appropriation of another's property with the intent to permanently deprive the victim of that property. The key distinction between extortion and other theft crimes involves the use of threats to obtain the property. Extortion will continue as long as persons have secrets they believe should continue to be hidden and are willing to pay another person not to expose this information to the public view.

BRIBERY

Bribery is the best-known crime involving official corruption. There are two basic types of bribery: First, it is bribery to give a public official money or property of any value in exchange for an agreement by the official to do or refrain from doing something that is against or in contradiction to an official duty. Second, it is bribery for a public official to agree to do something that is in contradiction to his or her duty in exchange for money or property of any value.

The key element in bribery is the agreement, not the act or the failure to act. The crime is completed when the agreement is made, even if the act never takes place. A few states require the acceptance of money or property in addition to the agreement. Unlike with extortion, the thing agreed to by the officer need not be within the scope of the officer's authority or employment. While extortion involves illegal payment for doing the right thing, bribery calls for doing or not doing the wrong thing or something contrary to the powers of the office. Most states have made bribery a felony and make it a crime to offer a bribe or to solicit one.

Under common law, the bribe must have been directed toward a public official. Statutes have expanded the scope of bribery to include agreements to fix sports events, shave points on ball games, and to influence members of a jury or witnesses.

Commercial Bribery

In *Perrin v. United States* (444 U.S. 37 [1979]), the U.S. Supreme Court looked at the federal statute known as the Travel Act, which involves the crime of commercial bribery. The defendant and his codefendants were convicted of violating the Travel Act (18 U.S.C.S. § 1952), and for conspiring to violate the act (18 U.S.C.S. § 371). He and his codefendants were allegedly using the facilities of interstate commerce for the purpose of promoting a commercial bribery scheme through the exploitation of geological data. On appeal, the defendant alleged that bribery under the act only included the bribery of public officials and challenged the constitutionality of the commercial bribery statute. The court affirmed his conviction based on the generic definition of bribery rather than a narrow common law definition because the term encompassed conduct in violation of the state's commercial bribery statutes as well as the federal bribery law. The Court held that Congress intended bribery in violation of the laws of the state in which it was committed, as used in the Travel Act, to encompass conduct in violation of state commercial bribery statutes. Accordingly, the conviction was upheld.

HOW WOULD YOU RULE?

While walking home from school, thirteen-year-old F.R. tried to throw a rock at a stop sign. He missed and hit the defendant's car. The defendant followed F.R. home. Along the way, defendant swore at F.R. and threatened to run him over. He said he had a gun, "so don't play around with me."

When F.R. got home, he tried to get inside his house, but the front door was locked and he had forgotten his key. His parents were at work. The defendant backed his car into F.R.'s driveway, got out of the car, and told F.R. he wanted to talk to his parents. F.R. offered defendant $40 and his cell phone to go away. The defendant said he wanted the car fixed. The defendant pulled up his shirt and showed F.R. a gun, which was tucked in his waistband.

F.R.'s twin brother, A.R., arrived. A.R. got into the house through the garage or a side door. A.R. asked defendant to stay in the garage, but the defendant followed the boys into the house. When A.R. attempted to call his father, the defendant hung up the phone.

The defendant heard a noise and told the boys to go upstairs. The defendant followed the boys into their parents' bedroom, where he saw several jewelry boxes. He told the boys to "get a bag and give me all the goods." The boys got some garbage bags. The defendant pulled out his gun and touched the things he wanted the boys to put in the bags with the barrel of the gun. They went from room to room and took jewelry, sixteen handbags, three television sets, two hand-held video games, a laptop computer, clothing, money, tools, the telephone, and the boys' cell phones. The defendant hit A.R. in the face twice with the handle of the gun. When A.R. dropped a purse, defendant opened the gun's chamber and showed A.R. the bullets.

The defendant told the boys to back his car into the garage. While A.R. backed the car into the garage, defendant put his arm around F.R.'s neck and held the gun up against F.R.'s ribs. The boys loaded the items into the car. F.R. made a note of defendant's license plate number and called the police after defendant left.

The defendant was convicted of two counts of robbery and one count of extortion. As an appellate court justice, would you say there was there sufficient evidence to approve defendant's convictions of those crimes?

PEOPLE V. ROBEY, 2009 CAL. APP. UNPUB. LEXIS 8037, 3-4 (CAL. APP. 6TH DIST. OCT. 7, 2009)

Summary

Both robbery and extortion have their roots in early English common law. They share certain characteristics but differ in the manner and type of threats used to accomplish the crime.

Robbery is a violent crime that strikes fear in the hearts and minds of every person walking on our city streets late at night. Various scholars have attempted to classify robberies and robbers to better understand this offense. Robbery is a personal offense in that the offender confronts the victim and demands money or property. If there is a lapse of time between the taking of the property and the confrontation with the victim, courts may hold it is larceny and assault rather than robbery.

The timing, manner, and characteristics of the threat of immediate physical injury are key in determining whether the crime of robbery has occurred.

Extortion is similar to robbery in that it involves threats to the victim. However, there are several differences between extortion and robbery.

In extortion, the threat is of future harm rather than immediate physical injury. In addition, extortion may involve threats of ruin to personal reputation or business. Extortion is not as violent as robbery, but it is significantly more threatening than the other more traditional theft crimes such as false pretenses or embezzlement.

Additional Assignments

1. Read the selected cases and associated material for Chapter 9 posted at www.mycrimekit.com.
2. Complete the online study guide material for Chapter 9 posted at www.mycrimekit.com.
3. Discussion and thought questions:
   a. Describe the various types of robbers.
   b. Where is the most likely place for a robbery? Why?
   c. Should a simple purse-snatcher be treated the same as an armed robber? Why or why not?
   d. What is the key difference between robbery and extortion?
   e. Should we continue to have a specific crime such as extortion? Should it be considered under the general theft statutes?
   f. If a victim turns in someone who is attempting the crime of extortion, should the victim's secret that is the subject of the threats be made public? What if the victim is a public official? What if the victim is a millionaire?

Practicum

How does your home state classify the crimes of robbery and extortion?

Notes

1. See Sue Titus Reed, *Criminal Law*, 4th ed. (Englewood Cliffs: Prentice Hall, 2003), Chapter 7, which includes both robbery and extortion along with other traditional theft crimes such as larceny, false pretenses, burglary, and others.
2. See Joel Samaha, *Criminal Law*, 6th ed. (St. Paul, MN: West, 1999), Chapter 11, which has a separate subheading titled "Robbery and Extortion."
3. See Iowa Criminal Code, Chapter 711 (1978).
4. U.S. Department of Justice, *Uniform Crime Reports – 1997* (Washington, DC: U.S. Government Printing Office, 1998), 27.
5. See id., Tables 3.47 and 3.48, pp. 283–284.
6. Id., Table 3.8, p. 258.
7. See F. H. McClintock and Evelyn Gibson, *Robbery in London* (London: Macmillan, 1961), 15.
8. John Conklin, *Robbery and the Criminal Justice System* (New York: Lippincott, 1972), 1–80.
9. As reported in B. E. Witkin and Norman L. Epstein, *California Criminal Law*, vol. 2, 2nd ed. (San Francisco: Bancroft-Whitney, 1988), 720.
10. See *State v. Campbell,* 41 Del. 342, 22 A.2d 390 (1941).
11. *People v. Patton*, 76 Ill. 2d 45, 389 N.E.2d 1174 (1979).
12. The statutory definition of robbery has been extended in some states to include robbery by snatching. See Ga. Code Ann. § 26-1901 (1978).
13. *McLaughlin v. United States*, 476 U.S. 16 (1986).

14. *State v. Felix*, 153 Ariz. App. 417, 737 P.2d 393 (1986).
15. See *Thomas v. State*, 91 Ala. 34, 9 So. 81 (1891).
16. See *Mangerich v. State*, 93 Nev. 683, 572, P.2d 542 (1977).
17. *Nelson v. State*, 233 Ga. App. 385; 503 S.E.2d 335; 1998 Ga. App. LEXIS 903.
18. See MPC and Commentaries, Part II, § 222.1, p. 98.
19. See *United States v. Williams*, 621 F.2d 123 (5th Cir. 1980), holding extortion "under color of official right" incorporates the common law extortion, the taking of money by a public official not due him or his office for the performance or nonperformance of an official duty. 621 F.2d at 124.
20. William Blackstone, 4 *Commentaries* 141.
21. *United States v. Compagna*, 146 F.2d 524 (2d Cir 1944).
22. See *People v. Holder*, 119 Ill. App. 3d 366, 456 N.E.2d 628 (1983), cert. denied, 104 S. Ct 3511.
23. See *People v. Downey*, 120 Ill. App. 3d 456, 458 N.E.2d 160 (1983).

Theft and Other Crimes Involving Property

What you should know about theft and other property crimes. After reading this chapter, you should know

- The difference between the theft crimes.

- How to distinguish between embezzlement and larceny.

- Why a person cannot be convicted of both stealing and receiving the same stolen property.

- The differences between the crimes of counterfeiting and forgery.

- That there are two types of forgery crime.

- The issues involved with prosecuting identity theft.

Key Terms

After reading this chapter, you should understand the following key terms:

actual possession: An individual's actual physical possession of property.

asportation: The wrongful taking and carrying away of personal property in the crimes of larceny or kidnapping.

constructive possession: One's interest after willingly giving up temporary physical possession of property but retaining legal ownership.

conversion: Illegal use of someone else's property.

counterfeiting: The false making or materially altering of personal property such as money or paintings, which are not subject to forgery.

criminal simulation: The making of a false document or object that does not have any apparent legal significance.

embezzlement: Taking possession of property of another that has been placed in the thief's possession for safekeeping. Includes the violation of a trust.

false pretenses: Illegally obtaining money or other property from another by fraud or misrepresentation.

fixture: An item that is permanently affixed to the land.

forgery: The false making, materially altering, or uttering a writing that, if genuine, would either have legal efficacy or be the foundation of legal liability.

identity theft: The unauthorized use of another individual's personal identity to fraudulently obtain money, goods, or services, to avoid the payment of debt, or to avoid criminal prosecution.

intangible property: Property that has no intrinsic value but that represents something of value such as a property deed.

larceny: The trespassory or wrongful taking and carrying away (asportation) of the personal property of another with the intent to steal.

larceny by trick: The crime of larceny where the owner of the property is tricked into giving possession of personal property, but not title to the property, to the offender.

personal property: Any property of value that is subject to ownership and is not land or attached to the land (fixtures).

real property: Land and fixtures attached to the land, like houses.

robbery: The unlawful taking of property that is in the immediate possession of another by force or by threat of force. Also larceny from a person by violence or intimidation or by placing the person in fear of bodily injury or harm.

receiving stolen property: The act of receiving property that has been stolen by another person. In some states, it is referred to as "trafficking in stolen goods."

theft: The consolidated crimes of larceny, embezzlement, and false pretenses.

tangible property: Property that has a physical form and can be touched, such as goods, furniture, and jewelry. Movable property that can be taken and carried away.

trespassory taking: Wrongfully taking possession of property.

uttering: The offering, passing or attempted transfer of a forged instrument with the knowledge that the document is false and done with the intent to defraud.

The term **theft** is often used to refer to three different and distinct crimes: larceny, embezzlement, and obtaining property by false pretenses. These crimes will be discussed in this chapter, along with forgery, receiving stolen property, and identity theft. In examining theft crimes, the terms personal property, ownership, custody, control, and possession are frequently used.

Larceny was a common law felony. The origins of the other theft crimes can be traced to English misdemeanor statutes. Under early English common law, protection of personal property was limited to the crime of **robbery**.[1] Later, larceny was developed as a crime to handle the situations where the personal property was taken from the possession of another without consent and nonviolently by stealth. In recent years, there has been a trend among states to consolidate the offenses of larceny, embezzlement, and false pretenses into the crime of theft.

Personal property is generally defined as all property except land and buildings attached to land. Ownership is the highest form of interest that you may have in a piece of property. It confers complete and unlimited discretion over the property. While an owner may temporarily give up possessory rights in the property, he or she still retains legal title, the essence of ownership. Custody is the physical control of an item. It is less than possession. Custody of property confers no right to exercise discretion as to its use or handling. Possession of property occurs when a person has control of the property and discretion in the use and handling of that property. For example, if A owns a truck and leases it to B, A has ownership rights in the truck and B has possessory rights. If B hires C to drive the truck, C has custody of the truck when she is driving it, but not possession.

LARCENY

Larceny is a crime directed against the possession, not ownership, of property. It involves those who take personal property and carry it away from the person who has the right of possession. The actus reus of the crime is the taking and carrying away. The offense is completed when the personal property is taken and carried away. It is not necessary that any damage be done to the property.

The Elements of Larceny

The crime of larceny has five elements:

THE WRONGFUL TAKING   To constitute the offense, the taking must be wrongful, that is, "a **trespassory taking**." If the taking is with permission of the person who has the right of possession, then the crime committed, if any, is not larceny.

The most complicated issue is usually whether there has been a taking of the property. The wrongful taking must be the taking of possession rather than mere custody. As noted earlier, a person has possession when he or she has sufficient control over the property in a generally unrestricted manner. The line between custody and possession is often fuzzy and more technical than practical.

Actual possession of property means that the person is in physical control of the property. **Constructive possession** means that a person with the right of possession is not in actual physical control of the property, and someone else may have actual physical possession of it—that is, the property has been mislaid. Unless the property has been abandoned, it is in the actual or constructive possession of someone.

Generally, a person has mere custody of property when

- The holder has temporary and limited use of the property.
- The holder has received the property from his or her employer for use in the employment environment.
- The property is obtained by fraud.
- The holder is a bailee of the goods, which are packed in containers.[2]

Personal property entrusted to an employee by an employer in the course of employment is still considered in the constructive possession of the employer. This fiction originated in early common law to allow a master to punish his servant for taking the master's property.

Larceny

Defined

Common law larceny is the trespassory taking and carrying away of the personal property of another with the intent to deprive the other of the property permanently.[3]

Elements

The crime of larceny has five elements:

1. The wrongful taking.
2. And carrying away.
3. Of personal property.
4. Of another.
5. With the intent to permanently deprive.

CARRYING AWAY As we noted earlier, one key element of larceny is the carrying away or **asportation** of the property. An old law review article stated that virtually any movement of the property—even a "hair's breadth" away from the place where the defendant took possession of it—is sufficient to constitute the offense.[4] The carrying away must be directed toward carrying the property away from the possession of another. Moving a container in order to open it and steal the contents is not carrying away, but the process of taking possession of the property.

PERSONAL PROPERTY Larceny was designed to protect the possession of personal property. As we have said, the crime is completed when there is asportation, that is, the taking and carrying away. Since land cannot be taken and carried away, the crime of larceny does not protect land from wrongful taking. Items attached to the land (**fixtures**) tend to take on the characteristics of the land (**real property**), and they also are not subject to larceny as long as they are attached to the land. Once they are severed, however, things such as trees, crops, and lumber become personal property and are therefore protected by the larceny laws.

Practicum 10.1

Custody or Possession?

The defendant goes to the local new car dealer. He takes one of the cars for a test drive.

ISSUE: Does he have possession or custody?

The defendant has at least custody, but does he also have possession? Generally, if the defendant test drives the automobile with one of the salespersons in the car, the defendant has only custody and the car dealer retains possession (constructive). Suppose that, after test driving the automobile with the salesperson present, the defendant without permission drives off as soon as the salesperson gets out of the car. In this case, the defendant is guilty of larceny. If, however, the defendant gets permission to test drive the car alone and fails to return the car, he is probably guilty of obtaining the property by false pretenses. In the last example, the taking is nontrespassory and therefore not larcenous.

There is a degree of legal fiction attached to property that is converted from real property to personal property. For example, suppose D went into A's property and took lumber from a building owned by A. When the lumber was a part of the building, it was real property. D changed the nature of the lumber from real property to personal by detaching it. Since D was the first person to possess the property in its new state, he had constructive possession of the property, and taking it and carrying it away was not larceny. If, however, he left the lumber on the property, he would lose constructive possession, and possession would revert to the owner of the property. Accordingly, if D came back later to take it and carry it away, he would be guilty of larceny.

Under common law, a legal fiction also existed regarding the theft of animals and intangible personal property. For example, wild animals were not considered to be in the possession of anyone. Once the animal was killed, however, it became personal property and subject to protection by the law of larceny. Domesticated animals, except for horses and cattle, also were not protected by larceny statutes. The common law rules regarding animals have been changed by statutes, and animals are subject to the larceny laws.

Under common law, **intangible personal property** (e.g., checks, bonds, and notes) was not subject to larceny under the fiction that the document in question was only a piece of paper that evidenced a right to property, not property itself. Today, larceny statutes have included intangible personal property in the definition of personal property.

OF ANOTHER Property that the victim has no right to possess may still be stolen from him or her. For example, marijuana, which is contraband, is subject to the crime of larceny. In addition, a person may be guilty of larceny when she steals personal property from a person who has stolen the property from another. This concept is based on the legal fiction that, when two people's rights to possession of certain property are equal, the first in time prevails. That is, although neither thief had a right to possess the property, the first had a greater right of possession than the second. This concept also demonstrates that the larceny statutes are based more on history than on logic.

WITH THE INTENT TO PERMANENTLY DEPRIVE Larceny is also a specific intent crime in that the taker must know that his or her taking of the property is wrongful. For example, if a person takes personal property with the belief that the property belongs to him, there has been no wrongful taking, that is, no larceny. If a defendant takes property that is for sale, with the intent to pay for it later, she lacks the intent to permanently deprive the possessor of the property's value. In most states this would not be larceny. Taking property that is for sale without paying, however, raises the presumption that the taking was with the intent to steal. Accordingly, it would be up to the defendant to prove that she intended to pay for the property. In addition, if defendant lacked the current ability to pay for it, that fact would also be evidence that she intended to permanently deprive the possessor of the property. If one takes property that is not for sale, with the intent to pay fair market value for it, this is larceny.

New York Penal Code

155.00. larceny: definition of terms

The following definitions are applicable to this title:

1. "Property" means any money, personal property, real property, computer data, computer program, thing in action, evidence of debt, or contract, or any article, substance, or thing of value, including any gas, steam, water, or electricity, which is provided for a charge or compensation . . . [Note: This definition refers only to personal property; larceny does not cover real property.]

155.05. larceny: defined

1. A person steals property and commits larceny when, with the intent to deprive another of property or to appropriate the same to himself or to a third person, he wrongfully takes, obtains, or withholds such property from an owner thereof.
2. Larceny includes a wrongful taking, obtaining, or withholding of another's property, with the intent prescribed in subdivision one of this section, committed in any of the following ways:
   a. By conduct heretofore defined or known as common law larceny by trespassory taking, common law larceny by trick, embezzlement, or obtaining property by false pretenses;
   b. By acquiring lost property . . . without taking reasonable measures to return such property to the owner;
   c. By committing the crime of issuing a bad check . . .;
   d. By false pretenses . . .;
   e. By extortion. . . .

Practicum 10.2

The defendant wants to buy an automobile. He goes to a used car lot, which is closed. The defendant has purchased cars there before and knows that the dealer will give a 10 percent discount for cash. The defendant writes a check for what he thinks the car is worth, minus 10 percent. He slips the check under the door of the office and drives off.

ISSUE: Is the defendant guilty of larceny?

No. If the defendant honestly, even if unreasonably, thinks that he has purchased the car, he is not guilty of larceny.

Lost or mislaid property is subject to special rules regarding whether the finder is guilty of larceny for keeping the property. Mislaid property is property that was intentionally placed where it was found. Lost property is property that was unintentionally placed where it was found. Mislaid property remains under the constructive possession of its owner. Accordingly, when someone picks up mislaid property with the intent to keep it, he has committed the crime of larceny. Lost property is under the constructive possession of the owner, if the property has reasonable clues as to the ownership of the property.

Degrees of Larceny

Under early common law, there were no degrees of larceny. All larcenies were felonies. By statute in most states, larceny has been divided into grand larceny (a felony) and petty larceny (a misdemeanor), depending on the fair market value of the property taken. The dividing line in many states is that property valued at more that $100 is subject to grand larceny. In addition, in many states the nature of the property rather than the fair market value may also be used. For example, in California it is a felony to steal a horse, regardless of value.

EMBEZZLEMENT

The first general **embezzlement** statute was passed in 1799.[5] As we stated earlier, larceny requires a wrongful taking of personal property. To cover those situations in which there was a legal taking of property that was later wrongfully converted to the defendant's use, the crime of embezzlement was created in the eighteenth century. Under common law, embezzlement was only a misdemeanor. Presently, embezzlement is either a felony or a misdemeanor, depending on the value of the property embezzled.

Most of the rules applicable to larceny also apply to embezzlement. The chief difference between the two crimes is that, in the case of embezzlement, the embezzler is entitled to possess the property at the time of the taking, whereas the thief has no right to possess the property in question. Unlike larceny, the essence of the crime of embezzlement is the violation of a trust. Like larceny, embezzlement requires that the defendant know that his or her conduct is wrong when the property is appropriated. Accordingly, a "claim of right" defense (in which the defendant honestly claims a right to the property) applies to both crimes.

Embezzlement

Defined

Embezzlement is a crime against ownership. It consists of the **conversion** of property by someone to whom it has been entrusted. Another definition of embezzlement is the fraudulent conversion of the property of another, where the fraudulent conversion has been made punishable by statute.

Elements

Embezzlement involves at least the two following elements:

1. Defendant was entrusted with the personal property of another in a lawful manner.
2. Defendant fraudulently converted the property.

FALSE PRETENSES

Obtaining property by **false pretenses** is similar to larceny and different from embezzlement in that the taking must be wrongful. However, it is like embezzlement and unlike larceny in that possession must be given to the thief by the person in lawful control of it. When property is obtained by false pretenses, the title to the property is also transferred to the thief. The essence of this crime is that the owner of the property is induced to transfer title to personal property as the result of false pretenses. The false pretense must go to a material fact, not an opinion. The pretense also must be relied on by the victim. The false representation must go to an existing fact, not an opinion: A promise of future conduct is not fraudulent unless, at the time the individual made the promise, she had no intention of carrying out the promised conduct.

 Larceny by trick is similar to obtaining property by false pretenses, except that only possession, not title to the property, is passed to defendant. For example, suppose the defendant intends to steal a car, rents one for one day, and then sells the car. In this case, since the defendant got only possession of the property, not its title, it is larceny by trick.

False Pretenses

Defined

False pretenses is the act of obtaining title to property by making a material false representation with the intent to permanently deprive the owner of possession.

Elements

1. Obtaining title to property.
2. By making a material false representation.
3. With the intent to permanently deprive the owner of possession.

CONSOLIDATION OF THEFT OFFENSES

To eliminate some of the subtle distinctions between the various theft offenses, the trend is to consolidate them into a single theft offense. The statutory theft crime can be a lesser-included offense of aggravated robbery, as we see in *Moseby v. State, 2004 Tex. App. LEXIS 9166 (Tex. App. Houston 14th Dist. Oct. 19 2004)*. In many states, the prosecutor need only allege that the defendant "stole" the property. In other states, he must allege how the defendant stole the property. In the latter states, the prosecutor still faces the problem of alleging the correct type of theft involved. The Texas consolidated theft statute is one of those statutes where the prosecutor need only to allege that the defendant stole the property.

Texas's consolidated theft statute

Tex. Penal Code § 31.03 (2009) § 31.03. Theft

(a) A person commits an offense if he unlawfully appropriates property with intent to deprive the owner of property. (b) Appropriation of property is unlawful if:

   (1) it is without the owner's effective consent;

   (2) the property is stolen and the actor appropriates the property knowing it was stolen by another; or

   (3) property in the custody of any law enforcement agency was explicitly represented by any law enforcement agent to the actor as being stolen and the actor appropriates the property believing it was stolen by another.

Case on Point

Evans v. State

Texas Court of Appeals—San Antonio

Justice Duncan:

The Court noted that in a theft case, consent is not effective if it is induced by coercion. Tex. Penal Code Ann. § 31.01(3)(A). When a public servant is not involved, coercion is statutorily defined as follows: coercion means a threat, however communicated: (A) to commit an offense; (B) to inflict bodily injury in the future on the person threatened or another; (C) to accuse a person of any offense; (D) to expose a person to hatred, contempt, or ridicule; or (E) to harm the credit or business repute of any person. Tex. Penal Code Ann. § 1.07(9)(A)-(E). Each statutory definition of coercion requires that a defendant threaten to take some affirmative act: commit, accuse, inflict, expose, or harm.

   The appellate court reversed the conviction and noted that defendant's clients testified that she claimed bad fortune would befall their loved ones or her if they did not follow her instructions, which invariably included handing over money, merchandise, and gift cards to defendant and some of her relatives. Also, she harassed her clients until some of them had cleared their bank accounts and were far over their heads in loan and credit card debt. However, even when viewed in the light most favorable to the verdict, defendant's actions did not fall within a statutory definition of coercion under *Tex. Penal Code Ann. § 1.07(9)(A)-(E)* because (1) she never communicated to her clients in any manner a threat to commit an offense against them or their loved ones; (2) although she told her clients that their loves ones had cancer, were about to get cancer, or were generally in harm's way, she never told them she was going to inflict cancer or harm upon them; (3) she never accused a person of any offense; and (4) she never threatened to expose her customers or others to hatred, contempt, or ridicule. Because there was no evidence that defendant's actions fell within a statutory definition of coercion, she had to be acquitted of theft by coercion.

2006 Tex. App. LEXIS 11016.

RECEIVING STOLEN PROPERTY

Receiving stolen property is an aggravated form of being an accessory after the fact. The crime of receiving stolen property is directed at protecting against those persons who would benefit from thefts, even though they were not the ones who stole the property. In some states, the crime has been renamed "trafficking in stolen goods." Stolen property is property that was obtained as the result of a theft, burglary, robbery, or any other form of theft crime. The crime of receiving stolen property may be either a misdemeanor or a felony, based on the fair market value of the property in question.

The property must be stolen at the time that it is received. Accordingly, one cannot be guilty of stealing and receiving the same item. The goods must be received for a dishonest purpose. Therefore, a person who receives stolen property for the purpose of returning it to its owner or to proper authorities is not guilty of receiving stolen property.

FORGERY

At early common law, the term cheats was used to describe a group of misdemeanors that involved the use of false documents. Cheats included forgery, uttering forged documents, and counterfeiting. In most cases, the crimes of forgery and uttering forged documents have been incorporated into the single crime of **forgery**.[6]

The term making, when used in connection with forgery, includes any alteration of a document or writing. It also includes the unauthorized completion of a document such as a check or other negotiable instrument. **Uttering** is a term used to describe the acts of giving, offering, cashing, or passing, or attempting to do one of these acts. Material alteration of a document or other writing includes changing a word, a letter, a figure, or a decimal point. The legal effect of the change determines whether the alteration is material. For example, moving a decimal point is a simple alteration that has material significance.

Receiving Stolen Property

Defined

Receiving stolen property consists of a number of different legal concepts in addition to and separate from merely receiving stolen property. It includes receiving, concealing, continuing possession, buying, and transferring of stolen property.

Elements

The crime of receiving stolen property has two elements:

1. Receiving, concealing, possessing, purchasing, or transferring stolen property.
2. With the knowledge that the property is stolen.

Practicum 10.3

Receiving Stolen Property

Three juveniles were caught with stolen property. The juveniles identified the defendant Monasterski as their prospective fence. The FBI, with the permission of the owner, returned the property to the juveniles, who then sold it to the defendant. The FBI then arrested the defendant and charged him with receiving stolen property.

ISSUE: Is the defendant guilty of receiving stolen property?

The court held that, at the time the defendant received the property from the juveniles, it was no longer stolen property. Once the FBI received the property and obtained permission from the owner to set up the sting operation, the property was no longer stolen.[7]

Practicum 10.4

Defense to Receiving Stolen Property?

The defendant was stopped for speeding. The officer observed that the defendant was intoxicated. The officer also noticed a toolbox, a cell phone, and several identification badges bearing the name of someone other than the defendant. He was arrested for receiving stolen property. The defendant said he had used many drugs over the years and had myriad mental disorders so he could not have the intent of receiving stolen property because he did not know it was stolen.

*ISSUE: Can the fact the defendant was intoxicated and has a mental disorder constitute a defense to the charge of * receiving stolen property?*

The appellate court held that evidence of intoxication and mental disorders may be a defense to the crime of receiving stolen property since that crime is a "specific intent crime."[8]

Forgery

Defined

Forgery is falsely making, materially altering, or uttering a writing that, if genuine, would either have legal efficacy or be the foundation of legal liability, with intent to defraud or prejudice the rights of another. Forgery is generally a felony, probably based on the fact that it can do serious damage to our commercial system. Forgery may be committed by several methods:

- By creating a wholly new false document.
- By significantly altering an existing document.
- By endorsing a check or other instrument with a false endorsement.
- By filling in blanks on a check or other instrument when not authorized to do so.

Elements

The elements of the crime of writing, signing, making, or altering an instrument are as follows:

1. Falsely writing, signing, making, or altering an instrument.
2. That, if true, would have legal significance.
3. With the intent to defraud.

The elements of the crime of passing, attempting to pass, uttering, or giving a false instrument are as follows:

1. Passing, attempting to pass, uttering, or giving a false instrument.
2. That, if true, would have legal significance.
3. With the knowledge that the instrument is false.

Practicum 10.5

One federal court defined counterfeiting of money as an attempt to pass as money a reproduction of money that so resembles the real thing that a reasonable unsuspecting person would be fooled.

ISSUE:** *Does this mean that, if the defendant makes a poor quality of phony money that will not fool a reasonable person, it is not counterfeiting?*

The court held that feeding a black-and-white photocopy of a one-dollar bill into a change machine was not counterfeiting, since the reproduction would not fool a reasonable person.[9]

MONEY LAUNDERING

After completing a sale of cocaine, a dealer is left with "dirty money" in his hands. Because the money is evidence of his crime, he is susceptible to detection by law enforcement. More important to the trafficker, his profits could be seized. The trafficker therefore attempts to disguise the "dirty money" as legitimate, or "clean," money. That process is money laundering.[10]

The crime of money laundering is designed to combat the methods used criminals to hide, disguise, and legitimize their ill-gotten gains. Money laundering allows criminals to profit from their crimes; therefore, curbing money laundering eliminates those profits. Money laundering enables criminal organizations to realize profits from committing crime and to fund future criminal activity. Removing the financial incentive to commit crime and the financial ability to commit future crimes plays a major role in crime prevention. The International Monetary Fund estimates that laundered money generates $590 billion to $1.5 trillion per year, which constitutes approximately 2 to 5 percent of the world's gross domestic product.

Before September 11, 2001, international anti-money-laundering efforts were aimed at thwarting the proceeds of drug trafficking. After September 11, 2001, the international community's focus shifted from antidrugs to antiterrorism. Prior to 9/11, the focus was on funds that had been obtained by an illegal source, e.g., the drug trade. Now the focus includes legitimately obtained funds being used for the purpose of financing illegitimate activities, e.g., terrorism.[11]

The money laundering has three steps: placement, layering, and integration. Placement occurs when dirty money first enters the legitimate financial system by being deposited into a financial institution. This step is the most vulnerable to law enforcement detection because it involves the physical disposal of cash. While cash is anonymous—an attractive quality for criminal proceeds—it is bulky and difficult to physically transport. For example, forty-four pounds of cocaine worth $1 million equates to 256 pounds of street cash worth the same amount; the cash weighs more than six times the drugs.[12] In the United States, financial institutions must file currency transaction reports for each transaction that involves more than $10,000. When individuals transport more than $10,000 into or out of the United States, they must file a Report of International Transportation of Currency and Monetary Instruments. In addition, financial institutions in many countries must file a suspicious activity report when they suspect a transaction is illegal.

To counter the reporting requirement, money launderers often engage in "structuring." Structuring occurs when traffickers use many people to make small deposits totaling less than the mandatory reporting amount. They will also use family, friends, or acquaintances who are trusted in the community to conduct business on the launderers' behalf, thereby disguising the source of the illicit funds. Many launderers use a cash-intensive business, such as restaurants, to justify large deposits that exceed reporting requirements.

The layering step occurs when the launderer separates the illicit proceeds from their source through a series of financial transactions. During the layering process, the money-laundering individuals attempt to disguise the crime proceeds and hide the money trail. Layering is the most complex step of the laundry cycle because funds are typically moved

from one account to another. The final step of the money laundering process is integration. During integration, the illicit funds are returned to the legal economy and appear as legitimate business proceeds.

Case on Point

Abuhouran v. Grondolsky, 643 F. Supp. 2d 654 (D.N.J. 2009)

In 1992, the Bank of the Brandywine Valley ("BBV") failed as a result of thefts of more than $9 million engineered by a consortium of individuals including the three Houran brothers, led by Steve Houran. On October 3, 1995, Steve Houran, Tony Houran and five others were named in a 57-count indictment in the United States District Court for the Eastern District of Pennsylvania. Steve Houran was charged with 27 counts, including one count of engaging in a continuing financial crimes enterprise, 18 U.S.C. § 225; 15 counts of bank fraud, in violation of 18 U.S.C. § 1344; four counts of money laundering, in violation of 18 U.S.C. § 1956(a)(1); two counts of interstate transportation of stolen property, in violation of 18 U.S.C. § 2314; one count of conspiracy to commit perjury and to make false statements to a bank, in violation of 18 U.S.C. § 371; one count of conspiracy to commit money laundering and to transport stolen property in interstate commerce, in violation of 18 U.S.C. § 371; two counts of perjury, in violation of 18 U.S.C. § 1623; and a forfeiture claim, based on 18 U.S.C. § 982. On September 10, 1996, when his trial was scheduled to begin, Steve Houran entered a guilty plea to all charges against him.

Defendants were convicted of bank fraud and money laundering, but they asserted that they were actually innocent of money laundering because there were no profits from their fraudulent scheme to constitute proceeds of unlawful activity.

The court held that the defendants' money laundering was established since the funds they obtained from the bank through fraud constituted profits as proceeds of unlawful activity. The payments to maintain the business were not part of the underlying bank fraud which was complete when the bank, in reliance on the prisoners' fraud, turned over the funds to the defendants, and the money laundering was separate and apart from the bank fraud and took place after the bank fraud offense was completed. Further, the money laundering and the bank fraud were not so interrelated that the money laundering payments could not be deemed profits, and the operation of the business at a loss did not constitute an expense of committing the bank fraud and was not intended or necessary to promote commission of the bank fraud For purposes of money laundering, the proceeds of specified unlawful activity are the proceeds from the conduct sufficient to prove one predicate offense. Thus, to establish the proceeds element under the "profits" interpretation, the prosecution needs to show only that a single instance of specified unlawful activity was profitable and gave rise to the money involved in a charged transaction, and the government can select the instances for which the profitability is clearest. The fact finder does not need to consider gains, expenses, and losses attributable to other instances of specified unlawful activity, which goes to the profitability of some entire criminal enterprise. What counts is whether the receipts from the charged unlawful act exceed the costs fairly attributable to it.

COUNTERFEITING

Normally, when we think of **counterfeiting**, we think of phony money. Actually, many things—such as paintings—can be counterfeited. At common law the crime of forgery was limited to actions involving false documents. Counterfeiting was developed as a misdemeanor to cover those frauds involving property other than documents. Any item of personal property that is not subject to forgery is subject to counterfeiting. In limited cases, some property like bank bonds may be either forged or counterfeited. In many states, it is a crime to counterfeit labels that are attached to consumer goods.

The test for determining what constitutes counterfeit obligation is whether fraudulent obligation bears such likeness or resemblance to any genuine obligation securities issued under authority of United States as is calculated to deceive honest, sensible, and unsuspecting person of ordinary observation and care dealing with person supposed to be upright and honest. *United States v. Chodor (1973, CA1 Mass) 479 F2d 661*. For example, a bill was not counterfeit where it consisted of a Xeroxed reproduction of only one side of a federal note, printed on poor paper with bad ink that had pinkish color, since bill was insufficient to be imitation of and to resemble genuine article. *United States v Johnson (1970, CA9 Cal) 434 F2d 827*.

18 U.S. Code § 471. Counterfeiting obligations or securities of United States

> Whoever, with intent to defraud, falsely makes, forges, counterfeits, or alters any obligation or other security of the United States, shall be fined under this title or imprisoned not more than 20 years, or both.

IDENTITY THEFT

Identity theft has become the most important new theft crime of the twenty-first century. It is defined as the unauthorized use of another individual's personal identity to fraudulently obtain money, goods, or services; to avoid the payment of debt; or to avoid criminal prosecution. Although identity theft is a relatively new crime, all states and the federal government now have statutes specifically targeting the crime.

The Federal Trade Commission (FTC) runs a clearinghouse for complaints by identity theft victims. While the FTC has no authority to prosecute criminal cases, it helps victims by providing them with information to help resolve the financial and other problems that can result from such illegal activity. The FTC also refers victim complaints to other appropriate government agencies and private organizations for action.

If someone has used your name to open a credit card account or has used your identifying information—name, social security number, mother's maiden name, or other personal information—to obtain property, you have been the victim of identity theft. Various types of identity theft include the following:

- Taking over an existing credit card account and making unauthorized charges to it. Typically, the thief forestalls discovery of the unauthorized charges by submitting a change of address to the credit card issuer.
- Using computers to read and store information encoded on the magnetic strip of an ATM or credit card when the card is used at a store. The information is then recoded on another card identical to that of the original card.

• Obtaining personal information from an individual over the telephone or Internet connection and then using that information to set up fraudulent accounts with card issuers.

FEDERAL AND STATE RACKETEERING LAWS

It has been speculated that the name and acronym RICO were selected as a reference to the movie *Little Caesar*, which featured a notorious gangster named Rico. The original drafter of the bill, *G. Robert Blakey*, has refused to confirm or deny this rumor.

In 1970, the U.S. Congress passed the Racketeer Influenced and Corrupt Organizations (RICO) Act, Title 18 U.S. Code, Sections 1961–1968. At the time Congress's goal was to eliminate the profits of organized crime and destroy the Mafia. Prior to the 1980s, it was seldom used outside of cases against organized crime. Since then, it is almost never applied to the Mafia. It is currently used more often against individuals, businesses, political protest groups, and terrorist organizations.

The Racketeer Influenced and Corrupt Organizations (RICO) Act

RICO is aimed at repetitive criminality that either affects or utilizes enterprises in accomplishing its unlawful ends. The federal RICO statute, 18 U.S.C. §§ 1961–1968, prohibits any "person" from "investing in," "acquiring" or "conducting the affairs of" an "enterprise" engaged in or affecting interstate and foreign commerce by means of a "pattern" of "racketeering activity," including collection of an unlawful debt, and also prohibits conspiring to accomplish these goals.

In the preamble of the act, Congress stated that it had made the following findings:

(1) organized crime in the United States is a highly sophisticated, diversified, and widespread activity that annually drains billions of dollars from America's economy by unlawful conduct and the illegal use of force, fraud, and corruption;

(2) organized crime derives a major portion of its power through money obtained from such illegal endeavors as syndicated gambling, loan sharking, the theft and fencing of property, the importation and distribution of narcotics and other dangerous drugs, and other forms of social exploitation;

(3) this money and power are increasingly used to infiltrate and corrupt legitimate business and labor unions and to subvert and corrupt our democratic processes;

(4) organized crime activities in the United States weaken the stability of the Nation's economic system, harm innocent investors and competing organizations, interfere with free competition, seriously burden interstate and foreign commerce, threaten the domestic security, and undermine the general welfare of the Nation and its citizens; and

(5) organized crime continues to grow because of defects in the evidence gathering process of the law inhibiting the development of the legally admissible evidence necessary to bring criminal and other sanctions or

remedies to bear on the unlawful activities of those engaged in organized crime and because the sanctions and remedies available to the government are unnecessarily limited in scope and impact.

Congress then stated that the purpose of this Act was to seek the eradication of organized crime in the United States by strengthening the legal tools in the evidence-gathering process, by establishing new penal prohibitions, and by providing enhanced sanctions and new remedies to deal with the unlawful activities of those engaged in organized crime.

State RICO Acts

Most states have enacted RICO acts. Many of these statutes have both criminal and civil applications; however, some of them do not authorize private suits. While many of these statutes bear a structural resemblance to the federal RICO statute, there are significant differences between the state laws and the federal law. A number of the state laws, for example, incorporate many state law violations that are not encompassed by the federal RICO law. Some of the state RICO laws have longer limitation periods than the federal law and also authorize various types of relief to private litigants not available under federal law, such as recovery for personal injury and the right to equitable remedies. State RICO statutes also may have elements that are easier for litigants to establish. Criminal prosecutions under state RICO laws are often not subject to review by one agency, such as the U.S. Department of Justice, but can be commenced by any district attorney. State RICO statutes are also largely unaffected by amendments to the federal act, such as the Private Securities Litigation Reform Act of 1995, which effectively eliminated the use of securities fraud as a predicate act in federal civil RICO litigation. Some states have broadened their RICO laws by incorporating federal predicates in the statute. There are also state statutes that authorize the reward of punitive damages in addition to treble damages.

Case on Point

Defendant Payne contends that his convictions should be overturned on the grounds that there was insufficient evidence to prove that there existed a RICO enterprise. He contended that was a single narcotics conspiracy as alleged in the indictment, rather than a group of individual, independent drug dealers, and that he was a member of the conspiracy (and the enterprise) alleged in the indictment. The indictment alleged that from 1985 through January 2003 a number of associated individuals participated in and conducted the affairs of a **RICO** enterprise by; inter alia, distributing crack and powder cocaine and committing robberies and murders in furtherance of their drug distribution operations. **RICO** defines the term "enterprise" to include "any . . . group of individuals associated in fact." *18 U.S.C. § 1961(4).*

Payne contended that the evidence at trial merely showed a group of "neighborhood friends" who "may have given each other sporadic assistance."

Question: Did the indictment adequately describe a RICO enterprise?

The court held that the existence of a **RICO** enterprise may be proved by evidence of an ongoing organization, formal or informal, and by evidence that the various associates function as a continuing unit. An association-in-fact is oftentimes more readily proven by what it does, rather than by abstract analysis of its structure. The court affirmed the conviction.

See: *United States v. Payne,* 2010 U.S. App. LEXIS 116 (2d Cir. N.Y. Jan. 5, 2010)

Summary

The term theft refers to three distinct crimes: larceny, embezzlement, and obtaining property by false pretenses. Larceny was a common law felony, but the other theft crimes were prohibited by English misdemeanor statutes. At early English common law, protection of personal property was limited to the crime of robbery. Later, the concept of larceny was developed to handle nonviolent takings of personal property without consent. Many states have consolidated the offenses of larceny, embezzlement, and false pretenses into the crime of theft.

Larceny is a crime that concerns possession, not ownership, of property. It penalizes those who take personal property and carry it away from the person who has the right of possession. The taking must be wrongful (a trespassory taking). If the person with the right of possession consents to the taking, then the crime committed, if any, is not larceny.

Embezzlement is a crime against ownership. It is the fraudulent conversion of property by someone to whom it has been entrusted.

Receiving stolen property is an aggravated form of being accessory after the fact. It penalizes those persons who would benefit from the thefts even though they were not the ones who stole the property. In some states, the crime is called trafficking in stolen goods. The crime includes receiving, concealing, continuing possession, buying, and transferring of stolen property.

Forgery means falsely making, materially altering, or uttering a writing that if genuine would have legal significance, intending to defraud or prejudice the rights of another. Forgery is generally a felony.

Identity theft is the unauthorized use of another individual's personal identity to fraudulently obtain money, goods, or services; to avoid the payment of debt; or to avoid criminal prosecution.

Additional Assignments

1. Read the selected cases and associated material for Chapter 10 posted at www.mycrimekit.com.
2. Complete the online study guide material for Chapter 10 posted at www.mycrimekit.com.
3. Discussion and thought questions:
   a. Explain the differences between larceny, embezzlement, and false pretenses.
   b. Explain what is meant by "uttering" a forged document.
   c. Why can't a person be convicted of both stealing and receiving the same property?
   d. Why can't real property be the subject of common law larceny?
   e. What are the advantages of merging the common law crimes into the general theft crime?

Practicum

Conduct research on how your home state handles the crimes of larceny, embezzlement, and forgery as compared with the Model Penal Code.

Notes

1. Jerome Hall, Theft, Law and Society, 2nd ed. (Indianapolis: Bobbs-Merrill, 1952), and Nelson Kidd, "The Jurisprudence of Larceny," 33 Vand. L. Rev. 1101 (1980).
2. A bailee is a person who holds goods for another.
3. *United States v. Waronek*, 582 F.2d 1158 (1989).
4. Jerome Hall, *Theft, Law and Society* (Chicago: American Law Institute, 1952).
5. Hall, supra note 1, at 63.
6. L. M. Hudak and D. C. MacPherson, "Forged, Altered or Fraudulently Obtained Checks," 23 Prac. Law 73 (April 1977).
7. *United States v. Monasterski*, 567 F.2d 677 (1987).
8. People v. Reyes, 52 Cal App. 4th 975; 1997 Cal App. LEXIS 101.
9. *United States v. Martin*, 590 F.2d 104 (1990).
10. Alison S. Bachus, "From Drugs to Terrorism: The Focus Shifts in the International Fight Against Money Laundering After September 11, 2001," 21 Ariz. J. Intil & Comp. Law 835.
11. Id.
12. Id, p. 837.

Crimes against Habitation

Chapter Outline

What you should know about crimes against habitation. After reading this chapter, you should know

- The various types of burglars.

- The elements of the crimes of burglary, criminal trespass, and arson.

- Why burglary poses a special threat to citizens.

- How prosecutors establish the necessary intent to enter and commit a crime in the offense of burglary.

- Why we have a separate statute for criminal trespass.

- The motives or reasons involved in the crime of arson.

- The differences between criminal trespass and burglary.

Key Terms

After reading this chapter, you should understand the following key terms:

arson: The knowing and malicious burning of the property of another. In addition, the burning one's own property for the purpose of collecting insurance money.

burglary: The breaking and entering of a building, locked automobile, boat, or other structure with the intent to commit a felony or a theft.

constructive entry: An entry that occurs when the defendant causes another person or animal to enter a structure in order to commit the crime of burglary.

crime concealment arson: Arson committed in the hope of concealing another crime committed on the property that is burned.

criminal trespass: Criminal acts not amounting to burglary committed in buildings or structures open to the public.

curtilage: Common law term for the area surrounding the home, which includes separate buildings and structures necessary for the landowner to carry on his business.

excitement arson: Arson caused by persons who set fires simply because it excites them.

fence: A person who pays thieves for stolen property and then disposes of it to other parties.

junkie burglars: Burglars who wait for the opportunity to steal and quickly dispose of the stolen property to feed their drug habit.

juvenile burglars: Juvenile criminals who confine themselves to local neighborhoods chosen by chance, often operating at the direction of an older fence or burglar.

known burglars: Burglars, known to the police because of prior arrests, who plan their crimes but are not as adept as professionals.

night-time: That period between thirty minutes past sunset and thirty minutes before sunrise.

occupied structure: Any structure, vehicle, or place adapted for overnight accommodation of persons, or for carrying on business therein, regardless of whether a person is actually present.

professional burglar: A skilled burglar who exhibits the characteristics of a career criminal, planning crimes and concentrating on lucrative targets in order to earn a living by engaging in burglaries.

profit-motivated arson: Burning down a structure to collect on insurance that covers the destruction of the building.

revenge arson: Arson motivated by the desire to get even with another person or entity.

sabotage arson: Arson for purposes of sabotage, most common during labor strikes, prison riots, and other acts of civil disobedience.

sting operation: A police antifencing operation that is conducted to apprehend criminals who are attempting to dispose of stolen property.

vandalism arson: Arson to express hatred toward a particular group or culture.

young burglars: Offenders, usually in their late teens or early twenties, who do not plan as well as the known or professional burglar.

Two of the best-known property crimes at common law were burglary and arson. These were classified as offenses against habitation. The rationale behind classifying these crimes as felonies was to protect the innocent landowner in his home. Since only rabble roamed the countryside at night, the common law crime of burglary sought to protect the property owner from intrusion during the night. Arson was based upon the same principle, that of protecting a landowner from destruction of his home or other real property. A home is more than a mere dwelling where someone resides. It is a person's kingdom.

Modern statutes have enlarged the scope of both burglary and arson. These crimes are still considered serious, especially when the offense is committed upon an inhabited dwelling. Criminal trespass is included in this chapter for purposes of comparison with the other two crimes. It is not as serious as either burglary or arson, but to the victims it can be a very serious intrusion into their privacy. Since all three of these offenses involve real property, they have been grouped together in this chapter for emphasis and clarity. While it is true that burglary is a theft crime, it is a unique offense that deserves special and separate treatment.

BURGLARY

While burglary was a common law crime, it also existed as a punishable offense in ancient societies. Those who entered and carried away the treasures inside the tombs of the pharaohs were harshly punished when caught. This form of plunder existed as early as 100 BC in the Valley of the Kings in Egypt.[1]

While modern burglars do not steal from tombs, they are just as imaginative in that they will steal from any location that offers a profit. Just as there are different types of burglaries—residential, commercial, and industrial—so there is a wide spectrum of burglars. Marilyn Walsh, in her classic work *The Fence*, set forth a continuum of these offenders ranging from the most adept to the least organized.[2] The following is a listing of Walsh's typology of burglars:

Professional burglars are skilled burglars who exhibit the characteristics of a career criminal. These offenders plan their crimes and concentrate on lucrative targets since they earn their living by engaging in burglaries.

Known burglars are not as skilled as the professionals, nor are they as successful, although they may plan their crimes. The title is appropriate since these criminals are known to the police because of prior arrests.

Young burglars are usually offenders in their late teens or early twenties. They do not plan as well as known or professional burglars.

Juvenile burglars are under the age of sixteen. They confine themselves to local neighborhoods, which are chosen by chance. Many times these juvenile burglars will operate at the direction of an older fence or burglar.

Junkie burglars are the least organized offenders. They wait for the opportunity and quickly dispose of the stolen property to feed their habit.

Burglary

Defined

Burglary is entry into the dwelling of another with the intent to commit a crime.

Elements

The crime of burglary has four distinct elements:

1. Entry.
2. Into the dwelling.
3. Of another.
4. With the intent to commit a crime.

Other scholars have conducted research that supports Walsh's basic classification.[3] While descriptions or groupings may differ, it is clear that there are classes of burglars that range from the very good to the inept.

Once a burglar steals property, she must dispose of it. The **fence**, a dealer in stolen property, is a critical link in the crime of burglary as well as other property crimes. The professional fence is a full-time career criminal who buys and sells stolen property. Other fences occasionally buy or sell stolen goods to supplement their full-time law-abiding occupation.

People commit burglary for a variety of reasons, and they dispose of the property in a number of ways. We are all "victims" of the crime of burglary. If we are the actual victims, we feel a sense of outrage and loss. If we are the neighbors of the victims, we wonder if we will be next. All citizens pay higher insurance premiums because of this property crime. Just as there is no simple answer to the crime of burglary, there is no simple outline on the elements of the crime. While at first glance it may seem to be a rather straightforward property crime, the long history of burglary and its evolution has made any discussion of its elements interesting and complex.

The Elements of Burglary

The crime of burglary has four distinct elements:

THE ENTRY Early common law required "breaking and entering" for the crime of burglary to be complete.[4] However, today there is no requirement of damage to or destruction of the property during the entry into it. Opening a door or a window is sufficient. In fact, pulling open a screen door closed by a spring will constitute entry.[5]

Sidebar on Burglary: Sting Operations

A sting operation is a police antifencing operation that is conducted to apprehend criminals who are attempting to dispose of stolen property. The law enforcement agency sets up an undercover operation as a business and passes the word on the street through informers that it will purchase stolen goods. The "customers" are videotaped while delivering the property. After a time, the agency obtains arrest warrants and picks up the "customers" on charges ranging from burglary to receiving stolen property.

One of the most highly publicized sting operations was conducted in Washington, DC, under the cover name of PFF, Inc. (Police-FBI Fencing, Incognito), and resulted in numerous arrests ranging from burglary to murder.[7]

The offender does not have to enter the structure with his entire body for this element to be satisfied. If the defendant puts his hands inside while raising a window, courts will hold that entry has occurred.[6] There is a distinction between any part of the offender's body and any tools he may use to effect entry. The fact that a tool may have intruded into the structure does not establish entry within the meaning of this element, unless the tool was used to complete the crime. One court held that, where the defendant used a drill to bore a hole in the floor, which allowed grain to run out of the hole, there was sufficient entry for burglary when the tip of the drill "entered" the dwelling.[8] However, if the defendant used a drill to bore a hole in a door near the lock for the purpose of unlocking the door, courts have held that this did not satisfy the entry requirement, even though the tip of the drill intruded inside the dwelling during the boring.[9]

The entry must not be authorized or consented to for this element of burglary to be satisfied. If the defendant enters a department store that is open, she has not satisfied this element, since anyone can enter the store. If she commits a theft while inside, she may be guilty of larceny but may not be convicted of burglary. However, if, once in the building, the defendant enters a room or section not open to the general public and commits a theft, she has satisfied this element and may be convicted of burglary.

Sidebar on Burglary: Entry of Public Buildings

If a defendant enters a mall during normal working hours when the stores inside the mall are open to the general public and proceeds to go from one store to the next and commits the crime of theft inside each store, may the defendant be charged with the crime of burglary?

The entry element of burglary requires that the entry into the structure must not be consented to. On the surface, this requirement would preclude a burglary of any building during the time it was open to the public. However, the courts have construed this "consent to enter" invitation issued by department stores, malls, and other public buildings to mean there is consent to enter to carry on lawful business. The courts take the position that the consent to enter these businesses and institutions does not include consent to enter to commit a crime. As we will discuss later in this chapter, in these situations the issue is not the entry requirement but proving whether the defendant had the necessary intent to commit a crime prior to entry into the building.

INTO A DWELLING Under common law, burglary was limited to a person's home or those buildings within the curtilage. A **curtilage** was that area surrounding the home that included separate buildings and structures necessary for the landowner to carry on his business. Thus, a barn, stable, or dairy house were included within the definition of dwelling under common law.[10] Modern statutes have broadened this definition to include any structure. Many states impose an additional penalty if the structure that was burglarized was a dwelling. States vary in the definition of what constitutes a dwelling, but the majority require that it be occupied by persons in order to fall within this classification.

Many businesses are occupied only during the day, but they are now included within the scope of this element; thus, commercial stores may be burglarized. If industrial plants or warehouses are entered with the intent to commit a crime, they are burglarized. So long as there are four walls and a roof, this requirement is satisfied. In addition, the legislatures and courts have modified this requirement to adapt to changing technology. They have held that a motor home is a dwelling for purposes of burglary.[11]

OF ANOTHER The law of burglary was designed to protect the occupant of a building, not necessarily the owner. Thus the crime can be committed at a rental property by the owner if he enters without permission with the intent to commit a crime inside the building. However, one cannot be guilty of burglarizing his own home.[12]

Practicum 11.1

What Constitutes an Occupied Dwelling?

The Kennedys lived in Ulster County, New York. From January to mid-March, they were away from home traveling in Florida. On February 2, the defendants were arrested as they attempted to run from a rear door at the Kennedys' house.

The court found that the temporary absence of owners from their residence while on vacation does not cause the building to lose its character as a dwelling for purposes of the burglary statute.[13]

ISSUE: Does a one-month nonoccupancy of a residence cause a building to lose its character as a dwelling?

Practicum 11.2

Occasional Overnight Stay Constitutes a Dwelling?

The defendant broke into a building with offices. One of the offices had a bed in it that was used for occasional overnight stay.

ISSUE: Does an office with a bed used for occasional overnight stay constitute a dwelling?

The Court said that is does not constitute a dwelling within the definition of burglary. The fact that the bed was rarely used is not legally sufficient to support a finding that the building was a dwelling. The building must usually be occupied and currently used as a dwelling.[14]

Practicum 11.3

Weekend Home?

Mr. and Mrs. Highstreet of New Orleans, Louisiana, owned a weekend home in Waveland, Mississippi. The Highstreets tried to spend the night at their Waveland residence every second or third weekend, on average, but they lived most of the time in New Orleans. On May 19, they were informed by their son that the Waveland house had been broken into. At about 11 a.m. they arrived at the Waveland house and found that it had been entered. They informed the police and were asked to leave the scene, as the police were going to stake out the residence in the hopes of apprehending the thief if he were to return. At approximately 2:30 p.m. on the same day, the police arrested the defendant in the kitchen of the house.

ISSUE: Is a weekend home a dwelling for purposes of burglary?

The court held it was clear that more is required than that a house be built to serve as a place for human habitation in order for it to qualify as a dwelling. When a dweller has moved out with no intention of returning, the place is not a dwelling within the meaning of the statute. To render a building a dwelling, it must be a habitation for humans and usually occupied by some person lodging in it at night. The seasonal or intermittent use of a residence, according to the weight of authority, does not prevent it from becoming a dwelling. The view that occupancy need not be continuous is likewise shared by many courts. It is accepted that a person may simultaneously have two dwellings, either of which would be subject to burglary. Since the Highstreets spent nights at the Waveland house and intended to continue this practice, the residence was a dwelling for purposes of the burglary statute.[15]

Practicum 11.4

When Homeowner Is Absent?

Mrs. Leah Eubanks owned a house in Hinds County, Mississippi. Frances Jamison, attorney for Mrs. Eubanks, testified that on the day of the burglary, October 1, Mrs. Eubanks was in a nursing home. She had entered the nursing home in August. On December 11, Mrs. Eubanks would be ninety years old, and, according to Mrs. Jamison, she was getting senile and unable to care for herself.

Prior to being admitted to the nursing home, Mrs. Eubanks lived in the house and intended to return when her health permitted. According to Mrs. Jamison, the victim had returned to the house several times since her admittance to the nursing home. She went there to visit for an hour or two at a time and got her mail there. The last time anyone had spent the night in Mrs. Eubanks's home was in late July.

ISSUE: When the owner of a house has been placed in a nursing home, does the house still retain the classification as a dwelling?

The court held that the term dwelling house means, as it implies, a place where people dwell or reside. The intention of the residents is the material consideration. All of Mrs. Eubanks's personal possessions had remained in the home. Therefore, the court held that Mrs. Eubanks's house had retained its status as a dwelling during her forced stay in a nursing home.[16]

WITH THE INTENT TO COMMIT A CRIME The defendant must have the intent to commit a crime before she enters the building. Normally, burglary is committed with the intent to commit a theft, but any felony will suffice. Therefore, entry with the intent to commit robbery, rape, or murder will be burglary. The defendant does not have to complete the intended crime, only enter with the necessary intent. If a defendant entered with the intent of killing another but was unable to find the prospective victim, she would be guilty of burglary.[17]

The issue of proving that the defendant had the requisite intent prior to entry has caused problems for some courts. How do you prove what was in the offender's mind prior to entering the structure? One approach holds that an unexplained intrusion into the dwelling of another will support a finding of intent to commit theft.[18] Some statutes establish a prima facie presumption of the necessary intent based upon such unexplained entry.[19] One court held, "Under Michigan law, intent to commit larceny may be inferred from the totality of circumstances disclosed by the testimony. Such intent may be inferred from the nature, time, or place of the defendant's acts before and during the breaking and entering."[20]

As the discussion indicates, burglary is a complex crime that can be very difficult to analyze, depending on the circumstances. The drafters of the Model Penal Code (MPC) attempted to simplify this process when they set forth the modern position on the crime of burglary.

Practicum 11.5

Is a House a Dwelling If the Resident Has Died Prior to Entry?

Virgil Wagner died at home of natural causes. Several days later, his daughter-in-law went to his house and found items missing. The police investigated the case as a burglary and subsequently arrested the defendant. He stated that he noticed no one was home so he broke in to steal items to sell for drug money.

The court said that a dead body is not using a house for a "dwelling," and there is no way that a dead man is going to return or that he has "intent" of any kind. It follows that, at the time of Mr. Ramos's entry, the house was not occupied within the meaning of the burglary statute.[21]

> **ISSUE:** Is the house of a dead man considered a dwelling for burglary?

Model Penal Code (MPC 221.1)

The MPC defines burglary as follows:

1. *Burglary Defined.* A person is guilty of burglary if he enters a building or occupied structure, or separately secured or occupied portion thereof, with the purpose to commit a crime therein, unless the premises are at the time open to the public or the actor is licensed or privileged to enter. It is an affirmative defense to prosecution for burglary that the building or structure was abandoned.

Focus 11.1

Intent to Steal

The general rule of law is that intent to steal cannot be inferred from a single fact of an unlawful entry into a building. Additional circumstances must be considered, such as the following:

- Type of entry—Was it forcible?
- Manner of entry—Was there a breaking or splintering?
- Place of entry—Was it at the rear or side of the building?
- Type of building—Did the building contain items that a thief would be interested in stealing, such as cash, merchandise, or equipment?
- Time of entry—Was it the middle of the night or the middle of the day?
- Conduct of the defendant when interrupted—Did he or she attempt to hide or run?

State v. Barclay, 54 Wis.2d 651, 196 N.W.2d 745 (1971).

3. *Multiple Convictions.*   A person may not be convicted both for burglary and for the offense which it was his purpose to commit after the burglarious entry or for an attempt to commit that offense, unless the additional offense constitutes a felony of the first or second degree.

The code sets forth several specific definitions that are important in understanding its position regarding the crime of burglary. An **occupied structure** is defined as "any structure, vehicle, or place adapted for overnight accommodation of persons, or for carrying on business therein, whether or not a person is actually present."[22] The term **night-time** is defined as "the period between 30 minutes past sunset and 30 minutes before sunrise."[23]

The drafters of the MPC reviewed the history of the crime of burglary and pointed out that the initial development of the offense probably resulted from an effort to protect property owners from existing defects in the common law crime of attempt. Early common law did not punish a person for the crime of attempt unless the actor had embarked on a course of criminal conduct and was very near completion of the crime. This position meant that a perpetrator who was breaking into a dwelling to commit a crime would escape punishment if he was captured during the entry or was unable to complete the intended crime, since he had not progressed far enough down the path toward the ultimate criminal act to be charged with the crime of attempt. The development of the crime of burglary provided a solution to this dilemma and imposed criminal sanctions for the breaking and entry of a dwelling with the intent to commit a crime, regardless of whether the defendant was successful in completing the ultimate objective of the entry.

The MPC retained the crime of burglary but narrowed its coverage. The drafters reviewed the purpose behind maintaining the offense and restructured the scope of the crime. The code accomplishes this by redefining the nature of the entry, the structure or building covered by the offense, and the criminal purpose accompanying the entry. The language in the MPC establishes that entry into premises open to the public cannot be considered burglary even if it can be proved that the defendant had the intent to commit a crime prior to entry. The code narrows the definition of dwelling or structure that is covered by the statute and establishes an affirmative defense for entry into an abandoned building or structure. The rationale behind this narrow definition of dwelling was to restrict the application of the crime of burglary to situations considered the most dangerous to citizens. However, the code does not require the actual presence of people in the dwelling, since this is a matter of chance that the perpetrator has no control over. The final major change in the code deals with the objective of the perpetrator. The defendant must intend to commit a crime that would result in imprisonment. Thus, infractions or minor violations that are punished only by fines are excluded, and if the defendant entered to commit these offenses, the crime of burglary has not occurred.

The MPC retains and redefines the crime of burglary. It narrows the scope of the crime and does away with many of the precedents established by early common law and statutes. By limiting burglary to nonprivileged entry, it highlights the importance of the offense of criminal trespass.

Sidebar on Burglary: Is the Crime of Burglary Really Necessary?

Some scholars would argue that the crime of burglary is a holdover from English common law and that, with the change in the scope of the offense of attempt, there is no need to retain the crime of burglary. Since a defendant may now be charged with attempted theft or any other crime when she enters a building with the intent to commit that crime, some would argue that we no longer need the crime of burglary.

With the crime of theft or robbery, the intrusion into a home or office could be made an aggravating factor that would enhance any punishment. In addition, the crime of attempt covers most situations where the defendant fails to complete the crime once she has entered a home or office. Finally, the argument goes, the crime of criminal trespass could be used for the less serious situations.

The arguments in favor of retaining burglary as a separate offense include the following:

1. There is a long tradition that holds unauthorized entry into a dwelling with the intent to commit a crime should be punished as a separate and distinct offense.
2. A dwelling is considered a person's castle, and the person and his or her family have a right to feel secure in it.
3. The MPC and all states continue to punish some form of burglary.

Many states have specific statutes dealing with **criminal trespass**. The MPC sets forth a comprehensive statute concerning this crime. The code defines criminal trespass as follows:

1. *Buildings and Occupied Structures.* A person commits an offense if, knowing he is not licensed or privileged to do so, he enters or surreptitiously remains in any building or occupied structure, or separately secured or occupied portion thereof. An

offense under this subsection is a misdemeanor if it is committed in a dwelling at night. Otherwise, it is a petty misdemeanor.

2. *Defiant Trespasser.* A person commits an offense if, knowing that he is not licensed or privileged to do so, he enters or remains in any place as to which notice against trespass is given by:

   a. actual communication to the actor; or

   b. posting in a manner prescribed by law or reasonably likely to come to the attention of intruders; or

   c. fencing or other enclosure manifestly designed to exclude intruders. An offense under this subsection constitutes a petty misdemeanor if the offender defies an order to leave personally communicated to him by the owner of the premises or other authorized person. Otherwise, it is a violation.

3. *Defenses.* It is an affirmative defense to prosecution under this section that:

   a. a building or occupied structure involved in an offense under Subsection (i) was abandoned; or

   b. the premises were at the time open to members of the public and the actor complied with all lawful conditions imposed on access to or remaining in the premises; or

   c. the actor reasonably believed that the owner of the premises, or other person empowered to license access thereto, would have licensed him to enter or remain.

The MPC defines criminal trespass in such a manner as to penalize those persons who do not fall within the definition of burglary and yet commit crimes in buildings or structures open to the public. The purpose of all these prohibitions is to afford the property owner or person in possession of property a secure working and living environment.

Summary of Burglary

The crime of burglary has been expanded since its inception in early England. It prohibits entry into a structure with the intent to commit a crime. It is a serious offense because of the potential violence that awaits the inhabitants of any building that is targeted for burglary.

While on the surface it seems to be a relatively simple crime, proving the necessary intent can be difficult. This is especially true if the crime occurs in a building that is open to the public, and the defendant enters at the implied or express request of the owner of the premises. While some state might allow the defendant to be prosecuted for burglary if the intent element can be established, other states use the lesser crime of criminal trespass to prosecute these types of offenders. As long as there are willing fences, there will be a market for goods stolen during burglaries.

The State's witness reported suspicious activity at a pawnshop and informed police that he had seen a man and woman taking items from storage containers behind the pawnshop. Police contacted defendant at a mobile home where she was residing with her husband. They found stolen items from the pawnshop in the residence and the car. For purposes of establishing the offense of burglary, the storage containers fell within the "other building" provision in Idaho Code § 18-1401. Rather than limiting the definition of a building to a structure with walls and a roof; for purposes of the burglary statute, it is the legislative intent that a building is a structure which has a capacity to contain, and is designed for the habitation of man or animals, or the sheltering of property.

Case on Point

State v. Allen, 53 Idaho 603 (Idaho 1933)

The evidence showed that a lumber shed was torn down and hauled away. According to the testimony of the owner, at the shed was empty and contained no personal property, goods, or chattels at the time it was hauled away. A criminal complaint was filed, charging defendants with burglary. The court overturned the judgment below. There was no evidence in the record that either defendant actually entered the shed, either to tear it down or to take anything therefrom, or for any other purpose, or that they entered the shed at all. Thus, the convictions were based only upon circumstantial evidence that tended to show that the shed was torn down and hauled away in the daytime. Such an act could not, in and of itself, constitute the crime of burglary, in the absence of the required proof that there was an entry with intent to commit grand or petit larceny, or any felony, as required by Idaho Code Ann. § 17-3401. Where it was left wholly to conjecture as to the manner in which an entry was effected, if at all, the evidence was insufficient to prove beyond a reasonable doubt that a breaking and entry was committed. To warrant a conviction for burglary, the evidence must be sufficient to prove affirmatively and beyond a reasonable doubt that there was such a breaking and entry as are necessary to constitute burglary, and evidence that leaves it wholly to conjecture as to the manner in which an entry was effected, if at all, is insufficient.

    State v. Tarrant-Folsom, 140 Idaho 556 (Idaho Ct. App. 2004)

ARSON

Arson is an ancient crime that continues to take a human and economic toll on today's society. It may be committed with a single match or a complex electrical or mechanical device. There are numerous reasons or motives behind this crime. Charles McCaghy classified arson in six major categories:

> *Vandalism arson* occurs when the offender is using arson to express hatred toward a particular group or culture. Abandoned properties are the normal target for vandalism arsonists.

> *Profit-motivated arson* occurs when a person burns a structure to collect from an insurance company. This is a form of insurance fraud that is all too common in the United States.

Crime concealment arson is used in the hopes of concealing another crime that was committed on the property that is burned.

Sabotage arson is most common during labor strikes, prison riots, or other civil rebellion.

Revenge arson is motivated by the desire to get even, whether the object is an employer who fired the arsonist or a former spouse.

Excitement arson is committed by a pyromaniac, who sets fires because they excite him. There is no motive other than experiencing the feelings that result from setting a fire and watching a structure burn.[24]

Since the crime of arson may involve emotions, compulsive actions, or simple greed, explaining why people commit this offense is complex and presents overlapping classifications. There is no definitive classification of the reasons for starting fires. Other authorities have classified arson in three basic categories: vandalism, pyromania, and arson for profit or other crime concealment.[25]

Arson vandalism, like other acts of vandalism, is usually the work of juveniles. Fires set by juvenile arsonists do not represent isolated criminal behavior. These adolescent offenders are usually involved in other criminal activity. There are numerous explanations of why juveniles start fires. One source lists the following factors: below-normal intelligence; motor-neural complications, such as brain damage; unstable family relationships; insufficient parental guidance; and adverse peer influence.[26] Fires started by juveniles are crudely set, indicating a lack of sophistication and knowledge of the chemistry of fire on the part of the arsonist. Most fires started by juveniles occur during the day.

Arson

Defined

Arson is the malicious burning of the dwelling or structure of another.

Elements

The crime of arson has four distinct elements:

1. Maliciously.
2. Burning.
3. The dwelling or structure.
4. Of another.

Pyromaniac arsonists are a category in this scheme as well as in McCaghy's. The term *pyromaniac* is controversial in the behavioral sciences and the law. The pyromaniac receives some form of gratification from the act of setting fires and seems to act as a result of some form of compulsion. However, it is difficult both medically and legally to establish a specific pyromaniac personality.

Arsonists for profit or for other crime concealment purposes are simply persons who have committed a crime and are attempting to hide it behind a wall of flames or are using the fire to attempt to collect money from insurance companies. They are the most common form of arsonist and the easiest to understand, since their motive is simply obtaining money or hiding another criminal act.

The riots and arson in Los Angeles that accompanied the Rodney King trial in Simi Valley illustrate the difficulty in explaining why persons start fires. Rodney King was an African American who was brutally beaten by Los Angeles police officers. The beating was videotaped and shown around the world on various television networks. Four of the officers were charged with criminal activities and tried in Simi Valley, a white middle-class suburban community near Los Angeles. The jury acquitted three of the officers of all charges and acquitted the fourth officer of all but one charge, on which they were unable to reach agreement. Roving bands in Los Angeles began to destroy homes, shops, and businesses. This destruction included looting as well as setting 4,591 fires. During television interviews, some of the rioters claimed the looting and arson were to show their disgust with the acquittals, others said it was because they had been discriminated against in the past and were fed up, and still others joined in because everyone else was involved in looting and setting fires. These officers were tried again in federal court for violating Mr. King's federal civil rights. During the second trial, police agencies from around the state of California as well as members of the National Guard prepositioned themselves in the Los Angeles area prior to the verdict in an effort to avoid further arson and looting. These actions proved to be unnecessary because the jury found the officers guilty of violating Mr. King's rights.

Arson may appear to be a relatively simple crime to define, but the reasons for the offense are complex and varied.

The Elements of Arson

The crime of arson consists of four elements:

MALICIOUS ACTION The requirement of malicious action does not require a specific intent to commit arson. Rather, the law will infer the necessary intent if the act was done voluntarily and without excuse or justification and without any claim of right.[27] In an early case, a prisoner set fire to the building in which he was confined with the intent of burning a hole in the wall for the purpose of escaping. The court found him guilty of arson, stating that his action was malicious even though he did not intend that the entire building should be damaged by the fire.[28]

Simple negligence that results in the burning of a structure will not satisfy this element. The defendant must have intended to burn the building of another or commit an act under such circumstances that there is a strong likelihood of such a burning.[29]

BURNING There is no requirement that the burning consume or totally destroy the building. The traditional test is whether "the fiber of the wood or other combustible material is charred."[30]

It is immaterial how the defendant starts the fire—matches, gasoline, focusing the sun's rays through a magnifying glass—if the structure is charred as a result of the defendant's actions, this element of the offense is satisfied.

The element of burning also includes explosions. Many statutes specifically include explosions within the definition of burning for purposes of defining the crime of arson. These statutes apply even if the explosion did not cause a fire.

DWELLING OR STRUCTURE Like the early crime of burglary, the offense of common law arson applied only to a "dwelling." This early restriction was based upon the same rationale that limits burglary to dwellings—the protection of a person's home. The structures protected under arson have been greatly expanded from early common law and now include any dwelling, shop, or structure used by persons for living or conducting business.

OF ANOTHER Since arson is intended to protect the security of another's property, the burning of one's own property does not fall within the definition of the offense. However, as with the crime of burglary, it is possession or occupancy, not title to property, that determines whether the structure falls within the definition of this element. For example, it would not be arson for the owner of a house to burn the house. However, if the owner had rented the property to another person and then set it afire, it would be arson since the owner had title but not legal possession of the property at the time of the fire.

Practicum 11.6

What Constitutes a Structure?

On April 30, at approximately 3:30 p.m., the defendant met a friend while walking through Tulocay Cemetery in Napa, California. After drinking six beers each within a half-hour period, they entered the mausoleum, where the defendant's friend took out a lighter and lit one of the couches. The defendant testified that he set fire to a couch, too. The damage to the mausoleum consisted of burned couches and discoloration and spawling (buckling, cracking, and chipping) of the marble floor and plaster walls of the mausoleum.

The court held that under the statute the structure must be burned or consumed by fire. An item is consumed if it is destroyed or devastated in whole or part by fire. If the item is ravaged or ruined by the fire, it is consumed, though not reduced to ashes. Since the marble, plaster, and concrete were affected by the fire, the jury properly found the defendant guilty of arson.[31]

ISSUE: Was the structure burned within the meaning of the statute?

Practicum 11.7

Is Burning a Carpet Arson?

The defendant threw a brick through the window of a house. She then threw a fire bomb through the broken window, causing the curtains to immediately catch fire. A neighbor who lived across the street saw the fire. He entered through the broken window, threw the curtains on the lawn, and stomped out the burning carpet. The carpet was burned through the pad but the wood was not charred, and the wood around the window was also not charred.

> **ISSUE:** Was the burning of the carpet arson within the meaning of the statute?

The California court said that wall-to-wall carpet is attached to the floor and is customized for a particular place and cut to fit only that area. When "used for the purpose which it was designed" the carpet could become a permanent and integral part of the realty. Since it is part of the structure, burning it is considered arson of a structure.[32]

Practicum 11.8

Is Scorching a Wall Arson?

One of the owners of the London Lodge Motel in New Orleans observed the defendant walking past the motel with a plastic milk container in his hand. Because of prior trouble with the defendant concerning a tenant, the owner called the police. The owner observed the defendant pour a liquid from the container onto the ground next to the motel, take a match, and set the liquid on fire in two different places. Flames rose two to three feet into the air, and the grass against the side of the building burned. The building was a part of the motel where rooms were located and was constructed of brick and wood. The flames made contact with the building and scorched the wall. The owner ran to the fire and began stomping it out. The police arrived and arrested the defendant. The total damage to the building was $10.

> **ISSUE:** Was the scorching of the wall a burning within the meaning of the arson statute?

The court held that, although the damage to the building was slight, it was sufficient to support the conviction. It was foreseeable to the defendant that human life might be endangered. The dissent argued that there was no evidence of setting fire to any structure, and, while the defendant was surely guilty of some offense, it was not arson.[33]

Practicum 11.9

Is Burning a Light Fixture Arson?

At approximately 3:45 a.m., the defendant broke into the administration building at Roosevelt High School in Fresno, California. He then started a fire. There was no direct flame damage to the exterior of the building, and inside, two desktops, computers, telephones, and other items of paper had been burned. Also, a plastic light cover had melted.

The court held that a fixture is personal property affixed to realty so that it becomes an integral part of the structure. Because it is an integral part of the structure, a burning or charring or destruction by fire is all that is required to constitute a conviction of arson.[34]

ISSUE: Is the melting of an attached light fixture arson within the meaning of the statute?

With the invention of insurance, the burning of one's own home or business to collect the proceeds raised issues of whether such acts were prohibited by the traditional arson statutes. State legislatures responded to this phenomenon by amending arson statutes to include this type of conduct. These sections require proof of a specific intent to defraud the insurer.

The crime of arson has evolved from its common law origins to its present statutory form. While there are many similarities between the various statutes that define this crime, each state has enacted arson laws that contain minor differences. The drafters of the MPC attempted to establish a uniform definition for this dangerous property crime.

Model Penal Code (MPC 220.1)

The MPC defines arson as follows:

1. *Arson.* A person is guilty of arson, a felony of the second degree, if he starts a fire or causes an explosion with the purpose of:
   a. destroying a building or occupied structure of another; or
   b. destroying or damaging any property, whether his own or another's, to collect insurance for such loss. It shall be an affirmative defense to prosecution under this paragraph that the actor's conduct did not recklessly endanger any building or occupied structure of another or place any other person in danger of death or bodily injury.
2. *Reckless Burning or Exploding.* A person commits a felony of the third degree if he purposely starts a fire or causes an explosion, whether on his own property or another's, and thereby recklessly:
   a. places another person in danger of death or bodily injury; or
   b. places a building or occupied structure of another in danger of damage or destruction.

3. *Failure to Control or Report Dangerous Fire.* A person who knows that a fire is endangering life or a substantial amount of property of another and fails to take reasonable measures to put out or control the fire, when he can do so without substantial risk to himself, or to give a prompt fire alarm, commits a misdemeanor if:

   a. he knows that he is under an official, contractual, or other legal duty to prevent or combat the fire; or

   b. the fire was started, albeit lawfully, by him or with his assent, or on property in his custody or control.

4. *Definitions.* "Occupied structure" means any structure, vehicle, or place adapted for overnight accommodation of persons, or for carrying on business therein, whether or not a person is actually present. Property is that of another, for purposes of this section, anyone other than the actor who has a possessory or proprietary interest therein. If a building or structure is divided into separately occupied units, any unit not occupied by the actor is an occupied structure of another.

The code established degrees of seriousness by considering both the kind of property destroyed or imperiled and the danger to persons as a result of the act. Under the code, arson as a second-degree felony carries a maximum sentence of ten years. However, if the arson results in serious bodily injury to another person, the crime of aggravated assault may be added if the circumstances of the offense manifest "extreme indifference to the value of human life."[35]

The MPC includes explosions as well as burning within the definition of arson. Under the code, as well as under a majority of state statutes, the crime is complete when the explosion occurs, even if there is no fire or flame after the explosion.

The MPC has established a uniform and rational approach to the crime of arson. It classifies the crime as a serious offense by making it a second-degree felony. In addition, it allows for charging other crimes if, as a result of the act, persons suffer great bodily injury. Like many states, it includes explosions within the definition of arson even if no fire results from the bombing.

Summary of Arson

The crime of arson affects both property and personal rights. It can cause enormous financial loss to the victims of the crime. Unfortunately, arson can also claim lives. The scope of the offense has expanded from its common law origins and now encompasses business property as well as dwellings. The numerous fires started in the Los Angeles riots during 1992 clearly illustrate the fact that arson is still a dangerous offense that authorities must continue to confront.

While the elements of the offense appear relatively simple, the causes or reasons why persons engage in this crime are complex and varied. In many instances, arson is viewed as simply another property crime. However, the possibility of persons dying in the blaze make it a serious felony that requires law enforcement officials to be constantly aware of all aspects of this offense.

Sidebar on Explosions: Arsonist or Killer?

Persons who use bombs create a special kind of terror in the minds of citizens as well as law enforcement officials. These offenders may strike at any time and any place. For example, the world viewed with disgust the explosion of the Pan American flight over Scotland and the bombing of New York City's World Trade Center and Oklahoma City's federal building.

Bombings and arson are not a recent phenomenon in the United States. On December 2, 1956, patrons at the Paramount Theater in Brooklyn, New York, became victims of a bombing by a person known in the press and to the New York Police Department as the Mad Bomber. In a series of more than thirty incidents spanning sixteen years, the Mad Bomber terrorized the residents of New York City. At their wits' end, the police department finally turned to Dr. James A. Brussel, a New York City psychiatrist, for assistance. Dr. Brussel was able to review all the available information on the crimes and set forth a profile that eventually led the police to arrest fifty-three-year-old George Metesky as the Mad Bomber.[36]

And who is not familiar with the Unabomber? On April 3, 1996, the FBI's eighteen-year nationwide search for one of the most notorious bombers of this century ended with the arrest of a former University of California, Berkeley professor, Theodore (Ted) Kaczynski. The Unabomber mailed bombs that targeted universities and airlines starting in 1978. Sixteen bombs, most of them package bombs, were attributed to the Unabomber. In 1995, the Unabomber threatened to send another bomb unless his manifesto was published by some of the nation's leading newspapers. The "manifesto" was published by the *New York Times* and the *Washington Post* based upon a Department of Justice recommendation that they publish it out of a concern for public safety.

Persons who use bombs can attack any building at any time. A serial bomber can turn a calm city into a camp of terror. A bomb has no conscience, and when it explodes, it may injure, maim, or kill men, women, and children. Should there be a separate crime for bombers? Why?

When a person uses a bomb to accomplish a criminal goal, should the offender be charged with murder or arson if, as a result of the explosion, another person dies?

SPECIAL PROBLEMS IN CRIMES AGAINST HABITATION

Burglary and arson at first glance appear to be relatively simple, straightforward crimes that are easy to prosecute. However, there are unique characteristics of each of these offenses that any student in criminal justice should understand.

Apprehension of the Offender

While burglary is primarily a crime against property, offenders do not normally commit a single burglary and then return to a law-abiding lifestyle. Police should check their *modus operandi* files to determine if a pattern can be established from the burglaries that will assist them in apprehending the suspect. One scholar has suggested that law enforcement agencies should concentrate more on the criminal than on the crime.[37] Because many burglars commit more than one offense, the primary target of any burglary division should be the serial burglar. This approach requires an effective *modus operandi* file and a case management system that allows for prioritizing cases.

This authority suggests that effective case management involves recognizing that burglaries are mobile and concentrates on motive rather than geographic area.[38] While motive (why the offender commits the crime) is important, law enforcement agencies must not forget to check all leads, including the traditional "pin map," that may assist in isolating the target areas of the offender. Police should ensure that the narcotics division is informed of the status of burglaries, since many of these offenses are committed to pay for drugs.

Burglary investigation involves close coordination within the police department. It ties together the patrol officer who responds to the first call by the victim, the detective in the burglary division, and other officers within the department. Arson, on the other hand, may require assistance from personnel outside the police department.

Arson and Interagency Cooperation

Unlike burglary, arson is investigated by numerous agencies that may have overlapping jurisdiction. State fire marshals, local police, and fire departments may all be involved in investigating a single fire. Arson is a simple crime to define but a complex offense to establish. Traditionally, except for major cities that have their own arson investigation personnel, lack of training for the frontline law enforcement officers may hinder a criminal prosecution of an arson offense.

Although arson is a crime against habitation, many police departments tend to give it a low priority, believing that the fire department should be responsible for investigation of this offense. The problem with this approach is that fire department personnel are trained to either prevent fires or put them out, not to investigate why or how they were started and who started them. Rural areas and small cities rely on the state fire marshal's office to conduct arson investigation. These state offices are normally understaffed and unable to conduct a thorough investigation of every suspicious fire in the state. Some jurisdictions, like New York City, have experienced difficulties in the past between the police and fire departments regarding who should investigate arson crimes. New York City has established a joint task force made up of both police and fire marshals. This appears to be the trend around the country to better coordinate the investigation of this crime that strikes at both the pocketbook and the heart.

Summary

Burglary and arson are two of the best-known common law crimes. Both have been modified by legislative change to meet new social conditions. Both crimes endanger the inhabitants of property. While both crimes have relatively simple elements, each possesses its own unique problems in the criminal justice system. Burglars have been classified by Walsh's typology into five classifications: professional, known, young, juvenile, and junkie burglars. To combat the rising rate of burglaries, police engage in sophisticated sting operations where they pose as criminals interested in purchasing stolen property. Once the burglar has sold the officers the property, they arrest the offender, either immediately or at the end of the sting operation.

Each element of the crime of burglary offers complex issues that must be examined in light of all the facts. For example, it is impossible to see into an offender's mind and determine exactly what his intent was at the time of entry. Prosecutors and law enforcement personnel rely on the facts surrounding the entry to determine if the defendant had the necessary intent to commit a crime at the time of entering the structure.

Arson is a highly visible crime that continues to cause economic and personal loss. The motives surrounding the commission of this crime are as varied as the types of fires that may be started by the offender. McCaghy classified arsonists into six categories: vandalism, profit-motivated, crime concealment, sabotage, revenge, and excitement arsons. Other authorities have classified motives for arson into three broad areas: vandalism, pyromania, and arson for profit or other crime concealment.

Arson does not require a specific intent to start a fire with the purpose of burning a structure. The law will infer the necessary intent if the act of starting the fire was done without excuse or justification. It is not necessary that a fire burn the building to the ground; a simple charring of the structure is sufficient for the crime of arson. Each state has its own definition of the crime, however, and there are distinctions and differences among the states. The MPC has set forth standard definitions in an attempt to bring some uniformity to this area of law.

Both burglary and arson will continue to be high-profile crimes. Law enforcement will be pressured to arrest these offenders. As long as there are criminals on the streets, burglary and arson will continue to occur since both are easy crimes to commit.

Additional Assignments

1. Read the selected cases and associated material for Chapter 11 posted at www.mycrimekit.com.
2. Complete the online study guide material for Chapter 11 posted at www.mycrimekit.com.
3. Discussion and thought questions:
   a. What is the most common reason that criminals commit burglary?
   b. What should citizens do to protect their property from being the target for burglary?
   c. Should we concentrate on increasing patrols to prevent burglaries? Justify your answer.
   d. Should criminal trespass be a separate crime from burglary? Why or why not?
   e. Understanding that there are multiple reasons why individuals commit arson, what steps can we take to prevent it?
   f. Arson is considered as a serious crime, but many police departments give it a low priority. What steps can be taken to improve this situation?
   g. Should convicted arsonists be required to undergo counseling? Why or why not?

Practicum

Conduct research and report on how your state handles crimes against habitation. Also include what types of buildings may be subject to the crime of burglary.

Notes

1. C. W. Ceram, *Gods, Graves and Scholars: The Story of Archeology*, 2nd ed. (New York: Knopf, 1967), 159.
2. Marilyn Walsh, *The Fence* (Westport, CT: Greenwood, 1977).
3. See Harry A. Scarr, *Patterns of Burglary* (Washington, DC: Government Printing Office, 1973) and Carl Pope, "Patterns in Burglary: An Empirical Examination of Offense and Offender Characteristics," 8 J. Crim. Just. 39 (1980).
4. *State v. Boon*, 35 N.C. 244, 246 (1852).
5. *United States v. Evans*, 415 F.2d 340, 342 (5th Cir. 1969).
6. *State v. Allen*, 125 Ariz. 158, 608 P.2d 95, 96 (App. 1980).
7. "The Sting," *Newsweek*, March 15, 1976, 35.
8. *Walker v. State*, 63 Ala. 49 (1879).
9. *The King v. Hughes*, 1 LEACH 406, 168 Eng. Rep. 305 (1785).
10. *Devoe v. Commonwealth*, 44 Mass. 316, 325 (1841).
11. See *United States v. Lavender*, 602 F.2d 639 (4th Cir. 1979), which held a Winnebago mobile home in which a family lived while touring the United States was a dwelling within the meaning of a burglary statute.
12. *People v. Gouze*, 15 Cal. 3d 709, 524 P.2d 1365 (1975).
13. See *People v. Lewoc*, 101 A.D.2d 927, 475 N.Y.S. 2d 933 (1984).
14. *People v. Quattlebaum*, 91 N.Y. 2d 744; 698 N.E. 2d 421; 1998 N.Y. LEXIS 1428.
15. See *Gillum v. State*, 468 So.2d 856 (1985).
16. See *Course v. State*, 469 So.2d 80 (1985).
17. *Ziegler v. State*, 610 P.2d 251, 252 (Okla. Crim. 1980).
18. *State v. Hopkins*, 11 Utah 2d 363, 359 P.2d 486 (1961).
19. *State v. Bishop*, 90 Washington 2d 185, 580 P.2d 259 (En banc 1978).
20. *Goldman v. Anderson*, 625 F.2d 135, 137 (6th Cir. 1980).
21. *People v. Ramos*, 52 Cal. App. 4th 300; 1997 Cal. App. LEXIS 52.
22. MPC § 221.0(1).
23. MPC § 221.0(2).
24. Charles McCaghy, *Crime in American Society* (New York: Macmillan, 1980).
25. International Association of Chiefs of Police, Training Key #300, "The Arsonist," pp. 67–71.
26. *Id.*, p. 68.
27. *State v. Scott*, 118 Ariz. 383, 576 P.2d 1383, 1385 (App. 1978).
28. *Lockett v. State*, 63 Ala. 5 (1879).
29. Rollin M. Perkins and Ronald N. Boyce, *Criminal Law* (Mineola, NY: Foundation Press, 1982), 277.
30. *People v. Losinger*, 331 Mich. 490, 502, 50 N.W.2d 137, 143 (1951).
31. See *People v. Mentzer*, 163 Cal. 3d 482 (1985).
32. *People v. Ondrea M. Lee*, 24 Cal. App. 4th 1773; 1994 Cal. App. LEXIS 487.
33. See *State v. Williams*, 457 So.2d 610 (1984).
34. In re *Jessed*, 221 Cal. App. 3d 161; 1990 Cal. App. LEXIS 614.
35. MPC § 220.1, p. 10.
36. For an excellent discussion of this case and the use of behavioral sciences in the apprehension of bombers, see Joseph J. Chrisholm and David Icove, "Targeting Bombers," *Police Chief* 42 (October 1991).
37. Paul Goodwin, "A Modern Approach to Burglary Investigation," *Law and Order* (October 1989): 89.
38. *Id.* at 90.

Crimes against Public Morals

Chapter Outline

What you should know about crimes about public morals. After reading this chapter, you should know

- The essential elements necessary to constitute prostitution.
- The issues involved with victimless crimes.
- The test used to determine if an item is obscene.
- The elements of extortion, bribery, and blackmail.

- The differences between bribery and extortion.
- The problems involved in enforcing our gambling statutes.
- The federal gambling statutes.

Key Terms

After reading this chapter, you should understand the following key terms:

bigamy: The crime of marrying one person while still legally married to another person.

devadasis: Prostitutes in India who enjoyed a high social standing.

gambling: Games of chance.

incest: Unlawful sexual intercourse with a relative through blood or marriage.

lascivious: That which is obscene or lewd or tends to cause lust.

lewdness: Obscene behavior.

Miller test: A three-pronged test for determining if material is obscenity, developed in the *Miller v. California* case.

obscenity: Sexually explicit material that falls outside the protection of the First Amendment, and therefore, may be punished under a criminal statute.

pandering: The act of soliciting a person to perform an act of prostitution.

pimping: Aiding, abetting, counseling, or commanding another in the commission of the crime of prostitution. Includes the act of procuring a prostitute for another.

polygamy: The state of having more than one wife or husband at the same time.

pornography: Material that displays sexual activities but is protected by the First Amendment and may not be prosecuted.

prostitution: Solicitation of, or act of, engaging in commercialized sex, including deviate sex.

prurient interest: Interest that tends to excite lust or lewd behavior.

public morals offenses: Offenses that offend the community's morals, normally including obscenity, prostitution, gambling, and public corruption. Prohibited because they violate our traditional values and thus affect "public morals."

soliciting prostitution: The act of asking, enticing, or requesting another to commit the crime of prostitution.

victimless crimes: An offense committed against the social values and interests represented in and protected by criminal law and in which the parties to the offense willingly participated in it.

Historically, the term *public morals* originated in medieval days when the monarchs and the churches were jostling for jurisdiction over nonviolent sexual conduct. The churches, which considered themselves the guardians of public morals, labeled certain activities offensive and claimed jurisdiction over these violations. The primary crimes were adultery, sodomy, indecent exposure, and prostitution. Presently, **public morals offenses** include the crimes of obscenity, prostitution, gambling, and public corruption. The laws regarding public morals are generally justified as attempts to protect traditional values.

OBSCENITY

The term **obscenity** comes from the Latin word *caenum* (filth). **Pornography** is derived from the Greek word *porne* (prostitute) and *graphein* (to write). Obscenity and pornography are two distinct concepts. The law punishes the sale, possession, and distribution of obscene material, and, while it may regulate pornography, it does not make the sale, possession, or distribution of it a crime. Municipalities, for example, may regulate where pornographic material is sold.

They may restrict the location of adult bookstores and theaters to certain zones within the city. Within the bookstores or theaters, the sale and viewing of pornographic material would be legal, but the sale or viewing of obscene material would be a criminal offense. The problem arises when police attempt to prosecute a person under the obscenity statutes. Obscenity is a concept that has evolved during the growth of our nation. At one time, such works as Henry Miller's *Tropic of Cancer*, James Joyce's *Ulysses,* and D. H. Lawrence's *Lady Chatterley's Lover* were considered obscene.

The First Amendment established the right of a private citizen to express himself without fear of prosecution by the government. This right of expression includes the right to produce, distribute, and sell material. This is the case even if a majority of the population disagrees with the position or thoughts set forth in that material. In a series of three cases, the U.S. Supreme Court has established the rules regarding obscenity.

During 1957, the Court held in *Roth v. United States* that, while the First Amendment protected material with even the slightest redeeming social importance, obscenity was utterly without redeeming social importance.[1] This standard stood for nine years, and in 1966 the Court was called upon once again to define obscenity. In *Memoirs v. Massachusetts* the Court held that for a book or other publication to be outside the protection of the First Amendment it must be utterly without redeeming social interest.[2] As these two cases indicate, the standard for determining whether material was obscene was rather vague and hinged upon a concept of socially redeeming importance or interest. In 1973, the Court overturned its previous decisions and finally established a detailed test to determine whether material was obscene. In *Miller v. California*, the Court set forth the three-pronged test, now called the **Miller test**, that guides the police in their determination of obscenity.[3] This test forms the basis for the elements of the crime listed in the beginning of this section.

Obscenity

Defined

Obscenity is any description, account, display, or material depicting sexual activity that an average person applying contemporary community standards would find (that the work), taken as a whole, appeals to the prurient interest and depicts or describes, in a patently offensive way, sexual conduct specifically defined by state law and, taken as a whole, lacks serious literary, artistic, political, or scientific value.

Elements

The elements of the crime of obscenity are as follows:

1. An average person applying contemporary community standards would find that the work, taken as a whole, appeals to the prurient interest.
2. Determine that the work depicts or describes, in a patently offensive way, sexual conduct specifically defined by state law.
3. Conclude that the work, taken as a whole, lacks serious literary, artistic, political, or scientific value.

Obscenity is material that falls outside the protection of the First Amendment, and therefore, may be punished under a criminal statute. Pornography is material that, while it may display sexual activities, is protected by the First Amendment and may not be prosecuted. Assuming that pornographic material does not violate criminal law, does the viewing of explicit sexual matter harm our society? Just as the Supreme Court found it difficult to define obscenity, so does our society have problems with the answer to this question.

One school of thought is that so long as minors are not allowed to view this material, people should be able to decide for themselves. This position finds support in our history—certain banned books are now looked upon as classics. If our government is allowed to control what we see, read, and hear, the argument goes, who controls our government?

Another position is that there is no direct link between pornography and violent crimes. In 1970, the National Commission on Obscenity and Pornography conducted a study of all scholarly works on the effects of pornography and concluded that there was no clear relationship between pornography and violence.[4] In 1986, the *Attorney General's Commission Report on Pornography* called for governmental regulation of this material, but it also found no direct evidence that pornography caused antisocial behavior.[5] In a 1973 article recognized as a classic study in this area, Berl Kutchinsky found that the rate of sex offenses actually declined after pornography was legalized in Denmark.[6]

The opponents of pornography argue that the showing of explicit sexual activity degrades women. In addition, they point to the Attorney General's Commission Report on Pornography indicating that men who view movies depicting violence, sadism, and women who enjoy being raped are more sexually aggressive toward female victims.[7] In support of this position, other studies have found that men who view violent pornographic movies are more likely to act aggressively toward women.[8]

The literature in this area seems to suggest that, while pornography by itself may not be harmful or cause men to act aggressively toward women, when the theme of the pornographic material includes violence, rape, and aggression, there is a correlation between viewing this type of material and acts or feelings of aggression toward women. Just as the findings in this area are confusing, so are the three elements composing the crime of obscenity technical and complex.

The Elements of Obscenity

The elements of the crime of obscenity are as follows:

AN AVERAGE PERSON APPLYING CONTEMPORARY COMMUNITY STANDARDS WOULD FIND (THAT THE WORK), TAKEN AS A WHOLE, APPEALS TO THE PRURIENT INTEREST In 1987, the Supreme Court held in *Pope v. Illinois* that a work is obscene if an average person applying national standards would find the material lacking in any social value.[9] In addition, the Court held that the average person is defined as a reasonable person viewing the material. This person must consider the entire work and determine that it appeals to the prurient interest. **Prurient interest** is that which tends to excite lust or **lewdness**; that is, lewd behavior.

DETERMINE THAT THE WORK DEPICTS OR DESCRIBES, IN A PATENTLY OFFENSIVE WAY, SEXUAL CONDUCT SPECIFICALLY DEFINED BY STATE LAW For material to be deemed obscene, the state must specifically define the prohibited acts. An Illinois statute defined obscenity this way: "A thing is obscene if, considered as a whole, its predominate appeal is to prurient interest, that is, a shameful or morbid interest in nudity, sex, or excretion, and if it goes substantially beyond customary limits of candor in description or representation of such matters."[10]

CONCLUDE THAT THE WORK, TAKEN AS A WHOLE, LACKS SERIOUS LITERARY, ARTISTIC, POLITICAL, OR SCIENTIFIC VALUE The material must not have any serious literary, artistic, political, or scientific value for a conviction under an obscenity statute. The producers of obscene material will argue that the persons engaging in the prohibited activity are acting and that, therefore, the work has literary or artistic appeal. In these types of trials, experts will testify regarding the history of literature and the banning of earlier classics and that the material being considered by the jury should not be suppressed.

Obscenity is a complex issue that has been studied by various authorities for a number of years. Material that depicts sexual activity has a group of supporters who rally to the call of freedom of expression. In addition, there are other groups that believe sexual material should be banned under all circumstances. The drafters of the Model Penal Code (MPC) conducted an extensive study of this area of the law when they established the code sections dealing with obscenity.

Model Penal Code (MPC 251.4)

The MPC attempted to reflect current social mores and, if possible, to include in the law provisions that would maintain some relation between legal standards and changing customs. In addition, the code attempted to reflect modern views about the scope and purpose of the penal law. Conduct that many believe to be sinful and immoral should not be made criminal. It was thought to be unjust and impractical to jail people for behavior widely tolerated by society.

The MPC defines obscenity as follows:

> Material is obscene if, considered as a whole, its predominant appeal is to prurient interest, that is, a shameful or morbid interest, in nudity, sex, or excretion, and if in addition it goes substantially beyond customary limits of candor in describing or representing such matters. Predominant appeal shall be judged with reference to ordinary adults unless it appears from the character of the material or the circumstances of the dissemination to be designed for children or other specially susceptible audience. Undeveloped photographs, molds, printing plates, and the like, shall be deemed obscene notwithstanding that processing or other acts may be required to make the obscenity patent or to disseminate it.

The code specifically establishes an affirmative defense to a charge of obscenity if dissemination was restricted to noncommercial dissemination to personal associates of the actor. The code attempts to prevent commercial exploitation of ordinary members of society caught between normal sex drives and curiosities, on the one hand, and powerful social and legal restraints on overt sexual behavior, on the other.

Child Pornography

Classifying a photo of a child as obscene and in violation of child pornography laws is constitutional even though the same photo would not be considered as obscene if the child were an adult. The courts have limited child pornography to prohibit only images of real children, not virtual images. In *New York v. Ferber (458 U.S. 747, 102 S. Ct. 3348, 73 L. Ed. 2d 1113 [1982]),* the Supreme Court upheld against First Amendment attack a state child pornography statute that did not purport to prohibit virtual images but only images of real children. The Court in Ferber upheld the state statute against First Amendment attack, even though the statute prohibited material that would not be obscene, because the production of child pornography utilizing real children necessarily harmed the children.

The burden of proof is on the government to prove that a pornographic image is of a real child under the Child Pornography Prevention Act of 1996 (18 U.S.C.S. § 2251 et seq.). The government at all times has the burden of proof by a preponderance of the evidence at sentencing, and the defendant has no burden. The evaluation of the sufficiency of the evidence is done on the record as a whole, not on "bright line" tests.

Summary of Obscenity

Obscenity is an act that our society has deemed necessary to criminalize. The distinction between obscene and pornographic material is slight and can be perceived only by reviewing the elements of the crime of obscenity to determine if the material falls within the scope of those elements. There are arguments on both sides regarding whether explicit sexual material is harmful to either the viewer or other members of society. We must walk a fine line between punishing the attempt to distribute obscene material and restricting a citizen's rights to express ideas.

PROSTITUTION

Prostitution is said to be the world's oldest profession. In early England, it was considered an ecclesiastical offense and was, therefore, not considered a common law crime.[11] In some early cultures, prostitutes enjoyed a high social standing. The **devadasis** in India were an example of prostitutes who were looked upon with approval for their education, training, and skill at entertaining. During the Middle Ages, prostitution was not a crime. Prostitutes were taxed and provided a steady source of revenue to the king. In the early American colonies, the Protestant ethic was introduced, and the concept of sin was translated into legal restraints. Thus, prostitution became a crime.

In the United States, the act of intercourse is not a crime by itself. It is the act of solicitation and payment for sexual services that is regulated. Most states punish prostitution as a misdemeanor, and prostitutes rarely spend any length of time in jail if convicted of plying their trade.

The Elements of Prostitution

The crime of prostitution has three elements:

SOLICITING OR ENGAGING IN The crime of prostitution punishes both partners. Thus, the male who **solicits** a female prostitute is equally guilty. The crime is also gender neutral and thereby applies to male prostitutes. If a prostitute does not accept an offer of sex for money, she cannot be convicted of this crime. However, the person who made the offer is guilty under this definition.

Prostitution

Defined

Prostitution is the solicitation of, or act of, engaging in commercialized sex, including deviate sex.

Elements

The crime of prostitution has three elements:

1. Soliciting or engaging in.
2. Any sexual activity, including deviate sex.
3. For the purpose of commercial gain.

ANY SEXUAL ACTIVITY, INCLUDING DEVIATE SEX The crime includes masturbation, sexual intercourse, sodomy, and any other physical sexual activity between members of the same or different sexes. It does not include paying someone to dance or strip for a group or a private person, nor does it include massages that are given for compensation. While these latter activities may be fronts for prostitution rings, they are legal so long as no physical sexual activity takes place. A new sexual activity that is becoming a billion-dollar enterprise is so-called phone sex. This business offers phone numbers that anyone can call and for a fee either talk to another person or listen to that person describe sexual activities. This form of sexual activity is not covered by the crime of prostitution.

FOR PURPOSES OF COMMERCIAL GAIN The solicitation or sexual activity must be engaged in for money or some other form of compensation. Simply asking someone to have sex because a person wants to engage in sexual activities is not prostitution.

Prostitution is an age-old activity and is still considered a crime. Even with society's modern morals regarding sexual activity, prostitution still flourishes. The drafters of the MPC attempted to establish some order in this area by examining all aspects of the crime of prostitution.

Model Penal Code (MPC 251.2)

The MPC defines prostitution and related offenses as follows:

1. *Prostitution.* A person is guilty of prostitution, a petty misdemeanor, if he or she:
   a. is an inmate of a house of prostitution or otherwise engages in sexual activity as a business; or

   b. loiters in or within view of any public place for the purpose of being hired to engage in sexual activity . . .

2. *Promoting Prostitution.* A person who knowingly promotes prostitution of another commits a misdemeanor or felony. . . . The following acts shall constitute promoting prostitution:

   a. owning, controlling, managing, supervising, or otherwise keeping, alone or in association with others, a house of prostitution or a prostitution business; or

   b. procuring an inmate for a house of prostitution or a place in a house of prostitution for one who would be an inmate; or

   c. encouraging, inducing, or otherwise purposely causing another to become or remain a prostitute; or

   d. soliciting a person to patronize a prostitute; or

   e. procuring a prostitute for a patron; or

   f. transporting a person into or within this state with purpose to promote that person's engaging in prostitution, or procuring or paying for transportation with that purpose; or

   g. leasing or otherwise permitting a place controlled by the actor, alone or in association with others, to be regularly used for prostitution or the promotion of prostitution, or failure to make reasonable effort to abate such use by ejecting the tenant, notifying law enforcement authorities, or other legally available means; or

   h. soliciting, receiving, or agreeing to receive any benefit for doing or agreeing to do anything forbidden by this section.

Section 2 of the code is directed at those who procure prostitutes for customers. These persons are commonly known as pimps, and their activity is called **pimping**. The code attempts to cover the entire range of activities that pimps engage in when they "market" their "stable of girls or boys." The state of Nevada has legalized prostitution under certain conditions. One famous brothel in Nevada, the Mustang Ranch, even sold shares of stock to the general public before it went into bankruptcy. Prostitution and its related activities such as pimping remain a crime in the majority of U.S. states. It flourishes even in this era of AIDS and probably will continue so long as customers are willing to pay money for sexual favors and as long as there are persons willing to perform those favors in return for compensation.

Summary of Prostitution

Prostitution is basically sex for sale. The crime includes the offer to engage in sex for pay as well as the actual sexual activity. The act applies to both the customer and the prostitute. Prostitutes may be either male or female and may service members of the same or opposite sex. Statutes make it a crime for a third party to **pander** or offer to procure a prostitute for another. Even though they commit a crime, persons convicted of this and related crimes spend very little time in jail, even if they are repeat offenders.

INCEST, BIGAMY, AND POLYGAMY

Article I. Incest

Incest is the crime of having unlawful sexual intercourse with a relative through blood or marriage. The elements of the crime are:

1. Sexual intercourse
2. with a relative through blood or marriage.

In one interesting case, *Hendry v. State*, 571 So. 2d 94 (Fla. Dist. Ct. App. 2d Dist. 1990), the father allowed his daughter to be legally adopted by a third person. He then married his former daughter. When the state brought charges against both the daughter and the father for incest, they contended that at the time they got married they were no longer relatives. The defendants moved to dismiss the charges against them. The trial court denied the motion, and the defendants appealed. The appellate court affirmed the denial, holding that the biological fact of the defendants' lineal consanguinity was not nullified by the adoption which terminated legal relationships between an adopted person and his or her natural parents. The incest statute applied to defendants' relationship was *Florida statue § 826.04*:

> **§ 826.04. Incest**
>
> Whoever knowingly marries or has sexual intercourse with a person to whom he or she is related by lineal consanguinity, or a brother, sister, uncle, aunt, nephew, or niece, commits incest, which constitutes a felony of the third degree. . . . "Sexual intercourse" is the penetration of the female sex organ by the male sex organ, however slight; emission of semen is not required.

Article II. Case on Point

In *Deal v. Romero, 2009 U.S. App. LEXIS 17195 (10th Cir. N.M. July 31, 2009)*, the defendant Deal confessed to having sexual intercourse with his daughter during a videotaped interview with the police (common law crimes of incest and rape of a child). He was convicted by a jury of twelve counts of criminal sexual penetration in the second degree, nineteen counts of criminal sexual penetration in the third degree, ten counts of criminal sexual contact of a minor, one count of intimidation of a witness, one count of child abuse (or in the alternative contributing to the delinquency of a minor), and thirty-six counts of incest.

Based on those offenses, what sentence would you pronounce if you were the judge in his case?

Note: Deal was sentenced to a total of 108 years in prison, all but sixty years suspended. The New Mexico Court of Appeals affirmed and the New Mexico Supreme Court denied certiorari review.

Article III. Bigamy

Bigamy is the crime of marrying one person while still legally married to another person. An example of a bigamy statute is the following Ohio statute. Under the Ohio statute, which is similar to most state statutes, the offense is committed when the bigamous marriage takes place in that state, or, regardless of where the marriage took place, when the bigamous couple cohabit in that state.

Intent is a necessary element of the crime of bigamy, and innocent mistake, good faith, reasonable diligence, and honest belief in the right to enter into a second marriage is a complete defense to a charge of bigamy *(Kontner v. Kontner, 103 Ohio App. 360, 139 N.E.2d 366 (1956)).* The Ohio code says:

Ohio Revised Code Annotated § 2919.01. Bigamy

(A) No married person shall marry another or continue to cohabit with such other person in this state.

(B) It is an affirmative defense to a charge under this section that the actor's spouse was continuously absent for five years immediately preceding the purported subsequent marriage, and was not known by the actor to be alive within that time.

Article IV. Polygamy

Polygamy is the crime of state of having more than one wife or husband at the same time.

In many prosecutions for polygamy, the defense of religious beliefs is often used as a justification for multiple marriages existing at the same time. The courts are uniform in holding that religious beliefs are not a legal defense in prosecutions for polygamy. As noted in *State v. Fischer, 219 Ariz. 408, (Ct. App. 2008),* the defendant's prosecution for sexual conduct with a minor for marrying and having a child with the seventeen-year-old victim did not violate his right to religious freedom under First Amendment because article 20, paragraph 2 of the Arizona Constitution prohibited the recognition of polygamy or plural marriage by the state under all circumstances without exception, and therefore was both facially neutral and nondiscriminatory in effect.

The Arizona State Supreme Court stated in the Fischer case that the Free Exercise Clause of the First Amendment to the U.S. Constitution was made applicable to the states through the Fourteenth Amendment. The free exercise of religion encompasses two concepts—the right to believe and profess whatever religious doctrine one desires and the right to the performance of (or abstention from) physical acts for religious reasons. The first was absolute but, in the nature of things, the second cannot be. Thus, the government was prohibited from any regulation of religious beliefs as such, and the government may not penalize or discriminate against individuals or groups because of their religious views. In contrast, the right to engage in actions or conduct prompted by religious beliefs or principles is not totally free from legislative restrictions. Conduct remains subject to regulation for the protection of society. The freedom to act must have appropriate definition to preserve the enforcement of that protection.

Arizona State Constitution, article 20, paragraph 2: Polygamous or plural marriages, or polygamous co-habitation, are forever prohibited within this state.

GAMES OF CHANCE

Games of chance are more commonly referred to as **gambling**. Like other crimes discussed in this chapter, gambling is supported by a large segment of the population who enjoy it and see nothing wrong in it. Probably a majority of American males have placed at least one illegal bet on a sporting event during their lifetime. In addition, "games of chance" are being used by many states as a method to raise public revenues.

At common law, gambling was not a crime unless committed in such a manner that it became a public nuisance. Accordingly, for a game of chance to be illegal, there must be a specific law or ordinance prohibiting it. In all states, however, there are now restrictions on gambling. Many states have state-controlled lotteries that are very similar to "numbers" operations that have illegally existed in most major cities for many years. Other states allow betting on horse races. The definition of what is legal gambling and what is illegal varies in each state. Two things are apparent regarding gambling: (1) It is highly regulated in each state, and (2) any gambling not authorized by a state's gambling statutes and regulations is a crime.

Practicum 12.1

What Is Compensation?

The case becomes more complex if a business-person takes a companion on a date and gives that companion an expensive gift with the expectation that sex will be provided as a result of tendering the gift. Is this compensation? What if the gift was a necklace worth $1,000? What if the gift was a diamond ring worth $2,000, and the sales receipt was included in the box with a statement that the store would make a full refund? Is it compensation if the gift was a gift certificate worth $500 redeemable in cash or merchandise at the local jewelry store?

In 1978, a study on the enforcement of gambling laws in the major U.S. cities, funded by the Law Enforcement Assistance Administration, concluded the following:

1. The illegal gambling industry in the United States was growing.
2. The legalization of commercial gambling has not been shown to reduce illegal gambling.
3. Social gambling has generally been decriminalized by society.
4. Upgrading the penalties for convicted gambling operators would not significantly reduce gambling.[12]

Federal Gambling Laws

While most gambling activities are regulated by state and local government, there are several federal statutes that also limit gambling activities. The key federal statutes are listed below:

Title 18 U.S. Code, Section 1955 prohibits conducting, financing, managing, supervising, directing, or owning an interest in an illegal gambling business that is in violation of a state or local law.

Title 18 U.S. Code, Section 1084 prohibits the interstate or foreign transmission by wire communications facility of wagering information by persons engaged in betting or wagering activities that are illegal by state or local law.

Title 18 U.S. Code, Section 1952 has similar prohibitions on the use of the U.S. Postal Service.

Title 18 U.S. Code, Section 1953 regulates the interstate transportation of gambling devices.

Title 18 U.S. Code, Section 1082 regulates the operation of gambling ships.

Internet Gambling

The United States is considered as a nation of gamblers. It is estimated that Americans wager more than $630 billion annually on state-sanctioned gambling activities such as lotteries, riverboat casinos, and horse- and dog-track betting. The National Gambling Impact Study Commission (NGISC), created by Congress to study the social and economic effects of gambling in the United States, reported, "Commercial gambling has become an immense industry. Governments are now heavily involved and increasingly active in pursuit of gambling revenues."[13]

Gambling prohibitions in the United States have existed from the time of colonial independence. After the Civil War, some states legalized various forms of gambling to help boost the Southern economy. The Great Depression brought another wave of gambling in the United States as thirty-eight states introduced state lotteries. New Jersey and Nevada, in particular, have legalized casino gambling, and Missouri, Indiana, and Illinois have legalized riverboat casino gambling. The only states with total prohibitions on gambling are Hawaii and Utah. Despite the increased legalization of gambling activities that are state approved, many states have enacted new laws criminalizing Internet gambling or have applied existing gambling laws to prevent Internet gambling.

Because of the international nature of Internet gambling—with a website located in one country and a gambler in another—federal law is the primary vehicle used to prohibit Internet gambling in the United States. There are three federal statutes used in an attempt to prohibit Internet gambling: The Wire Act of 1961 makes it illegal for gambling providers to offer or to take bets from gamblers over telephone lines unless it is authorized by a particular state. The Travel Act prohibits travel or the use of mail or any facility in interstate or foreign commerce with intent to distribute the proceeds of any unlawful activity or otherwise promote, manage, establish, carry on, or facilitate the promotion, management, establishment, or carrying on, of any unlawful activity. The Illegal Gambling Business Act makes it illegal to operate certain gambling enterprises that violate the law of a state in which the business is conducted. In addition to those acts, the federal government exerts pressure on financial institutions; as a result, the eight largest U.S. credit-card-issuing banks voluntarily block credit card use for Internet gambling.[14]

At least fifty-four countries now allow some form of Internet gambling. Accordingly, owners of Internet casinos have moved outside the jurisdiction of the United States under the assumption that they will not be prosecuted. Should the United States and the various states allow Internet gambling?

PUBLIC CORRUPTION

The offenses traditionally referred to as public corruption crimes include extortion and bribery. Extortion and bribery are also discussed in Chapter 9. Bribery generally involves an attempt to extract money or property from another by the misuse of public office.

Bribery

Bribery, as discussed in Chapter 9, is perhaps the best known of the public corruption crimes and is often associated with organized crime. At common law, bribery was a misdemeanor, but in most states it is now a felony. To establish the crime of bribery, there must be an agreement to do the act. The agreement, not the act, is the gist of the offense. At common law, an offer without an agreement is at most an attempted bribery. The crime is completed with the acceptance of the money or thing of value. For example, a public official who agrees to commit an act but later refuses payment is still guilty of bribery. Jury members, including grand jury members, and witnesses are considered public officials for the purpose of the bribery statutes. In addition, several states have enlarged the crime of bribery to include not only official duties of a public officer but also the activities of sports referees, umpires, and athletes.

Unlike for extortion, the act agreed to need not be within the scope of the official's duties. While extortion involves illegal payment for doing a lawful act, bribery involves doing or not doing a wrongful act.

Summary

Crimes committed against public morals cover a broad range of activities. Some would argue that law enforcement should spend its time hunting down hardened, violent criminals rather than waste the taxpayers' money on consensual acts that occur in private among adults. However, most law enforcement officials believe these crimes are serious, and the law should be enforced. In addition, other groups believe crimes such as obscenity and prostitution demean women and contribute to a view in society that women are playthings to be used and abused. By actively enforcing the criminal codes in this area, we send a message that these types of acts will not be tolerated in our society.

Games of chance and political corruption have been with us since the beginning of recorded history. All one has to do is pick up a daily paper to see that politicians are still being charged with violating criminal statutes. These crimes may not cause physical injury to another person, but they weaken our national honor and set examples for our youth that are not in anyone's best interest.

Additional Assignments

Discussion and thought questions:

a. Explain the difference between bribery and extortion.
b. What is the test to determine if a book is obscene?
c. Should gambling be a crime? What types of gambling are authorized in your state?
d. What arguments can you state to justify the elimination of prostitution as a crime? Should it be a crime?
e. What is the difference between obscene material and pornography?
f. What arguments can you present for strict enforcement of the prostitution and obscenity statutes?

Practicum

Conduct research on your state laws and draft your definition of obscenity based on those statutes. Also, what distinction does your state make regarding obscenity when the material is available to juveniles?

Notes

1. *Roth v. United States*, 354 U.S. 476 (1957).
2. *Memoirs v. Massachusetts*, 383 U.S. 413 (1966).
3. *Miller v. California*, 413 U.S. 15 (1973).
4. *The Report of the Commission on Obscenity and Pornography* (Washington, DC: U.S. Government Printing Office, 1970).
5. *Attorney General's Commission Report on Pornography* (Washington, DC: U.S. Government Printing Office, 1986), 2158.
6. Berl Kutchinsky, "The Effect of Easy Availability of Pornography on the Incidence of Sex Crimes," 29 J. Soc. *Issues* 95 (1973).
7. *Attorney General's Report,* supra note 5, p. 1005.
8. Edward Donnerstein, "Pornography and Violence Against Women," 347 *Annals N.Y. Acad. Sci.* 277 (1980).
9. 107 S. Ct. 1918 (1987). There is a question in this case as to whether the Court, by using "national" rather than "community," meant to change the standard.
10. See *Ward v. Illinois,* 431 U.S. 767 (1977), upholding the constitutionality of the statute in an obscenity prosecution.
11. It was an ecclesiastical offense because it involved either fornication or adultery, and these acts were left to the spiritual court. William Blackstone, , IV *Commentaries* 65.
12. G. R. Blakey and H. A. Kurland, "The Development of Federal Law of Gambling," 63 *Cornell L. Rev.* 923 (1978).
13. Jonathan Schwartz's 2005 essay: "Click the Mouse and Bet the House: The United States' Internet Gambling Restrictions Before the World Trade Organization," *U. Ill. J. L. Tech & Pol'y* 125, p. 124.
14. Jonathan Godfried, "The Federal Framework for Internet Gambling," 10 *Rich. J. L. & Tech.* 26, P1 (2004). Retrieved April 28, 2007, from http://law.richmond.edu/jolt/v10i3/article26.pdf.

CHAPTER 13

Narcotic and Alcohol Offenses

Chapter Outline

Narcotic Offenses
Possession
Possession for Sale
Sale of a Controlled Substance
Medical Marijuana Laws

Alcohol Offenses
The Alcohol Problem

Public Drunkenness
Driving Under the Influence

Solutions
Prevention of Alcohol Abuse

What you should know about Narcotic and Alcohol Offenses. After reading this chapter, you should know

- The problems that face our society as a result of drugs and alcohol.

- The controlled substances statutes.

- The difference between the crimes of possession, possession for sale, and sale of controlled substances.

- The different types of alcohol-related crimes.

- The various proposed alternative solutions to narcotic and alcohol offenses.

Key Terms

After reading this chapter, you should understand the following key terms:

blood alcohol level: A medical and legal term used to express the level of alcohol in a person's blood, expressed in terms of milligrams of alcohol per milliliter of blood.

cannabis: A group of drugs produced from the leaves of Cannabis sativa, including marijuana, hashish, and hash oil.

Cannabis sativa: Scientific name for the marijuana plant.

central nervous system depressants: A group of drugs that depress the functional state of the central nervous system, including alcohol, barbiturates, and tranquilizers.

central nervous system stimulants: A group of drugs that increase the functional state of the central nervous system, including cocaine, crack, amphetamines, methamphetamines, and "ice."

controlled substance: A specifically defined bioactive or psychoactive chemical substance that is under the purview of criminal law.

crop eradication: The systematic effort to destroy plants that produce the raw material that is manufactured into a narcotic drug.

crop substitution: Effort to motivate farmers in foreign countries to grow domestic food crops for commercial markets instead of poppies, coca bushes, or cannabis plants.

crucial alcoholic phase: Point at which the drinker's loss of control becomes complete, there is isolation from others, and life becomes centered on alcohol.

designer drug: A chemical substance that (1) has a potential for abuse similar to or greater than that of controlled substance, (2) is designed to produce a desired pharmacological effect, and (3) is produced to evade the controlling statutory provisions of a criminal law.

driving: Movement of a vehicle in some direction, including steering and controlling the vehicle while in motion.

drug: Any of a wide variety of substances having a physical or psychotropic effect on the human body.

final or bottom alcoholic phase: Point at which a drinker experiences emotional disorganization or impaired thinking.

hallucinogens: A group of drugs that produce hallucinations, including LSD and peyote.

heroin: A highly addictive drug and the most widely abused and most rapidly acting of the opiates. Heroin is processed from morphine, a naturally occurring substance extracted from the seedpod of certain varieties of poppy plants.

inhalants: Volatile substances that produce chemical vapors that can be inhaled to induce a psychoactive, or mind-altering, effect. Inhalants include a broad range of chemicals found in hundreds of different products that may have different pharmacological effects.

intermediate alcoholic stage: Point at which an individual who drinks has occasional blackouts coupled with a compulsion to drink and lose control.

marijuana: A green, brown, or gray mixture of dried, shredded leaves, stems, seeds, and flowers of the hemp plant (Cannabis sativa). Cannabis is a term that refers to marijuana and other drugs made from the same plant. Other forms of cannabis include sinsemilla, hashish, and hash oil. All forms of cannabis are mind-altering (psychoactive) drugs.

narcotic analgesics: A group of drugs that depress the central nervous system and relieve pain without producing loss of consciousness, including morphine, codeine, heroin, and methadone.

precursor chemical: A chemical that may be used in the manufacturer of a controlled substance.

phencyclidine: A synthetic drug that removes the feeling of physical pain and may act as a depressant, stimulant, psychedelic, or tranquilizer. Also known as PCP.

prealcoholic phase: Point at which a person has an occasional drink as a means of reducing tension.

under the influence: Condition in which alcohol or drugs have affected the nervous system, brain, or muscles so as to impair to an appreciable degree the ability to operate a motor vehicle in a manner like that of an ordinary, prudent, and cautious person in full possession of his facilities using reasonable care and under like circumstances.

W hile most introductory texts in criminal justice mention drugs and alcohol offenses, they do not examine these crimes in any detail. However, considering the impact these offenses have on society, it is critical to include them in any discussion of criminal law. A brief discussion of crime with any law enforcement professional will soon be consumed by the topic of drug and alcohol crimes. While drugs are illegal, alcohol is a legal depressant that any adult can purchase. However, its misuse can lead to death and destruction of property. This chapter will examine some of the more common drug and alcohol offenses as well as set forth some of the proposed solutions to these problems.

NARCOTIC OFFENSES

Narcotic offenses have been widely publicized in the media. This publicity ranges from multimillion-dollar drug busts to stories of drug overdoses by young children. These crimes are relatively simple to define, but debate rages about both the causes and cures of drug-related offenses.

Narcotic offenses run the gamut from simple possession of marijuana to the sale of heroin. Offenders vary from a neighbor supplying marijuana for an afternoon party to a Miami drug lord planning distribution of heroin throughout the United States. Today many segments of our society use or have used narcotic drugs.

Narcotics and their use are not a new phenomenon in our society. Opium was used by such noted physicians as Hippocrates.[1] Widespread use of these narcotics led to a serious drug abuse problem in the United States as early as 1924. The use and abuse of drugs has continued to this date.

Focus 13.1

Drugs and Alcohol: Some Definitions

The following is a brief list of some of the more common **drugs** used in our society. It is not intended to cover all the various types of drugs encountered by law enforcement officials. Rather, it should be used as an introduction to the vast array of drugs that are available on the streets of our nation.

Central Nervous System Stimulants

Central nervous system stimulants are drugs that increase the functional state of the central nervous system.

Cocaine is a psychoactive alkaloid produced from the coca leaf. The coca shrub thrives in several regions of the South American Andes. Cocaine was first isolated from the coca leaf by Albert Niemann of Germany in 1860. It is a very powerful natural drug, the use of which produces euphoria, restlessness, and excitement. Cocaine can be sniffed into the nostrils or injected. The resulting euphoria is short-lived, and heavy users must constantly snort the drug to maintain the feeling. "Speedballing" is the practice of mixing cocaine and heroin for the purpose of obtaining a distinct high. "Freebasing" refers to the conversion of street cocaine to freebase, or pure cocaine. This substance is then sprinkled on a cigarette or smoked in a pipe. Freebase enters the bloodstream through the lungs, and the high is felt before the smoke is exhaled.

Crack is refined cocaine that comes in rock form. Crack is an off-white color resembling pieces of soap. The word crack comes from the crackling sound made when it is smoked or from its occasional resemblance to cracked plaster. The popularity of crack is that it renders cocaine smokable. When smoked, it produces an immediate high.

Amphetamines are synthetic drugs that stimulate the central nervous system. The use of these drugs produces an intense physical reaction, including increased blood pressure, breathing rate, and elevation of mood. Some of the more commonly known amphetamines are Benzedrine, Dexedrine, and Methedrine. Extended use of this drug can result in exhaustion, anxiety, and depression.

Methamphetamines are a form of amphetamine that has been called the poor man's cocaine. They have various street names, including meth, speed, or crystal. They have been produced illegally for decades and may be manufactured in homemade laboratories. They may be injected, inhaled, or taken orally.

Ice is smokable methamphetamine. Ice was initially reported in Hawaii in 1985 and supposedly has become its greatest drug problem. The slang term "ice" was due to the drug's appearance, generally a clear, crystal-shaped form that looks like glass. In some areas this narcotic is also known as crank. Ice has the same properties as methamphetamine, but through a recrystallization process the rocklike crystals can be smoked. The ice form of methamphetamine is highly addictive.

Central Nervous System Depressants

Central nervous system depressants are drugs that decrease the functional state of the central nervous system.

Alcohol refers to ethanol, which is a psychoactive ingredient found in alcoholic beverages. Consumed orally, it produces a wide range of symptoms depending on the individual and the amount ingested. These symptoms can range from euphoria to aggressive behavior.

Barbiturates are defined as barbituric acid derivatives used in medicine as sedatives and hypnotics. Barbituric acid was discovered by Adolf Baeyer in Germany in 1864. Some of the more commonly abused barbiturates are amobarbital (Amytal), known on the street as blues or blue devils; pentobarbital (Nembutal), known as nembies, yellows, or yellowjackets; and secobarbital (Seconal), known as reds, red devils, or Seccy. Barbiturate use can produce a state of intoxication. There may be an initial loss of inhibition, euphoria, and behavioral stimulation. Barbiturates may produce drowsiness and sleep.

Tranquilizers are antipsychotic agents generally used to treat schizophrenia and acute psychosis. However, many laypersons use the term to refer to the benzodiazepine drugs Librium and Valium. These drugs were originally manufactured to treat various symptoms of anxiety. Their use produces drowsiness, light-headedness, and other impairments of mental and physical activities.

Hallucinogens

Hallucinogens are drugs that produce hallucinations.

LSD is a synthetic drug also known as lysergic acid diethylamide-25. This substance stimulates cerebral sensory centers and promotes a full range of visual hallucinations. The drug may induce feelings of anxiety and panic, and some users have experienced flashbacks even after discontinuing use of the substance.

Peyote is a small cactus that grows naturally in Mexico and the southwestern portion of the United States. It contains mescaline, a hallucinogenic substance named after the Mescalero Apaches, who first used it. Peyote produces a wide range of hallucinations including colors, geometric patterns, and out-of-body sensations.

Narcotic Analgesics

Narcotic analgesics are drugs that depress the central nervous system and relieve pain without producing loss of consciousness. The most common narcotics are derivatives of opium. Similar to coca leaves, opium has a long history of use. Long before 4,000 BC, opium was known for its medicinal qualities, and it was used as a narcotic in Sumerian and European cultures 6,000 years ago. Opium is produced from the opium poppy flower. People first learned to smoke opium in China, and the practice quickly spread to many parts of the world.

Morphine is the principal psychoactive alkaloid in opium. It was first produced in 1805 and named after the Greek god of dreams, Morpheus. Morphine is ten times stronger than opium and is used by physicians to relieve pain. It produces an elevation of spirits and then drowsiness. Morphine is a highly addictive drug.

Codeine is another derivative of opium that may be used legally under a doctor's orders. It is present in many pain-relieving prescription drugs. It can produce drug dependence of the morphine type and therefore is considered highly addictive.

Heroin was first produced in 1874 by an Englishman, D. P. Wright, and is twenty-five times stronger than morphine. It is one of the more commonly used drugs in the United States. Users quickly build up a tolerance and must use more of the drug to obtain the same effect. It is sold as a powder and mixed before being injected into the bloodstream. There are numerous forms of heroin: "Mexican Brown" is sold in the western United States and is pink-brown in color. It is usually a fine powder with dark brown flecks. The color may vary from light brown to chocolate. "Persian Heroin" is tan or reddish in color. It is not water soluble; rather, lemon juice or vinegar is added prior to cooking in the traditional spoon. "Black Tar Heroin" began appearing in the United States about 1979. This drug is especially desired on the streets because of its purity, about 93 percent. There are numerous street names for Black Tar, including gum, goma, and Mexican Mud.

Methadone is a synthetic drug that is used to assist heroin users in breaking their habit. Some states have established methadone clinics where heroin users may go to obtain the drug legally in lieu of purchasing heroin on the streets. Methadone is considered highly addictive. The withdrawal following extended use of methadone is more prolonged but less intense than that of heroin.

Demerol is a synthetic drug that is used by the medical profession. It is usually administered before and after operations as a method of controlling pain.

Phencyclidine

PCP, or **phencyclidine**, is a synthetic drug. It was first discovered in 1956 by researchers at Parke, Davis and Company. The PCP sold in the United States is made in illegal laboratories. PCP in its pure state is a clear liquid. In solid form, it is a powder that may be white or have a yellowish or brownish tint. It may act as a depressant, a stimulant, a psychedelic, and a tranquilizer. It also removes the feeling of physical pain. The user's pain threshold is dramatically increased, and therefore, traditional police restraints may be ineffective against a person under the influence of PCP.

Cannabis

Cannabis is produced from the leaves of **Cannabis sativa**, a weedlike plant that is grown throughout the world. The active ingredient in cannabis is tetrahydrocannabinol (THC). Prolonged use can cause distortion in auditory and visual perception. Small doses produce a "high" or excitement that gives way to drowsiness.

Marijuana is produced from the leaves of cannabis. It is called pot, dope, and other names. Normally it is smoked as a cigarette or in a pipe.

Hashish is a concentrated form of cannabis that is produced from the unadulterated resin from the female plant. It is also called hash.

Hash oil is a liquid form of hashish that is considered a very powerful form of the drug. The concentration of THC in this oil may be as high as 90 percent.

Scholars have pointed out that drug use undermines the health, economic well-being, and social responsibility of drug users. In addition, drug trafficking threatens the civility of city life and undermines parenting. Finally, law enforcement professionals acknowledge that the police can accomplish little by themselves. The drug problem will require more resources than simply putting more cops on the street.[2] The offenses may be simple, but they affect every segment of our society.

There is no Model Penal Code (MPC) provision setting forth elements of crimes involving narcotics and dangerous drugs. The federal Comprehensive Drug Abuse Prevention and Control Act of 1970 as amended is one set of statutes that govern narcotics and dangerous drugs.[3] A majority of states have adopted the Uniform Controlled Substances Act, which was approved by the National Conference of Commissioners on Uniform State Laws. The following elements and definitions draw upon these acts in discussing the various narcotic crimes.

Possession

THE PERSON HAS POSSESSION OR THE RIGHT TO EXERCISE CONTROL OVER A CONTROLLED SUBSTANCE The term *possession of the **controlled substance*** is used in its ordinary meaning. The duration of the possession is immaterial. If the offender had possession for any period of time, this element is satisfied. This element also includes dominion or control over the substance. The control aspect of this element may be actual possession or constructive possession. Courts have held defendants liable when the substance has been found on their persons, in their presence or custody, or in an area over which they have control. However, mere access to the place where the narcotic or dangerous drug is located is insufficient to establish that the defendant had possession or exercised the right of control over the controlled substance.

Practicums 13.1 to 13.3 examine the issue of possession.

THE POSSESSION IS UNLAWFUL The possession of a controlled substance is not unlawful if there is a statutory exception allowing the person to possess the substance. Under certain conditions, particular persons, such as manufacturers, druggists, or medical personnel, may be authorized to possess narcotics or dangerous drugs.

THE PERSON HAS KNOWLEDGE OF SUCH POSSESSION OR CONTROL A more accurate term for describing the defendant's mental state might be awareness or knowledge of the presence of the substance. Knowledge of such possession is an essential element of the crime, since possession without such knowledge is not possession in the legal sense of the word. The mere presence of the person where a controlled substance is found is insufficient to establish that he knowingly possessed the item. The amount of the substance is in usable form. While there is some debate regarding the necessity of including this element, the better view would seem to hold that it is a critical part of the crime. Generally speaking, in order to establish that the possession was criminal, the substance must be of a quality and quantity that is usable as a narcotic. The amount need not be sufficient to produce the drug's effect or in sufficient concentration to stimulate the nervous system.

Possession

Defined

Possession of a narcotic is the unlawful possession or right to exercise control over a controlled substance.

Elements

The crime of possession has four elements:

1. The person has possession or the right to exercise control over a controlled substance.
2. The possession is unlawful.
3. The person has knowledge of such possession or control.
4. The amount of the substance is in usable form.

Practicum 13.1

The defendant and a co-occupant of his residence were arrested for possession of marijuana. Both parties had equal access to the area where the narcotic was hidden. The co-occupant denied knowing that the drugs were on the premises. The defendant had previous narcotic convictions. When told that the co-occupant was being booked for possession, the defendant replied, "Well, you don't want to book her for that."

ISSUE: Did the defendant's statement prove he had possession of the narcotic?

The court held that the jury was entitled to accept the disclaimer of the co-occupant and find that the defendant was guilty of possession based upon his statements and prior convictions.[4]

Possession for Sale

Possession of a controlled substance is a serious crime in both the federal and state criminal justice systems. Another crime that is considered just as serious and more dangerous to society occurs when the offender is arrested with a large amount of narcotics or dangerous drugs. In these situations, some jurisdictions allow the charging of a crime distinct from and carrying more severe penalties than possession. Even though the offender may not have been caught selling the drug, these statutes allow charging her with possession of a controlled substance for sale.

The first three elements of this offense are identical to the crime of simple possession. All the factors that go into determining whether the defendant has committed the crime of possession of a controlled substance apply to this crime. If any of the three elements is missing or cannot be proved, it does not matter that the offender may have had a boxcar full of narcotics or drugs.

Practicum 13.2

The defendant and another person occupied a bedroom together. Two police officers were conducting a search of the apartment when the defendant arrived home. Upon observing the officers in the bedroom, the defendant fled the scene.

ISSUE: Did the defendant's conduct establish knowledge of possession of the controlled substances?

The court held that the defendant's suspicious behavior when he became aware of the presence of the police officers was sufficient to establish knowledge for purposes of convicting him of possession of a controlled substance.[5]

Practicum 13.3

The defendant shared an apartment with his wife and their four children as well as another adult. The officers discovered heroin in the base of the defendant's basketball trophy on a bureau in their bedroom. The defendant's arm bore needle marks indicating he had administered narcotics to himself in the past.

ISSUE: Was there sufficient evidence to establish possession by the defendant?

The court held that evidence that the defendant was a user of narcotics at the time of his arrest as well as the facts surrounding the location of the heroin were sufficient to establish possession.[6]

THE AMOUNT IS IN EXCESS OF WHAT IS NORMALLY CONSUMED BY A SINGLE INDIVIDUAL This element replaces the one listed under possession of a controlled substance that requires the substance to be in usable form. In this crime, the amount necessary for a conviction is not minute or simply a trace of the narcotic or drug. This element may also be proved if the defendant offers to sell some of the drugs to an undercover agent. In some jurisdictions, narcotic officers qualify as expert witnesses and testify that in their opinion the amount possessed by the defendant is in excess of that usually held by a person for his or her own personal use. Factors such as the amount of the substance, its packaging in smaller amounts, and statements by the offender may be used to establish this element. Some jurisdictions have a rebuttable presumption that the substance is held for sale if it exceeds a certain minimum amount.

Focus 13.2

Proof of Possession and/or Control

As the practicums indicate, no clear line can be drawn to distinguish between circumstances that establish possession or custody and control of a controlled substance and those situations in which there is insufficient evidence to link the offender with the drugs. However, the courts will consider the following factors that will support a finding that the defendant had possession of the controlled substance:

Factors Indicating Possession

1. Incriminating statement made by the defendant, linking her to the drugs.
2. The defendant's incriminating or suspicious behavior.
3. The fact that the defendant has sold drugs or is a known user of narcotics.
4. The defendant's proximity at the time of arrest to the area where the drugs were found.
5. The fact that the drugs were found in the defendant's personal belongings or in an area under her exclusive control.

Possession for Sale

Defined

Possession of a narcotic for sale is the unlawful possession or right to exercise control over a controlled substance in an amount in excess of what is normally consumed by a single individual.

Elements

The crime of possession for sale has four elements:

1. The person has possession or the right to exercise control over a controlled substance.
2. The possession is unlawful.
3. The person has knowledge of such possession or control.
4. The amount is in excess of what is normally consumed by a single individual.

Sale of a Controlled Substance

UNLAWFUL As with the crime of possession, the law exempts those persons who may lawfully sell controlled substances. Thus, the sale of drugs by a pharmacist based upon a physician's prescription is not a violation of the statute.

SALE OR TRANSFER This element includes transfers without consideration. A defendant may give the substance to another without receiving anything of value and still be convicted under this definition. Sale or transfer includes selling, transferring, giving, or disposing of a controlled substance to another person. This element is complete even if no words are spoken by the parties. A defendant may be approached by a purchaser who shows him money and accepts a package of narcotics and hands over the money to the defendant. This element has been proved even though the defendant and the purchaser did not negotiate the price or communicate in any other manner.

OF A CONTROLLED SUBSTANCE The substance must be a narcotic or dangerous drug. Some jurisdictions have separate crimes for the sale of items represented to be controlled substances. However, for a conviction of selling a controlled substance, the item must be a prohibited substance in usable form.

WITH KNOWLEDGE OF THE NATURE OF THE SUBSTANCE As with the crime of possession, the offender must know that she is selling a controlled substance.

As the above discussion indicates, narcotic offenses are common crimes that occur in every city and on many street corners in the United States. Top federal, state, and local leaders have declared a "war on drugs" in an effort to combat the rising tide of possession, use, and sale of narcotics within the United States. The crimes are relatively simple to define and prosecute. However, the "cure" for this phenomenon is a complex issue that will be addressed later in this chapter.

Medical Marijuana Laws

In 1996, the states of California and Washington passed the first state laws that permitted individuals to possess and use marijuana for medical purposes. The California statute exempted prosecution for the possession or cultivation of marijuana if it was solely for the patient's medical treatment. The patient must have the approval of a physician, and the physician must certify that the patient's health will benefit from medical treatment with marijuana. The state also established a voluntary patient registry system where caregivers and patients are given special ID cards that may be verified with an 800 number. Patients with approved ID cards may possess up to eight ounces of marijuana.

Sale of a Controlled Substance

Defined

Sale of a controlled substance is the unlawful sale or transfer of such a substance.

Elements

The crime of sale of a controlled substance has four elements:

1. Unlawful.
2. Sale or transfer.
3. Of a controlled substance.
4. With knowledge of the nature of the substance.

Some states have enacted laws that permit patient use of marijuana. These laws vary among the states. The state laws do not require employers to allow patients to smoke on the job, and it appears that employers may establish a drug-free policy and are free to terminate any person who smokes marijuana on the job.

The state laws do not affect federal law banning the use of marijuana. The U.S. Food and Drug Administration (FDA) still considers marijuana a controlled substance with a very high potential for abuse and contends that the drug has no accepted medical use. The American Medical Association does not support the medical use of marijuana and advocates further study on this issue.[7]

In *United States v. Oakland Cannabis Buyers' Co-op* (532 U.S. 483 [2001]), the U.S. Supreme Court stated that, even though permitted by state law, medical necessity was not a defense to federal prohibition of marijuana use, since controlled substances statute unambiguously classified marijuana as having no medical benefits warranting exception. The Court also stated in *Gonzales v. Raich* (545 U.S. 1 [2004]) that the regulation of marijuana under the Controlled Substances Act (CSA; 21 U.S.C.S. § 801 et seq.) was squarely within

Congress's commerce power under the U.S. Constitution, Article I, Section 8, U.S. because production of marijuana meant for home consumption had a substantial effect on supply and demand in the national market.

ALCOHOL OFFENSES

Until several years ago, alcohol offenses were looked upon as "victimless" crimes, since everyone had a drink now and then. The formation of MADD (Mothers Against Drunk Driving) and the ensuing publicity surrounding the effects of driving and drinking have raised the public's awareness regarding not only "drunk driving" but other alcohol-related offenses. This section will briefly examine some of the more common alcohol-related crimes.

The Alcohol Problem

There is no doubt that we as a society have an alcohol problem. The extent of the consumption of alcoholic beverages is staggering. There are approximately one hundred million Americans who occasionally drink an alcoholic beverage and between nine and ten million individuals who can be classified as alcoholics.[8] Of this startling figure, an estimated eighteen million American adults and several million children are experiencing physical, mental, and social problems related to the consumption of alcohol. These problems include cirrhosis of the liver, certain types of cancers, emotional disorders, interpersonal conflicts, and alcohol-related violence.[9]

Alcohol takes its toll in human lives; even though the number of alcohol-related fatalities is declining, the number of deaths attributed to driving under the influence in a two-year period was more than the entire number of deaths suffered during more than ten years of warfare in Vietnam.[10]

Alcohol and its effects are a continuing social and criminal problem that affects every law enforcement department and every citizen in the United States. Not only do its effects play havoc with personal lives and fortunes, its consumption under certain circumstances may lead to arrest and conviction for the commission of a crime.

Public Drunkenness

Public drunkenness has been present in American society since the establishment of the colonies. The Puritans stocked their ship the *Arabella* with ten thousand gallons of wine, forty tons of beer, and only eleven tons of water.[11]

A person does not normally become a chronic drunk in one or two days. While numerous models describe the transition from occasional drinker to public drunk, one of the most accepted is E. M. Jellick's medical model. The stages of alcoholism include the **prealcoholic phase**, when the person has an occasional drink as a means of reducing tension; the **intermediate alcoholic stage**, when an individual drinks and has occasional blackouts coupled with a compulsion to drink and loss of control; the **crucial alcoholic phase**, when the loss of control becomes more complete, the drinker is isolated from others, and his life becomes centered on alcohol; and the **final or bottom alcoholic phase**, when the drinker experiences emotional disorganization or impaired thinking.[12]

Public Drunkenness

Defined

Public drunkenness is the state of being intoxicated to the degree that one is unable to care for oneself in a public place.

Elements

The crime of public drunkenness has three elements:

1. Being intoxicated.
2. To the degree that one is unable to care for oneself.
3. In a public place.

BEING INTOXICATED Simply having a few drinks before the football game does not make a person a drunk. As we will discuss later, there are degrees of intoxication. For this aspect of the offense to be satisfied, the level of intoxication must reach the degree set forth in the next element.

TO THE DEGREE THAT ONE IS UNABLE TO CARE FOR ONESELF The consumption of alcohol must reach a level where the person cannot function. Normally, he will have slurred speech, stagger while attempting to walk, or, more commonly, pass out from the consumption of alcohol. The offender will have severely impaired reasoning and be unable to function in a normal manner.

IN A PUBLIC PLACE It is not a crime to become this severely intoxicated in the privacy of your own home. The offense must be committed in a public place. Subways, bus stations, streets, alleyways, and empty fields are common locations where police will find persons so intoxicated that they are classified as public drunks.

We have come to accept public drunkenness as a disease instead of a crime. In order to treat rather than punish, some states do not classify public drunkenness as a criminal offense. Police officers who discover a person who is drunk may contact a social service agency and place the person in its care until she has sobered. Other jurisdictions treat the offense as a civil matter and commit the person to a detoxification center to "dry out." Whether it is classified as a crime or a civil matter, public drunkenness is a serious issue that we must address within our society.

Driving Under the Influence

Every state has a law that prohibits driving a motor vehicle while under the influence of alcohol or drugs. The purpose of these statutes is to protect every person lawfully on a public road or highway and to reduce the hazards of prohibited operation of a motor vehicle to a minimum. Unlike public drunkenness, which requires the person to be extremely intoxicated, driving under the influence requires only that the driver be influenced in his or her mental or physical operation of the vehicle.

Driving Under the Influence

Defined
Driving under the influence is driving or operating a motor vehicle on a public street or highway while under the influence of alcohol or drugs.

Elements
The crime of driving under the influence has three elements:

1. Driving or operating a motor vehicle.
2. Upon a public street or highway.
3. While under the influence of alcohol or drugs.

DRIVING OR OPERATING A MOTOR VEHICLE The defendant must be the driver or engaged in the operation of a motor vehicle. Simply being intoxicated while a passenger in an automobile is insufficient for purposes of this element. **Driving** usually is defined as movement of the vehicle in some direction and means steering and controlling the vehicle while it is in motion.

It may be an offense, depending on the wording of the statute, simply to "operate" the vehicle while **under the influence** of alcohol or drugs. Operation may include sitting in a vehicle with its engine running and the transmission in park. Some cases have held that the vehicle need not be in motion to constitute operation.[13]

Practicums 13.4 to 13.6 examine various factual situations that involve driving or operating a motor vehicle. For purposes of these practicums, you should assume that the defendant is intoxicated to the degree that all other elements of the offense have been satisfied.

Some statutes define motor vehicle very broadly for purposes of this crime. Many states prohibit the driving or operation of motorcycles, motorbikes, motor homes, bicycles, boats, and even horses. The purpose behind this broad prohibition is to ensure that other drivers are protected from any activity that may cause an accident or injury.

UPON A PUBLIC STREET OR HIGHWAY The offense must be committed upon a public street, road, or highway to satisfy this element of the offense. A public road or street is one that is open for use or is used by the public for motor vehicle or pedestrian traffic. Courts have found public park roads or thoroughfares in fairgrounds open to the public, and therefore, public streets within the meaning of the statutes.

Practicum 13.4

Driving?

In a state that requires the driving of a vehicle as part of the offense, an officer observed a vehicle, with its motor running, on the side of a deserted road approximately ten miles from the nearest residence. The defendant was passed out in the back seat.

ISSUE: Do these facts establish driving?

The courts in these situations will look to determine if there was sufficient evidence to establish that the defendant was in control of the vehicle and had driven it to that location.

The fact that the incident occurred on a deserted road and the defendant was in the car normally will carry weight. The defendant must then rebut this evidence and put forth facts that raise a reasonable doubt in the minds of the judge or jury. Normally, defendants in these situations contend that someone else was the driver, and they were merely intoxicated passengers. However, the location of the defendant in the car will be considered vital in establishing this element. What if the defendant was passed out in the passenger's side of the front seat? What if he was slumped over the wheel?[14]

WHILE UNDER THE INFLUENCE OF ALCOHOL OR DRUGS Many statutes define "under the influence" in a variety of ways. One example states that the defendant is under the influence if it can be proved that the alcohol or alcohol and drugs have affected the nervous system, brain, or muscles so as to impair to an appreciable degree the ability to operate a motor vehicle in a manner like that of an ordinary, prudent, and cautious person in full possession of his faculties using reasonable care and under like circumstances.

Practicum 13.5

Operating a Vehicle

In a state that prohibits operation of a vehicle while under the influence, an officer observed a vehicle moving on a public road in an erratic manner. After stopping the car and approaching the driver's side, the officer observed a ten-year-old behind the wheel and the defendant in the passenger seat. The defendant was obviously intoxicated and stated that the minor was her son.

ISSUE: Was the defendant operating the vehicle within the meaning of the statute?

In this situation, the courts will hold the defendant was not "operating" the vehicle. She may have legal custody or control of the vehicle by virtue of the relationship with the driver and may be charged with contributing to the delinquency of a minor, but she will probably not be convicted of DUI.[15]

Practicum 13.6

Operating a Vehicle?

Under the same statute as in Practicum 13.5, the officer discovered the defendant in the vehicle with its engine running, but the gearshift was in the park position and the emergency brake was on.

ISSUE: Was the defendant operating the vehicle within the meaning of the statute?

The courts may find this element of the offense has been satisfied in these types of factual situations. The vehicle does not have to be in motion for the defendant to be operating it within the meaning of these statutes if the accused set in motion the operative machinery of the vehicle for purposes of putting it in motion.[16]

Proof that the defendant was under the influence may be given by the officer's testimony. The officer would testify regarding the defendant's driving pattern, behavior, and performance on any field sobriety test. While this method may result in a conviction, the more common method of proving this element of the crime involves establishing the defendant's blood alcohol level. **Blood alcohol level** is a legal and medical term that is expressed in milligrams of alcohol per milliliter of blood. This level has been translated into the ability or fitness to operate a motor vehicle based upon several broad categories or zones of impairment.

Law enforcement agencies use a variety of tests to establish the blood alcohol level. The three most common are blood, breath, and urine tests. Blood tests involve drawing a sample of blood from the defendant and having it chemically analyzed. Breath tests require the defendant to blow into a machine that analyzes the alcohol content of his breath. Urine tests use a urine specimen taken from the defendant and then analyzed like a blood sample. Each of these tests is voluntary in that the police cannot obtain the sample without the defendant's consent. Many states, however, provide for loss of the defendant's driver's license if he refuses to provide a sample of blood, breath, or urine for analysis.

Some states have enacted presumptions that shift the burden of proving this element. If the driver of the vehicle has tested for a certain blood alcohol level and it can be shown that this level existed during the operation of the vehicle, the offender must prove she was not under the influence. This level varies from state to state, but most statutes establish .08 to .10 blood alcohol level as a presumptive indication that the defendant was under the influence of alcohol, drugs, or both at the time of the operation of the motor vehicle.

Driving under the influence is an offense that can be just as destructive as use of drugs. Thousands of innocent citizens are killed or maimed each year as a direct result of drunk drivers. State legislatures have responded to calls for reform by such groups as MADD and have increased penalties for this offense and shifted the burden of proof to the offender by lowering the blood alcohol level as it relates to the presumption of driving while under the influence.

This section has examined the alcohol problem and offenses that involve consumption of alcohol. Drug and alcohol crimes continue to occupy a high percentage of law enforcement's time and energy. Local, state, and federal elected officials have all sounded the call to battle against these types of crimes. The next section will examine some of the proposed solutions to drug and alcohol offenses.

SOLUTIONS

The solutions to drug and alcohol abuse are complex and subject to wide-ranging debate. The following discussion is not intended to provide a comprehensive examination of all possible intervention techniques available to society. Rather, it is an effort to list some of the more common initiatives that are presently being used by law enforcement agencies and public and private institutions.

INTERNATIONAL AGREEMENTS As early as 1912, nations were enacting international agreements to prohibit certain types of drugs. The International Opium Convention was signed at The Hague, the Netherlands, in 1912. The League of Nations enacted conventions similar to the 1912 agreement in 1925, 1931, and 1936. In 1961, the United Nations Single Convention on Narcotic Use consolidated most of these earlier agreements.

In addition to these international conventions, there are numerous other treaties, agreements, protocols, and resolutions between various nations designed to reduce the supply of illegal drugs. These agreements include the Permanent Secretariat of the South American Agreement on Narcotic Drugs and Psychotropic Substances, initiatives by the Organization of American States, the South Pacific Commission, and the Pan-Arab Bureau for Narcotic Affairs of the League of Arab States, just to name a few. The purpose of all these agreements is to combat the growth, distribution, and sale of prohibited drugs.

PREVENTION OF ILLICIT DEMAND Prevention and reduction of the demand for illegal drugs involve a multifaceted approach that combines law enforcement activities, intervention in the workplace, and education.

Law enforcement activities. The main purpose of law enforcement activities in the United States is to reduce the demand, control supply, and suppress trafficking in illegal drugs. Any law enforcement administrator will tell you that police working by themselves cannot stop the sale of illegal drugs. Therefore, other measures have been employed by our government to wipe out drug use.

Education. We have undertaken a concerted effort to educate our young children on the dangers of using drugs. This information is taught in our classrooms and transmitted into our homes by television. Many of us have seen the television commercial of the egg frying in the pan and the admonition regarding drug use. "Just Say No to Drugs" is a common phrase that can be heard throughout our school systems.

Testing in the workplace. The federal government has passed mandatory drug testing for certain federal employees. We have all seen the signs in various businesses: "Drug-Free Workplace." Many businesses now require as a condition of employment that prospective employees submit to a drug test prior to being hired.

CONTROL OF SUPPLY By attempting to control the supply of illegal drugs, nations are focusing their efforts on the growers of the raw material. Growers of opium poppies, coca bushes, and cannabis plants are the targets of these efforts. However, controlling the supply of such goods is a complex and difficult task.

Crop eradication. Crop eradication refers to the systematic effort to destroy those plants that produce the raw material that is manufactured into narcotic drugs. In addition, there are planned activities that search out and destroy cannabis plants. These plants are destroyed either by physically uprooting them or by spraying them with herbicide. These efforts are taking place both domestically and internationally.[17]

Crop substitution. Crop substitution seeks to motivate farmers in foreign countries to grow domestic food crops for the commercial market instead of poppy, coca, or cannabis plants. Most of these programs have been failures. The main reason for such a lack of success is the difference in price between the prohibited plants and regular farm produce—sometimes as much as fifty to one.[18]

Rural economic development. Crop substitution alone does not appear to be effective in controlling the narcotic problem. Some countries are attempting to combine this measure with rural economic development programs aimed at controlling the supply of drugs. These programs offer redevelopment activities within areas controlled by the state. Thus, local police are better able to monitor the activities of the farmers. In addition, the farmers can live closer to home and enjoy the benefits of civilization. Colombia and Thailand are two of the countries that are actively engaged in these types of programs.[19]

SUPPRESSION OF ILLICIT INTERNATIONAL TRAFFICKING Drug traffickers have employed and continue to employ every conceivable organizational, strategic, and tactical measure to transport their product to market. Some authorities have suggested certain methods to suppress these efforts.

Interdiction of major drug networks. International treaties permit states to stop the entry of drugs inside their boundaries by extraterritorial means. The U.S. Coast Guard, the Border Patrol, and the Drug Enforcement Administration target known routes of drug dealers. The theory behind this strategy is to cut the lines of supply and make it more expensive to purchase the drugs on the streets.

Forfeiture of assets. Federal law allows law enforcement agencies to seize as contraband certain classes of property used by persons found to possess or deal drugs. Items subject to seizure include cars, homes, apartment complexes, commercial establishments, and boats, to name a few. State and local agencies may participate in these activities. The items seized are auctioned off, and the proceeds are funneled back to the various law enforcement activities for specified purposes.

Extradition. Drug traffickers habitually seek haven in a country that has no extradition treaty with a principal consuming nation. The United States has entered into several extradition treaties aimed at apprehending drug leaders and bringing them to trial. Colombia's Medellín cartel suffered a major defeat when one of their ringleaders, Carlos Lehder, was successfully extradited to the United States in 1987. The seizure and transportation of President Noriega of Panama to the United States for trial in 1991 is a striking example of the government's attempt to bring to trial those who are ringleaders in the international trade of narcotics.

Numerous initiatives are being undertaken on both the international and national levels to attack the drug problem. They range from traditional law enforcement activities to drug education programs. The profit from dealing drugs is enormous, and the need for drugs by an addict is overpowering. This war on drugs will continue, grow, and adopt new strategies as long as narcotics continue to invade our shores and harm our citizens.

Prevention of Alcohol Abuse

Some authorities believe that alcohol-related crimes are only symptoms of a much larger problem. They argue that we as a society must address alcohol abuse and its causes if we are to stop the carnage that is occurring on our nation's roads and highways as a result of drunk drivers. What causes alcoholism is a multifaceted issue that is beyond the scope of this text. However, we can address some of the programs that are aimed at preventing alcohol abuse. There are numerous theories regarding how to prevent alcohol abuse. Jan Howard, Mary Ganikos, and Jane Taylor set forth the following typology of some of the more common prevention strategies.[20]

SOCIALIZATION APPROACHES Socialization approaches are based upon the theory that the transfer of knowledge, values, and norms from one group to another person will cause the recipient to internalize what has been taught and act accordingly through self-control mechanisms.

School-based interventions. These programs include instruction in the hazards of alcohol consumption, refusal skills, and social skills. They normally are taught in grammar and high schools. In general, school-based programs have had very limited success.[21]

Driver education programs. There are two primary types of educational interventions that focus on the prevention of drinking and driving: the school-based program aimed at primary prevention and programs for drunk driving offenders, a form of secondary prevention.

Media interventions. Mass communication is a common approach to the prevention of alcohol problems. Historical data indicate that counter-advertising on television concerning smoking practices was an effective strategy.[22]

Health warning labels. The new warning labels on alcoholic beverages may act as a form of deterrence. These labels express the official concern of the U.S. government regarding the consumption of alcoholic beverages.

Primary healthcare providers. There is some authority to support the theory that providers of care could play an important role in preventing alcohol abuse.[23] These efforts may be effective in patients with emerging problems, where health intervention might detect the problem, offer counseling, and give treatment.

SOCIAL-CONTROL APPROACHES Social-control approaches target self-control. However, they do so by establishing external situations that allow for restricted choice.

Economic disincentives. There are a number of studies to indicate that increases in the price of alcoholic beverages directly correlate with decreases in the number of alcohol-related traffic accidents.[24] The surgeon general has recommended increased taxation as a means of mitigating the drunk-driving problem.[25] Other economic disincentives include the availability of civil lawsuits for the sale of alcoholic beverages at public facilities to persons who are under the influence. If these persons are subsequently in an accident, the victims may have a right to sue the tavern owner who served the drunk driver the last drink or drinks.

Restricted availability. A number of authorities have stated that restrictions on the availability of alcoholic beverages reduce alcohol problems.[26] Other interventions include restrictions on the number and type of establishments that are allowed to sell alcoholic beverages.

Punishment. Violations of alcohol-related laws are punishable by license revocation, fines, and imprisonment. The revocation of an offender's driver's license is usually an administrative matter and may be carried out independent of any criminal charges. Some states have established minimum sentences for drunk drivers that require them to spend a certain number of days in jail.

The above typology sets forth a brief analysis of some approaches to solving or combating the alcohol problem that faces our society. This is a complex problem that will take a determined effort by not only law enforcement departments but by state, local, and national agencies as well. We must continue this "war on alcoholism" if we are to prevent further death and destruction on our roads and highways, as well as in our homes in the form of domestic abuse.

Summary

Narcotic and alcohol offenses are commonplace in our society and drain our social and financial resources. The drug problem is well documented in our classrooms, on the streets, and in prisons. There is a clear link between drug use and street crime—the majority of all theft crimes are drug-related. Law enforcement, then, has a dual purpose in stopping drug use: It will decrease street crime as well as stop the flow and use of narcotics in this country.

The crime of possession of a controlled substance appears on the surface to be a simple offense to prove. However, issues include whether the offender had control of the narcotic. Courts will look at a variety of factors, including statements, behavior, prior sales of drugs, and other aspects of the defendant's background.

Possession of a narcotic for sale is simply an extension of the crime of possession, with the added element that the amount of drugs is such that the defendant intended to sell them to another person. This aspect of the offense is usually proved by testimony of a police officer who qualifies as an expert witness regarding the use and sale of narcotics. Normally, officers who are assigned to vice and/or narcotic divisions are used for this purpose.

Sale of a controlled substance is the crime of physically selling a drug to another person. The sale does not have to involve an exchange of money. The crime is complete with the transfer of the drug for any consideration.

The alcohol problem has been with us since the early days of our nation. While we accept social drinking, there are those among us who progress from social drinking to alcoholism. This may cost them their families, friends, and fortunes. Many states treat drunkenness as a disease and, instead of arresting the individual, place him or her in a detoxification facility.

Drunk driving is a misnomer. The offense of drunk driving really involves driving under the influence of alcohol or drugs. States have enacted laws that establish a presumptive level of intoxication. This blood alcohol level may range from .08 to .10. The establishment of MADD has assisted in educating the public regarding the seriousness of driving under the influence. More and more persons are beginning to understand the nature of this offense and to act accordingly.

The solutions to the drug and alcohol problems that face our nation are complex and multifaceted.

There will continue to be a raging debate about the virtues of legalizing drugs. This is an emotional and hard-fought issue with proponents and opponents waging a battle of words and statistics. We have undertaken numerous measures in our war on drugs and alcohol. They include general law enforcement activities, interdiction of drugs, and education about the evils of drugs and alcohol. There is no doubt that the drug and alcohol problem will continue to be of primary importance to citizens, educators, law enforcement departments, and elected officials for the foreseeable future.

Additional Assignments

1. Read the selected cases and associated material for Chapter 13 posted at www.mycrimekit.com.
2. Complete the online study guide material for Chapter 13 posted at www.mycrimekit.com.
3. Discussion and thought questions:
   a. In your view, which is the more serious offense: possession for sale or sale? Why? Are they not basically the same offense, with the exception that the offender actually sold the drug in one crime and not the other?
   b. Should public drunkenness be a crime?
   c. If alcoholism is a medical disease, should we not treat rather than punish the person who is suffering from this disease?
   d. Since it is legal to have one drink and then drive, why is it a serious offense for the driver to be drinking that one drink while she drives? Justify your answer.
   e. How should we approach the question of legalization of certain controlled substances? Explain.

Practicum

You are elected governor of your state. What steps would you take to control the substance abuse problems in your state?

Notes

1. Hippocrates was an early Greek doctor who at one time was believed to have written the Hippocratic Oath. This oath pledges service to the patient and establishes high moral and ethical standards for those in the medical profession.
2. Mark H. Moore and Mark A. R. Kleiman, "The Police and Drugs," *Perspectives on Policing* (U.S. Department of Justice), September 1989.
3. See 21 U.S.C. 801 *et seq.*
4. See *Evans v. United States,* 257 F.2d 121 (9th Cir. 1958).
5. See *State v. La Barre,* 292 Minn. 228 (1972).
6. See *State v. Harris,* 159 Conn. 521 (1970).
7. *USA Today,* April 17, 2007, p. 2B, Col. 2.
8. Ken Liska, *Drugs and the Human Body,* 3rd ed. (New York: Macmillan, 1990), 218.
9. Jan Howard, Mary L. Ganikos, and Jane A. Taylor, "Alcohol Prevention Research," in *Drug*

and Alcohol Abuse Prevention, ed. Ronald R. Watson (Clifton, NJ: Humana Press, 1990).

10. *Fatal Accident Reporting System 1989: A Decade of Progress* (Washington DC: U.S. Government Printing Office, 1991), Table 2–2, p. 2–2.

11. H. Lee, *How Dry Were We: Prohibition Revisited* (Englewood Cliffs, NJ: Prentice-Hall, 1963).

12. E. M. Jellick, *The Disease Concept of Alcoholism* (New Brunswick, NJ: College and University Press, 1960).

13. See *Gallagher v. Commonwealth*, 205 Va. 666, 139 S.E.2d 37 (1964).

14. See *State v. Blaine,* 148 Vt. 272, 531 A.2d 933 (1987).

15. See *State Dept. of Public Safety v. Juncewski,* 308 N.W.2d 316 (1981).

16. Compare *State v. Hedding,* 122 Vt. 379, 172 A.2d 599 (1961) and *Commonwealth v. Plowman,* 28 Mass. App. Ct. 230, 548 N.E.2d 1278 (1990), upholding convictions, with *Ferguson v. City of Doraville,* 186 Ga. App. 430, 367 S.E.2d 551 (1988), which stated merely occupying a parked car is not sufficient for this element.

17. See John Whitehead, "U.S. International Narcotics Control Programs and Policies," *Dept. of State Bulletin,* 1986.

18. See James Painter, "Bolivia's New President Faces an Old Problem: How to Control Coca Growing," *Latinamerica Press,* 1989.

19. See "Where Poppies Once Stood," *Far Eastern Econ. Rev.* 10 (1984).

20. Howard, Ganikos, and Taylor, supra note 12, pp. 1–19.

21. J. M. Moskowitz, "The Primary Prevention of Alcohol Problems: A Critical Review of the Research Literature," *J. Stud. Alcohol* 50, 54–88 (1989).

22. Office on Smoking and Health, "Smoking Control Policies, in Reducing the Health Consequences of Smoking: 25 Years of Progress: A Report of the Surgeon General's Centers for Disease Control, Rockville, MD (DHHS publication No. [CDC] 89-8411) (1989), 461–536.

23. R. L. DuPont, "Teenage Drug Use: Opportunities for the Pediatrician," 102 *J. Pediatr.* 1003 (1983).

24. D. Coate and M. Grossman, "Change in Alcoholic Beverage Prices and Legal Drinking Ages: Effects on Youth Alcohol Use and Motor Vehicle Mortality," 12 *Alcohol Health Res. World* 22 (1987).

25. Office of the Surgeon General, "Surgeon General's Workshop on Drunk Driving Proceedings," December 14–16, 1988 (Washington, DC: Government Printing Office, 1989), pp. 8–11.

26. H. Abadinsky, *Drug Abuse* (Chicago: Nelson-Hall, 1993).

CHAPTER 14

Special Crimes and Offenses

Chapter Outline

Child Abuse
  Physical Child Abuse
  Child Neglect
  Child Sexual Abuse

Elder Abuse
  Definition
  Sexual Assault
  Other Violent Crimes

Fraud
Burglary

Spousal Abuse
  Definition
  Physical Abuse
  Sexual Abuse
  Emotional Abuse

What you should know about special crimes and offenses. After reading this chapter, you should know

- The difference types of abuse.
- The extent of each form of abuse.

- Why emotional abuse is a significant but misunderstood type of abuse.

Key Terms

After reading this chapter, you should understand the following key terms:

child neglect: The negligent treatment or maltreatment of a child by a parent or caretaker under circumstances indicating harm or threatened harm to the child's health or welfare.

child sexual abuse: Sexual exploitation or sexual activities with children under

circumstances that indicate that the child's health or welfare is harmed or threatened.

elder: A person sixty-five years or older.

elder abuse: Conduct that results in the physical, psychological, material harm, neglect, or injury to an elder.

extrafamilial sexual abuse: Exploitative sexual contact with perpetrators who may be known to the child (neighbors, babysitters, live-in partners) or unknown to the child.

intrafamilial sexual abuse: Any type of exploitative sexual contact occurring between relatives, including incest.

material abuse: In the context of elder abuse, the exploitation or use of resources.

physical child abuse: Any act that results in a nonaccidental physical injury by a person who has care, custody, or control of a child.

spousal abuse: Any intentional act or series of acts that cause injury to the spouse.

This chapter deals with special types of crimes that involve intimates. Its format is also different in that it does not have boxes with definitions and elements. Rather, these crimes and their definitions have already been discussed and analyzed in the preceding chapters. This chapter takes those crimes and applies them to people we know and love—family members or intimates with whom we live. We decided to include this special chapter because of the focus and notoriety brought about by cases we read about every day that involve family members or acquaintances.

CHILD ABUSE

Physical Child Abuse

Is a parent unfit or considered abusive if, while bathing his one-year-old daughter, she slips from his grasp and hits her head against the faucet, causing a cut over her eye requiring two stitches? Is this child abuse? While some might blame the father for not being alert to that possibility, others would not classify him as a child abuser. Accidents happen. They are a part of growing up, and painful as they may be to the parent and the child, they are part of a normal, healthy relationship. Thus, not all injuries sustained by children can be classified as child abuse. If not all injuries are child abuse and parents have a right to inflict corporal punishment on children as a form of discipline, how do we draw the line and define physical injuries to children?

Numerous authorities have defined child abuse. Part of the problem in this area has been the continued struggle to agree on what the term child abuse means. Pagelow, Van Hasselt, Gelles, and other scholars in the field have excellent discussions and definitions of this condition.[1] For purposes of this text and ease of understanding, we have accepted the following definition: **Physical child abuse** may be defined as any act that results in a nonaccidental physical injury by a person who has care, custody, or control of a child.

There are two key aspects to this definition—the act is intentional or willful and the act resulted in a physical injury. An accidental injury does not qualify as child abuse. In the example we set forth above, an accidental slip in a bathtub would not qualify as child abuse even if the child received an injury that required several stitches. Child abuse as discussed in this chapter is manifested by physical injury that can be proved or documented. Simply yelling at the child is not child abuse within the meaning of this definition. Nor is spanking the child on the hand, the face, or the buttocks if those acts did not result in a physical injury that can be documented. While it is true that any form of spanking causes injury in the form of pain and some trauma to the child, unless the force is sufficient to leave marks, most medical and legal authorities will not classify these acts as child abuse. This lack of a clear definition is part of the problem of physical child abuse.

Practicum 14.1

When Is It Child Abuse?

- The mother leaves a six-month-old child in the car seat to run into a local convenience store to buy a pack of cigarettes. Would your answer be any different if she was buying baby formula?
- The father spanks his three-year-old son with a belt, saying, "My father did it to me and I turned out OK."

- The mother lets her eight-year-old watch nudity, sex, and violence on the late-night cable channel.
- A three-year-old child is playing catch with his older brother in his front yard next to a busy street, runs into the street to retrieve the ball, and is hit and injured by a car.

The physical battering of children is not a new phenomenon. Children have suffered trauma at the hands of the their parents and caretakers since the beginning of recorded history. In Egypt, upon the birth of Moses, the pharaoh ordered the death of all male children. King Herod also ordered infanticide on a large scale when Jesus was born.

Early history records the practice of burying infants alive in foundations of buildings and bridges.[2] Excavations of Canaanite dwellings have uncovered jars of infant bones in the foundations of buildings.[3] Although officially outlawed, this practice continued in seventeenth-century Europe, and children were found buried in the foundations of London Bridge.

Plato (428–348 BC) and Aristotle (384–322 BC) both urged the killing of infants born with birth defects. Children with birth defects, female infants, and the children of poor families were killed as a matter of course several hundred years before the birth of Christ. In Rome, the law of the Twelve Tables prohibited raising a child with a defect or deformity. In Sparta, infants were examined by a local council of elders that had the power to throw those children considered unfit into a canyon.[4]

Infanticide was not the only form of abuse practiced by early civilizations. During the Middle Ages, families would often mutilate or sever limbs from children so as to make them more effective beggars. The histories of the European school systems are filled with records detailing beatings and abuse by teachers inflicted on their young charges.

The Industrial Revolution was characterized by repeated maltreatment of children. Young children were forced to work long hours under inhumane conditions in factories or other heavy industries. Many were beaten, shackled, or starved to force them to work harder at their tasks.

In 1874, an eight-year-old child named Mary Ellen Wilson was discovered by a social worker to have been beaten and starved by her adoptive parents. The worker referred the case to the New York Police Department, who refused to take any action because there were no laws on the books that addressed the abuse of children by their parents or caretakers. In an effort to save the child, the city filed charges against the caretakers utilizing a statute that prevented cruelty to animals. The adoptive mother was sentenced to one year in jail, and the resulting publicity surrounding Mary Ellen's plight led to the formation of the Society for the Prevention of Cruelty to Children in 1875.

From this beginning, we have expanded our concern and care for abused children. Every state has laws preventing the physical abuse of children. The phenomenon of child abuse has generated many studies. One of the most commonly cited of these studies was conducted by the American Association for Protecting Children. The information contained in this annual report indicates that in 1982 almost one million children were abused and neglected.[5] Other studies report figures ranging from 200,000 to four million. Some researchers even take the position that there is no method of obtaining reliable data in this field.[6] Even the federal government has failed to establish standards for reporting child abuse. The FBI's Uniform Crime Reports (UCR) is the accepted method of reporting crimes on a nationwide basis. The UCR publishes crime statistics reported by 16,000 law enforcement agencies. However, it provides no specific information on crimes against children. With the exception of murder, the UCR does not list the victim's age. The National Center on Child Abuse and Neglect (NCCAN), a division within the U.S. Department of Health and Human Services, has commissioned studies to provide a national estimate of the incidence of child maltreatment.

Many authorities believe that the number of reported cases of child abuse is only the tip of the iceberg. This is particularly true for those children between the ages of twelve and nineteen. This age group is far less likely than younger victims to report crimes, especially when the offender is not a stranger.[7] Part of the problem with determining the magnitude of physical child abuse may have something to do with the definition itself.

By defining the characteristics or hallmarks of physical child abuse differently, the research data itself can differ significantly. Researchers select their sample populations based upon criteria that differ from scholar to scholar and study to study. Some social scientists view physical child abuse in the context of determining whether the child is "at risk," while those working in the criminal justice field emphasize physical evidence. This multifaceted approach to understanding physical child abuse presents both problems and opportunities for growth. As mentioned earlier, the problem is reaching consensus on the definition of physical child abuse and how we respond to it. The opportunities for growth are based upon the premise that professionals can and should learn from each other. The social worker may learn of the difficulties in proving certain types of abuse while at the same time teaching the prosecuting attorney to accept the seriousness of a situation that might not otherwise be apparent from a legal perspective. The next section will address the issue of child neglect, an area that is even more emotional and hard to define.

Child Neglect

In the past forty years, there have been numerous texts, articles, and studies that deal with the subject of neglect. The literature runs the gamut from examining assessment techniques of neglect[8] to listing all the different forms of this abuse.[9] Except for rare instances, child neglect does not receive the public attention that child sexual and physical abuse generates. Part of the reason for this lack of emphasis may lie in the definition and nature of child neglect.

Child neglect is the negligent treatment or maltreatment of a child by a parent or caretaker under circumstances indicating harm or threatened harm to the child's health or welfare. While this appears at first glance to be a simple and straightforward statement, it covers a wide range of activities or omissions that impact on the physical and emotional well-being of a child. At what point does mere inattention or lack of knowledge translate itself into child neglect? The above definition would require an act or omission that results in harm or threatens to cause harm to the child's health or welfare. This act or omission may be physical or psychological. A strict interpretation of this definition would require that parents or caretakers guard their children like prisoners. However, this is unrealistic because children are mobile. They get into drawers, cabinets, and every corner in the house and yard. Therefore, we are dealing with a continuum that stretches from momentary inattention to gross inaction.

Momentary inattention————Gross action or inaction

Somewhere on this line, acceptable parenting ends and child neglect begins. While there is no clear point that establishes neglect, it is a common form of child abuse. The next section addresses another aspect of child abuse, the issue of sexual abuse of children.

Some scholars have stated that child neglect is the most common form of maltreatment. According to Arthur Green, in the State of New York, the reported cases of neglect outnumbered those of physical abuse by eleven to one in 1987.[10] Other studies indicate that physical abuse is more prevalent than neglect. No matter who is right, child neglect is an important topic all professionals should understand. Neglect is less obvious than physical or sexual abuse, and it may continue for years without any outsider even being aware that the child they see daily is a victim. It has many faces, forms, and appearances. There are serious cases in which a child's life is threatened and more mundane acts by which the child is simply neglected on a daily basis.

Child Sexual Abuse

Child sexual abuse is sexual exploitation or sexual activities with children under circumstances that indicate that the child's health or welfare is harmed or threatened.[11] This definition includes inappropriate sexual activities between children and adults. The inappropriate behavior may be between family members or between a stranger and the victim. **Intrafamilial sexual abuse** includes incest and refers to any type of exploitative sexual contact occurring between relatives. **Extrafamilial sexual abuse** refers to exploitative sexual contact with perpetrators who may be known to the child (neighbors, babysitters, live-in partners) or unknown to the child.[12]

One of the major problems with this definition is the requirement that the child be harmed. From a legal perspective, harm to the victim is not an element of the crime of child sexual abuse. If certain physical acts occur, the crime is complete. In criminal proceedings it is not necessary to prove that the perpetrator intended to or actually harmed the child. However, this definition is useful in exploring the consequences of child sexual abuse, and retaining the requirement of an injury to the child will allow for such a discussion.

The following acts are examples of child sexual abuse: exposing one's sexual organs to the child, voyeurism, touching the sex organs of the child, mutual or self-masturbation with the child, oral sex, intercourse, and anal sex. In addition, allowing the child to view or participate in pornographic or obscene movies is considered child abuse.

Child sexual abuse may be distinguished from rape in that the perpetrator may use a variety of different "techniques" to achieve the objective of sexual gratification. Rape normally involves sexual acts as the result of force or fear. Child abuse offenders may also use force or fear; however, they also employ other pressures or influences to accomplish their goal. These actions include manipulation of the child (psychologically isolating the child from other loved ones), coercion (using adult authority or power on the child), force (restraining the child), threats or fear (informing the child that if she tells, no one will love her).[13]

The American people have a widespread interest in child sexual abuse. However, the true magnitude of this problem is difficult to establish. There is a general agreement among both scholars and professionals in the field that the incidence of child sexual abuse reporting is understated.[14] Estimates on the number of child sexual abuse vary from source to source. Finkelhor's 1979 study of 796 college students indicated that 19 percent of the females and 9 percent of the males had been subjected to sexual abuse as a child.[15] A later study by Finkelhor of 521 Boston parents indicated that 15 percent of the females and 6 percent of the males had been sexually abused by the age of 16.[16] Russell's survey of 930 San Francisco women found that 28 percent had been victims of child sexual abuse before the age of 14.[17] In 1985, the *Los Angeles Times* conducted a random survey of 2,627 adults across the United States. The survey revealed that 27 percent of the women and 16 percent of the survey participants had been molested as children. The total percentage (combining men and women) for those who suffered child sexual abuse was 22 percent.[18] In 1991, researchers came to the conclusion that as many as 10 percent to 15 percent of all boys and 20 percent to 25 percent of all girls had experienced at least one instance of sexual abuse prior to the age of 18.[19]

Rape in America, which was published by the National Victim Center, indicates sexual violence occurs at a much higher rate than previously expected.[20] It illustrates that sexual violence is still a major problem in America. Based upon this study, the National Victim Center estimates there are at least 12.1 million women in the United States who were subjected to sexual violence as a child or adult.

Using some of these statistics, we can project the possible prevalence of child sexual abuse in the United States today.[21] The most conservative estimate indicates 10 percent of all women and 2 percent of all males have been molested. Our census indicates a population of 60 million minors within the United States. Using these figures, we can project that there are 210,000 incidents of child sexual abuse that occur every year. Comparing this number with the 44,700 cases reported to professionals clearly indicates a lack of reporting of this type of abuse.[22]

While the figures may vary from study to study regarding the types and incidence of child sexual abuse, there is some agreement among researchers that the following classification of offenders is a valid estimate:[23]

Classification	Percentage
Strangers as the offender	Approximately 8–10 percent
Family members as the offender	Approximately 47 percent
Other acquaintances as the offender	Approximately 40 percent

The true extent of child victimization is unknown; however, simply discussing this subject raises our awareness and makes it more likely that we will acknowledge its existence. Professionals must not simply be aware that it occurs; they should have a basic understanding of some of the more common theories dealing with the causes of child abuse.

ELDER ABUSE

While we became aware of certain forms of family violence in the 1960s and 1970s, it wasn't until the 1980s that the plight of elder victims entered our national consciousness as a problem that must dealt with. One of the first studies dealing with elder abuse was published in 1979. Block and Sinnott titled their work "The Battered Elder Syndrome: An Exploratory Study." They contacted twenty-four agencies in Maryland and surveyed 427 professionals and 443 elders. They found twenty-six cases of elder abuse. Unfortunately, the study went no further, but it was the first step in the long process of recognizing that elders can be victims of family violence.[24] By 1988, the research examining elder abuse consisted of over two hundred research papers.[25] Today, that number continues to rapidly expand. Although there are several problems in the study of elder abuse, defining the term itself and determining its extent are two of the most controversial and difficult to resolve.

Practicum 14.2

Abuse or Support?

- A fifty-five-year-old son has his ninety-year-old mother living with him. The mother has a habit of wandering away from the house. He locks her in her room at night from 7 p.m. until morning. There is no bathroom in her room.
- A twenty-year-old takes care of her grandmother, age eighty-five. After combing her hair, she takes $40 from her purse as payment. The grandmother sees her do it but says nothing because she is afraid the granddaughter will stop visiting her if she complains about the money.
- A husband and wife are taking care of the wife's eighty-five-year-old mother. The husband requires the mother to take a shower each night while he stands at the open bathroom door watching her.

There is a continuing failure to report and act on this form of abuse, and Decalmer lists two major factors that may contribute to this failure:

1. There is a failure to understand the size, severity, and nature of the problem because of the conflicting definitions of elder abuse.
2. The number of controlled studies and the case reporting methods that are used in most of the research in this area has produced difficulties in estimating the true extent of the various acts of abuse and neglect.[26]

In addition, methodology and sampling procedures differ from study to study. Some research focuses on the elderly population, other studies examine agency records, and still other investigations poll professionals. As a result, there are no definitive figures that are accepted by all scholars and researchers.

Definition

The term elder abuse was first used during congressional hearings in the late 1970s. The House Select Committee on Aging, chaired by Representative Claude Pepper (The Pepper Commission), examined the mistreatment of the elderly and introduced the term "elder abuse" to the nation.[27] However, coining a term does not always clearly define the parameters for the scholars and professionals trying to do the research.

Some scholars, while examining elder abuse, have included persons under the age of sixty in their research while others simply include everyone who is over the age of sixty regardless of the circumstances.[28] Well-respected authorities defined elder abuse as occurring only between those who share a residence with the victim, while in other studies out-of-home caretakers were included.[29] The debate, confusion, and inability to agree on any acceptable conceptual framework from which to study elder abuse continues to cause problems in this area.

In an effort to clarify this confusion, some authorities attempted to develop a list of definitions involving abuse of the elderly by establishing typologies. Unfortunately, these typologies lacked uniformity and resulted in more confusion. Hudson and Johnson pointed out that some typologies differed considerably in defining neglect, while others classified withholding of personal care as physical abuse, psychological abuse, or both.[30] As a result of this continuing confusion, other researchers began to attempting to frame the definition of elder abuse from a conceptional perspective. For example, some scholars placed the issue of elder abuse within the broad category of inadequate care.[31] However, the same problems that were faced in trying to establish an acceptable typology were present in the effort to conceptualize the entire issue.[32]

Several prominent scholars, including Wolf, Pillemer, and Godkin, subsequently distilled these various definitions down to a multifaceted definition that classified elder abuse into five areas:

1. Physical abuse includes the infliction of physical pain or injury, physical coercion, sexual molestation, or physical restraint.
2. Psychological abuse includes the infliction of mental anguish.
3. Material abuse includes the illegal or improper exploitation and/or use of funds or resources.
4. Active neglect includes the refusal or failure to undertake a caretaking obligation.
5. Passive neglect includes the refusal or failure to fulfill a caretaking obligation.[33]

The above discussion clearly illustrates the difficulty in attempting to define the term elder abuse and helps to explain the continuing scholarly debate and controversy. Based upon this confusion and conflict, a simple, clear definition of elder abuse may not be possible. However, for purposes of consistency with other definitions contained in this text, **elder abuse** is defined as conduct that results in the physical, psychological, material, neglect, harm, or injury to an elder. This definition applies both to domestic as well as institutional abuse.

Material abuse in the context of elder abuse refers to the exploitation or use of resources. An **elder** is a person sixty-five years or older. The initial age determination of sixty-five is based upon common acceptance of that age by most authorities, scholars, and professionals.[34] This age group may be further subdivided into those between sixty-five and seventy-five, who are called the young-old, and those above sixty-five, who are referred to as the old-old.[35]

Elder abuse can occur in a domestic or institutional setting. Pillemer and Moore point out that despite two decades of state and federal regulation of nursing homes, abuse of the elderly still occurs on a regular basis.[36] The focus of this section will be on the domestic abuse aspect of this form of violence, since more research has been done in this area. However, abuse of the elderly in nursing homes and long-term care institutions is a fact of modern life and should not be forgotten or overlooked when considering the overall plight of the elderly in our society.

This section will examine a few of the more common crimes that are committed against elders. Not only are elders preyed upon by family members because of their frail condition, they are also prime targets for certain kinds of criminals who seek easy targets.

Sexual Assault

For many elderly women who were raised during a time when sexual matters were never discussed publicly, becoming a victim of a sexual assault can be a traumatic experience that the elder is not able to process. Some elders are still surrounded with embarrassment about sexual activity and have never discussed it even with their children. To these elders, the thought of having to discuss sexual acts in public is unthinkable. Many older victims believe it is the worst form of lost dignity. They may experience shame in discussing the case or participating in a medical examination with law enforcement officers present. They may have been required to perform sexual acts they have never participated in before, which only adds to the humiliation.

Elderly rape victims often sustain injuries different from those experienced by younger victims. Vaginal linings are not as elastic as those of younger women because of hormonal changes. This may cause increased sexual trauma including infections, bruising, and tears that never fully heal. More alarmingly, many elders have brittle bones, such as the pelvis and hips, that can be more easily broken or crushed by the weight of the rapist.

Other Violent Crimes

Elder victims are the least likely to be physically injured during the commission of a violent crime. However, if they are injured, these injuries tend to be more serious because of their frailty and aging bodies. Bones of the elderly become more brittle with advanced age and break more easily than those of a twenty-year-old. One study points out that, when elders are physically injured during a violent crime, they are twice as likely as any other age group to be seriously injured and require hospitalization.[37] However, the elderly as a whole are significantly less likely than younger age groups to become the victim of most types of crime including violent crime.[38] This may be because they are not as mobile and do not go out in public as much as their younger counterparts and therefore are not as easily approached or victimized.

Most homicide victims over the age of sixty-five were killed during the commission of another felony and were more likely to be killed by a stranger. The elderly are also less likely to protect themselves during the incident and may suffer injuries that younger victims would avoid. A purse-snatcher may cause a younger victim to stumble and regain her stability, while the same incident may cause an elderly victim to fall and break her hip.

Fraud

The elderly are targeted for crimes involving finances more than any other victim population. While elderly victims may not sustain any physical injury as a result of this type of crime, the psychological impact can be devastating. The loss of one's entire life savings can create severe and debilitating depression. Many victims blame themselves for the loss and because of this can suffer additional health problems relating to depression such as loss of appetite, decreased interest level, increased withdrawal, and diminished sleep. Some victims feel ashamed that they didn't recognize the "con" and become reluctant to report the crime because they think family members will blame them for mismanagement of their funds and seek to terminate their financial independence.

A majority of the elderly live on fixed incomes, and the impact of a financial crime can be devastating to them. They may lose their life savings and even their homes. This may result in the loss of their independence that many elderly people value more than money itself.

Burglary

For many of the elderly, the home becomes the center of their world as they gradually lose friends and their own mobility. They retire from jobs, family members begin to die, and outside activities decrease due to increasing physical or mental limitations. This imposed isolation explains, in part, why a majority of the elderly are victimized near or in their homes.

The loss of certain possessions, especially those that have sentimental value, can have a great impact on an older person. The loss of other material items, such as televisions, can further restrict an elder's outside contact with the world. Many victims may want to relocate after a burglary but may not have the financial ability to do so. Once their home has been invaded, they may never feel safe again.

SPOUSAL ABUSE

There is probably no more misunderstood form of violence than spousal abuse. Richard J. Gelles has published a series of *Domestic Violence Factoids* that are statements, or sound bites, used by various individuals or agencies when discussing family violence.[39] Gelles points out that many of these statements have taken on a life of their own and are presumed to be true or accurate. In many instances, this "truth" is based upon misinterpretation or faulty analysis of research. The following are some of these factoids and Gelles's response:

> DOMESTIC VIOLENCE IS THE LEADING CAUSE OF INJURY TO WOMEN BETWEEN THE AGES OF 15 AND 44 IN THE UNITED STATES—MORE THAN CAR ACCIDENTS, MUGGINGS, AND RAPES COMBINED.

Gelles points out that as good a sound bite as this statement is, it is simply not true. The actual research that this statement is based upon was a small survey of only one emergency room and the authors of the study stated that domestic violence may be a more common cause of emergency room visits than car accidents, muggings, and rapes.

THE MARCH OF DIMES REPORTS THAT BATTERING DURING PREGNANCY IS THE LEADING CAUSE OF BIRTH DEFECTS AND INFANT MORTALITY.

Gelles responds that the March of Dimes knows of no such study.

NATIONALLY, 50 PERCENT OF ALL HOMELESS WOMEN AND CHILDREN ARE ON THE STREETS BECAUSE OF VIOLENCE IN THE HOME.

Gelles states that this factoid can be attributed to Joseph Biden, a senator at the time, but there is no actual published scientific research supporting these figures.

THERE ARE NEARLY THREE TIMES AS MANY ANIMAL SHELTERS IN THE UNITED STATES AS THERE ARE SHELTERS FOR BATTERED WOMEN AND THEIR CHILDREN.

Gelles indicates that while this is another great sound bite, there is no verified count of either type of shelter.

As the above discussion indicates, there is still a great deal of misinformation and controversy surrounding spouse abuse. These factoids should not be interpreted to mean that spousal abuse is not a serious and deadly problem. It is, however, to understand this form of violence, we must base our knowledge on facts or theories that are accepted within the various professions that deal with spousal abuse, not sound bites.

Definition

There is no clear single definition of spousal abuse. Different authorities include different acts within their definition, and some authorities have established levels of spousal abuse. They categorize spousal abuse into two forms of violence. The lesser forms include yelling and throwing things and the more severe include striking and hitting.

As Practicum 14.3 indicates, there are shades of gray in any situation, and reasonable people may disagree as to what constitutes spousal abuse. For purposes of this chapter, **spousal abuse** is defined as any intentional act or series of acts that cause injury to the spouse. These acts may be physical, emotional, or sexual. Spouse is gender neutral; therefore, the abuse may occur to a male or female. The term includes those who are married, cohabiting, or involved in a serious relationship. It also encompasses individuals who are separated and living apart from their former spouse. While there is some disagreement regarding the exact definition of spousal abuse, all scholars and authorities agree it exists. The next section will examine the extent of this form of family violence.

Practicum 14.3

Human Nature or Abuse?

- A boy is upset at his girlfriend who is late for a date. He calls her lazy and irresponsible.
- During a date, the male takes his date's arm and steers her to an entrance, commenting that she is stupid for not seeing that this is the fastest way to leave the theater.
- A couple who are living together while attending college get into a yelling match, with each of them calling the other names.
- The same couple's argument escalates and the female throws a textbook at her male friend. It misses and strikes the TV.
- During a heated argument, the male grabs the female by the arms and shakes her.

- A husband yells at his wife and calls her dumb after she overdraws the bank account, causing him to bounce a check.
- The husband does not allow his wife access to any funds after she bounced three checks and almost caused him to lose his job at the bank.
- The wife is tired and wants to sleep, but the husband forces her to engage in sex.
- The wife does not enjoy anal sex, stating that it hurts her, but the husband forces her to engage in it once a month.

While it is true that the definition of spousal abuse is gender neutral, and in fact men can be battered by women, most of the victims of spousal abuse are women. In 1977, Suzanne Steinmetz presented a paper titled "The Battered Husband Syndrome." This presentation was the basis for an article dealing with husbands who are battered.[40] Steinmetz's research, which was widely publicized in the media, claimed that men were abused at a far greater rate than previously believed. Steinmetz went even further and claimed that wives abused their husbands more often and more severely than vice versa. This claim was attacked by feminists, professionals, and scholars. In 1988, Steinmetz and Lucca published a follow-up article discussing husband battering in more detail.[41] In this article, they continued to assert that husbands are battered and concluded that all forms of violence must be prevented by placing greater emphasis on changing the attitudes and values of a society that glorifies violence.

One of the results of Steinmetz's position is the acknowledgment that both parties in an abusive relationship need to be evaluated. There have been studies to indicate that there are higher levels of female aggression by women toward their spouses than previously thought.[42] However, the type and severity of aggression is different from that experienced by women. As Campbell points out, most authorities agree that the detrimental effects of abuse affect women disproportionately.[43] Furthermore, Campbell states that gender inequity is a significant risk factor in battering.

While it may be true that some men are abused by women in an intimate relationship, the majority of all abuse is inflicted by men. Therefore, the remainder of this chapter will examine the abused from the perspective of women as the victims.

One of the more surprising results of some of these studies is the indication that spousal abuse may have declined by as much as 20 percent in recent years. There are several explanations for this apparent decline. One is the existence of shelters for women who are abused. This escape valve allows them an option to escape an abusive relationship. Another is the widespread publicity that has occurred in recent years about spousal abuse. A third possible explanation is more effective punishment and better treatment for the assaultive partner.[44] While the incidence of spousal abuse may be declining, many scholars believe its severity is increasing. Even with a decline in the number of reported cases in recent years, this form of family violence is still prevalent and requires any professional to be familiar with the nature and dynamics of spousal abuse.

As with other subjects in this area, there is disagreement on the different types of spousal abuse. Many of the studies have focused solely on physical abuse, documenting the number of times a husband strikes his wife, while others have looked at sexual violence in a marriage. Still others examine the psychological or emotional abuse a spouse suffers at the hands of her tormenter. Finally, some classify abuse as a property form and discuss the financial dependence imposed by the abuser. No matter how many types or variations one employs, it is important to realize that they all work together to form a net that completely encompasses the woman in a world of physical violence, sexual violence, emotional violence, or all three.

For purposes of clarity, spousal abuse in this chapter is classified as physical, sexual, or emotional abuse. Within each area there are degrees of severity and differences. A woman may suffer from one or all forms of spousal abuse.

Determining who has suffered what type of abuse is more of an art than a science. Two major types or techniques are relied upon in assessing spousal abuse: self-reporting and interviews. The Conflict Tactics Scale self-report developed by Straus contains eighteen items that measure or assess reasoning and aggression during conflicts within a family. Another self-report is the Spouse Specific Aggression Scale, which measures psychological but not physical aspects of abuse. These inventories allow for a quick and confidential screening of physical and verbal abuse.

Additionally, there are checklists that allow for answers or information that may not be obtained in a clinical setting. The disadvantages of these inventories are that they fail to provide information on how aggression is related to, or interacts with, control and power in the relationship.

Another form of gathering information is the clinical interview. For any interview to be successful, it requires the interviewer be knowledgeable in the various forms of spousal abuse. (You cannot ask what you don't know.) The interview process allows for assessment of the effects of abuse as well as the dynamics of power and control in the relationship. The main disadvantage to the interview process of gathering information should be obvious—the spouse or spouses must agree to be interviewed. Since one of the characteristics of spousal abuse is isolation, the interview process is limited to those situations in which one or both of the spouses come forward and agree to be interviewed.

Physical Abuse

Physical aggression may take the form of "minor" acts that escalate over time. It may begin with an arm being grabbed, a dish thrown, or a slap to the arm or face. This aggression increases in severity until the victim has no way out of the relationship. Only the perpetrator's imagination is the limiting factor in the infliction of physical abuse on the spouse. The following is a list of the more common forms of physical abuse suffered by spouses:

Striking acts. The abuser may strike the face, arms, body, or legs of the spouse. The violence may be delivered with an open or closed hand. These acts include punching with his fist.

Throwing or destruction of property. The abuser may throw dishes, small appliances, and so forth, at the spouse, or he may go on a rampage and simply destroy household property.

Control or choking acts are also common. Choking is a common form of abuse. It sends a very clear message that the abuser is stronger and more powerful. Choking allows the batterer to control the spouse and have her beg for mercy.

Repeated beating using objects. Use of belts, sticks, or other objects during the assault is not uncommon. Using the same object allows the abuser to completely control the victim simply by laying his hand on the object.

Humiliation violence. Some abusers will require their victims to assume certain positions for the imposition of violence. Having the victim undress before yelling and beating her adds to the feeling of helplessness.

As the above discussion indicates, there are numerous forms of physical violence. The results of these acts will leave certain physical marks or injuries on the women. In the event that they require medical treatment, the physician should be alert to the possibility of abuse if an injury is not consistent with the medical history given by the spouse. The second form of spousal abuse, discussed below, is even harder to detect.

Sexual Abuse

Physical violence is often accompanied by sexual abuse. Sex on demand or after physical assaults is very common. Since the woman does not believe she has any choice or free will, she will submit to the abuser's demands. Additionally, she may fear that a refusal to engage in sexual activity will cause the abuser to react violently.

Sexual acts that humiliate or degrade the wife are not uncommon. The husband may demand oral sex without any regard for his spouse's feelings or beliefs. Anal intercourse is common form of sexual abuse. The abuser may say things to the spouse or require her to say things that are degrading to her. Some abusers may require their spouses to share sex with friends or coworkers.

Violence during the sexual act may occur. The abuser may engage in sexual activities in a violent and forceful manner that is intended to injure or hurt his spouse. This is a form of physical abuse that is accomplished by use of sex.

Sometimes, *sex will occur after a physical altercation.* This may be loving and caring and an attempt by the abuser to "make up" for the aggression. This offers false hope to the abused spouse and is intended to make her believe that the abuser is really sorry and the physical acts will not occur again.

Sexual abuse may provoke intense emotional and physical reactions in the abused spouse. This intensity and humiliation may become additive and be looked upon as a form of release. It may, on occasion, take on a narcotic effect for the abused spouse.

At one time in our history, a man had a "right" to sex with his wife. There was no such thing as spousal rape. Today, we have laws that prevent this form of assault, and the topic of rape was discussed in more detail in other chapters in this text. Sexual abuse may not leave physical scars visible to the naked eye, but certainly it will leave emotional scars that may be even longer lasting and more devastating.

Emotional Abuse

Emotional abuse is far more than a husband simply calling his wife degrading names. This form of spousal abuse has far-reaching consequences for the victim and leaves scars that require long-term treatment. Emotional abuse includes many different acts that all contribute to a feeling of helplessness and inability.

The batterer may engage in verbal dominance. At first, the spouse may believe this is simply ego or a strong person speaking. However, in time, she learns her opinions, feelings, and thoughts carry no weight, and if, in fact, she expresses herself at all, she is subject to verbal and possibly physical abuse.

Isolation is a common form of emotional abuse. The abuser may isolate the victim by limiting her access to money, use of the car, or other normal activities. He talks negatively about her family and friends thereby making it uncomfortable for the spouse to maintain outside relations. Isolation forecloses feedback from others. The only feedback she receives is from the abusing partner, who distorts both his and her realities, leaving her feeling dumb, lazy, and unattractive. After a time, the abused spouse comes to accept these statements as true.

Guilt is a common form of emotional abuse. The abuser usually blames the spouse for his assaultive behavior with the rationale that, if she had only carried out her duties better, he would not have had to hit her. After a time, the abused spouse begins to accept these pronouncements and blame herself for the battering.

Fear is common form of emotional abuse. The abuser may threaten to reveal secrets or private information to family and friends, or the batterer may threaten the spouse with a beating when he gets home. The spouse then waits hours for the expected assault. The abuser may threaten to harm her or her family if she ever leaves him or does anything else he does not approve of.

Humiliation is another common form of emotional abuse. The spouse may be put down in front of friends, family, or children. In extreme cases, the abuser may require her to perform degrading acts in public, such as having sex in front of friends or her children, requesting permission before leaving the room or going to the bathroom, and so on. This type of emotional abuse destroys the spouse's sense of self-worth and ability to resist further acts of control by the abuser.

Using fear, guilt, and isolation, the abuser will promote the *feeling of helplessness* within the spouse. This further ties the victim to the abuser. She believes there is no way to break the cycle and is, therefore, trapped.

One aspect of emotional abuse that deserves special attention is *financial dependence*. The abuser may require the spouse to work and turn her check over to him. He will control all finances and ensure she never has any funds that he does not approve. The abuser may control the funds in order to isolate the spouse, deny her opportunities to improve herself, or demean her. This financial dependence adds to the spouse's feeling of helplessness and entrapment. Even if she wanted to leave, she would have no money with which to support herself or to even rent a room for a night.

Emotional abuse is a serious form of spousal abuse. While it leaves no physical scars, it can bind the abused spouse to the perpetrator far more effectively than chains or ropes.

Summary

Family violence is a newly emerging form of criminal activity. These types of crime strike at the heart of our relationships and are a very emotional experience for both the victim and the law enforcement officer who investigates these criminal acts. We are becoming more knowledgeable regarding the dynamics of these special crimes, and with that knowledge comes responsibility to act accordingly when investigating these crimes.

Child abuse can occur anywhere and at any time. It may be physical, neglect, sexual, or a combination of all three forms of abuse. It may occur to a six-week-old baby or to a young teenage girl. Elder abuse is one of the most tragic forms of family violence. It occurs after the victim has led a life full of vigor and energy. It happens in the twilight of our life and can add sorrow and pain to our remaining years. Spousal abuse is one of the most common forms of family violence. It happens behind closed doors and involves dynamics that make it hard for the victim to leave.

These special crimes desire special attention because they can happen to our families, our friends, or neighbors. Blacks, whites, Latinos, and Asians are, have been, and will continue to be both perpetrators and victims of family violence.

Additional Assignments

1. Read the selected cases and associated material for Chapter 14 posted at www.mycrimekit.com.
2. Complete the online study guide material for Chapter 14 posted at www.mycrimekit.com.
3. Discussion and thought questions:
   a. Why are these crimes important to understand? How are they different from the "regular" crimes that are discussed in other chapters of the book?
   b. Should there be special punishment for child abusers? Should certain abusers be given second chances with their children? Which form of child abuse is the most serious? Why?
   c. Describe the different forms of elder abuse, and list the common characteristics that appear in all forms of elder abuse.
   d. Why do women who are victims of spousal abuse stay with the abuser? List the reasons.
   e. Which type of special crime is the most serious? Why?

Practicum

Is there a local shelter for abused women in your home city? Research the nearest shelter in your area. How is it funded? How do women know of its location and rules?

Notes

1. See, for example, V. B. Van Hasselt et al., eds., *Handbook of Family Violence* (New York: Plenum Press, 1988).

2. S. Radbill, "A History of Child Abuse and Infanticide," in R. Helfer and C. H. Kempe, eds., *The Battered Child,* 2nd ed. (Chicago: University of Chicago Press, 1974).

3. C. F. Potter, "Infanticides," in *Dictionary of Folklore, Mythology and Legend,* Vol. 1, ed. M. Leach (New York, Funk & Wagnalls, 1949).

4. N. C. Sorel, *Ever Since Eve: Personal Reflections on Childbirth* (New York: Oxford University Press, 1984).

5. American Association for Protecting Children, Inc., *Highlights of Official Child Neglect and Abuse Reporting* 1983 (Denver: American Humane Association).

6. R. Uviler, "Save Them from Their Saviors: The Constitutional Rights in the Family," in *Child Abuse: An Agenda for Action*, ed. G. Gerber, C. Ross, and E. Zigler, 147–155, 151 (New York: Oxford University Press, 1980).

7. U.S. Department of Justice, Bureau of Justice Statistics, *Criminal Victimization in the United States, 1987* (Washington, DC: U.S. Government Printing Office, 1989), Table 4.

8. R. T. Ammerman and M. Hersen, *Assessment of Family Violence* (New York: John Wiley & Sons, 1992).

9. J. Myers, *Evidence in Child Abuse and Neglect,* 2nd ed. (New York: John Wiley & Sons, 1992).

10. Arthur H. Green, "Child Neglect," in *Case Studies in Family Violence*, ed. R. Ammerman and M. Hersen (New York: Plenum Press, 1991), 135.

11. This is a shortened version of the definition contained in the Child Abuse Prevention and Treatment Act of 1974, which is one of the most widely adopted statutes defining child sexual abuse.

12. D. A. Wolfe, V. V. Wolfe, and C. L. Best, "Child Victims of Sexual Assault," in *Handbook of Family Violence*, ed. V. B. Van Hasselt et al. (New York: Plenum Press, 1988).

13. J. R. Conte, "Victims of Child Sexual Abuse," in *Treatment of Family Violence*, ed. R. T. Ammerman and M. Hersen, 64–65 (New York: John Wiley & Sons, 1990).

14. C. R. Hartman and A.W. Burgess, "Sexual Abuse in Children: Causes and Consequences," in *Child Maltreatment*, ed. D. Cicchetti and V. Carlson, 98 (New York: Cambridge University Press, 1989).

15. D. Finkelhor, *Sexually Victimized Children* (New York: Free Press, 1979).

16. D. Finkelhor, *Child Sexual Abuse: New Theories and Research* (New York: Free Press, 1984).

17. D. Russell, *Rape in Marriage* (New York: Macmillan, 1982).

18. L. Timnick, "22% in Survey Were Child Abuse Victims," *Los Angeles Times*, August 25, 1985.

19. Friedrich, Grambsch, Broughton, Kuiper, and Beilke, "Normative Sexual Behavior in Children," 88 *Pediatrics* 456 (1991).

20. D. G. Kilpatrick, C. N. Edmonds, and A. K. Seymour, *Rape in America: A Report to the Nation* (Arlington, VA: National Victim Center, 1992).

21. D. Finkelhor, *Child Sexual Abuse*, supra note 16.

22. The figure of 44,700 comes from the *National Incidence Survey of 1981. See National Study of the Incidence and Severity of Child Abuse and Neglect: Technical Report Number 1,* K. Bergdorf and J. Edmonds, eds. (Washington DC: DHHS Publication No. (OHDS) 81-30326, 1981).

23. Hartman and Burgess, "Sexual Abuse of Children," 98–99.

24. M. R. Block and J. D. Sinnott, "The Battered Elder Syndrome: An Exploratory Study," Center on Aging, University of Maryland (1979).

25. B. Schlesinger and R. Schlesinger, eds., *Abuse of the Elderly: Issues and Annotated Bibliography* (Toronto: University of Toronto Press, 1988).

26. Peter Decalmer and Frank Glendenning, eds., *The Mistreatment of Elder People* (London: Sage, 1993) 35.

27. "Elder Abuse," Infolink, National Victim Center 1 (17) (Washington, DC, 1992).

28. Karl Pillemer and J. J. Suitor, "Elder Abuse," in *Handbook of Family Violence*, ed. V. B. Van Hasselt et al. (New York: Plenum Press, 1988).

29. Compare M. R. Block and J. D. Sinnott, "The Battered Elder Syndrome: An Exploratory Study," Center on Aging, University of Maryland (1979) with S. Steinmetz and D. J. Amsden, "Dependent Elders, Family Stress and Abuse," in

Family Relationships in Later Life, ed. T. H. Brubaker, (Beverly Hills, CA: Sage, 1983).

30. M. F. Hudson and T. F. Johnson, "Elder Abuse and Neglect: A Review of the Literature," in *Annual Review of Gerontology and Geriatrics*, ed. C. Eisdorfer et al. (New York: Springer, 1986).

31. T. A. O'Malley, H. C. O'Malley, D. E. Everitt, and D. Sarson, "Categories of Family-Mediated Abuse and Neglect of Elderly Persons," *Jour. of Amer. Ger. Soc.* 362.

32. Id.

33. See R. S. Wolf and K. A. Pillemer, *Helping Elderly Victims: The Reality of Elder Abuse* (New York: Columbia University Press, 1989) and M. A. Godkin, R. S. Wolf, and K. A. Pillemer, "A Case-Comparison Analysis of Elder Abuse and Neglect," 28(3) *Inter. Jour. Aging and Human Development* (1989), 207.

34. R. Bachman, "Elderly Victim," *Special Report, Bureau of Justice Statistics* (Washington DC: U.S. Department of Justice, 1992).

35. M. D. Pagelow, *Family Violence* (New York: Praeger, 1984), 359.

36. K. A. Pillemer and D. W. Moore, "Abuse of Patients in Nursing Homes: Findings from a Survey of Staff," 29(3) *The Gerontologist* 314 (1989).

37. *Elder Victimization* (Washington DC: Bureau of Justice Statistics, 1987).

38. *Highlights from 20 Years of Surveying Crime Victims, 1973–1992* (Washington DC: Bureau of Justice Statistics, October 1993).

39. Richard J. Gelles, *Domestic Violence Factoids,* http://www.umn.edu/mincava/factoid.htm (file created October 16, 1995).

40. S. Steinmetz, "The Battered Husband Syndrome," 2(3/4) *Victimology* (1978), 499.

41. S. K. Steinmetz and J. S. Lucca, "Husband Battering," in *Handbook of Family Violence*, ed. V. B. Van Hasselt (New York: Plenum, 1988).

42. K. D. O'Leary, J. Barling, I. Arias, A. Rosenbaum, J. Malone, and A. Tyree, "Prevalence and Stability of Physical Aggression Between Spouses: A Longitudinal Analysis," 57 *Journal of Consulting and Clinical Psychology* (1989), 263.

43. J. Campbell, "Violence Toward Women: Homicide and Battering," in *Vision 2010*, ed. R. J. Gelles (Minneapolis, MN: National Council on Family Relations, 1995).

44. E. W. Gondolf and E. R. Fisher, "Wife Batterings," in *Case Studies in Family Violence*, ed. R. T. Ammerman and M. Hersen, 273–274 (New York: Plenum, 1991).

Sentencing and Punishment

Chapter Outline

What you should know about sentencing and punishment. After reading this chapter, you should know

- The various purposes behind sentencing in the United States.

- The constitutional issues that are involved in sentencing.

- The different types of sentences and the advantages and disadvantages of each type.

- The concepts behind each form of incarceration and the alternatives to incarceration.

- The various types of rights available to victims of crimes.

- The legal, moral, and ethical issues surrounding the imposition of the death penalty.

- Why the U.S. Supreme Court prohibits the execution of individuals for crimes they committed as juveniles.

Key Terms

After reading this chapter, you should understand the following key terms:

Auburn System: Prison that segregates prisoners based upon criminal conduct and behavior while in custody.

community service: A form of restitution where the offender must work, without pay or for minimum wage, in a social service agency for a specified number of hours.

concurrent sentence: Situation in which two or more sentences are to be served at the same time.

consecutive sentence: Situation in which one of two or more sentences are to be served after completion of the first sentence.

determinate sentence: Type of sentence that establishes a specific time that the offender will serve in prison.

deterrence: Theory of punishment based upon the concept that criminal sanctions convince the public that they should not commit crimes because they could be punished. Fear of punishment is viewed as a primary deterrent to crime.

diversion: Theory of punishment that diverts offenders from more severe forms of punishment if they agree to attend counseling or educational programs, and they do not commit the same or similar offenses within a specified period.

due process: Concept requiring fairness in legal proceedings. Procedural due process concerns the procedures used in the criminal justice system. Substantive due process examines whether the process is fair and reasonable.

equal protection: Concept requiring that all persons be treated the same, without regard to race, creed, color, or sex.

fine: A monetary punishment requiring the offender to pay a specified sum.

forfeiture: Process whereby a criminal's assets become the property of the government.

incapacitation: Theory of punishment based upon the concept of removing the offender from society. Prevents criminals from continuing their criminal activities and protects law-abiding citizens from further criminal acts by this specific person.

indeterminate sentence: Process that sets a minimum and maximum term that the defendant may serve. Known as indeterminate because the offender's actual time in prison is not known or determined at the time of sentencing.

jail: Locally administered penal institution that holds offenders before and after conviction.

plea bargain: Agreement between the prosecutor and the defense attorney to allow the defendant to plead guilty to a lesser offense than the one charged.

presumptive sentencing: Form of sentencing that establishes a minimum and maximum sentence and a fixed point within that range that is the usual or presumed sentence for a certain class of crimes.

prison: Penal institution administered by the state or federal government.

proportionality: Requirement that a sentence must impose punishment proportionate to the offense.

rehabilitation: Theory of punishment that focuses on reduction or elimination of the offender's crime-committing propensity after release from confinement.

restitution: Court-ordered reimbursement of victims of crimes by the offender.

retribution: Theory of punishment based upon the concept of just desserts, holding that those who violate the law deserve to be punished.

sentencing: Process by which a judge imposes punishment on a person convicted of a crime or crimes.

suspended sentence: A criminal sentence that is suspended by the court on the condition that the offender satisfies certain terms and conditions set forth by the court.

victim impact statement: A statement that a crime victim may present to the court for consideration in determining the sentence that should be imposed on the defendant for the crime.

zero tolerance: A policy that is often used by schools to indicate that any violation of a specific policy will not be condoned and the offender will immediately be expelled; in the case of criminal defendants, probation or suspension will be revoked upon the violation of any of the conditions of probation or suspension.

Understanding the elements of the various crimes is only part of the body of law in criminal justice. Once the police have arrested the offender and the judge or jury have found him or her guilty, the next step in the process must take place. A defendant must be sentenced to a certain punishment for the crime. As we will discuss, this sentence may be as light as a suspended sentence or as harsh as the death penalty.

What constitutes a correct or appropriate punishment has been subject to heated debate in our society since the original thirteen colonies were established. Various forms of sentencing and punishment have been tried in our quest to stop crime and to protect our lives and property. This chapter will examine various aspects of sentencing and punishment, including the history, purpose, and types of sentences.

INTRODUCTION TO SENTENCING

While Focus 15.5 may generate heated discussion concerning the death penalty, that form of punishment is only one aspect of the entire body of law that affects the sentencing of criminals. The death penalty and its legality and morality will be discussed along with victim rights later in this chapter. However, before we can engage in an informed examination of these emotional and complex legal issues, we must lay the foundation by examining the other aspects of this complex criminal procedure.

History

One cannot discuss sentencing without reviewing the history of punishment. Our views and beliefs regarding punishment have changed as we have matured as a civilization. Early humans used banishment or exile as the primary form of punishment. This "sentence" withdrew the support and safety of the tribe or group from the individual, and he was considered an outcast. In ancient Rome, punishment for violent crimes was looked upon as a right of the victim's family, not a prerogative or obligation of the state.

The concept of family vengeance carried over into the Middle Ages (500–1100 AD). Family blood feuds remained the primary method of settling wrongs between parties. During the feudal period, when medieval lords ruled over large tracts of land and many peasants, the forfeiture of land and property became the accepted method of punishing a wrongdoer.

During the fifteenth century, our belief regarding punishment once again changed. The king was looked upon as the dispenser of justice and punishment.[1] It was during this period that the concept of capital punishment by the state gained widespread acceptance. Executions, torture, branding, and flogging were commonly accepted sentences.

As civilization expanded and immigrants crossed the Atlantic during the sixteenth century, there developed a need for industrial and manufactured goods. Our perception of appropriate punishment changed to match the needs of society and included the phenomenon of forced labor. Persons convicted of crimes were sentenced to perform manual labor at various public or private institutions. It was also common during this period to deport a criminal to the colonies or other countries. Australia is famous as a country that started out as a penal institution.

After the American Revolution (1776), we moved away from extensive use of corporal and capital punishment and began to accept imprisonment as a viable sentencing option. Capital punishment did not disappear as an accepted sentence; rather, we acknowledged the fact that imprisonment would also serve our needs as a society.

Various concepts of incarceration were used during this period. Jails and prisons began to be constructed on a wide scale. The **Auburn System** of prisons was established in New York. This type of prison segregated prisoners based upon criminal conduct and behavior while in custody. Some inmates were held in constant isolation, others were allowed to perform occasional labor, and the largest group of prisoners worked together during the day and were placed in individual cells only during the evening.[2] The Auburn System was to become the forerunner of today's penal institutions.

During the Civil War, the concept of prison industries was introduced to corrections. Prisoners were forced to work for either public or private institutions for little or no compensation. Convicts were used to produce clothing, shoes, and furniture.

Since the Civil War, the concept of sentencing and incarceration has undergone radical changes. Private reform movements, legislative action, and judicial decisions have modified our concepts of punishment. The following sections discuss some of the modern principles regarding sentencing and several constitutional safeguards imposed by our form of government.

Purpose

Before we can discuss the purpose or purposes of sentencing, we must define the term. The definition depends upon one's perspective of the reason or purpose for sentencing. However, rather than address intent or purpose, we have accepted a more legalistic definition. **Sentencing** is the process by which a judge imposes punishment on a person convicted of a crime or crimes.[3] The various types of sentences will be discussed later in this chapter, as will incarceration and its alternatives.

There are as many different views on the objectives of sentencing as there are scholars.[4] However, the most commonly accepted purposes of sentencing involve either one or a combination of the following rationales: deterrence, rehabilitation, incapacitation, retribution, and diversion. **Deterrence** is based upon the concept that criminal sanctions convince the public that they should not commit crimes because they could be punished. Fear of punishment is viewed as a primary deterrent to crime. Since both law-abiding citizens and criminals are reasoning beings, the consequences of committing a crime and facing a variety of punishments act as a deterrent to crime. Proponents of this theory argue for quick and punitive sentencing as a means of controlling crime. The validity of this position is based upon the premise that punishing one offender for a crime will deter others from committing the same type of crime.

Rehabilitation focuses on reduction or elimination of the offender's crime-committing propensity after release from confinement. Rehabilitation attempts to modify the offender's conduct by administering some form of treatment under the supervision of criminal justice personnel. Rehabilitation efforts include vocational training, mental health counseling, educational opportunities, and termination of alcohol or drug dependency. These activities may occur while the offender is in custody or on supervised parole or probation.

Incapacitation is the removal of the offender from society. This prevents an individual criminal from continuing criminal activities and protects law-abiding citizens from further criminal acts by one specific person. Incapacitation implies warehousing the offender. Penal institutions simply become holding facilities to keep criminals off the streets.

Retribution is an ancient rationale for punishment. The biblical saying "an eye for an eye, a tooth for a tooth" is an early example of retribution. Many believe that retribution is a form of revenge by society. K. G. Armstrong has made a logical argument that retribution is not vengeance. He states that revenge is personal, while retribution involves lawful action on the part of the state to protect its members.[5] A second theory of retribution involves the concept of "just desserts," the premise that those who commit criminal acts deserve to be punished. Andrew Von Hirsh, in his classic work *Doing Justice*, sets forth the idea of just deserts as a model to guide criminal justice. He states, "To say someone 'deserves' to be rewarded or punished is to refer to his past conduct and assert that its merit or demerit is reason for according him pleasant or unpleasant treatment."[6] Since the offender has committed a crime, society has a right to inflict an equal form of punishment on that person.

Diversion is the concept of diverting offenders from more severe forms of punishment if they agree to attend counseling or educational programs, and they do not commit the same or similar offenses within a specified period.

The Model Penal Code (MPC) has adopted three of these rationales and directs the sentencing court to consider incarceration, deterrence, or rehabilitation when imposing a sentence.[7]

At one time or another, each of the above theories has gained prominence in our society and become the guiding principle for imposing sentences. Today many of the concepts are used in conjunction with each other to accomplish one or more of the purposes of sentencing. However, it is immaterial which premise sentencing is based upon if the procedure or effect of a sentence violates an offender's basic constitutional rights. The next section will briefly review these protections.

Constitutional Issues

The U.S. Constitution and its amendments set forth a series of individual rights that the government cannot infringe upon. When an offender is sentenced to imprisonment, certain of these rights are lost. For example, felons lose the right to vote while incarcerated, and in some states they never regain that right even after release from the institution. However, when a person is sentenced, certain other constitutional rights and protections remain. This section will briefly examine those rights that may be affected during sentencing or punishment.

THE FOURTEENTH AMENDMENT TO THE CONSTITUTION The Fourteenth Amendment requires equality in sentencing and mandates that all individuals receive procedural due process. The pertinent portion of the amendment reads:

All persons born or naturalized in the United States, and subject to the jurisdiction thereof, are citizens of the United States and of the State where they reside. No State shall make or enforce any law which shall abridge the privileges or immunities of citizens of the United States; nor shall any State deprive any person of life, liberty, or property, without due process of law; nor deny to any person within its jurisdiction the equal protection of the laws.

Due process is the principle that a person may not be deprived of life, liberty, or property without lawful procedures. In *United States v. Grayson*, a federal district court judge imposed a stiffer sentence on the defendant based upon the judge's opinion that he had committed perjury when he testified in his own behalf. Grayson argued that he was being denied due process of law because he was never tried for perjury. The Supreme Court ruled that there is no protected right to commit perjury, and the sentencing judge could consider Grayson's truthfulness or lack thereof in imposing a sentence.[8]

Equal protection is the principle that all persons are entitled to the same treatment under the law regardless of their race, creed, religion, or sex. A court may not sentence or punish individuals who are convicted of the same or similar crimes in distinctly different ways based solely upon their sex or race. Lower court decisions and state statutes that imposed different sentences on males and females have been overturned as a denial of equal protection.

THE EIGHTH AMENDMENT TO THE CONSTITUTION The Eighth Amendment prevents excessive punishment as well as any form of punishment that may be deemed cruel and unusual. The amendment reads as follows:

Excessive bail shall not be required, nor excessive fines imposed, nor cruel and unusual punishment inflicted.

While we as a nation have moved a long way from the type of punishment imposed upon Francis Townley (see Focus 15.1), legal issues are still raised during sentencing and the subsequent punishment imposed by that procedure. Traditionally, cruel and unusual punishment has been raised in death penalty cases and will be discussed in more detail under the section dealing with that form of sentencing. Courts will examine a variety of factors when determining whether a sentence constitutes cruel and unusual punishment.

Focus 15.1

Cruel and Unusual Punishment

Francis Townley and others were convicted of high treason for waging war against their king. The following is the sentence and punishment imposed for such crimes:

Let the several prisoners above-named return to the gaol of the county of Surrey from whence they came and from thence they must be drawn to the place of execution and when they come there they must be severally hanged by the neck but not till they be dead for they must be cut down alive then their bowels must be taken out and burnt before their faces then their heads must be severed from their bodies and their bodies severally divided into four quarters and these must be at the king's disposal.[9]

Proportionality has been interpreted by courts to mean that a sentence imposing punishment must be proportionate to the offense. If a sentence is out of proportion to the crime, the courts may hold that it violates the prohibition against cruel and unusual punishment and is thus void. The issue of proportionality may also be raised when examining the length of the sentence imposed and comparing it to the type of crime committed.

In *Solem v. Helm,* the U.S. Supreme Court addressed this issue when it was asked to decide if the Eighth Amendment prohibited the imposition of a life sentence without possibility of parole for conviction of a seventh nonviolent felony.[10] By 1975, Jerry Helm had been convicted of six nonviolent felonies. In 1964, 1966, and 1969, he was convicted of third-degree burglary. In 1972, he was convicted of obtaining money under false pretenses. In 1973, he was convicted of grand larceny. In 1975, he was convicted for a third time of driving under the influence of alcohol. In 1979, Jerry Helm was convicted of writing a check without sufficient funds. The amount of the check was $100. In South Dakota, where the trial took place, the usual sentence for nonsufficient funds offenses was five years in prison and a $5,000 fine. However, because of his prior convictions, Helm was classified a habitual criminal and sentenced to life without possibility of parole. The Supreme Court reversed the decision, holding that such a sentence under these circumstances amounted to cruel and unusual punishment. The court set forth guidelines to be considered when determining whether a sentence is proportionate to the crime: (1) the gravity of the offense and the harshness of the penalty; (2) the sentences imposed on other criminals in the same jurisdiction; and (3) the sentences imposed for the commission of the same crime in other jurisdictions.

Practicum 15.1

Jail Overcrowding: Is It Cruel and Unusual Punishment?

Two or more prisoners were placed in a fifty-square-foot cell that contained sleeping bunks, a toilet, and a sink. This was their entire living space when they were not working, exercising, or carrying out some other activity in the institution.

ISSUE: *Are such conditions cruel and unusual punishment?*

The U.S. Supreme Court has stated that conditions of confinement must not involve wanton and unnecessary infliction of pain, nor may they be grossly disproportionate to the severity of the crime warranting imprisonment. To the extent that such conditions are restrictive and even harsh, they are part of the penalty that criminal defendants pay for their offenses against society.[11] Is it cruel and unusual punishment to deny an inmate the right to watch TV? Does it make any difference if the program is a daily soap opera or a national news broadcast?

Penal living conditions have been a fertile ground for challenges based upon a violation of the Eighth Amendment. Jail overcrowding occurs when inmates are placed in such crowded conditions as to constitute inhumane or cruel treatment. This normally occurs when inmates are placed two to three in a single cell or have to sleep on the floor because of lack of bed space. Numerous state prisons and local jails have been sued over the issue of jail crowding. Many of these institutions entered into consent degrees, agreeing to either build new facilities or limit the number of inmates to the spaces available. These actions have caused taxpayers to spend huge sums of money on new penal construction or have required local sheriffs or wardens to release inmates prior to the completion of their terms.[12]

The above discussion has briefly examined the history, purpose, and constitutionality of various aspects of sentencing and punishment. This area of the law is continually being modified as new court decisions are rendered. However, certain basic principles regarding the types of sentences and how they are imposed have remained constant.

TYPES OF SENTENCES

There are numerous types or varieties of sentences. The three main types of sentences are indeterminate, determinate, and presumptive. Each of these procedures has been adopted by different legislative bodies and hailed by its proponents as the "cure" to crime. Prior to discussing each of these sentencing practices, we should review some common techniques or procedures that affect the crime the defendant is sentenced for, the amount of time actually spent in confinement, and some sentencing options available to the court.

Plea bargaining is an accepted practice in state and federal courts. A **plea bargain** is an agreement between the prosecutor and the defendant (by her attorney) to plead guilty to a lesser offense than the one charged. Plea bargaining may also involve dismissing several charges or counts in exchange for a plea of guilty to one of the charges. The effect of a plea bargain is to guarantee to the defendant that she will receive a lesser sentence than if she had been convicted of all the crimes or the most serious crime charged. Plea bargaining has generated heated debate between those that support its use and those that claim it deceives the public and allows criminals to escape the full consequences of their acts.[13] The following list sets forth some of the more common arguments in favor of and opposed to plea bargaining.

Advantages of Plea Bargaining:

- It ensures conviction for a crime. A bird in the hand is better than two in the bush.
- The criminal court system is overcrowded, and without plea bargaining, we could not handle all the crimes that are committed every day.
- We can plea bargain with a defendant in exchange for testimony against other criminals. This allows the state to obtain convictions that might not be possible without accomplice testimony.

Disadvantages of Plea Bargaining:

- It allows criminals to escape mandated punishment for all the crimes with which they are charged.
- If the system is overcrowded, we need to provide for more judges. Bargaining away crimes is not an answer to an economic issue.
- We should require guilty pleas to all crimes, and the defendant's testimony for the government may be considered in sentencing.

As the foregoing discussion indicates, plea bargaining is part of our criminal justice system. It occurs every day in crowded courtrooms across the nation. It will continue to be the subject of controversy within and outside the criminal justice sentencing process.

Even with a plea bargain, the court may retain the discretion to impose a **concurrent** or **consecutive sentence**. If the defendant has been convicted or has pled guilty to more than one offense, the sentencing judge must determine whether the sentences will run consecutively or concurrently. In concurrent sentencing, two or more sentences are to be served at the same time. If the defendant is already serving time in jail or prison, a sentence for another crime may be added to run concurrently with the already existing sentence. In consecutive sentencing, one of the two or more sentences is to be served after the completion of the other sentence. In other words, concurrent sentences are served at the same time and consecutive sentences are tacked on one after the other. The determination of whether to impose concurrent or consecutive sentences is often completely within the discretion of the sentencing court. The judge will usually review several factors in making the decision. These factors include the defendant's prior criminal record, the seriousness of the offenses, the probability of rehabilitation, and any other information that will assist the judge in imposing sentence.

Sentencing courts have the option of imposing a sentence, then suspending the effect of that sanction. A sentence may be suspended on the condition that the offender satisfy certain terms and conditions set forth by the court. A **suspended sentence** imposes a threat of incarceration upon the offender if he fails to abide by the terms and conditions in the court order. As we will discuss later in this chapter, suspended sentences are used in lieu of incarceration on the condition that the offender pay a fine, make restitution, or engage in some other activity such as community service. These options are some of the alternatives available to the sentencing judge. However, the length of time the defendant will serve in prison is usually established by statute. These state and federal laws may take three basic forms: indeterminate, determinate, and presumptive. The following section will briefly review each of these alternatives.

Indeterminate Sentences

Early prison sentences were for a fixed term, and the inmate faced harsh living conditions and physical punishment while incarcerated. Reformers such as Enoch Wines and Zebulon Brockway espoused the principle of rehabilitation and reformation. By 1900, states were adopting minimum and maximum ranges of imprisonment, called **indeterminate sentences**. The minimum time was usually one year and the maximum could be as long as life imprisonment. This type of sentencing was known as indeterminate because the offender's actual time in prison was not known or determined at the time of sentencing. The rationale for this type of sentencing was that it permitted the parole board to make individualized decisions regarding release based upon the prisoner's rehabilitation while in prison.

For most of the twentieth century, state and federal statutes authorized judges to impose sentences within these wide ranges. The judge's decision on the amount of time a person was to serve was rarely overturned on appeal. Typically, a judge might impose a sentence such as, "You are hereby sentenced to not less than five years and not more than twenty-five years at hard labor with the State Department of Corrections." Even though the judge imposed this range of years upon a defendant, federal or state parole boards had authority to release the offender at any time after a parole hearing. Normally, these boards acted when the defendant had served approximately one-third of the sentence.

Indeterminate sentencing is still an accepted practice in many states. However, by the early 1970s, indeterminate sentencing had come under attack by criminologists, law enforcement groups, and legislatures.[14] The wide disparity between sentences, as well as concerns about whether rehabilitation was possible, led to reform movements that established determinate sentence laws.

Determinate Sentences

Determinate sentences establish a specific time that the offender will serve in prison. Parole boards have been eliminated or their power curtailed. An example of determinate sentencing is the Federal Sentencing Reform Act of 1984. Among other reforms, the act established the U.S. Sentencing Commission to develop guidelines that scale punishment to the gravity of the offense and the defendant's criminal background.

The Sentencing Commission set up a range for each criminal offense. If there are special factors present in a particular case, the guidelines allow judges to depart from the "mandated" sentence. Many of these mitigating or aggravating factors are listed in the guidelines. If a court does depart from the mandated or recommended sentence, that action may be appealed to review the reasonableness of the imposed sentence. Under these guidelines, federal prisoners are no longer released from prison by the U.S. Parole Commission. The act requires federal judges to impose prison sentences that are served in full, except for time off that each prisoner earns for good behavior. Offenders are supervised following their release only if a judge requires it as part of the original sentence.

When the Federal Sentencing Reform Act was passed, some federal judges claimed it deprived them of the ability to exercise their judicial discretion at the time of sentencing, but the U.S. Supreme Court in *Mistretta v. United States* upheld the act's constitutionality.[15] The Court held that Congress had acted in a constitutional manner and that the guidelines developed by the Sentencing Commission were appropriate and could be applied to all federal criminal cases.

In 2005, the U.S. Supreme Court, in *United States v. Booker (543 U.S. 220 [2005])*, greatly expanded the judicial discretion of federal judging in federal criminal cases when it declared that the federal sentencing guidelines were only advisory and were not mandatory. The Court also determined in *United States v. Fanfan (125 S.Ct. 125 [2005])* that the sentencing guidelines wrongly forced a federal judge to increase punishment based on the judge's factual findings, which violated a defendant's right to a jury trial.

Presumptive Sentences

A form of determinate sentencing is the **presumptive sentencing** procedure. Presumptive sentencing establishes a minimum and maximum sentence and a fixed point within that range that is the usual or presumed sentence for a certain class of crimes. However, depending on the facts of each case, the sentencing judge may vary from that presumptive sentence while remaining within the range provided by the statute. Most presumptive sentencing schemes set forth certain factors that allow the judge to set either the lower or higher sentence within the range. Mitigating or aggravating factors allow the sentencing court to retain some flexibility in sentencing while providing certainty to victims, citizens, and society in general that all classes of offenders will be treated the same.

States vary in how they have established the presumptive sentencing procedure. For example, a presumptive sentence in Minnesota might be forty-nine months, but the judge may impose a sentence between forty-five and fifty-three months without leaving the presumptive range established by the legislature. In California, the presumptive sentence for a number of crimes is three years, but a judge may make findings and sentence the offender to either two or four years depending on the mitigating or enhancing factors present in the specific case.

Presumptive sentencing attempts to reduce differences in sentences imposed by different judges for similar crimes. It also limits judicial discretion in sentencing while leaving the judge some latitude to tailor a sentence within a certain range depending on the facts of the crime. Finally, presumptive sentencing seeks to ensure that criminal defendants serve a specified sentence.

Each of the above options involves sentencing the offender to a period of incarceration. The cost effectiveness of placing individuals in jails or prisons is one of the continuing debates in our society. However, some individuals are so violent and dangerous that society is safe only if they are behind bars. The following section will review the various forms of incarceration and some alternatives to imprisonment.

INCARCERATION AND ITS ALTERNATIVES

The desire to place all criminals in confinement is not realistic, cost effective, or even attainable. Some crimes are more serious than others and should be treated differently. Even the most conservative of us would not demand that a petty thief be sentenced to state prison. This disparity in the nature of crimes has led to a wide variety of sentencing options. This section will discuss incarceration, probation, parole, and other sentencing options.

Jails

A **jail** is a local penal institution that is used to hold offenders before and after conviction. Jails hold persons convicted of misdemeanors or less serious offenses. In addition, defendants are confined in the local jail pending the outcome of the trial. Traditionally, jails are under the supervision of the local sheriff and staffed by the sheriff's deputies. However, as local budgets shrink, local law enforcement administrators have begun to hire nondeputized personnel to supervise inmates in jails. A jail may be the block concrete structure we all see in the downtown area or an honor camp where inmates serve time without the constraints of bars and fences. Because of overcrowding, many local sheriffs have begun the process of "booking and releasing" nonviolent prisoners. This procedure ensures that there is a record of confinement on the defendant's criminal record and yet frees up bed space for the more serious offenders.

If the crime is a felony, the offender is usually committed to a more stringent form of incarceration. The following section briefly discusses the various types of prisons used in the United States today.

Prisons

A **prison** is a state or federal penal institution. Prisons are usually reserved for the more serious offenders who have committed felonies. These penal facilities are administered in various ways. In the majority of states, they are under the control of a state agency that ensures uniformity of administrative policies and programs. In other states, the local warden is responsible for the administration of the prison and answers to a board of trustees or managers. In these latter situations, the warden is a very powerful figure and controls the operation and management of the institution.

Prisons hold the most violent of society's criminals. Mass murderers, rapists, robbers, and other hardened criminals are placed in prisons. Many of these individuals are repeat offenders who have served prior prison terms. The next section will discuss how an inmate may obtain an early release from prison.

Probation and Parole

While a certain segment of our society would prefer that all defendants be incarcerated, our jails and prisons are already full. As we mentioned earlier in this chapter, jail and prison overcrowding has led to the early release of many nonviolent offenders. Two of the more common alternatives to incarceration are probation and parole.

Probation is the release of a convicted offender back into society under the supervision of an agent of the court. Probation is usually imposed in addition to a period of incarceration, but that imprisonment is fully or partially suspended on the condition that the offender abide by certain terms and conditions of probation.

The theory on which probation is founded is that a majority of offenders do not need time in prison or jail. These offenders are not hardcore criminals, nor are they a menace to society. Further, one argument in support of probation is that sending a young offender to jail or prison is similar to sending that person to a college on crime. In most institutions, the newcomer to crime will learn to become a more hardened and sophisticated criminal.

The goal of probation is to impose some degree of control over the offender and to use community-based programs to effect rehabilitation. Probation may be summary or supervised. Summary probation does not involve any active supervision, while supervised probation entails periodic visits and reviews of the probationer's activities by an agent of the court. Probation is normally granted to those offenders who are not violent or a threat to society.

Once a person has been sentenced to prison, there is another alternative available for early release. Parole is the release of a convicted offender back into society, prior to the expiration of the prison sentence, under the supervision of an agent of the state or federal government. Parole is normally granted by a parole board or commission. These groups hold hearings and review the files of those prisoners who are eligible for parole. Depending on the jurisdiction and sentence, some prisoners can be eligible for a parole hearing after serving as little as one year in prison. However, some offenders have committed such outrageous and dangerous crimes that, even though they may have a right to a parole hearing, many boards or commissions will not grant them an opportunity to return to society.

The goal of parole is to release the prisoner from incarceration and allow him to become a productive member of society. Once the offender is released from prison, the parole agent supervises the person's progress to gauge his readjustment and rehabilitation. However, this supervision has lessened in recent years as the state and federal governments have made budget cuts that affect the operation and functioning of parole departments across the nation.

Probation and parole are two of the more common methods used by the courts to relieve the overcrowding of jails and assist in the rehabilitation of offenders. These procedures are employed in lieu of initial or extended imprisonment. There are other alternatives to incarceration that punish the offender and help restore or make society whole for the crimes committed by these persons.

Fines, Forfeitures, and Restitution

Alternatives to incarceration deal with financial penalties that are levied against the offender. The theory behind these sanctions is to hit the defendant where it hurts—in the pocketbook. In addition, these sentencing techniques punish the offender and yet do not require the taxpayer to foot the bill for feeding and housing her in a penal institution.

A **fine** is an offender's monetary payment to the court as a form of punishment. Traditionally, fines are most commonly used for the less serious offenses such as misdemeanors. However, large fines may be imposed for white-collar or corporate criminal acts. Ivan Boesky, the Wall Street millionaire who violated stock trading rules, was fined in excess of $100 million. The corporate firm of Drexel Burnham Lambert paid a fine of $650 million as part of a sentence involving violation of federal securities laws.[16]

Courts may impose fines in lieu of imprisonment. Many times, courts will order the offender to serve time in jail but suspend the sentence on the condition that he pay a fine. There is a continuing debate regarding the effectiveness of fines in deterring future criminal acts. However, a new form of "fine" seems to be effective in preventing petty thefts—a civil action available to the victim. This alternative is not imposed during sentencing but can be brought independent of any criminal action. Statutes in many states now authorize commercial establishments to file simple civil actions against petty thieves and to seek damages, ranging from the value of the item stolen up to $500.[17]

While technically not a sentencing option, forfeiture of property used during a crime is another form of criminal punishment. **Forfeiture** involves the seizure of property related to or used in the commission of a crime. Forfeiture laws are designed to punish defendants financially by causing a loss of property owned or controlled by the offender.

Federal law authorizes government agents to seize boats, automobiles, and real property used in drug dealing. Once the property is seized, a forfeiture hearing is conducted, and the government may then dispose of the property. Originally enacted to apply to narcotic offenses, these laws have been expanded to include forfeiture of property involved in white-collar crime.

Zero tolerance is the concept that even a small amount of drug contraband will trigger the use of the forfeiture procedure. Million-dollar yachts have been seized on the basis of a few ounces of marijuana. Some scholars argue that this zero tolerance process is being abused by the federal government.[18]

Focus 15.2

Parole: Should Some Offenders Ever Be Paroled?

Charles Manson, Squeaky Fromm, and Sirhan Sirhan are names that immediately come to mind as criminal defendants whose parole would cause an outcry from the general public. However, there are other less known, and in many instances more dangerous, prisoners who are granted parole hearings each year. The following is a brief description of two such criminals. To date, neither of these offenders has been granted parole.

Edmund Emil Kemper III, known as the Coed Killer, began his killing at the age of fifteen when he walked up behind his grandmother and shot her in the back of the head. He shot her two more times and then repeatedly stabbed her. He was placed in Atascadero Mental Hospital for the Criminally Insane. He was able to master the necessary skills to convince the parole board, against the advice of the hospital psychiatrists, to release him after five years. He weighed in at 280 pounds and was 6 feet 8 inches tall at the time of his release.

At the age of twenty-three, Kemper started killing again. This killing spree would last a year and claim eight more victims. He picked up hitchhikers, then shot, stabbed, and strangled them. He cannibalized at least two of his victims, cutting off parts of their legs and cooking the flesh in a macaroni casserole. He decapitated all of his victims and saved body parts for sexual acts. He was finally captured and confessed to the killings. Kemper was sentenced to life imprisonment and was denied parole at his first parole hearing in 1980.

Jerry Brudos started on his path of crime at the age of seventeen when he assaulted a girl at knifepoint and forced her to disrobe while he took pictures. He was caught and sentenced to a mental hospital for eight months. After his release, Brudos finished high school, served in the military, and became an electronics technician. He began his odyssey of crime and death by assaulting four women and raping one of them. At the age of twenty-eight, Brudos started killing. He raped, killed, and mutilated his victims. One victim's foot was severed and placed in a freezer, and Brudos would dress the foot in a spike-heeled shoe. Other victims suffered amputation, sexual acts, and electric shock.

Brudos was eventually captured and confessed that he enjoyed the killings, especially how the victims looked when they were dead. Brudos was sentenced to Oregon State Prison for the murders in 1969 and is now granted a parole hearing every year. He has not given up hope that someday he may be paroled.

Should Kemper or Brudos ever be paroled? Why? If they are completely cured, why not?

Restitution is the reimbursement of victims of crimes. It normally takes the form of financial repayment to the individual victim. The judge may order the defendant to pay a fine to the court to repay society and restitution to the victim as a condition of probation. Another form of restitution is **community service**. The offender must work, without pay or for minimum wage, in a social service agency for a specified number of hours. Some states have attempted to enact specific statutes that allow the victim of the crime to pursue civil actions against the criminal to recover losses independent of any restitution ordered by the court.

Focus 15.3

Restitution

David Richard Berkowitz, also known as the Son of Sam, was front-page news from 1967 to 1977. He caught and held the attention of millions of people in New York and across the nation as he went on a killing spree using a .44-caliber handgun to shoot thirteen young men and women in New York City. Six of his victims died and seven were severely injured.

Berkowitz was tried, convicted, and sentenced to three 24-year terms for his crimes. New York State enacted a far-reaching "Son of Sam" statute that required felons to turn over any proceeds received from book or film royalties to their victims who had obtained a civil judgment against them within a five-year period. However, the U.S. Supreme Court struck down the statute as a violation of the First Amendment's freedom of expression clause.[19]

New York and other states have revised their Son of Sam statutes to comport with the Supreme Court's decision.[20] Under certain circumstances, these more narrowly drawn statutes allow victims of crimes to receive funds that have been generated by books or movies dealing with the criminal act that caused them injury.

Should convicted criminals be able to profit as a result of their acts? Why do you believe the court struck down the Son of Sam statute? Should victims of crimes be entitled to any more protection than any other person in our society?

Jails, prisons, and other alternatives to incarceration are methods society has adopted to punish the offender for her crime against society. All of these procedures are aimed at reducing crime and thereby benefitting society. One of the long-forgotten parties in the criminal justice system is the individual victim of the crime. We have now begun to acknowledge this person's rights in the area of criminal law. The next section will discuss this newly emerging area in the field of criminal justice.

VICTIMS' RIGHTS

We as a society have come a long way in recognizing that there is a third party to any criminal action. Traditionally, the People, in the form of the prosecutor, presented the case against the defendant. The victim of the crime was looked upon merely as another witness to assist in presenting evidence to obtain a conviction. Today, there is a groundswell of voices crying out that we must consider the victim in the prosecution and sentencing of criminal defendants. Law enforcement agencies have begun to accept the role that the victim plays in the criminal justice system and are becoming more sensitive to their needs and desires.[21]

Over the past twenty years, various states and the federal government have enacted laws that provide victims of crimes with certain rights. These rights include providing monetary compensation from the government or criminal and allowing victims to attend hearings and provide the court with input regarding the impact of the offender's actions on their lives. In 1982, California voters passed an initiative that made victim rights a part of its constitution. Seven other states followed California's lead and enacted legislation protecting victims and establishing a bill of rights for them. Since then, most states have passed amendments creating victim bills of rights.

Victims' Bill of Rights and Other Remedies

In August 1992, the National Conference of Commissioners on Uniform State Laws adopted the Uniform Victims of Crime Act, which is aimed at establishing uniformity in the way victims are treated. The commissioners had researched this area of the law and determined that numerous states had enacted laws giving victims certain rights. However, there was no uniformity or clear pattern set forth in all these statutes. The uniform act is divided into three sections: victim rights, victim compensation, and restitution.

The victims' rights section establishes the principle that the victim may be present at any public court proceeding. The victim has a right to submit a victim impact statement and be informed of the release date of the offender.

The compensation section requires crime victims or their survivors to be compensated by the state for physical or emotional injuries. The compensation would not exceed $25,000, but it could be reduced if the victim received other funds such as insurance proceeds or restitution from a civil judgment.

The restitution section permits a court to enter a judgment against the defendant for the victim's direct economic losses. These losses can include medical expenses, loss of income, and even burial expenses.[22]

The National Organization for Victim Assistance (NOVA) has been a strong proponent of victim rights and continues an active campaign.

In addition to passing laws that give victims rights within the criminal justice system once a crime has occurred, more and more states are passing laws to prevent or curtail potential crimes. After several well-publicized cases in which the offenders harassed and then killed the victims, several states have passed "stalking laws." At least thirty-seven states have statutes that prohibit anyone from willfully following or harassing another and making a threat against that person with the intent of causing the victim to fear for his or her safety. Illinois has a very strict stalking law that classifies stalking as a felony. The punishment for a violation of this statute can be a fine up to $10,000 and a jail term of up to three years.

Focus 15.4

Crime Victims' Bill of Rights

A crime victim has the following rights:

1. The right to be treated with fairness and with respect for the victim's dignity and privacy.
2. The right to be reasonably protected from the accused offender.
3. The right to be notified of court proceedings.
4. The right to be present at all public court proceedings related to the offense, unless the court determines that the testimony by the victim would be materially affected if the victim heard other testimony at trial.
5. The right to confer with an attorney for the government in the case.
6. The right to restitution.
7. The right to information about the conviction, sentencing, imprisonment, and release of the offender.

Source: United States Victims' Rights and Restitution Act of 1990.

Other states have adopted a procedure that requires the offender to wear an electronic ankle bracelet that triggers an alarm if he goes near the person he is accused of harassing. In Littleton, Colorado, the district attorney's office is using this technique in domestic violence situations. The offender is given the option at pretrial hearings and upon conviction of wearing the bracelet, going to jail, or posting a bond.

One of the more common provisions in victims' rights statutes or constitutional amendments is the use of victim impact statements. The next section will briefly describe this procedure that allows victims to become the third party in criminal proceedings.

Victim Impact Statements

A **victim impact statement** allows the victim to present evidence, either orally or in writing, for the court to consider when imposing sentence on the offender. At one time the constitutionality of these statements was questionable, but in *Payne v. Tennessee*, the U.S. Supreme Court reversed its previous position and held that the victim impact statement is simply another form or method of informing the sentencing authority about the specific harm caused by the crime in question.[23] In *Payne*, the defendant had stabbed a two-year-old child and her mother to death in 1987. A second child, aged three, was severely wounded and witnessed the deaths of his mother and younger sister. The defendant was convicted of both murders, and at the sentencing phase, the child's grandmother testified that he continued to cry out daily for his dead mother. The Court's decision lends authority to the position that victim impact statements have a legitimate place in the criminal justice system.

The Uniform Victims of Crime Act provides the following:

(a) Before imposing sentence, the court shall permit the victim to present a victim-impact statement concerning the effects of the crime on the victim, the circumstances surrounding the crime, the manner in which the crime was perpetrated, and the victim's opinion regarding appropriate sentence. At the victim's option, the victim may present the statement in writing before the sentencing proceeding, orally under oath at the sentencing proceeding, or both.

(b) The court shall give copies of all written victim-impact statements to the prosecutor and the defendant.

(c) The sentencing court shall consider the victim-impact statement along with other factors, but if the victim-impact statement includes new, material, or factual information upon which the court intends to rely, the court shall adjourn the sentencing proceeding or take other appropriate action to allow the defendant adequate opportunity to respond.[24]

Victim impact statements are now an accepted part of our sentencing process. As more and more states adopt victims' bills of rights, we will see more involvement of victims in our criminal justice system. They may truly become the third party in a criminal proceeding.

THE DEATH PENALTY

The execution of convicted criminals is not a new form of punishment.[25] Today thirty-six states and the federal government have criminal statutes that authorize the imposition of this ultimate sanction. Since 1976, more than five hundred offenders have been executed, and approximately

2,300 inmates await this final sentence on death rows throughout the United States. The backgrounds of these inmates hardly inspire confidence in our criminal justice system's efforts at rehabilitation: 99 percent of all death row inmates are male, 57 percent are white, 66 percent had prior felony convictions, and 10 percent had previous homicide convictions.[26]

Methods of imposing death vary by jurisdiction. The majority of states authorize execution by lethal injection. The electric chair is the second most common method of carrying out the sentence. Other methods include the gas chamber, hanging, and the firing squad. The majority of Americans support the imposition of the death penalty for certain crimes. The constitutionality of the death penalty is an issue that has been argued and decided by every state and federal court at one time or another.

Constitutionality

The history of the constitutionality of the death penalty has been one of changing positions by the U.S. Supreme Court. In 1972, in *Furman v. Georgia*, the Court ruled that the death penalty as imposed was cruel and unusual punishment.[27] As a result of this decision, many states had to reenact death penalty statutes in an attempt to do away with any arbitrary and capricious methods of imposing it. In 1976, the Court upheld the death penalty in *Gregg v. Georgia*, finding that the jury acted properly in considering aggravating circumstances in imposing the sentence.[28]

The following are some of the aggravating and mitigating circumstances that are present in many of our death penalty statutes.

AGGRAVATING CIRCUMSTANCES Prior conviction of a violent felony, a case involving the felony-murder rule, multiple murder, murder for profit, murder of a peace officer or public official, killing to avoid arrest, torture during the commission of a murder, or killing during an escape constitute aggravating circumstances.

MITIGATING CIRCUMSTANCES Mitigating circumstances include no significant prior criminal record, extreme mental or emotional illness, minor participation in the killing, or youth at the time of the murder. In *McLesky v. Kemp*, the Supreme Court upheld the imposition of the death penalty on a black defendant despite evidence that black criminals who kill white victims are more likely to receive the death penalty than white killers who murder black victims.[29] Many authorities believe that this case puts to rest the last of many constitutional issues surrounding the death penalty. The fact that the death penalty has been found constitutional does not stop the debate about whether it is morally and ethically reasonable or just. The next section will briefly review the more common arguments raised by proponents and opponents of the death penalty.

Opponents and Advocates

Opponents of the death penalty list numerous ethical, moral, and legal reasons that it should be abolished. On the other side of the argument, advocates for imposing the death penalty have just as many reasons for maintaining or expanding its use. The discussion in the preceding section indicates that, for the moment at least, the U.S. Supreme Court has clearly stated that, if certain procedural safeguards are followed, the death penalty is not a violation of the Eighth Amendment's prohibition against cruel and unusual punishment. However, legality is not the only reason for opposition to the death penalty, nor do death penalty proponents rest their arguments solely on the fact that it is legal.

Focus 15.5

The Death Penalty: An Appropriate Sanction?

On September 2, 1974, a convicted inmate named Coker escaped from the Ware Correctional Institution in Waycross, Georgia. At the time of his escape, Coker was serving time for murder, rape, kidnapping, and assault. At approximately eleven o'clock that evening, Coker entered the house of the Carvers through an unlocked kitchen door. He threatened the occupants with a board. He tied up Mr. Carver and then proceeded to rape Mrs. Carver. He stole the Carvers' car and left the house, taking Mrs. Carver with him. Coker was soon arrested, and Mrs. Carver was released without any further injury. A jury convicted the defendant of escape, armed robbery, vehicle theft, kidnapping, and rape. The Georgia statute authorized the imposition of the death penalty for rape if the jury found certain aggravating factors to be present. After deliberating, the jury determined that the specified aggravating factors were present and imposed death by electrocution. Coker appealed the death sentence, and the U.S. Supreme Court held that while the death penalty was not cruel and unusual punishment within the meaning of the Eighth Amendment, imposition of the death penalty for rape of an adult woman is grossly disproportionate and excessive punishment and is, therefore, forbidden by the Eighth Amendment's ban on cruel and unusual punishment.[30]

      Should the death penalty be imposed only for murder? What about a serial rapist who "specializes" in young female children? List the crimes that you believe are appropriate for imposition of the death penalty. After reading this section, review your answers. Are they the same?

      What about cost? Is the cost of execution or the cost of keeping a criminal in prison for life without possibility of parole an argument that should be made in support or in opposition to the death penalty? There are numerous other arguments regarding capital punishment. List as many as possible and justify your position.[31]

Focus 15.6

Should Young Criminals Be Subject to the Death Penalty?

This question was considered by the U.S. Supreme Court in *Roper v. Simmons*.

Roper v. Simmons 543 U.S. 551 (2005) (Excerpts from opinion)

At age 17, Christopher Simmons committed a capital murder. He was tried after he had turned 18, he was sentenced to death. . . . This court held, in Atkins v. Virginia, 536 U.S. 304, that the Eighth Amendment prohibited the execution of a mentally retarded person. Simmons filed a petition for post conviction relief, arguing that Atkins' reasoning established that the Constitution prohibits the execution of a juvenile who was under 18 when he committed his crime. The Missouri Supreme Court agreed and set aside Simmons' death sentence in favor of life imprisonment. It held that, although Stanford v. Kentucky, 492 U.S. 361, rejected the proposition that the Constitution bars capital punishment for juvenile offenders younger than 18, a national consensus had developed against the execution of those offenders since Stanford. . . .

While drawing the line at 18 is subject to the objections always raised against categorical rules, that is the point where society draws the line for many purposes between childhood and adulthood and the age at which the line for death eligibility ought to rest. Stanford should be deemed no longer controlling on this issue. . . . The United States is the only country in the world that continues to give official sanction to the juvenile death penalty. . . . The Eighth and Fourteenth Amendments forbid imposition of the death penalty on offenders who were under the age of 18 when their crimes were committed. The judgment of the Missouri Supreme Court setting aside the sentence of death imposed upon Christopher Simmons is affirmed. [Five justices supported the decision and four dissented.]

Summary

The sentencing and punishment of an offender is a necessary part of any criminal law discussion. As a nation, we have embraced several different concepts regarding the need for effective punishment. Deterrence, rehabilitation, incapacitation, retribution, and diversion are the main theories underlying the different forms of punishment.

Certain constitutional guarantees control the dispensing of justice and the imposition of punishment. We cannot discriminate in our sentencing based upon race, sex, or beliefs. The punishment must fit the crime and must be proportional to the offense for which it is imposed. The death penalty is not an appropriate sentence for sex crimes against adult women. However, an argument can be made that a serial rapist who targets young child should face the death penalty and that such a sentence is proportionate to the serious nature of the offenses.

Victim rights is a newly emerging field in the area of criminal law. Various jurisdictions have adopted victim bills of rights to guarantee that the victim of a crime will be treated with dignity and allowed input into the sentencing process. While we have come a long way in this area, there is still a great deal to be accomplished before the victim is truly the third party in any criminal proceeding.

The death penalty continues to generate controversy in our courts and homes. The Supreme Court has ruled that as it is presently imposed, the death penalty is constitutional. This has not stopped the debate as we search for the proper method to protect ourselves from vicious criminals. This subject will continue to occupy scholars and laypersons in the coming years.

Sentencing is the end of the criminal law process. However, it is not the answer to what is wrong in our society. Rather than react to crimes, we as a society must continue to find the cause of criminal activity and prevent it before it occurs. Only by approaching the issue in this manner, will we finally make our streets safe and our homes secure.

Additional Assignments

1. Read the selected cases and associated material for Chapter 15 posted at www.mycrimekit.com.
2. Complete the online study guide material for Chapter 15 posted at www.mycrimekit.com.
3. Discussion and thought questions:
   a. Why should we punish criminals? What should be our primary purpose in imposing punishments?
   b. Should a sentencing judge have discretion to tailor the sentence to fit the offender's background, or should offenders receive uniform sentences? Support your answers.
   c. Are fines an appropriate method of punishing an offender? Is community service a better option?
   d. What rights should victims have at the sentencing stage? Should they have a voice in whether the prosecutor accepts a plea bargain or a plea to a lesser offense? Justify your responses.
   e. Should executions be televised? Explain how you would set up such a procedure.

Practicum

Conduct research on the sentencing guidelines in your state. Include in your research the discretion that is given to the sentencing judge in felony cases. Does your home state have a "three strikes" law? How does it work?

Notes

1. George Rusche and Otto Kircheimer, *Punishment and Social Structure* (New York: Russell and Russell, 1939), 19.
2. Gustave de Beaumont and Alexis de Tocqueville, *On the Penitentiary System in the United States and Its Application in France* (Carbondale, IL: Southern Illinois University Press, 1964), 49.
3. See Richard Singer, "Sentencing," National Institute of Justice, Crime File (Washington, DC: U.S. Department of Justice, 1981).
4. See and compare Douglas Lipton, Robert Martinson, and Judith Wilks, *The Effectiveness of Correctional Treatment: A Survey of Treatment Evaluation Studies* (New York: Praeger, 1975) and Edwin Schur, *Radical Nonintervention* (Englewood Cliffs, NJ: Prentice-Hall, 1973).
5. K. G. Armstrong, "The Retributionist Hits Back," 70 *Mind* 471 (1969).
6. Andrew Von Hirsh, *Doing Justice* (New York: Hill and Wang, 1976), 15–16.
7. See Model Penal Code and Commentaries, Introduction to Articles 6 and 7, Part I, 6.01 to 7.09, p. 2.
8. *United States v. Grayson*, 438 U.S. 41 (1978).
9. "The Trial of Francis Townley," 18 *Howell's State Trials* 330, 350–351 (1746):.
10. *Solem v. Helm*, 436 U.S. 277 (1983).
11. See *Rhodes v. Chapman*, 452 U.S. 337 (1981).
12. See *Estelle v. Ruiz,* Docket No. 74-329 (E.D., Texas), where Federal District Court Judge William Wayne Justice has retained jurisdiction over the administration of the Texas state prisons since 1974. He appointed special masters to ensure that prison overcrowding was rectified.
13. Compare Robert Weninger, "The Abolition of Plea Bargaining: A Case Study of El Paso County, Texas," 35 *U.C.L.A. L. Rev.* 265(1987); and Gary Schulhofer, "Is Plea Bargaining Inevitable?" *Harv. L. Rev.* 1037 (1984).
14. See Marvin Frankel, *Criminal Sentences: Law Without Order* (New York: Hill and Wang, 1972).
15. *Mistretta v. United States,* 448 U.S. 361 (1989).
16. David Pauly and Carolyn Friday, "Drexel's Crumbling Defense," *Newsweek*, December 19, 1988, 44.
17. See Junda Woo, "Most States Now Have Laws Permitting Stores to Impose Civil Fines on Shoplifters," *Wall Street Journal,* September 9, 1992, B-1.

18. See David Fried, "Rationalizing Criminal Forfeiture," 79 *J. Crim. L. Criminology* 328 (1988).

19. *Simon and Schuster v. Members of the New York State Crime Victims Board,* 112 S. Ct. 501 (1991).

20. See 1992 N.Y. Laws 618 (to be codified at N.Y. Exec. Law 641[3][d]).

21. Gary L. Webb and James E. Hendricks, "Confronting Citizen Fear of Crime: Police Victim Assistance Training," *The Police Chief,* November 1992, p. 30.

22. See Uniform Victims of Crime Act, drafted by the National Conference of Commissioners on Uniform State Law, adopted in August 1992.

23. *Payne v. Tennessee,* No. 90-5721 (1991).

24. Uniform Victims of Crime Act 216.

25. See Arthur Koestler, *Reflections on Hanging* (New York: Macmillan, 1957), xi.

26. U.S. Department of Justice, Bureau of Justice Statistics, *Data Report,* 1988 (Washington, DC: Government Printing Office, 1989), p. 67.

27. *Furman v. Georgia,* 408 U.S. 238 (1972).

28. *Gregg v. Georgia,* 428 U.S. 153 (1976).

29. *McLesky v. Kemp,* 478 U.S. 1019 (1986).

30. *Coker v. Georgia,* 433 U.S. 584 (1977).

31. For an excellent discussion of both sides of the death penalty debate, see M. Ethan Katsh, ed., "Should the Death Penalty Be Abolished?" *Taking Sides, Clashing Views on Controversial Legal Issues* (Guilford, CT: Dushkin, 1993), 247–261.

CASE INDEX

SUBJECT INDEX